MW00465260

Praise for *Substance Abuse Treatment for Youth and Adults*

"David Springer and Allen Rubin have compiled a valuable practice guide for any professional who works with substance-abusing youth or adults. This is a volume that should be on every practitioner's bookshelf!"

C. Aaron McNeece, Dean, and Walter W. Hudson Professor (Emeritus),
College of Social Work, Florida State University

"This edited book is an important addition for clinicians wishing to incorporate the latest in evidence-based practices into their work with substance abusing clients. The detailed descriptions, case examples, and supportive materials in each chapter provide invaluable guidelines to both beginning and experienced clinicians. It is a book that belongs in the libraries of all substance abuse educators, students, and clinicians."

S. Lala A. Straussner, Professor and Director,
Post-Master's Certificate Program in the Clinical Approaches to Addictions Treatment,
Silver School of Social Work, New York University

"A major stumbling block to adoption of evidence-based practice in the real world of clinical practice has been the absence of clinician-friendly guides. Such guides need to be understandable, free of technical research jargon, infused with clinical expertise, and rich with real-life examples. Rubin and Springer have hit a home run with this series, which has all of these characteristics and more."

Edward J. Mullen,
Willma & Albert Musher Chair and Professor, Columbia University

Clinician's Guide to Evidence-Based Practice Series

Treatment of Traumatized Adults and Children
Allen Rubin and David W. Springer, Editors
Substance Abuse Treatment for Youth and Adults
David W. Springer and Allen Rubin, Editors

Substance Abuse Treatment for Youth and Adults

DAVID W. SPRINGER & ALLEN RUBIN, Editors

Substance Abuse Treatment for Youth and Adults

Clinician's Guide to Evidence-Based Practice

WILEY

John Wiley & Sons, Inc.

Library of Congress Cataloging-in-Publication Data:

Substance abuse treatment for youth and adults / editors, David W. Springer & Allen Rubin.

    p. cm.
  Includes bibliographical references and index.
  ISBN 978-0-470-24453-1 (cloth)
 1. Substance abuse—Treatment. 2. Youth—Substance use.
 I. Springer, David W. II. Rubin, Allen.
  HV4998.S83 2009
  616.86'06—dc22   2009008539

Printed in the United States of America

10 9 8 7 6 5 4 3 2 1

Contents

Series Introduction

ONE OF THE most daunting challenges to the evidence-based practice (EBP) movement is the fact that busy clinicians who learn of evidence-based interventions are often unable to implement them because they lack expertise in the intervention and lack the time and resources to obtain the needed expertise. Even if they want to read about the intervention as a way of gaining that expertise, they are likely to encounter materials that are either much too lengthy in light of their time constraints or much too focused on the research support for the intervention, with inadequate guidance to enable them to implement it with at least a minimally acceptable level of proficiency.

This is the second in a series of edited volumes that attempt to alleviate that problem and thus make learning how to provide evidence-based interventions more feasible for such clinicians. Each volume will be a how-to guide for practitioners—not a research-focused review. Each will contain in-depth chapters detailing how to provide clinical interventions whose effectiveness is being supported by the best scientific evidence.

The chapters will differ from chapters in other reference volumes on empirically supported interventions in both length and focus. Rather than covering in depth the research support for each intervention and providing brief overviews of the practice aspects of the interventions, our chapters will be lengthier and more detailed practitioner-focused how-to guides for implementing the interventions. Instead of emphasizing the research support in the chapters, that support will be summarized in an appendix. Each chapter will focus on helping practitioners learn how to begin providing an evidence-based intervention that they are being urged by managed care companies (and others) to provide, but with which they may be inexperienced. Each chapter will be extensive and detailed enough to enable clinicians to begin providing the evidence-based intervention without being so lengthy and detailed that reading it would be too time consuming and overwhelming. The chapters will also identify resources for gaining more advanced expertise in the interventions.

We believe that this series will be unique in its focus on the needs of practitioners and in making empirically supported interventions more feasible for them to learn about and provide. We hope that you will agree and that you will find this volume and this series to be of value in guiding your practice and in maximizing your effectiveness as an evidence-based practitioner.

David W. Springer, Ph.D.
Allen Rubin, Ph.D.

Preface

MENTAL HEALTH CLINICIANS are very likely to encounter a substance-abusing client in their work, with some estimations approximating that half of our clients have problems related to either their own or a family member's alcohol or drug abuse (Drake & Mueser, 1996; van Wormer & Davis, 2008). For substance abuse counselors, this number no doubt increases!

If you have been treating substance-abusing clients—or just reading about their treatment perhaps in anticipation of treating them—you probably have encountered many comments referring to empirically supported substance abuse interventions that are considered to be evidence-based. Such interventions include problem solving and social skills training, family behavior therapy, and motivational interviewing. You may also have encountered entire books on each of these interventions and wished you had more time to read them. Perhaps you've seen some research articles reporting outcome studies providing strong empirical support for one or more of these interventions and wished they provided more clinical guidance as to how you could provide them to your clients. Likewise, you may have read some books that contain chapters on various empirically supported substance abuse interventions, but have been disappointed with the brevity of specific practice guidelines in those chapters. That is because such books typically just provide very brief thumbnail sketches of the interventions, perhaps accompanied by rather lengthy reviews of the studies that supported each.

If you have had the above experiences and reactions, then this book is for you. Its very detailed, lengthy, how-to chapters—with case examples sprinkled throughout—are geared to practitioners who want their practice in treating substance-abusing clients to be evidence-based but who don't have the time to read each book on empirically supported interventions for substance abuse before feeling that they have enough knowledge to make decisions about which approach to adopt and enough guidance to begin providing the chosen intervention as they learn more about it.

This book is also geared to practitioners who may not have had the time to read research articles about empirically supported interventions for substance-abusing clients or who may be bewildered by some of the complex research concepts in those articles or by the diversity of findings from study to study. By reading this book, you will learn what interventions have had the best research support and how to provide them. That's because this book has been written in a user-friendly/practitioner-friendly manner for clinicians who want to learn such things without having to struggle with daunting research and statistical terms. For readers who do not want to accept our conclusions just based on our authority, however, this book provides an appendix that reviews the supporting research.

Another aspect of this book that makes it practitioner-friendly and that may enhance its value to practitioners is that every intervention chapter has been authored or co-authored by practitioners who have had extensive experience in the intervention and are clinical experts in it. As you read this book, you may be gratified by the extent to which the chapter authors are communicating more as practitioners and not as ivory tower researchers who don't understand the needs of practitioners. Although the book's editors are housed in academia, we have insisted that our chapters be written in ways that maximize their utility to practitioners. Moreover, we too have had extensive practice experience, and the lead editor has vast clinical experience treating substance-abusing adolescents.

Although the lengthy how-to detail in this book's chapters will not be as extensive as what you will find in an entire book devoted exclusively to the intervention being described in any particular chapter, it should be enough to get you started in providing the intervention and perhaps helping you decide whether you want to pursue further reading and training in that intervention. Toward the latter end, each chapter will also identify recommended additional readings as well as training options.

As mentioned above, this book's chapters detail how to provide clinical interventions whose effectiveness with substance-abusing clients is currently being supported by the best scientific evidence. Thus, the separate chapters cover the Adolescent Community Reinforcement Approach, problem solving and social skills training, family behavior therapy, motivational interviewing, cognitive behavioral coping skills therapy for adults, and Seeking Safety. In addition to the how-to's of the interventions, each chapter covers their indications and contraindications.

Key among the commonalities across these six interventions is the prerequisite that the interventions be provided in the context of a strong therapeutic alliance. The importance of the therapeutic alliance should not be underestimated, especially in light of the research supporting it as a necessary component of effective treatment with *any* specific intervention approach. Moreover, there is a widespread misconception that the guidelines for providing empirically supported interventions devalue the importance of the therapeutic alliance and the related misconception that evidence-based practice requires practitioners to function in a mechanistic way following cookbook-like manuals that disregard their practice wisdom and relationship skills. Readers will *not* find such guidelines in *this* volume. Instead, each chapter will reflect our emphasis on the importance of *both* the need to provide interventions that have had their effectiveness supported by the best research evidence as well as the need to choose, adapt, and provide those interventions in light of their practice expertise, their knowledge of idiosyncratic client characteristics and circumstances, and their relationship skills.

This book is timely as practitioners are increasingly being urged to provide empirically supported interventions and as those interventions are increasingly being required by third-party payers. Although evidence-based practice (EBP) has become part of the definition of ethical practice, various studies have shown that practitioners rarely engage in the EBP process. Various pragmatic factors have been cited regarding this concern—in particular, real-world time constraints and the difficulty practitioners have in obtaining the needed expertise to begin implementing the interventions with the best empirical support. This book aims to provide that beginning level of expertise in a manner that fits clinician time constraints.

ORGANIZATION

Following this Preface, Part 1 of this book examines the importance of engaging substance-abusing clients in treatment and the change process through the use of Motivational Interviewing (Chapter 1). Part 2 provides two chapters on treating substance-abusing adolescents, examining problem solving and social skills training (Chapter 2) and the Adolescent Community Reinforcement Approach (A-CRA) (Chapter 3). Part 3 explores treatment with families through family behavior therapy (Chapter 4), in which the primary client can be either an adolescent or an adult. It is worth noting that the Center for Substance Abuse Treatment (CSAT) funds sites all over the United States to implement A-CRA under the name "Assertive Adolescent Family Treatment," and this chapter could have just as easily been placed in Part 3 of the book on families. Part 4 provides two chapters that cover cognitive based interventions to treat adults. Chapter 5 addresses cognitive behavioral coping skills therapy for adults. Chapter 6 explores Seeking Safety (developed to treat clients who present with both a substance use disorder and/or posttraumatic stress disorder [PTSD]). The book concludes with a brief Afterword and two appendices. Appendix A reviews the research that provides the empirical support for the interventions covered in this volume. Appendix B describes in detail the evidence-based practice process for readers who would like more detail about that process than is covered in the Preface.

Regardless of which specific approach you use in treating substance-abusing clients, we hope this book helps you get started in making your treatment of substance abuse more evidence-based. In connection to becoming more evidence-based, we hope it also spurs you to pursue further reading, training, and searching for evidence regarding any interventions you decide to adopt or continue using. We would appreciate any feedback you can provide regarding the ways you have found this book to be helpful or any suggestions you may have for improving it. You can email such feedback to dwspringer@mail.utexas.edu or arubin@mail.utexas.edu.

REFERENCES

Drake, R. E., & Mueser, K. T.(1996). Alcohol-use disorders and severe mental illness. *Alcohol Health & Research World, 20*(2), 87–93.

Van Wormer, K., & Davis, D. R. (2008). *Addiction treatment: A strengths perspective* (2nd ed.). Belmont, CA: Brooks/Cole.

Acknowledgments

S PECIAL THANKS GO to four Wiley staff members who helped make this series possible. In alphabetical order they are: Peggy Alexander, Vice President and Publisher; Lisa Gebo, Senior Editor; Sweta Gupta, Editorial Program Coordinator; and Rachel Livsey, Senior Editor. For this particular volume, we appreciate the fine work of our chapter authors and the helpful feedback they provided to earlier drafts of the complete volume and for graciously lending their expertise in the writing of Appendix A. Two graduate students who helped at various stages of production also deserve special recognition: Angie Lippman and Melissa Torrente. Thanks also go to the following colleagues who reviewed our submitted manuscript and suggested improvements: Albert R. Roberts, Ph.D. (*deceased*), of Rutgers University; and Sherry Cormier, Ph.D., of West Virginia University.

About the Editors

David W. Springer, Ph.D., LCSW, is the Associate Dean for Academic Affairs and a University Distinguished Teaching Professor in the School of Social Work at The University of Texas at Austin, where he is also Investigator of the Inter-American Institute for Youth Justice and holds a joint appointment with the Department of Psychology. Dr. Springer's practice experience has included work as a clinical social worker with adolescents and their families in inpatient and outpatient settings and as a school social worker in an alternative learning center with youth recommended for expulsion for serious offenses. He currently serves on the editorial board of several professional journals and on the National Scientific and Policy Advisory Council of the Hogg Foundation for Mental Health. He has co-authored or co-edited several other books, including *Substance Abuse Treatment for Criminal Offenders: An Evidence-Based Guide for Practitioners* and *Handbook of Forensic Mental Health with Victims and Offenders*. Dr. Springer recently served as Chair of a Blue Ribbon Task Force consisting of national and regional leaders, which was charged with making recommendations for reforming the juvenile justice system in Texas. In recognition of his work with the Blue Ribbon Task Force, the National Association of Social Workers, Texas Chapter/Austin Branch selected Dr. Springer as the 2008 Social Worker of the Year.

Allen Rubin, Ph.D., is the Bert Kruger Smith Centennial Professor in the School of Social Work at The University of Texas at Austin, where he has been a faculty member since 1979. While there, he worked as a therapist in a child guidance center and developed and taught a course on the assessment and treatment of traumatized populations. Earlier in his career he worked in a community mental health program providing services to adolescents and their families. He is internationally known for his many publications pertaining to research and evidence-based practice. In 1997 he was a co-recipient of the Society for Social Work and Research Award for Outstanding Examples of Published Research for a study on the treatment of male batterers and their spouses. His most recent studies have been on the effectiveness of EMDR and on practitioners' views of evidence-based practice. Among his twelve books, his most recent is *Practitioner's Guide to Using Research for Evidence-Based Practice*. He has served as a consulting editor for seven professional journals. He was a founding member of the Society for Social Work and Research and served as its president from 1998 to 2000. In 1993 he received the University of Pittsburgh, School of Social Work's Distinguished Alumnus Award. In 2007 he received the Council on Social Work Education's Significant Lifetime Achievement in Social Work Education Award.

About the Contributors

Daniel N. Allen, Ph.D., is Associate Professor in the Department of Psychology and Director of the Neuropsychology Research Program at The University of Nevada, Las Vegas. His research interests include the neurocognitive effects of substance abuse, severe mental illnesses, and child traumatic brain injury and neurodevelopmental disorders. He has published extensively in these areas and is Fellow of the American Psychological Association (Division 40), National Academy of Neuropsychology, and Western Psychological Association. He is the recipient of several awards, including the Nelson Butters Award and Early Career Award from the National Academy of Neuropsychology, and the Morris Award and Barrick Scholar Award for research contributions from the University of Nevada, Las Vegas.

Ashley M. Austin, Ph.D., is Assistant Professor in the School of Social Work at Barry University. Dr. Austin completed postdoctoral training in the area of adolescent substance use problems at the Community-Based Intervention Research Group (C-BIRG) at Florida International University. Dr. Austin was a recipient of the 2008 National Institute on Drug Abuse (NIDA) Early Career Social Work Research Mentoring Initiative Award.

Brad Donohue, Ph.D., is Associate Professor in the Department of Psychology and Director of Achievement Center at the University of Nevada, Las Vegas. He is editor of the *Journal of Child & Adolescent Substance Abuse*, and was one of the developers of Family Behavior Therapy for substance abuse and its associated problems. He has directed projects funded by NIDA, NIMH, and SAMHSA, authored more than 100 professional publications, and is a recipient of several research awards, including UNLV's Outstanding Faculty Award, Western Psychological Association's Early Career Research Award, and the Barrick Scholar Award for Distinguished Research.

Mark D. Godley, Ph.D., received his MSW from the Worden School of Social Service and his Ph.D. from Southern Illinois University. Since 1987 he has served as the Director of Chestnut Health System's research and training institute and oversees the work of more than eighty research and training staff conducting NIH, SAMHSA, and foundation-funded research related to treatment and recovery for individuals with substance use disorders. Dr. Godley worked on the early clinical trials (1975–1982) of the Community Reinforcement Approach for alcohol use disorders and is currently leading an NIAAA funded study of Assertive Continuing Care.

Susan H. Godley, Rh.D., is a Senior Research Scientist and the EBT Coordinating Center Director at Chestnut Health Systems in Bloomington, Illinois. She is a CSAT and NIH funded investigator. She received her doctorate in rehabilitation from Southern Illinois University. Dr. Godley is the lead author of the Adolescent Community Reinforcement Approach (A-CRA) manual, one of the five Cannabis Youth Treatment (CYT) study treatment manuals, and was the principal investigator for one of the four CYT study sites. She is also the lead author on the companion case management manual used in the Assertive Continuing Care (ACC) approach.

Holly B. LaPota, is a clinical psychology doctoral student at the University of Nevada, Las Vegas. She serves as Assessment Coordinator at Achievement Center, where she organizes training seminars for assessment counselors and manages the administration of assessments in a NIDA-funded treatment outcome study involving HIV prevention and concurrent intervention for substance abuse and child neglect. Her research interests include the promotion of healthy lifestyles within the substance abuse and child neglect population. She also serves as editorial assistant for the *Journal of Child & Adolescent Substance Abuse.*

Robert J. Meyers, Ph.D., is Director of Robert J. Meyers, Ph.D. & Associates and a Research Associate Professor Emeritus in Psychology at the University of New Mexico's Center on Alcoholism, Substance Abuse and Addiction. Dr. Meyers helped develop the first Community Reinforcement Approach for the seminal study published in 1982 and has helped establish the adolescent version of CRA (A-CRA). Dr. Meyers also developed an approach for engaging resistant substance abusers to enter treatment, called Community Reinforcement and Family Training (CRAFT), which has been shown to be superior to more traditional interventions in several empirical studies.

Lisa M. Najavits, Ph.D., is Professor of Psychiatry, Boston University School of Medicine; Lecturer, Harvard Medical School; and affiliated with VA Boston and McLean Hospital. She is author of the books *Seeking Safety: A Treatment Manual for PTSD and Substance Abuse* (2002) and *A Woman's Addiction Workbook* (2002), as well as over 125 professional publications. She is currently president of the American Psychological Association Division on

Addictions. She is recipient of several awards including the 2009 Betty Ford Award for addictions research from the Association for Medical Education and Research in Substance Abuse; and the 2004 Emerging Leadership Award of the American Psychological Association's Committee on Women.

Danielle E. Parrish, Ph.D., is Assistant Professor in the Graduate College of Social Work at the University of Houston. Dr. Parrish recently completed postdoctoral training with the Health Behavior Research and Training Institute at The University of Texas at Austin, School of Social Work. Prior to obtaining her doctorate, Dr. Parrish worked as a clinical social worker with children, adolescents, and adults in a diverse array of public mental health settings including juvenile justice, infant mental health, and outpatient children's mental health. Most of her recent research and publications have focused on the implementation of evidence-based practice and the prevention of fetal alcohol spectrum disorders. She also serves on the editorial board of *Research on Social Work Practice*.

McClain Sampson, Ph.D., is a Research Assistant at the Health Behavior Research and Training Institute at The University of Texas at Austin, School of Social Work. She graduated in May 2009 with a Ph.D. in Social Work and earned her M.S.S.W. in 2005 from the University of Tennessee, Knoxville. Her scholarly research and presentations have focused on the efficacy of motivational interviewing in restricted and unrestricted settings. She has also assisted in the coordination of federally funded substance abuse research projects. Ms. Sampson is a motivational interviewing coach.

Jane Ellen Smith, Ph.D., is Chair of the Psychology Department and Professor at the University of New Mexico in Albuquerque, where she has also served as the Director of Clinical Training. She received her Ph.D. in Clinical Psychology from the State University of New York at Binghamton. She is also the first author of the book, *Motivating Substance Abusers to Enter Treatment: Working with Family Members*, and the co-author of the book, *Clinical Guide to Alcohol Treatment: The Community Reinforcement Approach*. She has received federal grants from NIAAA to test the CRA program with homeless individuals.

Nanette S. Stephens, Ph.D., a licensed clinical psychologist, is a research scientist and Director of Training with the Health Behavior Research and Training Institute at The University of Texas at Austin, School of Social Work. She has over eighteen years of experience integrating Motivational Interviewing (MI) in her work as a trainer, supervisor, researcher, clinician, and consultant. In addition, Dr. Stephens has been a therapist in several federally funded MI-based projects (e.g., preventing alcohol-exposed pregnancies, group therapy for cocaine users), and her other clinical and research interests have included working with families with histories of domestic violence and child maltreatment.

Mary M. Velasquez, Ph.D., is Professor, Associate Dean for Research, Director of the Center for Social Work Research, and Director of the Health Behavior Research and Training Institute in the School of Social Work at The University of Texas at Austin. Her areas of interest are the development and implementation of interventions using the Transtheoretical Model of Change and Motivational Interviewing and health behavior interventions including HIV prevention, prenatal health, mental health, alcohol and other substance abuse, smoking cessation, and prevention of fetal alcohol spectrum disorder.

Eric F. Wagner, Ph.D., is a Professor in the Stempel College of Public Health and Social Work at Florida International University, where he directs the Community-Based Intervention Research Group (C-BIRG). Dr. Wagner earned his Ph.D. in Clinical Psychology from the University of Pittsburgh, completed a postdoctoral fellowship at the Brown University Center for Alcohol and Alcoholic Studies, and is a licensed psychologist in the states of Florida and Rhode Island. Dr. Wagner was recognized for his early career achievements with the New Investigator Award from the Sixth International Conference on Treatment of Addictive Behaviors, as well as being selected to present at the Symposium in Honor of Enoch Gordis at the 25th Annual Scientific Meeting of the Research Society on Alcoholism. Dr. Wagner also is the creator and director of the DIONYSUS <dionysus.fiu.edu>, an annual conference devoted to science-informed approaches to real-life issues in drinking.

Substance Abuse Treatment for Youth and Adults

PART 1

ENGAGING CLIENTS IN TREATMENT AND CHANGE

CHAPTER 1

Motivational Interviewing

McCLAIN SAMPSON, NANETTE S. STEPHENS, and MARY M. VELASQUEZ

WHAT IS MOTIVATIONAL INTERVIEWING?

Many counseling approaches are based on the idea that if people receive enough information (or education) about their problems, they will change. As a consequence, counselors working with substance-abusing clients often rely on providing advice or teaching relapse prevention and other action-related tasks as their primary therapeutic strategies. For clients who are ready to change, these approaches can be effective. If clients are not ready to change their problem behaviors, however, this type of approach can quickly lead to resistance and a lack of progress. There are numerous reasons why a client who is not ready for change might present for treatment such as legal, marital, or job-related problems that have led to coercion or ultimatums that the client attend treatment or face significant consequences. At the same time, some clients who appear ready to change feel quite ambivalent because they may have some very strong reasons to stay the same. In these cases, counselors and clients alike are much better served when counselors refrain from persuading or offering immediate advice and instead utilize an approach that seeks to enhance and reinforce client motivation and commitment to change. This approach is embodied by the Motivational Interviewing (MI) counseling style.

Because the MI approach begins with the assumption that the responsibility for change lies within the client, the counselor's task is to create an environment that will enhance the client's intrinsic motivation for and commitment to change. In this type of environment, the counselor elicits the client's answers and solutions for change, rather than directs, suggests, or provides the answers. In other words, MI is not a top-down, authoritarian approach, but rather a client-centered, respectful, and collaborative endeavor that mobilizes the client's own resources for change. A second assumption of MI is that unremitting problems are more often due to a lack of this kind of mobilization (i.e., not being motivated to try) rather than to skills deficits (i.e., trying, but not having the necessary tools or skills) or "denial" (i.e., not trying because the client believes there is not a problem in the first place). A third assumption is that when faced with making a difficult change, ambivalence is typical and "normal," particularly for those who are initially reluctant or resistant to considering change. Thus, the central purpose of MI is to help shift these decisional uncertainties (i.e., ambivalence) in the direction of positive change by creating an atmosphere of respect and acceptance and enhancing the belief that change is possible.

William Miller and Stephen Rollnick (2002), the originators of MI, define MI as "a client-centered, directive method for enhancing intrinsic motivation to change by exploring and resolving ambivalence" (p. 25). The goal of MI is to *prepare* clients for change—not push or coerce them—by helping them work through their ambivalence about changing through the use of active listening and skilled feedback techniques. To build rapport, reduce resistance, and enhance motivation, the MI counselor elicits the client's own concerns about the problem behavior. As the clients—rather than the counselors— articulate reasons for change, their internal motivation is harnessed and augments their readiness to change.

As a counseling style, MI is client-centered, collaborative, and goal-oriented. That is, the counselor and the client work together to identify and address the client's specific behavioral goals. In this "dual expertise" approach, the counselor and the client are both viewed as experts who collaborate in the service of the client's goals and concerns in terms of what is important and possible in the context of their lives. Because the MI counselor recognizes that all clients—on some level—have the desire and wisdom needed to improve their lives and accomplish their personal goals, the counselor's job is to elicit answers and solutions from clients rather than directing or providing the answers (Rollnick, Miller, & Butler, 2008). Unlike some nondirective counseling styles where counselors continually "stay with" the clients and avoid providing any type of structure or guidance, MI sessions maintain a purpose, goal, and direction as counselors actively select the right moments in which to intervene with incisive strategies. MI specifically avoids argumentative persuasion and instead accepts the validity of the client's experiences and perspectives. This involves listening to and acknowledging (though not necessarily agreeing with or approving of) a broad range of a client's concerns, values, preferences, beliefs, emotions, styles, and rationales.

The MI approach embodies both a relational philosophy described as the MI Spirit, or a "way of being," with another (Miller & Rollnick, 2002) and a set of strategies and methods that are selectively utilized to develop and strengthen motivation. MI elements and strategies can be utilized in two phases. Phase I, typically most useful for clients who are more reluctant or ambivalent about change, incorporates strategies referred to as OARS (i.e., asking Open questions, Affirming, Reflecting, Summarizing) to build rapport, explore ambivalence, and increase readiness to change. While Phase II also incorporates the OARS strategies, they are utilized to strengthen a growing commitment to change and develop plans of action to accomplish change goals. These strategies will be addressed more fully in the MI counseling strategies section.

THE MYTH OF DENIAL

The substance abuse field has long maintained that most clients are resistant, or "in denial," about their use. We frequently hear that "alcoholics" and "drug addicts" are liars, pathologically defensive, and nearly impossible to work with, and until they "hit rock bottom," they will not change. As a result, traditional substance abuse interventions are often based on the idea that change is motivated only by the avoidance of negative consequences. This approach suggests that "alcoholics" will not change their drinking behaviors until the external consequences become sufficiently painful and distressing or until their denial is broken by direct confrontation. In contrast, Miller believes that this sort of approach is not only ineffective, but also detrimental to clients. Instead of seeing denial as characteristic of certain types of clients, he contends that denial is actually a reflection of the interpersonal relationship between the counselor and the client. He states:

> It takes two to deny . . . If you approach someone by saying, "you're an alcoholic, and you had better stop drinking," the natural human response is to deny. If you come to them in a respectful manner that assumes they make choices about their lives and it is in their hands, that they're smart people who have reasons for what they are doing and also have within them the motivation for change, you get a very different response (as cited in Jones, 2007, p. 34).

As evidenced by Miller's comments, practitioners of MI maintain that motivation for change is facilitated by exploring and amplifying clients' intrinsic motivations to move toward positive consequences, behaviors, or goals rather than by confronting them about the need to avoid negative consequences. Because very often people make difficult changes on their own, we believe that although counseling may help facilitate the change process, the motivation to change comes from within the client.

WHAT MOTIVATIONAL INTERVIEWING IS NOT

Upon receiving their first introduction to MI, many people with training in social work, counseling psychology, or other helping professions say, "Oh, that's what it is—I already use MI in my practice, and I have been using it for years." In other words, at first blush MI can appear to some to be simply an empathic approach that uses a set of "good listening skills." While empathy and listening are certainly foundational elements, reaching proficiency in MI—learning to apply its spirit and artful, strategic principles and skills— typically requires practice and feedback over time. Before we explore the various aspects of MI, we will discuss what MI is not.

First, MI is not directive in the traditional sense, which implies confrontation, persuasion, and indoctrination. Instead, the directiveness of MI is exemplified by sessions that are goal-focused as client and counselor explore specific behavioral goals together such as increased sobriety, improved parenting skills, or smoking cessation.

MI is not just being "warm and fuzzy," empathic, accepting, and genuine. While empathy and acceptance are essential to the practice of MI, this approach also incorporates directive (in the sense of goal-oriented) strategies and methods that are applied in the service of change.

We have also heard more than one counselor say that he or she is going to do MI with their next client. MI is not something that is done to a client; rather, it is both an art and a craft that integrate relational processes with a set of skills and strategies.

In addition, although numerous studies have documented significant behavior changes after a single MI session, MI is not a "snap your fingers" method that is always instantly transformative; instead, we have learned that MI sessions may simply plant a seed that facilitates more distal behavior changes.

MI is also not a hierarchical, top-down approach in which counselors are viewed as experts who dispense wisdom, advice, and solutions. The term *interview* itself connotes a desire for an egalitarian exchange that acknowledges and respects the right to socially responsible self-determination. In MI, counselors set aside their own goals and timetables and begin where their clients are, by inviting them to explore and set their own goals. In contrast to the counselor being viewed as an authority on the client's life and choices, the client is seen as a powerful agent who possesses an inherent will and ability to set meaningful goals and work toward their accomplishment. Therefore, rather than giving incentives, setting goals, and providing solutions for a client, the counselor's task is to elicit and foster those elements from the client. This relational and respective type of dialogue, which is the hallmark of MI, is of utmost importance in developing a strong working alliance with the client (Miller & Rollnick, 2002).

Finally, MI is not something a counselor continues to utilize until the client agrees to submit to changes seen as necessary or desirable by the counselor. In many instances, MI is often a relatively short-term process that utilizes the key component of highlighting discrepancies the client may feel between a current behavior and personal values, goals, and self-concept. As this aware-ness grows, a client's sense of agency is enhanced as he or she increasingly feels an ownership and investment in the development of change options and pathways. While this process of empowerment continues to be fostered by evoking the client's feelings, desires, and solutions for change, the counselor remains respectful and accepting of the client's choices rather than conveying an expectation that the client needs to and/or must change.

THEORETICAL UNDERPINNINGS OF MOTIVATIONAL INTERVIEWING

The concept of MI, which evolved from experience in the treatment of problem drinkers, was first described by Miller (1983) in an article published in *Behavioral Psychotherapy*. The fundamental concepts and approaches were later elaborated by Miller and Rollnick (1991) in a more detailed description of clinical procedures. MI draws on Festinger's (1957) concept of cognitive dissonance, Bem's self-perception theory (1972), the transtheoretical model of change (Prochaska & DiClemente, 1984), and the health belief model (Rosenstock, 1974). While MI has these theories at its roots, Miller explains that MI actually originated as young protégés observed his approach to enhancing clients' readiness to change in substance abuse treatment. As Miller began to describe to his colleagues what he did in treatment, the conceptual model for MI evolved (MINUET, 1999).

The earliest conception of MI drew heavily on the stages of change (SOC), first identified by Prochaska and DiClemente in the *Transtheoretical Approach: Crossing Traditional Boundaries of Therapy* (1984). The SOC represent the temporal, motivational aspects of the change process. According to this model, individuals often enter the change process in the *precontemplation* stage because they are unconvinced that they have a problem or are unwilling to consider change. Individuals who progress to the *contemplation* stage begin to consider making changes in the distant future. In the *preparation* stage, individuals have more proximal goals to change and begin to make commit-ments and develop plans to change. The *action* stage of change is character-ized by individuals changing the target behavior and adopting strategies to prevent relapse. And in the *maintenance* stage, the change is solidified and integrated into the individual's general lifestyle.

Clients vary widely in their readiness to change. Some may come to treatment having already decided to change. Others are reluctant or even hostile at the outset. In fact, some precontemplators are coerced into treatment by families, employers, or legal authorities. Most clients, however, are likely to enter the treatment process somewhere in the contemplation stage. They may be thinking about taking action, but still need consolidation of their motivation for change. The MI focus in this period, termed Phase I (Miller &

Rollnick, 2002), may be thought of as tipping the motivational balance (Janis & Mann, 1977; Miller, 1989). One side of the seesaw favors keeping the status quo, whereas the other favors change. The counselor's task is to create opportunities for shifting the balance in favor of change. MI is especially useful for clients in the earlier SOC because it promotes the exploration and resolution of ambivalence about change by highlighting and increasing an individual's perceived discrepancy between current behavior and personal goals and values (Miller & Rollnick, 1991, 2002). Thus, in MI, a client's ambivalence, which is common in the earlier SOC, can be used to enhance his or her intrinsic motivation to begin to initiate behavior change efforts.

Counselors have also found MI to be a very effective style to use with clients in the later stages as they prepare for change, take action, and maintain the change over time. Miller and Rollnick (2002) have called this Phase II of Motivational Interviewing. This is the point at which the client has made a decision to change. In this phase, the counselor's job changes from enhancing motivation to collaborative problem-solving and coaching as the client develops a workable change plan, anticipates barriers to change and ways to address them, and identifies potential support systems. Although most change strategies in this phase (the preparation, action, and maintenance stages) are more behavioral or action-oriented, we believe clients are more engaged, and ultimately more successful, when they are treated in the empathic, caring style that is inherent in MI. For clients in action and maintenance, by helping to increase self-efficacy and reinforcing accomplishments, MI promotes sustained, long-term change (DiClemente & Velasquez, 2002).

The SOC concept can assist counselors in that they may select and utilize very different strategies, depending on clients' stage of readiness for change. Rather than being conceptualized as discrete, static periods, the SOC are a useful template for understanding the dynamic change process. The SOC are also helpful for clients in that they provide a framework by which clients can better understand where they are, where they have been, and where they are going. It is important for counselors to remember that not only can a client's stage of readiness for changing a behavior fluctuate from day to day, but a client may also be in different stages for changing different behaviors. For example, a client might want to change her alcohol use but not be at all ready to give up her use of marijuana. The skilled MI counselor will be attentive to possible variations in a client's readiness for change and apply selective MI strategies in a flexible, adaptive manner.

WHY MOTIVATIONAL INTERVIEWING?

MI is one of the most carefully designed and rigorously studied treatments for substance abuse (see Appendix A in this volume for a summary of MI's effectiveness). Moreover, we believe that many elements of MI can often be effectively integrated with a number of other counseling methods. For example, the MI OARS strategies, to be discussed more fully later, are especially applicable to many other approaches. Expressions of empathy and respect of client personhood and autonomy—central MI constructs—are also congruent with other therapeutic models.

In addition, in today's climate counselors are being called upon to use strategies that are clearly specifiable. That is, there is a call in the behavioral therapies arena for providers to define the "active ingredients" or "mechanisms of action" that are being used in each therapeutic encounter. In MI, the strategies are clearly defined, and supervisors listening to recordings of client encounters can identify the extent to which MI is being used by the counselor in the session. Behavioral coding systems such as the Motivational Interviewing Treatment Integrity (MITI) scoring system (Moyers, Martin, Manuel, Hendrikson, & Miller, 2005) can be used to assess counselor adherence to the MI style and use of strategies. The MITI assesses treatment quality by coding global MI concepts such as *empathy* (the extent to which the counselor understands and/or makes an effort to grasp the client's perspective) and MI *spirit* (how much the counselor supports the client's autonomy, collaborates, and evokes the client's goals and concerns). In addition to these global ratings, several counselor behavioral counts are assessed, such as use of closed or open questions, simple and complex reflections, and MI-Adherent (e.g., affirming, asking permission to give information or advice, expressing support) or MI-Nonadherent responses (e.g., advising without permission, confronting, arguing).

THE FOUR GUIDING PRINCIPLES OF MOTIVATIONAL INTERVIEWING
Express Empathy

The expression of empathy, based on the teachings of the humanistic psychologist Carl Rogers (1951), is an essential building block for a MI session. In the MI approach, the counselor actively listens to and reflects the meaning and feelings conveyed by the client. The accurate expression of empathy by the counselor conveys not only an understanding, but also an acceptance, of the client's perspective and experience. Thus, the client feels heard and accepted rather than judged or discounted. This element sets the stage for building rapport and creating a safe environment rather than one that pushes for change in a particular direction. The following scenario demonstrates this principle.

CLIENT: My wife and I had a lot of trouble . . . we got into it when she pushed and pushed me about getting a different job.
COUNSELOR: You felt pushed to the limits. . . . It got out of control.

CLIENT: Yeah, but it shouldn't have happened like it did.

COUNSELOR: You wished it could have been handled in a different way.

CLIENT: I could have done better.

DEVELOP DISCREPANCY

Another critical component of MI involves creating opportunities for clients to develop and explore discrepancies between their current actions and their closely held values and life goals. Awareness of inconsistencies between ongoing behavior and deeply held values and beliefs is an important step in the change process. Unlike some traditional therapies that may focus only on the negatives of current behaviors, the process of developing discrepancies involves the client's consideration of both the pros and cons of the behavior change. As he or she is encouraged to explore the conflicting aspects of the issue, the pros or advantages of changing a behavior begin to outweigh the cons or disadvantages of changing, so that a "tipping" point is reached where the clients themselves articulate their own reasons for change. It is important to keep in mind that MI's directiveness is applied to resolving ambivalence rather than leading or pushing for change in a specific direction. When MI is skillfully executed, clients typically experience a heightened sense of discrepancy and have less reason to feel resistant (since the behavior pros and cons are initially given equal opportunity) than when they feel judged, coerced, or persuaded.

CLIENT: I feel two ways about this whole thing. I want to quit drinking, but I'd feel lost without it . . . it's like a friend I can count on.

COUNSELOR: You would feel at a loss if you gave up alcohol, and at the same time you really want a change. What are some of the good things for you about drinking?

CLIENT: Hmmm. Well, I guess it helps me put aside the troubles of this life . . . it helps me escape.

COUNSELOR: It helps you deal with a lot of difficulties. What might be some of the not so good things for you about drinking?

CLIENT: Wow. My wife is about to take off, and I can't see my kids right now. That hurts.

COUNSELOR: So while alcohol helps you take some "time off," your wife and children are important and you might lose them.

CLIENT: Yeah. That'd be terrible.

ROLL WITH RESISTANCE

Often during the change process, especially for clients who are initially less ready to change, resistance is expressed, either subtly or overtly. Rather than reacting with confrontation, argument, sarcasm, or defensiveness, the MI counselor "rolls" with the resistance in order to create positive momentum rather than a need for more resistance. For the MI counselor, expressions of client resistance or defensiveness are seen as a signal to shift strategies because confronting or focusing on the resistance (e.g., *"So why don't you want to talk about it?"*) can stall or divert progress and even amplify client defensiveness.

CLIENT: It's *my* life. Nobody has the right to tell me how to live it! You've never been in this position of having everybody boss you around.

COUNSELOR: You're exactly right. You are in charge of your life. You are really the expert on your life, and you are the only one who can decide the next steps. What would be helpful for us to talk about in this time we have?

SUPPORT SELF-EFFICACY

Although the MI approach assumes that each person has the ability to change, a person may lack confidence in—may not recognize—this inherent ability. Because people who present to treatment often have had multiple quit attempts and failures, confidence in their own ability to change is low. In MI, counselors work to enhance self-efficacy by offering their own beliefs about clients' capacity for change, conveying support and eliciting input from clients about previous successes. Importantly, promoting self-efficacy does not require the counselor to become responsible for creating the client's confidence or self-esteem, but rather the counselor elicits and mirrors the successes and progress that the client verbalized.

CLIENT: This has been so hard. I've tried so many times to make this work—to quit drinking once and for all.

COUNSELOR: You have really wanted things to be different—not drinking was terribly important to you. You kept trying. Tell me, what worked a while for you before—when you were successful for a period of time in terms of not drinking?

CLIENT: Well, I stayed away from bars and old friends who drank day and night.

COUNSELOR: So staying away from temptation helped you be successful. What else?

CLIENT: I also got the liquor out of the house. I just threw it away.

COUNSELOR: What a great strategy—sounds like it helped you meet your goal.

THE SPIRIT OF MOTIVATIONAL INTERVIEWING

Motivational Interviewing (MI) is best viewed as a communication style, an interpersonal dynamic, rather than a set of techniques that one can learn. In MI, the counselor strives to convey a spirit of collaboration, evocation, and support of autonomy throughout the session (Rollnick, Miller, & Butler, 2008). In collaborating with the client, the counselor does not assume an authoritarian role, but rather seeks to create a positive atmosphere of teamwork that is conducive to change. Consistent with a collaborative role, the counselor's tone is not one of imparting knowledge, such as wisdom or insight, but rather evoking—drawing out—the client's own expertise, understanding, and solutions. That is, change arises from within the client rather than being imposed from without. Because the responsibility for change is recognized as being owned by the client, the counselor openly acknowledges an appreciation and respect for the client's autonomy—the right and ability to make choices important for his or her life. MI counselors recognize that clients are always free to take their advice or not, and when MI is skillfully utilized, clients rather than counselors present the arguments and choice for change.

Counselors who conduct their sessions with this MI spirit often find that this approach initially surprises and disarms clients who come with expectations that they will have counselors who confront, persuade, or lead them step-by-step through an unwanted or minimally desired change process. For this reason, the counselor using MI typically introduces and models the MI spirit at the start of the first session, as in the following example:

COUNSELOR: I'm glad you came in today. Before we begin, is it OK if I take a few minutes to explain a little about how we will work together?

CLIENT: Sure.

COUNSELOR: While our focus today will be primarily on your substance use, I should explain right up front that I'm not going to be trying to change you. I hope that I can help you think about your present situation and consider what, if anything, you might want to do, but if there is any changing, **you** will be the one who does it. Nobody can tell you what to do; nobody can make you change. I may be giving you some information and maybe some advice, but what you do with all of that is completely up to you. I couldn't change you if I wanted to. The only person who can decide whether and how you change is *you*. How does that sound to you?

CLIENT: That sounds OK to me. I'm glad you're not going to lecture me.

MOTIVATIONAL INTERVIEWING COUNSELING STRATEGIES

Miller and Rollnick (2002) identify four specific clinical strategies that form the fabric of MI. These techniques are summarized by the acronym OARS: Open questions, Affirmations, Reflections, and Summaries.

ASKING OPEN QUESTIONS

Counselors work collaboratively with clients to guide the session by using open-ended questions to encourage clients to elaborate on their experiences and feelings. Typically, closed-ended questions such as *"You came here because your wife says you have a drinking problem?"* or *"Are you ready to make a change in your drinking?"* yield brief yes or no answers, whereas *"What brings you here today?"* or *"What are your thoughts, if any, about changing your alcohol use?"* invite a more thoughtful and potentially informative response. MI counselors approach clients with a genuine and open curiosity that reflects their active interest in clients' perspectives and goals and leave any preconceived notions, expectations, or agenda for change at the door. In an MI session, clients are encouraged to do most of the talking, and this type of Socratic questioning invites more engagement and participation from the client than a session that is filled with yes or no queries.

In MI, some types of statements, although put forward in a declarative form, actually serve as questions. For example, while *"Tell me about your concerns, if any, about your drug use"* does not end in a question mark, it still has the purpose of eliciting information, albeit in a nonstandard question format. In general, then, we consider these types of statements to be a type of MI open question.

COUNSELOR: What concerns, if any, do you have about your alcohol use? *(as opposed to: "Are you concerned about your alcohol use?")*

CLIENT: Well, I'm really doing just fine. My wife nags me a lot about my beer drinking, and my boss is really fed up—he says he may have to let me go if I don't get back on the wagon.

COUNSELOR: In some ways things are going really well for you, and at the same time you are a little concerned about how alcohol may be affecting your marriage and your job.

AFFIRMING

The use of affirmations contributes to building rapport and helping to enhance self-efficacy for the client. Simple affirmations such as *"It takes a lot of courage to be here, thank you"* can be a valuable way to acknowledge a client's accomplishments, however small. Often, it is a natural instinct for counselors to affirm behaviors they think clients should execute, such as decreased drinking. However, in MI, effective affirmations are a simple and straightforward way to recognize and highlight the client's strengths and efforts. The MI counselor avoids value-laden affirmations such as, *"It is good that you quit drinking in front of the children since that is bad for them to witness,"* and instead offers *"The children really benefit from seeing you as a father who does not drink and lose control.''* Affirmations are a way to assure clients that they are being heard and appreciated, not to inform them that their counselor approves or disapproves of their behavior. In addition, a way to polish affirmations is to omit when possible the "I" reference—as in *"I think your showing up at work was great"*—because the insertion of "I" can shift the focus from the client's valuing the new behavior to the counselor's approving of it. Also, we believe that affirming behaviors, as opposed to decisions or intentions, is likely to be more useful in terms of strengthening clients' intrinsic motivations and goals. And when executed most skillfully, affirmations are specific, spelling out the type of behavior that was admirable, courageous, or positive.

CLIENT: I really want to be sober. My kids deserve it.
COUNSELOR: Your children are really important to you. You want to be the kind of father they can look up to.
CLIENT: You know, I did stay away from the booze all last week, and I think they really were glad about that.
COUNSELOR: Staying away from liquor really made a difference. What a gift to your children!

REFLECTIVE LISTENING

Reflective listening is used to express an understanding of the client's perspective, goals, and concerns. In MI, reflections are also utilized strategically to provide direction to the session, to evoke and/or highlight client statements that promote change, and to foster personal exploration and insight. Additionally, selective reflections provide opportunities for the client to examine and begin to resolve feelings of ambivalence. Reflective listening is not just a simple exercise in repeating what the client has said, but rather, it requires the counselor to focus on and listen closely to what the client is saying and then to take a guess—in the form of a reflection—as to what the client was saying and feeling (Miller & Rollnick, 2002). The skilled use of reflections often results in less need to rely on questions to further the dialogue, as clients often respond to astute reflections by becoming more engaged in the session and wanting to continue the dialogue. We have also observed that, at times, the simplest, briefest reflections are the most powerful. Sometimes, counselors may be tempted to use a reflection as an opportunity to teach or make a point, and these longer types of reflections can interrupt the flow of the dialogue and shift the focus from the client to the counselor. It is important to point out that what appears "on paper" to be a reflection (e.g., *"You are really discouraged"*) can become in fact a closed question if the phrase ends with an upward inflection of the voice (e.g., *"You are really discouraged?''*). While this is not a fatal error, it can result in a missed opportunity to invite further and deeper exploration of an important issue.

CLIENT: I just feel depressed because I have no family or friends here and nobody to talk with.
COUNSELOR: You're feeling kind of isolated.
CLIENT: It's really hard. I feel like I'm outside of the circle. I have felt this way a lot for a lot of years . . . probably why I began to drink—the bottle was my friend.
COUNSELOR: Feeling like an outsider—the bottle was there for you.
CLIENT: Yeah, and I've really paid the price. The more I drank, the more I stayed to myself—shut myself off.
COUNSELOR: Drinking really kept you from reaching out to people. You'd really like things to be different now.

In this example, if the counselor had phrased the reflection as a question (e.g., *You feel isolated?*), the client may have shifted to a more "intellectual" mode of trying to explain or clarify for the counselor's benefit—so the counselor could "get it"—what he or she had meant rather than staying with and exploring more of the topic in the service of increasing the client's own awareness, understanding, and wisdom.

Reflections come in many forms such as simple, complex, and double-sided. Simple reflections are usually a repeat or rephrase of a client statement.

CLIENT: I'm sick and tired of this life—too many drugs, too much booze.
COUNSELOR: You're sick of all the booze and drugs.

Complex reflections, on the other hand, convey an understanding of what the client may be feeling behind the words and/or take the client's statement to a deeper level. In other words, this type of reflection captures the emotional and meaning subtext of the client's talk. It is often the case that a client's nonverbal expressions (e.g., posture, sighs, frowns, tears, voice pace, and inflection) provide more grist for the reflection mill than the actual word content of the client statement.

CLIENT: I just wish everyone would quit nagging me about my drinking; it really bothers me. *(irritated tone of voice, frown, quick pace of speech)*
COUNSELOR: It's none of their business—it makes you a little angry.
CLIENT: It really does—they just don't know what I've been through.
COUNSELOR: It's hard for them to really understand—they haven't walked in your shoes.

Consider the preceding examples as opposed to the following words, which are accompanied by entirely different body language and voice tone/pace.

CLIENT: I just wish everyone would quit nagging me about my drinking; it really bothers me. *(sagging shoulder, depressed affect, low voice, hesitating pace of speech)*

COUNSELOR: It's hard to hear. . . . makes you a little sad.

CLIENT: *(remains quiet for a moment)* I hate disappointing them again. They have such high hopes for me.

COUNSELOR: They know what you can do, can be. They have faith in you. You want to live up to that faith.

Using metaphorical reflections can also increase the depth of the dialogue and provide extra meaning and guidance for the client. For example, changing one's drinking habits can be described as "starting on a new journey" or "down a new road." This type of language creates an image of progress and turning points that can be incorporated and expanded in future discussions. Sometimes, it is the client who offers this type of metaphor or analogy, and as such, the counselor should be alert for opportunities to attend to and utilize the client's language.

CLIENT: I just wish everyone would quit nagging me about my drinking; it really bothers me. *(sagging shoulders, subdued voice, indications of sadness in facial expression)*

COUNSELOR: Everyone's worried. It makes you sad.

CLIENT: I feel like I've let them all down again and again and again.

COUNSELOR: You'd like them to be proud of you.

CLIENT: Yeah, I'd feel like an eagle, proud and soaring the skies, looking down and seeing them proud of me.

COUNSELOR: That will be wonderful—flying with pride.

CLIENT: It's a great picture in my mind. Making them proud.

A double-sided reflection acknowledges both sides of the client's ambivalence. In offering this type of reflection, it may be most effective to begin the reflection with the client's stated "pros" of the problem behavior and then end it with the "cons," such as the client's reasons or desire to change. This strategic ordering of the conflict issues leaves the client's arguments for change as a bridge for continuing the dialogue about why he or she feels it is important to change. Miller and Rollnick (2002) suggest using the conjunction "and" when summarizing ambivalence to give credence to the presence of two competing desires or behaviors.

CLIENT: My cocaine use isn't such a big deal; everybody I know does coke. It is kinda scary though when I think about what my doctor said.

COUNSELOR: You don't see a big problem with your cocaine use, and at the same time you are a little worried about it.

This approach conveys respect for the client's perspective, whereas the conjunction "but" could subtly discount the pros and give the appearance that the counselor is taking sides and arguing for the "con." Thus, the use of "and" as opposed to "but" is less likely to elicit defensiveness or resistance. Because MI counselors use reflections to highlight client ambivalence with the goal of increasing awareness and intrinsic motivation for change, they do so by capturing elements of the client's statements rather than supplying the counselor's own arguments, persuasions, or prescriptions for change.

CLIENT: Smoking pot really helps reduce my stress, but it does seem to bother my daughter.

COUNSELOR: On the one hand, smoking pot lowers your stress, and on the other hand it upsets your daughter.

CLIENT: I hate it when I disappoint her. I want her to look up to me.

Sometimes a reflection is presented as a reframed statement that can help the client think about his or her problem in a different way.

CLIENT: I've been to so many treatment centers, nobody thinks I can get sober.

COUNSELOR: You are persistent. This must be important to you.

CLIENT: Yeah, I guess so. I never thought of it that way. Maybe I can prove them all wrong—that'd make my day!

SUMMARIZING

Summary statements are a type of reflection that links two or more ideas the client has shared. Summaries are an effective way for counselors to communicate that they have been listening, and they underscore the client-centeredness of the session. At times, a counselor might provide a prelude to a summary such as *"Let me see if I'm hearing you right"* and end with *"Is that a fair summary, or is there anything that I missed?"* It is worth pointing out that a counselor should select aspects of client statements to include in a summary rather than gathering every element that the client has expressed. Examples of summary content might include client statements of a desire to change or reasons to change. A summary might also include client statements about significant issues in his or her life, feelings of ambivalence, or deep emotions.

CLIENT: I was surprised, but the urges are getting less these days. But when I go around the old neighborhood, it's really hard not to drink. I'll confess. I did slip a little last week. I just couldn't resist.

COUNSELOR: Some of the urges have lessened, which surprised you a little.

CLIENT: Yeah, I just hadn't expected that—it was kind of a relief.

COUNSELOR: A welcomed surprise.

CLIENT: For sure! But that slip worries me. I hate the thought of not being in control of what I do.

COUNSELOR: Being in charge of your life is really important—something you highly value. And the slip gives you some concern. Tell me about that.

CLIENT: It makes me mad. And worries me because if I don't get back on the right track, I'll lose custody of my kids again. I couldn't stand that. They are the most important thing in the world to me. Really the only thing that matters.

COUNSELOR: Your children are everything to you. Alcohol will mean you will lose them. That would be unbearable.

CLIENT: Yes! (tearful) Next time I'm staying away from that place—there's nothing good there for me.

COUNSELOR: Let us see if I've got it right. The urges are starting to calm down, which really surprises and pleases you. Part of you found it hard to resist when you got back to your old neighborhood, and at the same time part of you is really worried about the slippery slope—about how alcohol can interfere with the most important thing in your life, your children. You are determined to get back on track, and that track won't go through your old neighborhood. What did I leave out?

CLIENT: That says it all. I want to be on the right track to take me to my children.

While these four clinical strategies—asking open questions, affirming, reflecting, summarizing—are fundamental skills that are utilized in many types of counseling approaches, what differentiates their usage in MI is the strategic, directive application as a means to help clients explore and resolve ambivalence and move toward positive change.

ELICITING CHANGE TALK

When used effectively, the four MI strategies described in this chapter can be utilized to elicit client statements about *changing* the status quo (i.e., changing their current use of a substance) as opposed to statements, termed *sustain talk*, that advocate for *maintaining* the status quo (i.e., presenting reasons not to change). Client responses that are inherently self-motivating and promote change are termed *change talk* as these types of statements reflect the client's desire, ability, reasons, and need for change. The acronym "DARN" summarizes these elements (i.e., Desire, Ability, Reasons, Need).

Desire: This type of change talk reflects the client's wishes and longing for a change.

"I want things to be different."

"I want to have drugs out of my life once and for all."

Ability: This kind of statement expresses the client's belief that he/she has the resources—the skills and ability—to make a change.

"I stopped using once before, so I know I can stop again."

"When I put my mind to something, I can do it."

Reasons: These client responses indicate their personal reasons for making a change.

"I worry about how cocaine has hurt my health and drained my pocketbook."

"My health really scares me. Those latest liver function test results were frightening."

Need: Need statements reflect the recognition that change has become a necessity, a "must" that has to be accomplished.

"I've got to get off drugs—this has gone too far."

"I have to do this, to take crack out of my life once and for all."

Recognizing or "catching" client change talk—even, and perhaps most important, in its most subtle forms—is an essential task for MI counselors because it can be a sort of homing beacon that provides immediate feedback, indicating that the counselor is headed in the right direction (Miller & Rollnick, 2002). In utilizing the MI style and strategies, counselors also create opportunities that can elicit change talk. Some of these strategies include asking evocative open questions, exploring the good and not so good things about the current behavior, discussing the client's closely held values and beliefs, asking clients about past successes and looking forward to life without drugs/alcohol, and utilization of scaling rulers. These specific strategies will be discussed later in the chapter. Listed below are some examples of questions that elicit change talk.

If you were to choose to quit drinking, why might you want to? *(elicits Desire to change)*

What are the three most important reasons you might want to go to rehab? *(elicits Reasons)*

If you chose to quit, how might you begin? *(elicits Ability)*

What makes you think you might need to quit? *(elicits Need)*

Looking ahead, what might life be like for you when drugs are out of the picture? *(may elicit Reasons, Desire, etc.)*

In addition to recognizing and eliciting change talk, MI counselors respond to, highlight and reinforce these types of client statements by reflecting, asking for examples, and encouraging elaboration of their change talk.

CLIENT: It's my self-respect. I want to be able to look myself in the mirror.
COUNSELOR: To feel a sense of self-worth. *(reflection)* To be the type of person you'd respect.
CLIENT: It'd be the real me—not the me on drugs.
COUNSELOR: Give me an idea, a picture of what the real you might be like. *(asking for an example)*
CLIENT: Well, I'd show up for work on time. People could count on me.
COUNSELOR: Tell me more about that. What would that be like? *(open question inviting elaboration)*
CLIENT: It would be wonderful, so wonderful. I could hold my head high and look people in the eye. They would respect me. I'd respect me.
COUNSELOR: You would be back to the real you—the you that you can and want to be. *(reflection)*

As change talk increases in a session, clients often begin to generate more statements indicating their intention to change. These types of statements, referred to as *commitment talk*, which express the client's determination or resolve to make a change, are strongly related to positive outcomes (Amrhein, Miller, Yahne, Palmer, & Fulcher, 2003). This synergistic process can be represented as:

$$\text{MI style/strategies} \rightarrow \text{Desire} + \text{Ability} + \text{Need}$$
$$+ \text{Reasons} \rightarrow \text{Commitment} \rightarrow \text{Change}$$

As stated earlier, Miller and Rollnick (2002) describe two phases of MI. When considering how and when to utilize the tools just mentioned, it is important to keep in mind which phase the therapeutic session is addressing. The tasks in MI for Phase I focus on increasing awareness, amplifying and resolving ambivalence, and strengthening motivation. In the event that a client expresses a desire or intent not to change at the current time, the counselor acknowledges this decision, often with a summary of relevant statements the client has made, which might include expressions of ambivalence and subtle change talk. At that point, the counselor may offer an ending statement that indicates understanding, acceptance, and respect for the client's self-agency, such as *"Thank you so much for talking with me; from what you've told me, this is not the time, right now, to make any changes in your drug use; please feel free to come back and talk with me again should that be something that might be helpful for you."*

In Phase II, when clients sustain talk, resistance, and ambivalence begin to decrease, counselors generally invite clients to make a goal statement and begin to develop a change plan (Miller & Rollnick, 2002) that states the client's specific change goal, steps to accomplish it, ways others could help, possible barriers, and ways to address them. The counselor will continue to use reflective listening, express empathy, and explore the client's concerns, goals, and solutions as well as summarize, when appropriate, what transpired in earlier sessions that facilitated change talk or enhanced self-efficacy.

COUNSELOR: So, you've shared that although you have fun with your friends drinking and watching football, you end up making decisions and saying things you regret. You told me that your drinking has caused fights with your wife and recently it caused you to lose your job. Where does that leave you now?

This type of question is designed to elicit change and/or commitment talk such as "I guess things would be better if I didn't drink—it seems like it's time to do something different. . . . " When the client begins to verbalize change talk (e.g., "I want to figure out how to quit drinking so much," which indicates a desire to change), or even verbalizes something more tentative, the counselor can transition into suggesting a change plan by saying something like *"It sounds as if you would like to talk about how to move forward. I have an exercise that will help put into words your thoughts and goals for the near future. Would you be interested in that?"* The counselor may also want to use the importance and confidence-scaling rulers (discussed in a later section) to further assess how ready and confident the client is for change.

In sum, the task of the MI counselor is to help the client resolve ambivalence for change by tipping the balance in favor of change. The counselor enhances the client's own intrinsic motivations by recognizing, reinforcing, and asking for elaboration of those client responses that indicate desire, ability, need, reasons for, and commitment to change. Keeping this in mind, the challenge for the counselor is to avoid arguing for change, but rather to gently intensify ambivalence within the client. As the discrepancies between the client's current behavior and his or her values, goals, and larger concerns are highlighted and amplified, a shift toward increased motivation generally occurs. Accordingly, when the client's level of motivation and commitment to change increase, the MI counselor shifts from focusing on motivational enhancement strategies to using techniques to support and build commitment for change such as helping the client set goals and develop a specific change plan.

OTHER MOTIVATIONAL INTERVIEWING TOOLS

PROVIDING PERSONALIZED FEEDBACK

Another useful MI tool is the provision of personalized feedback, based on assessment, information from the scaling rulers (discussed in section: Using Scaling Rulers), or a clinical interview. Using this approach, the counselor first asks permission to give the client some feedback and then proceeds to present the information in a neutral manner. Through the use of personalized feedback, clients may see an aspect of their substance-using behavior about which they had not been aware. The counselor may wish to use open questions when providing feedback such as, *"The information you provided about your daily drinking habits puts you in the high-risk category. What do you make of that?"* The attempt to elicit feedback from clients should be done with the goal of encouraging an awareness of their behavior rather than trying to get them to change. When providing feedback, the counselor should carefully observe how it is impacting the client. Some people are strongly moved, others will tell you it is just what they expected. The counselor should be attentive to identifying issues that appear to be of special concern to the client and reflect the concern back to them. At times, as Rollnick, Mason, and Butler (1999) note, it is acceptable—even necessary—to give more informative feedback on the dangers of the behavior if the counselor feels ethically compelled to do so.

For example, in the case of a pregnant woman who is drinking heavily, a counselor might offer information by incorporating or wrapping it in an MI-style delivery. This type of delivery, sometimes termed the "elicit-provide info-elicit" method (Rollnick, Mason, & Butler, 1999) involves the following sequence of steps. First, the counselor elicits the client's interest in or knowledge about additional feedback. For example, the counselor may ask, *"What kind of things do you know about alcohol use during pregnancy?"*, *"Would you be interested in hearing some information that many have found very helpful about alcohol use during pregnancy?"*, or *"May I share with you some information that you might find helpful?"* It has been our experience that because clients feel invited into the discussion—rather than coerced or given no choice—they almost always agree to hear the information and generally are more engaged in the process. Second, the counselor proceeds to provide the information or advice. And finally, after providing the client with the recommendation or information in an MI style (e.g., non-judgmental, empathic, emphasizing choice), the counselor should turn the discussion back to the client by eliciting her thoughts and reactions, such as *"I can see that's new information to you . . . what are your thoughts about that?"*

ELICIT:

COUNSELOR: Could I share some thoughts and information that I have with you?
CLIENT: Sure.

PROVIDE:

COUNSELOR: Because we know from research that alcohol use during pregnancy can have serious effects on the developing baby, my strong advice would be to not drink during the remainder of your pregnancy. Of course, what you do with this advice is entirely up to you.

ELICIT:

COUNSELOR: What are your thoughts about this?

THE "TYPICAL DAY" EXERCISE

Another useful tool that elicits information about frequency of use and possible motivations for use is the typical day exercise (Rollnick, Mason, & Butler, 1999). In addition to this type of information, this kind of query often results in a broader and deeper pool of information, much of which the counselor might not have thought to explore. This type of exercise is also often very helpful in the initial interview because it conveys a nonjudgmental and genuine, empathic interest in learning about the client and his or her life. In this exercise, the counselor asks the client to describe a typical day in his or her life, keeping substance use the question's focus.

COUNSELOR: Describe for me a typical day when you are using alcohol, starting with when you wake up in the morning, then from morning till noon, then noon till you go to bed. *(open question)*
CLIENT: Well, I wake up about 8—I can sleep late since there is nobody living with me. I just run on my own schedule. Well, I really don't have a schedule now that I think about it—I just wander through the day.
COUNSELOR: Your day usually doesn't have a plan. *(reflection)*
CLIENT: Nope. It just wanders. Sometimes to get me going I have a couple of beers and a cigarette, around 8:30 or so. I go check my garden and then usually have a couple more beers. I get thirsty when I'm pulling weeds and stuff.
COUNSELOR: You have a garden—that must be really nice. *(affirmation)* And taking care of the garden sometimes makes you thirsty; you want a beer. *(reflection)*
CLIENT: And I fix something easy for lunch—I really don't eat much. But I do enjoy some more beer then or maybe some wine, too.

Counselor: And from lunch till bedtime? *(open question)*

Client: More of the same, I guess. I sleep off and on during the afternoon, watch some TV. I like some of those reality shows. Sometimes I skip dinner or just eat cold leftovers. I've lost a good bit of weight lately—just don't like eating by myself. It's boring. Now that I think about it, my whole life is boring.

Counselor: Your life feels empty at this point—you'd like it to be better. *(reflection)*

Client: Yeah, eat, sleep, drink beer—that's all now . . . I need a real life . . . something to look forward to.

The counselor gleaned much helpful information from this exercise—far more than a *"How much do you drink?"* type of question—such as the quality of the client's current life, some possible health problems related to weight loss, drinking patterns (alone, throughout day, beer preference), and eating habits.

Values Clarification Exercise

Using this exercise, the counselor asks the client about the values that are most important to him or her (Miller & Rollnick, 2002). He or she may say, *"So that I can get to know you a little better and understand what kinds of things are most important to you, if it's OK, I'd like to ask you about some of the things you value most in your life."* Or the counselor could say something like, *"Many people have different ideas about what is most important to them in their life—they have different kinds of values. Some highly value family, some achievement, some good health. Other people have other kinds of values. What kind of things do you value most?"* The counselor continues to explore this issue and ask for elaborations, such as *"Tell me more about that"* or *"Give me an example of what that might look like for you."*

A variation of this exercise is to utilize a card-sorting procedure. Clients are provided with a number of cards, each of which has a value printed on it (e.g., family, health, security, freedom, learning, beauty, status, fun, friends, job success, sobriety, being a good parent, helping others, love, spirituality), and are asked to sort the cards into three piles (i.e., not important at all, important, highly important). Next, clients are asked to take the cards from the "highly important" pile and discard the others, then sort them into three new piles (i.e., not important at all, important, highly important). This is repeated until the final "highly important" pile has approximately five to eight cards that represent the client's most primary values. The counselor may take one of these "most important" cards and ask the client about it, about how the value plays out in his or her life or how he or she might like it to be manifested. If a good rapport has been well established, and the counselor senses that the client feels accepted, understood, and valued, the counselor might continue with open questions expressed in a genuinely interested manner. Ideally, this is a time for discussion rather than asking leading questions such as, *"How does your substance use fit with the values?"* or *"What are your thoughts about how much you value self-respect (i.e., one of the values the client noted) and alcohol?"* There are a number of ways to modify this exercise. For example, the counselor might opt to use a five-pile card sort, instead of three piles. The counselor can use ready-made sets of cards (which can be obtained from www.motivational interview.org and other sources) with preprinted values. Counselors can also create sets with values more pertinent and individualized for specific types of client issues, settings, or therapeutic agendas. A copy of the value cards can be found on the Motivational Interviewing website (Miller, Baca, Matthews, & Wilbourne, 2001).

COUNSELOR: *(after giving card-sort exercise instructions)* Tell me about these five values you've selected: security, creativity, time alone, freedom, and nature. How about "creativity"?

CLIENT: I like to make things with my hands. And I love going to museums—it just gives me a thrill, a high really.

COUNSELOR: What kind of things do you make?

CLIENT: I carve little statues, little wooden ones of animals. They are really cool, I think.

COUNSELOR: What a fine gift—to be creative! *(affirmation)*

CLIENT: It makes me feel really good—like I count for something. Sometimes I even sell a few.

COUNSELOR: Make a little money from your craft. *(reflection)* How about "freedom"? Tell me a little about that. *(open question)*

CLIENT: Freedom to be me. To be in control of *my* life—to be free to go here and there as I please. That probation officer, that's what bugs me so much about her—she's always asking about my business, telling me what I have to do and not do. That stinks!

COUNSELOR: You'd like the p.o. [probation officer] to be out of your life; it's really frustrating to have her on your back all the time. *(reflection)*

CLIENT: You're telling me! If I could just get clean and sober, I could get rid of her and her meddling once and for all. But that's easier said than done. This habit is so hard to kick.

COUNSELOR: You really want to be drug-free. That would help *you* be you free. But it's a real challenge. One way you would know you were making progress toward your goal of no drugs would be to have that p.o. out of your life. *(complex reflection)*

USING SCALING RULERS

Scaling rulers are simple yet effective tools for assessing readiness to change that most counselors can learn and implement. Rollnick, Mason, and Butler (1999) first suggested the use of these rulers for counselors in medical practices, but they are applicable in a wide range of settings. The Readiness Ruler (shown in Figure 1.1) offers a quick and simple way of assessing a client's change stage. The ruler's four marks correspond to the precontemplation, contemplation, preparation, and action SOCs. The counselor shows the client the ruler and simply asks, *"Which point on this line best reflects how ready you are at the present time to change your drinking/drug use?"* Be sure the term *change* is defined so that it is clear to the client the type of change that is being assessed (e.g., type of substance, abstinence, reduction). Use of the readiness ruler rounds out the counselor's understanding of the client's motivation and allows for full exploration of the problem behavior. Clients must believe, however, that they can endorse any point on this ruler without being judged and that the purpose of this exercise is to assist in developing the best treatment plan for them. For example, if this tool is to be used in a setting in which clients are mandated to treatment, it is important that the philosophy of the program not be punitive so that clients understand that they will not be penalized if they are in an earlier change stage.

Figure 1.1 shows an example of a ruler used to assess a client's readiness to quit drinking. Each ruler should clearly specify the target behavior, as in this example. This is because a client may be at one point for quitting drinking and at another for quitting cocaine use, so readiness rulers would need to be completed for both behaviors.

Likewise, if the target behavior is for an outcome other than abstinence, such as a reduction in drinking, the client and counselor should be clear about the target outcome. For example, in one study we conducted, the target

Make a slash mark on the line that most closely reflects how ready you are at the present time to quit drinking.

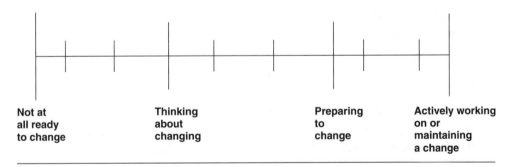

Figure 1.1   Change Ruler

behavior was for women to drink "below risk levels" as identified by the National Institute on Alcohol Abuse and Alcoholism. In that case, we used the definition of risk drinking as the target behavior (i.e., "How ready are you to drink below risk levels? Risk levels for women are defined as no more than four drinks per occasion or no more than seven per week."). In most cases, the client sets her or his own readiness goal prior to completing the ruler.

Other examples of scaling rulers that are often used in MI are Importance and Confidence rulers. Rollnick, Mason, and Butler (1999) note that along with readiness to change, two other related key elements are how important a specific change is to a client and how confident the client is about his or her ability to change. The idea is that if change feels *important* to a client, and the client has the *confidence* to achieve that change, he or she will feel more *ready* to make the change and will be more likely to succeed.

In addition to assessing the importance, confidence, and readiness to change, scaling rulers are an excellent way to elicit change talk from clients. When the OARS strategies are integrated into the session, the scaling rulers become powerful tools for enhancing the client's motivation to change. For example, using the Importance Ruler (see Figure 1.2) a counselor asks: *"How important is it for you to stop smoking now?"* The client marks a slash on the ruler (see below) to indicate his or her judgment of importance. The counselor can use a ruler with no numbers and slash marks only, or he or she may find it helpful to number the scale from 1 to 10, with 10 representing "extremely important." Then, the counselor asks (for example), *"Tell me why you rated the level of importance a 4 and not a 2?"* This question tends to elicit the client's own reasons for wanting to stop smoking. The counselor should listen carefully, reflect these reasons, and probe for any additional reasons. The client will thus hear his or her own reasons for wanting to change, which is motivating and, therefore, reinforces a change attempt. Additional scaling questions that can be used are *"What would have to happen for you to move up from a ___ to a ___?"* or *"What concerns do you have about [current behavior]?"* or *"If you were to change, what would it be like?"*

On the line below, please mark an "X" at the point that best reflects how **important** it is for you to quit smoking.

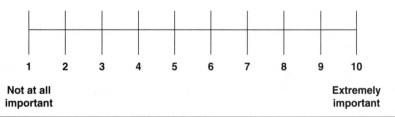

Figure 1.2 Importance Ruler

On the line below, please mark an "X" at the point that best reflects how **confident** you are that you can quit smoking.

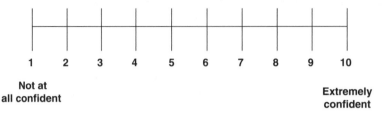

Figure 1.3 Confidence Ruler

Next, the counselor may assess the client's confidence in his or her skills to make the desired change (see Figure 1.3). For example, with a target behavior of drinking cessation, the counselor might ask, *"On this scale from 0 to 10, how confident are you that you can quit drinking?"* As before, the counselor follows up with the second question, which is (for example), *"Help me understand why you are a 3 and not a 0 (or another number below the first one given)."*

No matter how low clients' ratings of importance and confidence are, when compared with a lower number, they will likely have at least one reason why it might be important to change or how they might be able to make a change. Reasons for or ability to change may be elicited by simply asking, *"Why did you choose a 4 and not a 3?"* Additional scaling questions that can be used to explore and enhance a client's confidence are, *"Tell me about a time in the past when you have made a similar change. What did you do then to strengthen your confidence?"* or *"How could you move up higher, so that your score goes from x to y?"* or *"What would make you more confident about making these changes?"* Thus, MI strategies, such as the OARS, are used with the rulers to explore and build the client's levels of importance of and confidence in making a change.

A CASE EXAMPLE

COUNSELOR: We have about 45 minutes together today. Would it be OK if we spend a few minutes talking about your cocaine use? *(ask for permission)*. One thing I'd like say at the outset is that I will not be trying to make you change. Whatever you do with the information we talk about will be up to you. *(emphasizing choice)* How does that sound? *(open question)*

CLIENT: That sounds really good, but I don't think I have a problem with cocaine. I mean, I only use it on the weekends, and I'm not an addict. I'm only here because I have to be.

COUNSELOR: (*Nods*) You don't want to be here, and you feel this might be a waste of time for you. (*reflective listening, avoid argumentation*)

CLIENT: Yeah. I don't think I have a problem. The only reason why I'm in trouble in the first place is because I got caught with the stuff in my car.

COUNSELOR: I understand you don't want to be here, and I appreciate your coming here anyway. Since you are here already, could you tell me a little bit about your cocaine use? (*express empathy, affirmation, open question to roll with resistance*)

CLIENT: Well, like I said, I only use it on the weekends. Mostly with my friends, when we're hanging out or at parties. It's just a way to relax, you know? Work is so stressful right now, and it's not like I smoke every day, and I know tons of people who smoke more than I do. So I don't get why they are making such a big deal about it. I wouldn't be here if the cop who caught me would just cut me some slack.

COUNSELOR: You mentioned that you wish ''they'' wouldn't make such a big deal about it. Tell me more about that. (*open question*)

CLIENT: Well, the cop and the judge. And my girlfriend and my supervisor at work. They're always getting on my case about getting high on the weekends, and how it's illegal and not good for me.

COUNSELOR: I see. What else? (*open question to encourage elaboration*)

CLIENT: My girlfriend really freaked out when I came home high one night because I almost crashed into our garage. She started saying stuff like how much more I party these days and how irresponsible I've become and that she can't marry someone like this. And yeah, I guess I've been partying a bit more than I used to, but it's not like I quit my job to be a dope head.

COUNSELOR: So you've noticed that you have been partying more and that your girlfriend is getting worried about you. You also mentioned your supervisor—how does he fit into all of this? (*reflection, summary, open question*)

CLIENT: My supervisor found out because I came to work high one time and couldn't concentrate in our meeting. He said he noticed that my quality of work wasn't what it used to be, and he wanted me to get help because he wouldn't want to fire me. He's been really good to me, trying to help me out at times. I wouldn't want to get fired either.

COUNSELOR: Your cocaine use has extended beyond the weekends. (*reflection*)

CLIENT: Yeah, I guess I use a little during the week, too, but mostly on the weekends.

COUNSELOR: OK. Let me see if I understand. Both your girlfriend and your boss have expressed concerns about you because you seem different now that you have been using cocaine more often. They're both important to you, and you are concerned that both of them might leave you if you don't stop using. *(summary)*

CLIENT: Yeah, I'm worried. On top of that, now I'm on probation and have to come here.

COUNSELOR: It must be a very stressful time for you. To help me understand a little bit more, give me an idea of what a typical day is like when you are using cocaine. *(open question)* Start with when you first get up.

CLIENT: Well, like I said, it's usually the weekend when I use. I get up pretty early on Saturday, but I'm usually really beat, so sometimes I use a bit to get me going. I just hang out then, feeling kinda bored usually, but looking forward to getting the evening going.

COUNSELOR: So you use a bit in the morning. . . . What about from noon till early evening, dinner time? *(open question)*

CLIENT: I may do a couple of lines. It just depends on how much money I have. The more money, the more cocaine. *(laughs)* But it's the evening when things really get going. . . . me and the guys usually really get going and sometimes things get a little out of hand. . . .

COUNSELOR: A little out of hand. . . . ? *(open question)*

CLIENT: Well, we've gotten into a couple of fights—that's what got me in trouble with the cops.

COUNSELOR: You are really dealing with a lot right now. *(express empathy)* Tell me, how would your life look like right now if you were not using cocaine anymore? *(open question)*

CLIENT: Well, I guess I wouldn't be here. And I wouldn't be in trouble at work. My girlfriend wouldn't be talking about leaving me—we'd probably be talking about getting married, too. We've been together for a while, and I was thinking about asking her to marry me before all this came up. And yeah, I'd probably be saving some money, too.

COUNSELOR: Using cocaine, even just on the weekend and a little during the week, is making it difficult for you to do some of those things, like save money and ask your girlfriend to marry you. *(reflection to develop discrepancy)*

CLIENT: I guess. I just never thought that partying a little would cause so much trouble.

COUNSELOR: OK, you've told me some not so good things about your use of cocaine. What are some good things about it? You mentioned that it helps you through stressful times. *(decisional balance exercise, open question, reflection)*

CLIENT: Huh. No one has asked me that before. Well, like I said, it helps me have a good time and not be so stressed out. My life is stressful. When I use cocaine, I like how all my friends and I just have a good time, without a care in the world. And everything is just more fun when I'm high, and it's so depressing when I'm not.

COUNSELOR: So you enjoy yourself more when you're high because it's a way of socializing with your friends, and you don't feel so stressed out. Everything is more fun and you don't worry so much about your problems. What else? *(summarize, open question to encourage elaboration)*

CLIENT: Not much, I guess. I just really like how I'm relaxed and everything is good in the world when I'm high.

COUNSELOR: Earlier you told me some not so good things about using cocaine, like your girlfriend is upset with you and you might lose your job. What else might be not so good about your use? *(open question to elicit change talk)*

CLIENT: Well, it's costing a whole lot of money. It's getting more and more expensive. And sometimes my heart gets jumpy, and I feel like it's going to jump out of my chest. And I can't seem to remember as much anymore—I'm always forgetting errands I have to run or things I have to do at work. I'm not quite as responsible these days.

COUNSELOR: Besides causing problems with your girlfriend and work, using cocaine sometimes makes you nervous and anxious and your heart starts beating too fast. And your memory seems to be affected by it, too. You also worry that you're becoming less responsible. What else? *(summary, open question)*

CLIENT: I think that's it. But I can't imagine myself not using a little on the weekends. I mean, that's what I do with my friends.

COUNSELOR: You're not sure about how you'd spend the weekends without cocaine, and at the same time you are beginning to have a few worries about how it affects some of your important relationships——your girlfriend and your supervisor——and there are also the memory trouble and maybe some cardiac problems. *(double-sided reflection)* If you were to decide to make a change in your cocaine use, what might that look like? *(open question)*

CLIENT: Well, if I *did* decide to, I guess I'd try not using on a Saturday. But that would be pretty tough.

COUNSELOR: So a first step would be to have a Saturday without cocaine.

[reflection] Let's take a minute, if it's OK, and think about how important it is right now for you to make that kind of change, on a scale from 1 to 10, with 1 being not important at all and 10 being highly important. *(asking permission, assessing importance with a scaling ruler)*

CLIENT: Hmmmm. I guess maybe it would be around a 6 or 7, I guess a 7.

COUNSELOR: So about a 7. Tell me about that. Why a 7 and not a 5, for example? *(open question to elicit change talk)*

CLIENT: Well, it's more important than a 5 . . . you know, my girlfriend, and my job. And that memory thing really ticks me off. I'm way too young to have that going on.

COUNSELOR: There it is again, how important those relationships are in your life. And the memory issue is a concern, too. *(reflection)*

CLIENT: Yeah, and there's the money, too. That's getting to be a big problem.

COUNSELOR: A concern about money, as well. *(reflection)* In terms of confidence, I'm wondering where you'd put yourself on the same kind of ruler, with 1 being not confident at all that you could make this first change and 10 being extremely confident. *(assessing confidence with scaling)*

CLIENT: Now this is tough. *(laughs nervously)* I can usually do what I put my mind to, but this will be hard. Cocaine has been such a regular part of my weekend life.

COUNSELOR: It will be a challenge. *(reflection)* . . . what number? *(open ruler question)*

CLIENT: Oh, I don't know . . . I guess around a 5.

COUNSELOR: So about halfway. Why a 5 and not a 3? *(open question)*

CLIENT: Like I said, I'm pretty hardheaded and can usually do what I decide to do. But I'm not saying it'd be easy for sure.

COUNSELOR: When you determine to do something, you carry through with it. *(reflection)* What could happen that might make you even more confident, say move you from a 5 to a 6 or 7? *(open question)*

CLIENT: I guess if I could make some kind of other plans for a Saturday, doing something entirely different. Yeah, that might work.

COUNSELOR: So kinda putting yourself in charge of the day, planning something different, new. *(reflection with a reframe emphasizing choice, control)*

CLIENT: Sorta sounds fun now that I think about it. Maybe something with my girlfriend. She would be *really* surprised and like that!

COUNSELOR: It sounds like it might be something fun to try. *(reflection)*

> We're about out of time. We've talked about some good things and some not so good things about your cocaine use. I'm not here to tell you what to do, but to help you in any way I can. I'm confident that if and when you make a decision and commitment to stop using cocaine, you'll find a way to do it. The decision is up to you, though. I appreciate your willingness to share your experiences with me, and I'm looking forward to learning more about you next time we meet. *(reflection, emphasis autonomy, support self-efficacy, affirmation)*

INDICATIONS AND CONTRAINDICATIONS FOR MOTIVATIONAL INTERVIEWING

There are surprisingly few contraindications in the literature for using MI because it appears to be effective and appropriate across cultures, populations, settings, and behaviors. There are, however, ethical issues to consider when using MI. For example, MI may not be appropriate in situations where the counselor's role involves coercive power to influence the client's behavior and outcomes. This is particularly true when coercive power is combined with a personal investment in the client's behavior (Miller & Rollnick, 2002). Counselors may face dilemmas in this regard, which can create conflicting interests. For example, social workers or probation officers often function as both helpers and controllers/enforcers (International Federation of Social Workers, 2004), and the way in which the use of MI meshes with the legal power they hold over their clients must be taken into consideration. This is particularly true in cases such as those where social workers serve as child protective service caseworkers or with substance abuse counselors working in settings where clients are mandated to treatment. Miller and Rollnick (2002) suggest that in these types of interactions, counselors advise clients that they have two different roles in the situation. For example, the counselor may say something like, *"On one hand, I represent the court, to ensure that you know the terms required to have your children returned to you, and I must honor that role. My other role is to help you make changes in your life that will be beneficial. What I hope is that by working together I can help you make these positive changes. I am required by law to report the outcomes of our time together to the court, but I will also support you in your efforts."*

HOW TO LEARN MOTIVATIONAL INTERVIEWING

MI can be thought of as both an art and a craft. It is "artful" in terms of its spirit and the cadence and flow of the counselor-client dialogue; as a craft, it offers selective strategies that can be applied to a variety of behaviors and situations. Much like learning and refining any new skill or approach, MI proficiency is enhanced by practice and feedback.

A first step can simply be reading one or more of several books and resources that are available (e.g., *Motivational Interviewing: Preparing People for Change*, Miller & Rollnick, 2002; *Motivational Interviewing in Health Care: Helping Patients Change*, Rollnick et al., 2008; *Group Treatment for Substance Abuse*, Velasquez, Maurer, Crouch, & DiClemente, 2001; *Treatment Improvement Protocol (TIP) Series 35*). Some individuals participate in MI workshops or group trainings, such as those offered by a cadre of expert presenters from the Motivational Interviewing Network of Trainers (MINT). These workshops typically provide opportunities for a variety of learning experiences such as didactic presentations, role plays, observation, videos, and demonstrations. The www.motivationalinterview.org website provides a list of these trainings that are available in many countries.

Another excellent learning process involves practice with "standardized patients/clients" who are actors trained to deliver a series of scripted scenarios about a problematic behavior such as alcohol misuse. The practice sessions with these "patients/clients" are videotaped and reviewed by MI experts who provide immediate feedback and suggestions as how to fine-tune the MI delivery.

Some counselors find it helpful to meet with their colleagues to brainstorm and problem-solve about applying MI with more challenging clients or situations. They also can view and discuss one or more of the excellent MI videos that are available from the www.motivationalinterview.org website. Additional ideas for making these discussions most useful include scheduling regular meetings focused on strengthening MI skills, reviewing and coding MI elements from taped MI sessions (i.e., after obtaining written client consent, of course), and discussing specific readings on MI.

A particularly valuable learning tool is the use of the coding schemes such as the MITI 3.0 (Moyers et al., 2005), mentioned earlier. These coding systems allow for the provision of highly specific feedback (e.g., frequency of open questions, reflections, ratio of questions to reflections in the session) as well as broader impressions of how much the session conveyed the MI "spirit." As the learning process continues, many counselors report that listening to their own audiotapes and counting or coding their use of certain MI strategies or skills greatly increases their awareness of their strengths as well as areas that could be improved.

Finally, some counselors form their own MI-support peer groups that meet regularly to review their use of MI. Some programs or agencies that utilize MI-based interventions provide counselors with knowledgeable and highly experienced MI coaches who observe live sessions and/or review session tapes and discuss with the counselors their use of MI elements. Sometimes sessions can be uploaded to a secure website, which only the coach can access, and then the coach views the session—and perhaps codes MI session elements—and provides specific feedback to counselor and/or brainstorms with the counselor specific issues in the session.

TAILORING MOTIVATIONAL INTERVIEWING TO THE POPULATION

MOTIVATIONAL INTERVIEWING WITH INVOLUNTARY CLIENTS

There has been considerable interest in the use of MI in circumstances that are legally mandated. Some examples might be MI conducted in criminal justice settings, court-mandated programs such as drunk-driver or drug treatment programs, or child protective service (CPS) encounters. While it may at first seem counterintuitive to use a style that emphasizes client choice in these settings, research shows that it can be very effective with mandated clients (Fromme & Corbin, 2004). The reality is that clients do have choices. They can choose to follow the rules while incarcerated or not to follow the rules; while on probation they can choose actions that will determine whether they return to jail; they can choose or not choose behaviors that will result in forfeiting their driver's license or even their children. Indeed, when presented this way—that is, letting clients know that they do indeed have options—clients often have a much more favorable response to the intervention. Most people who are mandated to treatment are used to being intimidated and coerced, and they typically play very little part in making their own decisions. When counselors using MI listen to clients in a respectful manner and elicit their ideas about change, the clients are often quite surprised and become much more engaged in the process. The important message to deliver when working with mandated clients is that they have responsibility for and freedom of choice.

Presenting the style and rationale for MI at the beginning of the first session or encounter helps the client set aside any preconceived notions and fears about being confronted or coerced and to feel more at ease. For example, these opening remarks can set the tone in an MI encounter with a substance-abusing client:

> Before we begin, let me just explain a little about how we will be working together. I'm not going to be telling you what to do. I hope I can help you think about your substance use and consider what, if anything, you might want to do, but if there is any changing to be done here, you will be the one who does it. Nobody can tell you what to do, and I wouldn't even attempt to do that. I've been asked to give you some information, and I may give you some advice, if you'd like for me to, but what you do with it is completely up to you. The only person who can decide to change, and if so, how to change, is you. How does that sound to you? (Miller, Zweben, DiClemente, & Rychtarik, 1992, p. 50).

Helpful responses counselors can use with resistant clients in mandated settings might include:

I hear what you're saying about not wanting to be here. Given that we have this time together, what, if anything, would you like to change about your drug use?

No one can change your drug use for you. Only you can do it. You will decide whether you will use your time in this place to think about changes. Many clients do decide to make a change, but that's completely up to you.

You can decide to go on using just as you have been, or choose to make a change. You are the expert on your life and your choices.

Importantly, the tone that these types of statements are conveyed in is critical. Such statements can easily come across as a subtle lecture, sarcastic, or "preacherly" if not offered in a neutral, empathic, and genuine manner that conveys to the client that he or she does have a choice and that the choice that is made will be acknowledged and accepted by the counselor.

Although MI counselors emphasize personal autonomy and choice, a discussion of choice may well need to include information about consequences that the choice may entail. It is perfectly acceptable (and ethical), therefore, for counselors to inform clients that although they will not try to make them change, there may still be clear consequences for their actions. For example, given a particular choice, clients may end up having their probation revoked, losing their children, or giving up their employment.

An MI way of providing information about likely consequences—which is a variation of the elicit-provide-elicit process described earlier—might be:

I've been asked by the court to give you some information. Sometimes, clients have found this information to be really helpful. I don't know if that will apply to you, but if it's OK, I'd like to share it with you. Of course, what you do with the information is entirely up to you. The court is requiring 90 days of attendance at AA meetings. If that requirement it not met, then your parole will be revoked. What are your thoughts about that? What might be the next step, then, for you?

In the MI style, the counselor conveys that it is the client's choice whether to face those consequences because only the client can decide to change. One useful strategy that emphasizes this choice is asking the client to anticipate what the long-term results might be if he or she chooses to continue using the substance of concern (e.g., "If you were to continue your use, just as it is now, where might you be in five years? What would be the likely consequences?"), or if he or she decides to stop using (e.g., "If you were to decide to stop using, how might *things be better, be different for you in five years?''*) Another strategy that can be particularly helpful with mandated clients is to construct a formal "decisional balance" sheet by having the client generate the pros and cons of change. What are the good things about continuing to use drugs? What are some of the not so good things?

ADAPTING MI TO GROUPS

A significant strength of the MI approach is that it is a style that can be adapted to a number of venues and modalities, including groups (Velasquez, Stephens, & Ingersoll, 2006). Adding MI groups to the continuum of care for substance abusers can present some challenges, however. One consideration is the philosophy of the treatment program that is seeking to add an MI component. A philosophy that is punitive or includes assumptions that individuals are powerless to make change and that immediate abstinence is essential is not consistent with MI, which emphasizes personal choice and supports successive approximations toward a goal as a means of building self-efficacy. Because differing philosophies can be confusing for clients and staff alike, MI counselors are advised to seek open dialogue with peers and supervisors about ways to resolve any contradictory beliefs about treatment and the nature of change. A more detailed discussion of implementation issues in group MI can be found in Ingersoll, Wagner, and Gharib (2000) and in Velasquez, Maurer, Crouch, and DiClemente (2001).

Beyond philosophical issues, there are also challenges that stem from adapting a highly individualized approach such as MI for a group. In individual interventions, the MI counselor seeks to understand the client's perspective and to draw out the client's arguments for and commitment to change, rather than inserting the counselor's opinions and biases. In a group format, all members of the group are encouraged to share views and experiences as a means of providing learning opportunities for the group. If member feedback comes across as judgmental, critical, or self-interested, however, rather than empathic, it can engender resistance within the group. To counter this possibility, in group therapy as in individual MI, the counselor works to create an atmosphere of mutual respect and collaboration, models positive ways of providing feedback, and gently redirects less helpful comments and responses made by group members. In group MI, counselors must also attend to group processes rather than slip into a mode of conducting individual therapy within the group. Because group members are often diverse in terms of their target behaviors, SOC, reasons for change, and self-efficacy, the MI process of understanding and eliciting reasons for change for each group member might serve to emphasize the group's heterogeneity rather than its commonalities, which is one factor believed to be curative about the group therapy process (Yalom & Leszcz, 2005). This concern may be ameliorated, however, by the counselor's continual fostering of the MI spirit of affirmation, acceptance, and respect for different experiences and perspectives.

The counselor employing MI in a group setting should be highly skilled and experienced both in MI and in group therapy processes. The effectiveness of MI in group-based treatments is likely to be maximized by incorporating some of the following provisions:

1. Present the style and spirit of MI when opening the group.

   Before providing introductions and agreeing on group "rules" (e.g., not interrupting, avoiding monopolizing, arriving on time), it is helpful to present an overview of how the group will be conducted. Counselors can begin by telling members that they are here to help them learn more about themselves and whether there are any changes they would like to make. Counselors may also offer assurance that while they have some knowledge and skills that may be helpful, if there is any changing to be done, the members will be the ones to do it. In other words, the responsibility for change will be up to each member, and the counselor(s) will not try to force him or her to change in any way. Members can be told that although the counselor will serve as the group facilitator, each member will play an important role in helping other group members. The motivational approach of the group can be explained by emphasizing that members will help facilitate change in one another through supportive interactions. Thus, unlike some models of substance abuse treatment, this group will explicitly avoid confrontations and, instead, offer an environment of empathy, acceptance, and respect for individual differences. Counselors may also note that research indicates that a supportive, empathic manner is much more effective than a confrontational one. Since this type of group may be a new experience for some members, counselors will want to ask them to talk about their reactions to this approach. Often, the members are pleasantly surprised to learn that they won't be lectured to or forced to discuss anything against their will. Counselors should keep in mind that norms are established early in the course of a group and are not easily changed; thus, the ground rules of the group should be made explicit at the beginning of each session. For example, tactfully informing members at the outset that hostile or dominating speech is not part of this group's style will help discourage disruptions and the possibility of one member dominating the group.

   Some counselors find it helpful to use the acronym "OPEN" in starting the group (Velasquez, Stephens, & Ingersoll, 2006):

Open with group purpose: to learn more about members' thoughts, concerns, and choices

Personal choice is emphasized

Environment is one of respect and encouragement for all members

Nonconfrontational nature of the group

The following sequence of the opening of an actual first session illustrates the introduction to group MI as well as the counselor's use of empathy, open questions, reflective listening, and affirmation. This group was conducted as part of a project funded by the National Institute on Drug Abuse (RO1 DAO15453) to study the effects of a stage-based group treatment for cocaine abusers. The intervention is based on the group sessions detailed in *Group Treatment for Substance Abuse: A Stages of Change Therapy Manual* (Velasquez, Maurer, Crouch, & DiClemente, 2001).

COUNSELOR: This is likely to be kind of a different group from some of the other groups you've been in. In this group we will use a style called "Motivational Interviewing." Some of the groups in which you may have participated in the past have probably been confrontational, where the members tell another member what they *have* to do or "call each other out" when they suspect another person needs to be challenged or is not honest. In this group, rather than confronting each other, we support one another. We're a group that offers each other respect, empathy, and acceptance. Acceptance really means our hearing what the other person has to say—we don't have to approve of what that person says, but we respect each person's position and interact in a caring manner. Is that OK with everyone? *(group introduction with emphasis on nonconfrontational tone of the group)*

MEMBER A: Yes, I kind of like the idea that we will respect each other and that no one is going to get on my case. Maybe we can all work together to find solutions for each other. I know I sure need to do something different.

COUNSELOR: You got it exactly right—respect. *(affirmation)* It's kind of a relief that someone won't be talking at you, getting on your case. *(reflection)* We're really here to be supportive of each other, to talk about what kind of changes we'd each like in our life, what kind, if any, changes in your alcohol use. We won't be trying to make you change or telling you what to do, because if there is any changing to be done, any decisions to be made, it will be your choice. What you do with the information and things we talk about will be up to you. *(giving information with emphasis on personal choice and responsibility)* Could we start with you, B? *(asking permission)* What are some things you hope to get out of our group? *(open question)*

MEMBER B: I was sober a long, long time. But then off the wagon I went. I'm still off, and it's way too tough right now. This life, the way it is now, is way too hard. I'm tired of this. Beat down.

COUNSELOR: You're tired of being so down, so tired. You want it to be different. *(reflection emphasizing momentum)* So one of your goals for being in the group is. . . . ? *(open question, shifting focus to goals)*

MEMBER B: I need some help. Some of that support like you talked about. I need a new life.

COUNSELOR: You want to get something to help you move on. You're tired of being so tired. *(reflection)* What about you, D? *(open question, turning topic to another member)*

MEMBER D: This is my fourth time to try to shake the bottle habit. I've been drinking since I was 12 years old. Didn't really have much trouble with it till I had a couple of DUIs. Then everything went down for me. Lost my driver's license, then my job. My wife and I fight constantly . . . money problems all over us.

COUNSELOR: Alcohol cost you a lot—trouble with the law, money problems, and marital conflict. You've been through so much. *(reflection, support)* There seem to be some common themes here today—a lot of losses, feeling really down and low, wanting a real change, a new beginning. I really appreciate everyone's input—it takes a lot of courage to be so open with people you've just met. *(summary, affirmation)* *(looking at Member C)* What do you hope to get from this group experience? What changes are you thinking about?

MEMBER C: I'm not sure about all this. I don't know if I really belong here. I drink a lot, yeah, but not so much that it's really a problem.

COUNSELOR: You're a little puzzled—maybe you don't really fit with this group right now. Alcohol hasn't ever caused you any trouble. *(amplified reflection)*

MEMBER C: Well, *(laughs)* I wouldn't say *no* troubles—I got into some fights a while back, trouble with the cops. And there is this liver thing—I don't understand it very much, but . . .

COUNSELOR: On the one hand, you're not sure if this is the right place for you, if alcohol is really something you should be concerned about, and on the other hand there are some thoughts, a little worry, about some health issues and maybe legal troubles before. *(doubled-sided reflection capturing ambivalence)*

MEMBER A: Me, too. There are some good things, you know, about drinking for me. Helps me relax and also be more friendly. You know, sociable. It helps me get away from all the stuff in my life.

COUNSELOR: It sounds like some benefits for you about using alcohol include being relaxed, makes it easier to be with people. *(reflection,* *rolling with resistance)* Since you're here today, I'm wondering what concerns, if any, you might have about using alcohol? *(open question, shifting to decisional balance process)*

MEMBER A: I don't know. Other people, you know. They keep on talking about it. They say it's gotten out of hand.

MEMBER C: Out of hand?

MEMBER A: Yes. It's really kind of taken over my life.

COUNSELOR: Part of you sees some real pros—some reasons—for drinking, and part of you thinks that it may have gone a little too far, that you've lost control of your life. Of yourself. *(double-sided reflection, amplified)*

MEMBER A: I worry about that. And so do the people I care about.

2. Focus on collaboration and creating an atmosphere of partnership.

Counselors should avoid the "expert" trap by focusing on collaboration and creating a "partnership" atmosphere. Chairs should be arranged in a circle whenever possible, and in the case of groups with two facilitators, avoid having both facilitators sit side-by-side as this creates an "expert" segment of the circle. In general, in the spirit of collaboration, before offering suggestions or information about coping techniques, for example, MI counselors will ask the group members what their solutions have been or what they have seen work with other people.

COUNSELOR: So you've tried to quit before.

MEMBER D: Oh, yeah. For sure!

COUNSELOR: When you quit before, I wonder what worked for you then. What helped you with the quit? *(open question asking for member's past solutions)*

MEMBER D: Well, I'd spent a lot of time with my old buddies, from years ago. We used to go to the bar on 3rd Street and have a lot of fun together. Well, it started out as fun, but sometimes it got us in trouble—cops came. My girlfriend was not happy when she had to bail me out again. So when she said, "Quit or get out," I decided not to go back to the old places. . . . I tried to get some new buddies from work to hang out with.

COUNSELOR: You changed some of the places where you would go. What a good strategy. *(reflection, affirmation, collaboration in considering past successful strategies, building self-efficacy)*

MEMBER D: Yeah, it really worked for a while. As a matter of fact, I began to wonder why I'd ever hung out with those losers. All they did was laze around. And I wasn't the real me when I was with them. I hated myself then.

COUNSELOR: You didn't act like the person you know you really are. That was really hard to see. You want to be the "real" you. *(reflection)* What else did you do that helped? *(open question)*

MEMBER D: Well, I threw all the booze out of the house. That really helped! It just wasn't around when I got stressed. But when the stuff, the stress, really got bad, I got some back again.

COUNSELOR: Getting the liquor out of the house was really effective. *(reflection)* Tell me about other ways you, or other people you know, have handled a lot of stress—maybe ways that didn't involve alcohol. *(collaborative open question)*

MEMBER A: One thing I did, it may sound silly, but when it got really bad, sometimes I'd start exercising, working out. I'd run around the block, do some push-ups. I don't know why, but that seemed to really help, get my mind off other stuff.

MEMBER D: Yeah. I might try that sometime. I do need to lose a little weight. *(laughs)*

COUNSELOR: Exercising, changing patterns like where we hang out, who we are around—sounds like those things have been really helpful at times, pretty good ways to deal with stress in a positive manner. *(summary)*

3. Use selective reflective listening to build motivation and reinforce change talk.

As with MI in an individual format, judicious reflections are the heart of MI group work. Reflections can help establish rapport, express empathy, decrease resistance, selectively highlight responses that are most relevant to the change process, support autonomy, and promote change talk. Simple reflections repeat or paraphrase the meaning of a statement, while more complex reflections amplify the meaning or give voice to feelings that underlie a statement. In groups comprised of members in different change stages, reflections are powerful tools for responding to one member and applying the member's response to benefit the group. While reflective listening can be challenging in a group format, it is still possible. When two counselors facilitate the group, one may focus on reflecting and the other monitor and attend to the group process.

In the following transcript, the counselors model empathy and affirmation (rather than confrontation) by selectively using reflections to reframe a client's relapse as a learning experience.

MEMBER D: Things were going good for me. I had gotten a new job, a good one that even had some benefits. I was pretty proud of myself, and my family was, too. And then, out of the blue, seems like, a buddy offered me some beer, and before I even thought about it, I was on my second six-pack. Then it was down, down . . . back to the old ways.

COUNSELOR: You had things going really good, but then there was a turn, took you almost by surprise. It just seemed to happen. *(reflection)*

MEMBER C: Kinda the same thing happened to me—I was sailing along, been sober for three years. Then one day I was feeling kinda low, lonely, really, and there was the bar across the street and . . .

COUNSELOR: Loneliness is a trigger for you. *(reflection)* One thing we know is that it is really pretty normal for a slip to happen when somebody is making a really hard change. Sometimes we call it a relapse—not a fatal error. *(giving information that a relapse is normative, not shameful)*

MEMBER B: I've been there . . . but you know I learned something out of all that. I could stop because I did!

COUNSELOR: You knew that you could be successful because you had been! *(affirmation, reflection of "ability" change talk)*

MEMBER B: I sure was—and it felt great. I got a lot of things back that I had lost. Like my self-respect for one thing.

COUNSELOR: Respecting yourself—that's something you really value, hold dear. Staying off alcohol brought that back. *(reflection of "reason" change talk)*

4. Use MI methods for handling resistance.

MI methods that diffuse resistance in individual counseling can likewise be used in groups. They also can serve as a model for how group members can relate to each other in a positive way. Group leaders use methods such as empathic reflecting, asking for elaboration on change talk, and validating personal choice and responsibility. If a negative, hostile comment is made by one member, selectively emphasize the most positive part of the comment, reframe the comment, and/or affirm the member (e.g., for his or her concern, experience, energy, passion, pain). At times, the reframe or affirmation may be followed by a diplomatic, empathic reminder about the policies of the group. For example:

> Some of you have been through so much, have so much hard-earned experience that it's probably hard at times to remember that in this special kind of group we try to not tell someone else what to do because we know it is a matter of a personal choice—we each are the experts on our own life. But I appreciate how much we want to pass on some of our hard lessons.

Also, "differential reinforcement" can be used by attending to positive, nonargumentative, or change talk responses. These selective reflections allow individuals to be heard and reinforced for their constructive comments.

A group decisional balance exercise described by Walters, Ogle, and Martin (2002) can also be used to defuse resistance. Using an MI style, ask group members to first brainstorm a list of reasons for not making a change (i.e., the "good things" about their drug use) and then to list reasons for making a change (i.e., the "not so good things" about their drug use). Then have one of the facilitators use the group's list to argue against change and invite the rest of the group to take up counterarguments about why change would be a good thing. Record the group's reasons, reinforcing comments and encouraging members to argue their points even more forcefully. In this way, the resistance is voiced and then channeled into change talk. After the debate, summarize the group's arguments for change, and then specific members can be asked to elaborate on their reasons. This process reinforces the change talk that was generated by group members.

Group members can also be taught simple reflecting listening skills (Ingersoll, Wagner, & Gharib, 2000). Using this approach, the counselor asks for a volunteer to offer a statement such as *"One thing I'd like to change about my life. . . . "* After modeling a reflection of the client's statement, the counselor coaches group members on how to make simple reflective statements. The counselor should point out that members can use reflective statements to check out their understanding of another member's statement. While group members are not expected to become experts at reflective listening, teaching basic reflective listening skills can help them avoid using confrontational tactics and feel safe enough to receive feedback from others.

The following transcript illustrates the use of selective reflections and defusing resistance.

Member D: *(angrily to the members)* You don't know what my life has been like—nobody can understand. I've been through stuff nobody could imagine.

Counselor: Nobody here has walked in your shoes. *(reflection)*

Member D: You got that right! And I ought to be able to do what I want to—it's my life. I tell my girlfriend that how much I drink or how or when I drink is none of her business.

Counselor: You are the one in charge of your life. It's really frustrating when somebody else tries to make decisions for you. *(reflection emphasizing choice)*

Member D: Yeah. *(more subdued)*

Member B: Hey, man, sounds like she really cares about you. I wish I had somebody who'd be on my case some of the time. I got nobody.

COUNSELOR: Sometimes nagging shows concern . . . maybe when people in our lives don't nag, they don't care. *(reflection, reframing nagging as concern)*

MEMBER D: She does care. She's stuck by me—and I haven't made it easy for her. I always thought I could control it, you know, control the drinking. I think I really did for a while. I could drink all I wanted and still keep my job, my woman.

COUNSELOR: It was going OK . . . then something changed. *(reflection)*

MEMBER D: Yeah, it just got out of hand. I hate not being in control of my life. I've got to get that back . . . the way it is now, I can't take it any longer.

MEMBER A: You know, what you need to do is just get it together! Try harder!

MEMBER D: Huh?

COUNSELOR: *(to Member A)* Sounds like trying harder has really worked for you, and at the same time B has had a different story—like we said at the beginning, B knows best what will work for him. And you, A, are the expert on your life. *(gentle redirect to not tell others members what to do)*

MEMBER A: That's true . . . so true.

MEMBER D: But thanks for caring enough to say something.

COUNSELOR: (to D and group) For some of you, seems like this is the time for a new chapter, a turn down another, a better road. *(reflection, use of metaphor)*

MEMBER D: It's time for me, for sure.

MEMBER A: I want things to be better, too. I guess we all do or we wouldn't be here.

5. Discuss stages of change and encourage members to identify their own stage.

The SOC (Prochaska & DiClemente, 1984) can be used as a useful model for assessing members' readiness to change and for tailoring the group interventions. For this reason, it is useful to educate group members about the stages by describing them and then presenting vignettes for a variety of behaviors to allow members to identify the change stage for each scenario.

Many members in the precontemplation or contemplation stages may be participating in the program as the result of pressure from others, so it is important for counselors to accept and acknowledge any resistance that is demonstrated by members to the idea of changing their substance use. There are several ways in which members may express resistance, such as being openly hostile, refusing to talk in group, or appearing to participate while tacitly feeling passive and resentful. As seen in the previous transcript, the way to defuse resistance is to "roll" with it by using motivational strategies. One example would be to acknowledge that because some group members might feel pressured to be there, feeling resistant, disinterested, or reluctant is completely normal. Members can also be told that because many of them may have shared similar experiences, the group will give them a chance to explore their own feelings about their substance use with others in the group who can understand their situation. Other members may feel demoralized because they have attempted to change many times. Providing them with information about the SOC and the number of change attempts that often occur before lasting change is accomplished often instills hope in members who feel discouraged.

The next excerpt describes an SOC discussion that helps to promote insight, explore ambivalence, and identify triggers for alcohol use. This transcript demonstrates how a counselor can provide didactic information in an MI style, and it also demonstrates how two counselors can work collaboratively.

COUNSELOR A: Let's look at this handout that shows different stages somebody can be in when they are thinking about changing a behavior. It could be cocaine use, eating better, or drinking less. As you can see, when people are not really thinking about changing, see no reason to, they are in the stage we call "precontemplation." When a little question happens, kind of like a little idea that "maybe I ought to do something different, I don't know for sure, but just maybe . . . ," we call that "contemplation"—just beginning to think about changing. *(provides information)*

MEMBER C: That describes me!

COUNSELOR B: You're beginning to think about things being different, changing your alcohol use. *(reflection)* The handout also shows somebody who is beginning to make some plans for changing, getting some ideas, and maybe finding resources that would help—this is called the "preparation" stage of change. Next, when people are actually making some changes, doing some things differently about the issue of concern (such as drug use), we say they are in the "action" stage. *(provides information)*

MEMBER E: Like coming here to group?

COUNSELOR A: Right! That's an action to help change your drinking. *(affirmation, reflection)*

COUNSELOR B: And finally, when the changes become kind of like a habit——take less effort to keep going, that's called the "maintenance" stage. The handout also shows that if a slip or relapse occurs, people don't become a "failure," somebody outside the change process. But rather, they often reenter the change cycle, sometimes by coming right back into action or for others back to contemplation. So change is a process for us all—not an either-or state. What do you make of that? How does this idea fit for you? (provides information, open question)

MEMBER C: I'd say I'm in action, too. I quit using two weeks ago.

COUNSELOR B: You've taken some action. *(reflection)* Who else? *(open question to engage other members)*

MEMBER D: Can you be in two places, two stages at one time?

COUNSELOR B: Tell us about it. *(open question)*

MEMBER D: Contemplation and preparation? See, I like doing pot, although I know I probably should cut down. But alcohol's a different thing, I'm coming to this group, I also go to AA. . . . I haven't quit, but I *have* cut down, and I'm planning on more, on cutting down to nothing.

COUNSELOR A: Thank you for that excellent example. *(affirmation)* You are exactly right—a person can be, in fact often is—in different stages for two different behaviors. Sometimes we're really motivated to change one behavior, but less concerned about another behavior. *(affirmation, provides information)*

MEMBER E: And for me, I just keep bouncing back and forth. One day I want to quit and the next I'm not so sure. *(laughs)* It's pretty confusing to tell you the truth. I don't know where I am.

COUNSELOR B: The word that describes what you're talking about is "ambivalence" . . . feeling two ways about something. That's really common in the early stages where you think "I know that *this* part is OK, but I'm not sure if *this* part is OK. I know I want to change this, and I'm not sure I want to change that." That sort of confusion. *(provides information, reflection)*

MEMBER A: Oh yeah! . . . confusion—

(General laugh from members)

6. Eliciting change talk around a group theme.

While it is common for members to have differing concerns, themes often emerge that are important to the majority of the members of the group. When this occurs, the counselor has an opportunity to elicit change talk related to this theme. An example follows around the change talk related to concerns that others have.

COUNSELOR: Who else? Who else has ideas about ways people in your life may have expressed concern about your drinking? *(open question)*

Some of you said that nagging you really seems to mean that they care. Some of you said that giving you an ultimatum—shape up or ship out, I think you said, C—meant that they wanted the "old" you back, the "you" you used to be. *(summary)* Anybody else have other people in your lives who have some concerns? *(closed question)*

Member A: My girlfriend, at least the one I used to have. She worried about my health all the time. I kept having these chest pains and aches in my stomach. She kept saying that the alcohol made it all worse.

Member C: People who care about you don't want to see you get hurt or hurt yourself. But if you keep using, you're gonna hurt them for sure. I sure did, over and over again.

Counselor: So when people worry about you, about your health and how you are doing. . . . It shows that they care. And it hurts when you hurt them, when your alcohol use affects those around you who care. *(reflection capturing group concerns)*

Member B: I can see them, my kids, feeling better, not so scared now that I'm on the right track. I am through with the bottle—it's out of my life!

Counselor: Your children feel more secure—you've made that happen by your decision. *(reflection, affirmation)* I'm wondering, in terms of what we've talked about today, if you had to choose the most important reason for making this hard change, what would that be? *(open question to elicit change talk)*

Member B: As I think about it, really stop and think, I think the most important reason is that it is for me. I'm the one who has to do it, for me. For my kids, too, sure, but they didn't get the payoff, the benefit, until I finally did something. I missed so much during all those years. Missed my kids growing up. So it is for me, and my future and my kids' futures.

Counselor: This is for you. You are the one on the front line. And most important, it is for your future—for what you will do and for your kids' future and their time with you, too. *(reflection)*

7. Group summaries.

Group summaries can be used to selectively emphasize the most relevant comments made by group members and to reinforce change talk. Summaries can be utilized strategically to review and highlight relevant information provided, relate a response by one member to an earlier comment from another member, and transition the group discussion to another area of focus (Miller & Rollnick, 2002).

This transcript contains examples of one type of change talk (i.e., reasons for wanting to change), which is subsequently repeated in a group summary.

COUNSELOR: All of us here have separate stories, different situations. When you think about your own life, what might be some reasons that you might want to stop drinking? *(open question eliciting change talk)*

MEMBER D: I've wasted so much money over the years, in and out of my hands in a flash.

COUNSELOR: The money was gone. *(reflection)*

MEMBER D: Yeah, there were so many things I needed it for—rent, child support, even food! But . . .

MEMBER A: For me, money, too. I need to finally build up a little nest egg for me and my brother. I also want to get off the booze so maybe I can see my kids again. I miss them so bad.

COUNSELOR: Money for you, and most especially your children—to get back in touch with them, be with them again. *(reflection)*

MEMBER A: I need to be the kind of father to them I never had.

COUNSELOR: Be a father they can respect, depend on. *(reflection)*

MEMBER E: I don't have any kids. I guess for me, it's money, too. But I'm going back to jail if I don't make a change. That's for sure, but I'm not going back there. I'll do whatever it takes. And for me, that's going to be the end of alcohol. But it's going to be hard, really hard.

MEMBER B: I've been there too many times, too. It sucks. I got to get my freedom back. Keep it back.

MEMBER E: I know you can do it, man. I know you can. It's hard. But we can do it.

COUNSELOR: You all have mentioned a lot of things—from money, to relationships, to your future, to freedom, staying out of jail. Those are powerful issues. Really central to your lives. Your openness and support for each other is really admirable. *(summary of group concerns/reasons to change, affirmation)*

8. Providing brief written feedback.

Although it can be harder to provide feedback in groups, it can be accomplished relatively easily through using brief written exercises that provide personalized feedback to members. For example, have group members take the Alcohol Use Disorders Inventory Test (AUDIT; Babor, Higgins-Biddle, Saunders, & Monteiro, 2001) or the Drug Abuse Screening Test (DAST; Skinner, 1982; Gavin, Ross, & Skinner, 1989), then walk them through the scoring. Counselors can describe what the scores mean and ask members if they would like to discuss them. Typically, as most group members share their scores, a lively discussion that generates change talk ensues. Even members who are quieter are likely to benefit from the feedback from their own assessment and information that others have disclosed. As the discussion continues, counselors will want to affirm members for sharing their information and selectively reinforce any change talk generated by the feedback.

CONCLUSION

In this chapter we have given an overview of the principles of MI as well as some specific tools to facilitate the change process. As we have seen, MI can be effectively utilized with many types of populations and varieties of settings. Our intention has been to educate readers on this evidence-based intervention so that they can determine how it may be applied with their specific clienteles or practice settings.

To use MI is to embody and convey empathy and respect for the client's sense of autonomy as well as facilitate a collaborative therapeutic process. The feedback we receive from clients, people who have completed our trainings, and graduate students is typically characterized by two themes. One theme is that they are glad to have a way to engage with clients that takes the responsibility for client change off them, as practitioners. Many people have made comments such as, *"For years I felt it was my responsibility to get the clients to change—I needed to push them to change. MI invites clients to take responsibility for their change and allows me to support their journey."* Another theme we hear involves the growing appreciation, from people who are beginning a more intensive exposure to and training in MI, that rather than being something they thought they were "doing" for years, the effective utilization of MI requires a learning process that offers opportunities for practice, feedback, and more practice.

There are many variations of MI in the professional fields of mental health and substance abuse. Although MI can be a successful complement or augmentation of another therapy, it is not just a set of skills or exercises. Instead, as Miller and Rollnick (2002) have noted, this approach is, above all, a "way of being" with another in the service of growth and positive change. In this process, clients are the center of their own change process, which is fostered by the foundational MI elements of respect, empathy, and acceptance and the utilization of selective and skilled strategies designed to promote and sustain constructive and meaningful behavior change.

RESOURCES

KEY READINGS

Burke, B. L., Arkowitz, H., & Menchola, M. (2003). The efficacy of motivational interviewing: A meta-analysis of controlled clinical trials. *Journal of Consulting and Clinical Psychology, 71*(5), 843–861.

Department of Health and Human Services. (1999). *Enhancing motivation for change in substance abuse treatment*. Treatment improvement protocol (TIP) series 35. DHHS Publication No. (SMA) 00-3460.

Miller, W. R., & Rollnick, S. (2002). *Motivational interviewing: Preparing people for change* (2nd ed.). New York: Guilford Press.

Velasquez, M., Maurer, G. G., Crouch, C., & DiClemente, C. C. (2001). *Group treatment for substance abuse: A stages-of-change therapy manual*. New York: Guilford Press.

Velasquez, M., Stephens, N., & Ingersoll, K. (2006). Motivational Interviewing in groups. *Journal of Groups in Addiction and Recovery, 1*(1), 27–50.

WEB-BASED RESOURCES

The Motivational Interviewing website. This website contains information about MI, trainings, links to MI-related information, and current research. Through this website one can also get information about the Motivational Interviewing Network of Trainers (MINT). The website can be accessed through: www.motivationalinterview.org/.

Center on Alcoholism, Substance Abuse, and Addictions. This website provides a slide show of the principles of MI as well as a slide show of clinical findings. The site also posts links to coding resources for practitioners who might be interested in coding their MI sessions. The website can be accessed through: http://casaa.unm.edu/mi.html.

Addiction Technology Transfer Center. This network was established by the Substance Abuse and Mental Health Services Administration (SAMHSA) and is compromised of fourteen regional centers. The network's mission is to improve the quality of addiction treatment and recovery services by connecting service providers, policy makers, and consumers to a rich network of evolving research. Some regional centers offer information and training on Motivational Interviewing. The main website: www.attcnetwork.org/index.asp has links to regional locations, training, and workshop information.

TIPS 35. Access an online presentation of the main points from the TIPS manual at: www.nadcp.org/preconference/Pre-Conf_Motivational_Interviewing.pdf.

REFERENCES

Amrhein, P. C., Miller, W. R., Yahne, C. E., Palmer, M., & Fulcher, L. (2003). Client commitment language during MI predicts drug outcomes. *Journal of Consulting and Clinical Psychology, 71*(5), 862–878.

Babor, T. F., Higgins-Biddle, J. C., Saunders, J., & Monteiro, M. G. (2001). *The Alcohol Use Disorders Identification Test: Guidelines for use in primary care* (2nd ed.) Geneva, Switzerland: World Health Organization. [Brochure].

Bem, D. J. (1972). Self-perception theory. In L. Berkowitz (Ed.), *Advances in experimental social psychology* (Vol. 6, pp. 1–62). New York: Academic Press.

DiClemente, C. C., & Velasquez, M. (2002). Motivational Interviewing and the stages of change. In W. R. Miller & S. Rollnick (Eds.), *Motivational interviewing: Preparing people for change* (2nd ed., pp. 201–216). New York: Guilford Press.

Festinger, L. (1957). *A theory of cognitive dissonance.* Stanford, CA: Stanford University Press.

Fromme, K., & Corbin, W. (2004). Prevention of heavy drinking and associated negative consequences among mandated and voluntary college students. *Journal of Consulting and Clinical Psychology, 72*(6), 1038–1049.

Gavin, D., Ross, H., & Skinner, H. (1989). The diagnostic validity of the Drug Abuse Screening Test in the assessment of DSM-III drug disorders. *British Journal of Addiction, 84,* 301–307.

Ingersoll, K. A., Wagner, C. C., & Gharib, S. (2000). *Motivational groups for community substance abuse programs.* Richmond, VA: Mid-Atlantic Addiction Technology Transfer Center, Virginia Commonwealth University.

International Federation of Social Workers. (2004). *Ethics in social work, statement of principles.* Retrieved December 1, 2008, from www.ifsw.org/en/p38000324.html

Janis, I. L., & Mann, L. (1977). *Decision making: A psychological analysis of conflict, choice and commitment.* New York: Free Press.

Jones, L. K. (May/June 2007). Motivational interviewing with substance abusers—the power of ambivalence. *Social Work Today, 7*(3), 34. Retrieved November 15, 2008, from www.socialworktoday.com/archive/mayjune2007p34.shtml.

Miller, W. R. (1983). Motivational interviewing with problem drinkers. *Behavioral Psychotherapy, 11,* 147–172.

Miller, W. R. (1989). Increasing motivation for change. In R. Hester & W. Miller (Eds.), *Handbook of alcoholism treatment approaches: Effective alternatives* (pp. 67–80). Boston: Allyn & Bacon.

Miller, W. R., Baca, J., Matthews, D. B., & Wilbourne, P. L. (2001). *Personal values card sort.* Retrieved November 2, 2008, from www.motivationalinterview.org/library/valuescardsort.pdf.

Miller, W. R., & Rollnick, S. (1991). *Motivational interviewing: Preparing people to change addictive behavior.* New York: Guilford Press.

Miller, W. R., & Rollnick, S. (2002). *Motivational interviewing: Preparing people for change* (2nd ed.). New York: Guilford Press.

Miller, W. R., Zweben, A., DiClemente, C. C., & Rychtarik, R. G. (1992). *Motivational enhancement therapy manual: A clinical research guide for therapists treating individuals with alcohol abuse and dependence* (Project MATCH Monograph Series, vol. 2). Rockville, MD: National Institute on Alcohol Abuse and Alcoholism.

MINUET. (1999). *Motivational Interviewing Newsletter: Updates, Education and Training, 6*(3). Retrieved September 8, 2008, from http://motivationalinterview.org/mint/Mint6_3.PDF.

Moyers, T. B., Martin, T., Manuel, J. K., Hendrikson, S. M. L., & Miller, W. R. (2005). Assessing competence in the use of motivational interviewing. *Journal of Substance Abuse Treatment, 28*(1), 19–26.

Prochaska, J. O., & DiClemente, C. C. (1984). *The transtheoretical approach: Crossing boundaries of therapy.* Illinois: Dow Jones-Irwin.

Rogers, C. R. (1951). *Client-centered therapy: Its current practice, implications and theory.* Boston: Houghton-Mifflin.

Rollnick, S. Mason, P., & Butler, C. (1999). *Health behavior and change: A guide for practitioners.* New York: Churchill Livingstone.

Rollnick, S., Miller, W. R., & Butler, C. (2008). *Motivational interviewing in health care: Helping patients change behaviour.* London: Guilford Press.

Rosenstock, I. (1974). Historical origins of the health belief model. *Health Education Monographs, 2*(4), 328–335.

Skinner, H. (1982). The Drug Abuse Screening Test. *Addictive Behaviors, 7,* 363–371.

Velasquez, M., Maurer, G. G., Crouch, C., & DiClemente, C. C. (2001). *Group treatment for substance abuse: A stages-of-change therapy manual.* New York: Guilford Press.

Velasquez, M. M., Stephens, N., & Ingersoll, K. (2006). Motivational Interviewing in groups. *Journal of Groups in Addiction and Recovery, 1*(1), 27–50.

Walters, S. T., Ogle, R., & Martin, J. (Eds.). (2002). Perils and possibilities of group-based motivational interviewing. In W.R. Miller & S. Rollnick (Eds.), *Motivational Interviewing: Preparing people to change* (2nd ed., pp. 377–390). New York: Guilford Press.

Yalom, I. D., & Leszcz, M. (2005). *The theory and practice of group psychotherapy* (5th ed.). New York: Basic Books.

PART 2

ADOLESCENTS

CHAPTER 2

Problem Solving and Social Skills Training*

ERIC F. WAGNER and ASHLEY M. AUSTIN

SOCIAL CONTEXT OF ADOLESCENT SUBSTANCE ABUSE

There is absolutely no doubt that *social modeling* in primary social groups, such as friends and family members, significantly influences the development of adolescent health risk behaviors like substance abuse (Barkin, Smith, & Durant, 2002). Teenagers with substance use problems have more friends who (a) are substance users or (b) approve of adolescent substance use than teenagers without substance use problems. And teenagers with substance use problems have more family members who (a) are substance users or (b) approve of adolescent substance use than teenagers without substance use problems. Acknowledging these social context differences is a key first step toward appreciating the multitude of factors that may influence the success of adolescent substance abuse treatments targeting social interactions.

D'Zurilla and Nezu (1999) define *social problem-solving* as "the self-directed cognitive-behavioral process by which a person attempts to identify or discover effective or adaptive solutions to problems encountered in everyday living" (p. 10). Almost all problems in everyday living occur in an individual's primary social contexts, which typically are friends and family members for the teenager. Adolescent social problem-solving skills have been shown repeatedly and unequivocally to predict adolescent problem behaviors including substance abuse (Kuperminc & Allen, 2001). Compared to developmentally matched peers, substance-abusing adolescents have been found to utilize less effective strategies for resolving interpersonal conflicts (Allen, Aber, & Leadbeater, 1990; Allen, Leadbeater, & Aber, 1994; Freedman, Rosenthal, Donahue, Schlundt,

*Acknowledgment: Preparation of this chapter was supported in part by NIAAA grants R01 AA013369 & R01 AA013825.

& McFall, 1978), and less sophisticated approaches to perspective-taking (Leadbeater, Hellner, Allen, & Aber, 1989). Among general population adolescent samples, impulsive/careless and avoidant problem-solving styles have been shown to be particularly predictive of adolescent substance use (Jaffee & D'Zurilla, 2003).

Rinn and Markle (1979) define *social skills* as

> a repertoire of verbal and nonverbal behaviors by which children affect the responses of other individuals (e.g., peers, parents, siblings and teachers) in the interpersonal context. This repertoire acts as a mechanism through which children influence their environment [i.e., their social context, including friends and family] by obtaining, removing, or avoiding desirable and undesirable outcomes in the social sphere . . . the extent to which they are successful in obtaining desirable outcomes and avoiding or escaping undesirable ones without inflicting pain on others is the extent to which they are considered "socially skilled" (p. 108).

This particularly inclusive definition highlights the bidirectionality of the association between social skills and social context (i.e., "environment," "social sphere"), as well as invokes the notion of avoiding consequences to self and others as a critical component of social skillfulness.

TYPICAL CLINICAL APPLICATIONS

Treatments informed by social modeling perspectives of adolescent substance use problems typically target the following: (1) increasing knowledge about the consequences of substance use, (2) fostering social and self-regulative skills for resisting substance use, (3) providing guided practice and corrective feedback to build self-efficacy, (4) expanding nonuser social support, and (5) addressing social norms favoring alcohol and other drug use (Barkin et al., 2002). Social norms include (1) descriptive norms, which are beliefs concerning "typical" use among teenagers; and (2) injunctive norms, which are beliefs regarding friends' and parents' approval of use (Borsari & Carey, 2003).

In regard to social problem-solving perspectives, Donohue and colleagues (Azrin, et al., 2002) have developed an adolescent substance abuse treatment based primarily on empirically supported problem-solving interventions (e.g., D'Zurilla, 1986; D'Zurilla & Goldfried, 1971; Kendall & Braswell, 1985, 1987; Kendall, Padawer, Zupan, & Braswell, 1985; Spivack, Platt, & Shure, 1976). Individual Cognitive Problem Solving (ICPS) is designed expressly for adolescents with alcohol or other drug problems and includes the following social problem-solving skills elements: (1) "stop and think," which involves focusing attention and concentration; (2) "state the problem," which involves defining the details and circumstances of the problem situation; (3) "what are all of my choices?" which involves brainstorming options to responding to the problem; (4) "if I were to carry out this choice, what are the possible good or bad things that could happen?" which involves evaluating the relative merits of the various options; and (5) selecting for action the option that maximizes positive and minimizes negative consequences.

Treatments informed by social skills training models are of two types (Michelson, Kazdin, Sugai, & Wood, 2007). The first type views social skills problems as skills deficits and assumes that children do not have the requisite skills to interact well with others. The goal of social skills training is to build the requisite skills to overcome social behavior problems. The second type of social skills training assumes that emotional or cognitive states interfere with children expressing socially skilled behavior in social interactions. In this case, the goal of training is to build motivation to engage in competent problem-solving strategies, rather than to build the skills. Most social skills training programs targeting substance-abusing adolescents, including the program described in this chapter, rely primarily on the remediation-of-deficits model rather than inhibited-expression model. This is for two reasons: (1) the acquisition of more mature and adaptive social skills is a hallmark developmental goal of adolescence, and (2) substance-abusing teenagers demonstrate less effective strategies for resolving interpersonal conflicts, less sophisticated approaches to perspective-taking, and more impulsive/careless and avoidant problem solving, all of which speak to social skills deficits among substance-abusing youth.

Assertiveness training has received particular attention in the social skills training literature. Fodor (1992) has taken assertiveness training and described how to apply it to adolescents, with an emphasis on the remediation of social skills deficits. The fours steps in Fodor's assertiveness training with teens include:

1. *Feeling Training*: Addressing how to distinguish anger, excitement, anxiety, and general upset, and their respective triggers.
2. *Rights*: Addressing the following questions: What types of rights do adolescents have in schools, in families, and with friends? (Adolescent rights might include freedom to make choices, express themselves, not to be labeled, make mistakes, and be included in the decision-making process in school and family.)
3. *Goals*: Addressing the following questions: What does the teenager want to achieve? What does she or he want to end up with? What would success in reaching the goal bring?

4. *Skills*: Addressing how to express oneself clearly and keep feelings of upset, anxiety, and anger under control, as well as any cognitive factors interfering or inhibiting assertive responding.

INDICATIONS AND CONTRAINDICATIONS

Treatments based on social modeling, social problem-solving, or social skills training perspectives focus on the individual and his or her interactions with the environment. These treatments assume that through education, training in social skills, training in problem-solving skills, and/or building motivation for engaging in social skilled behaviors, social adjustment will increase and substance use will decrease. Since these treatments are "psychosocial" in nature, clients with severe mental illnesses or co-occurring disorders may be more likely to derive benefit from more intensive and/or more pharmacologic treatments (i.e., severe mental illness is a contraindication for treatments based solely in social modeling, social problem-solving, or social skills training). And since these treatments focus on individual adolescents, they may be contraindicated for clients whose substance use problems are related to broader systemic problems; such clients would likely benefit more from intensive family interventions (see Chapter 4).

Given the preceding, it is notable that these treatments have been shown to be successful with adolescent substance-abusing clients with co-occurring conduct disorder, which is a particularly common and vexing co-occurring diagnosis encountered in adolescent substance abuse treatment settings. Moreover, given normative, developmentally graded maturation of social skills throughout adolescence into emerging adulthood, even the most sophisticated and worldly of teenagers can benefit from treatment designed to improve their social problem-solving and social skills.

GUIDED ADOLESCENT PROBLEM SOLVING (GAPS)

Guided Adolescent Problem Solving (GAPS) is a brief intervention for substance use and related problems among adolescents. It was developed by our research group, and a recently completed, large-scale randomized clinical trial supports its effectiveness (NIAAA R01 AA013369; PI: Wagner). GAPS is based on theory, empirical research, and specific strategies associated with problem-solving and social skills training for adolescents struggling with substance use and related behavior problems. It should be noted that while the primary focus of GAPS is to facilitate the development of problem-solving abilities and social skills necessary to make healthy choices related to substance use and aggressive behaviors, GAPS incorporates Motivational Interviewing (MI) components (see Miller & Rollnick, 2002) in order to maximize client therapeutic engagement. MI has been identified as a developmentally appropriate approach for adolescents, particularly those teenagers who may exhibit resistance (e.g., adolescents with co-occurring substance use and aggressive behavior) (see Winters, Leitten, Wagner, & O'Leary Tevyaw, 2007). For a detailed exposition on MI, please see Chapter 1.

GAPS's five sessions are devoted to preparing clients to deal with the challenges associated with reducing their alcohol and other drug (AOD) use and violent/aggressive behaviors by developing the necessary problem-solving strategies and social skills. As noted earlier in the chapter, the program relies primarily on the remediation-of-deficits model rather than the inhibited-expression model of social skills training. The GAPS program focuses on bolstering clients' abilities to demonstrate effective problem-solving and social skills across a variety of contexts, including (1) coping with triggers for AOD use and violent/aggressive behavior, (2) coping with stress, (3) responding to social pressures to use, (4) navigating challenging interpersonal relationships, and (5) identifying and establishing appropriate short and long term goals for change.

Overview of the GAPS Intervention Program

Weekly individual intervention sessions are provided for 50 minutes for five consecutive weeks. The ultimate goals of the program are to (1) help clients stop or reduce alcohol or other drug use and (2) help clients stop or reduce violent/aggressive behaviors. The primary objectives of the GAPS program are as follows: (1) to help the adolescent learn about his or her substance use, (2) help clients set weekly goals for reducing or stopping use, and (3) foster the development and utilization of effective problem-solving and social skills (in lieu of substance use). GAPS is a manualized and sequential intervention, with each session reviewing and building upon previously discussed topics, as well as introducing new topics. At the beginning of the intervention program, clinicians emphasize the importance of constructive client participation in session activities. Clinicians remind clients that "they are here to identify, explore, and solve problems related to their substance use and that the goal is to help them learn about their substance use and to develop the skills necessary to make the changes they have identified as important."

The following section describes the topics, activities, and goals associated with each of the five sequential GAPS sessions.

Session 1   After paperwork and introductions, the first session begins with a brief overview of the GAPS program. Clients are informed that (1) GAPS stands for Guided Adolescent Problem Solving and (2) the ultimate goal of GAPS is to help adolescents stop or reduce alcohol or other drug use, as well as stop or reduce aggressive/violent behaviors. It is further explained that GAPS involves five 1-hour sessions and is based on learning about one's own alcohol and other drug use and aggressive/violent behaviors, setting goals for reducing or stopping substance use, setting goals for reducing or stopping aggressive/violent behavior, and developing specific skills to attain these goals. Clients are informed that (1) they will have handouts and other materials to use in every session; (2) these handouts will be kept in a GAPS manual that will remain with the clinician until the program is completed; and (3) at the end of the program the client will take home the manual, which will be filled with a host of useful material completed by the client. Finally, clients are reminded that the more they put into the program, the more they will get out of it.

At this point in the initial session, the clinician asks the client to complete the first worksheet, which is entitled "Things That Are Important to Me" (see Figure 2.1). Clients are asked to check off the items in each category that best apply to her or him. The clinician explains that this activity is important for two reasons: (1) It reminds the client about the types of things that are important to him or her, and (2) it helps the clinician better understand the client and the things that he or she feels are important. Once the client has completed the worksheet, the clinician and client review it together, discussing the client's responses in terms of (1) how they relate to his or her alcohol/drug use or violent/aggressive behaviors and (2) how his or her substance use or violent/aggressive behavior currently interferes with any of the things the client has deemed important.

The next activity associated with session 1 is the "Decision to Change" (see Figure 2.2). This *decisional balance* exercise is intended to help clients evaluate the pros and cons of changing alcohol or drug use, as it allows clients to tally and discuss the full range of pros and cons associated with changing or maintaining their substance use behaviors. The client is asked to select as many of the responses for each of the four categories (Good things about using; Less good things about using; Less good things about stopping or reducing; and Good things about stopping or reducing) that are true for him or her. Once the client has completed the activity, the clinician and client discuss the individual pros and cons, with specific attention to any ambivalence about changing alcohol or other drug use. When ambivalence is identified (e.g., "my drinking is a source of conflict between me and my family" vis-à-vis "I have more fun at parties when I drink"), the clinician asks questions such as, "What would it take for you to change at this very moment?" or "What is it going to take to *tip the scale* for you to decide to change?"

Sometimes it is also helpful to discuss a client's current level of weekly use in terms of material costs. The weekly material costs associated with substance use reported by clients can be multiplied by four in order to estimate a month's expense, and by twelve to estimate a year's expense. The client is

GOOD RELATIONSHIPS:

_____ Friends (to have close, supportive friends)

_____ Tolerance (to accept and respect those different from me)

_____ Faithfulness (to be loyal and reliable in relationships)

_____ Positive interactions (getting along well with other people)

Other: _____

_____

POSITIVE ATTITUDE:

_____ Self-esteem (to like myself just as I am)

_____ Hope (to maintain a positive and optimistic outlook)

_____ Setting and achieving goals (to know what I want to do and find ways to do it)

Other: _____

_____

SPIRITUALITY:

_____ Inner peace (to experience personal peace)

_____ Self-knowledge (to have a deep, honest understanding of myself)

_____ Religion (to know and understand God's will)

Other: _____

_____

GENERAL LIFESTYLE:

_____ Adventure (to have new and exciting experiences)

_____ Industry (to work hard and well at my life tasks)

_____ Simplicity (to live life simply, with minimal needs)

_____ Peace (lack of conflict)

Other: _____

_____

CREATIVITY/KNOWLEDGE:

_____ Creativity (to have new and original ideas)

_____ Knowledge (to learn and possess valuable knowledge)

Other: _____

_____

ANYTHING ELSE: Other: _____

_____

_____

Figure 2.1 Things That Are Important to Me

In making a decision to change, it can be helpful to think about the *good things* and *less good things* about using alcohol and/or drugs. Check the items in each box that apply to you.

Good things about using	Less good things about using
❏ I don't have to deal with my problems ❏ I feel more confident ❏ I have something to do when I am bored ❏ I fit in with my friends ❏ I have more fun at parties ❏ It helps me calm down and relax	❏ I feel guilty or ashamed ❏ I don't like the way I look and feel after use ❏ It is a source of conflict between me and my family ❏ It is a source of conflict between me and my friends ❏ I will have money problems ❏ I will continue to feel anxious and depressed ❏ I will harm my health ❏ I will have legal problems
List any others: _____ _____	List any others: _____ _____

Less good things about reducing or stopping	Good things about reducing or stopping
❏ I will feel more depressed and/or anxious ❏ I won't have anything to do when I'm bored ❏ I won't have any way to relax ❏ I will have to change my social life ❏ I won't fit in with some friends ❏ I don't know if I can make change stick	❏ I will feel more in control over my life ❏ I will gain more self-esteem ❏ It will improve my relationship with my family ❏ I will have more money ❏ I will have fewer problems at work and/or school ❏ It will make it easier to achieve life goals
List any others: _____ _____	List any others: _____ _____

Figure 2.2 Decision to Change

then asked to reflect upon what he or she would buy with that amount of money, which arguably would be available should he or she choose not to use. The goal of this exercise is to encourage the client to take an honest look at some of the financial and material *cons* associated with his or her substance use, with the hope that this may help *tip* the scale toward changing alcohol or other drug use.

The clients are next asked to complete the "Goals for Change Questionnaire" (see Figure 2.3), which elicits clients' reports of how important changing substance use is to them and how confident they are that they will be

---

We'd like to know your opinions about your substance use...

1. Right now, how important is it to you to reduce or stop your substance use? (If you've already stopped, rate your importance of staying substance free.)

0--------------25---------------50---------------75---------------100

| Not important at all | Less important than most of the other things in my life | About as important as most of the other things in my life | More important than most of the other things in my life | The most important thing in my life |

Write your goal importance rating (from 0 to 100) here: _____

2. Right now, how confident are you that you will reduce or stop your substance use? (If you've already stopped, rate your confidence in staying substance free.)

0--------------25---------------50---------------75---------------100

| Not confident at all | A little confident | Somewhat confident | A lot confident | Definitely confident |

Write your confidence rating (from 0% to 100%) here: _____

Please indicate which substance(s) you've rated (check all that apply):
[ ] Alcohol   [ ] Marijuana   [ ] Other Drugs_____

Figure 2.3 Goals for Change

successful in making changes. Clients are asked (1) Why did you give that particular rating (vs. a higher or lower rating)?, (2) What other goals are you currently working on?, (3) Do or don't the other goals take precedence over the changes in substance use?, and (4) How might changes in substance use affect your achieving these other goals? It is important that clients begin to recognize the interconnectedness of substance use with other aspects of their lives. Clinicians should also discuss why it is important to think about setting goals, stressing that goals provide something to focus on, strive for, and feel good about once accomplished. At this point, the clinician may explore clients' earlier goals, and how they thought, felt, and acted while achieving the goals.

Next, the client is introduced to the "Session Check-In" (see Figure 2.4), and told that he or she will complete the form at the start of each session. The Session Check-In helps clients to identify (1) the days of the week they used substances or thought about using, (2) the types of situations in which they wanted to use (e.g., "because I was angry or upset"), (3) their goals for the next week (e.g., "use fewer days of the week"), and (4) the skills they used to "cope" with their urge to use (e.g., "thought about the consequences," "did something else"). This exercise allows clients to keep track of their use and helps them identify the habits, tendencies, and patterns that characterize their use; it also helps clients become more aware of what they do when they decide *not* to drink or use other substances (e.g., thinking about consequences of use, leaving a place where substances might have been available, and/or assertively communicating that they didn't want to use).

With respect to the Weekly Change Goal on the Session Check-In, clinicians ask clients to think about what they would like to accomplish in terms of reducing use this week. For example, a clinician may say something like the following: *"Selecting a goal for the next session can be like an experiment, finding some way of reducing use and/or risk. While ideally it would be best if you did not drink or use other drugs at all, if you decide to drink or use other drugs, it is important to make changes that will reduce some of the associated risks of using."* Essentially, the clinician's' job here is to help clients generate specific, feasible, risk-reducing substance use goals about which clients are motivated and invested. This can include reducing the amount or frequency of substances used (e.g., no more than two beers per drinking day; only drink on weekends), change in the number of substances used (e.g., marijuana only versus marijuana and cocaine), circumstances of use (e.g., not using when driving), or pattern of use (e.g., use only on Saturdays instead of Fridays and Saturdays). The final component of the Session Check-In is the weekly rating, whereby the client rates his or her mood over the past week from 0 (lousy) to 10 (fantastic). If it is a high rating, clinicians reinforce what might have contributed to a good week and explore how clients can sustain

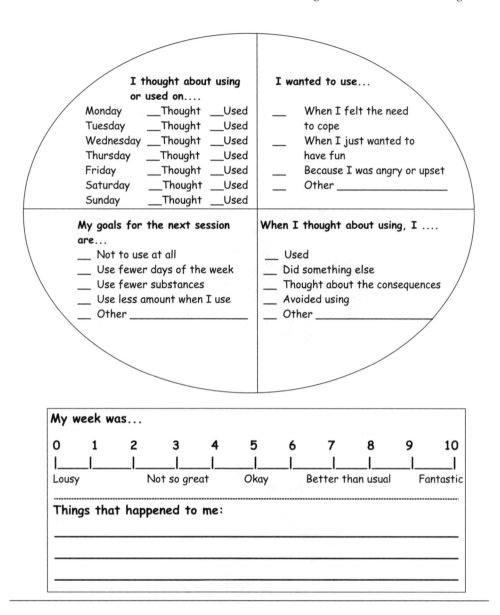

Figure 2.4   Session Check-In

non-substance-use-related factors contributing to a good week. For a low weekly rating, clinicians and clients discuss how factors that led to a bad week can be changed, especially those factors directly associated with their alcohol or other drug use.

Session 1 concludes with the Personalized Feedback Summary (see Figure 2.5), which is a printed report based on a client's alcohol and other drug use and aggressive/violent behaviors during the three months prior to intake. The summary report uses data collected via the Timeline Followback

Prepared for: _____

ALCOHOL Use

Use the following graphs to see how much you drink as compared to other youth.

Drinks of alcohol in the last month

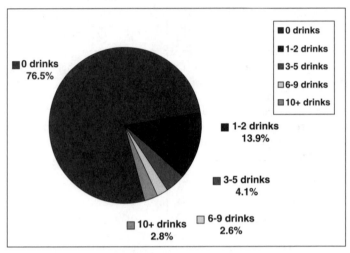

Drinks of alcohol in the last six months

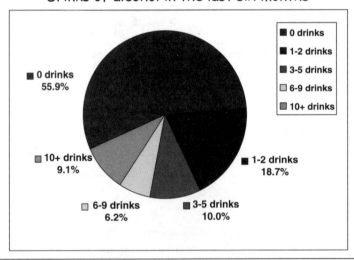

Figure 2.5   Personalized Feedback Summary: Where Does Your Drinking Fit In?

(TLFB; Sobell & Sobell, 1992, 1996) assessment method and compares them to normative data from national, statewide, and local epidemiological databases concerning adolescent risky behaviors. In our case, we have developed software that provides a direct comparison of a client's reported substance use and aggressive/violent behavior to normative data obtained in large-scale epidemiological studies involving same-gender and same-age adolescents. National data (e.g., the Montoring the Future Study data, www.monitoring thefuture.org), statewide data (e.g., state summaries from the Youth Risk Behavior Surveillance Systems, www.cdc.gov/HealthyYouth/yrbs), and/or local community data may be used for these comparisons, which can be made by simply reading through the available data rather than by using software specifically designed for this purpose. Our Personalized Feedback Summary provides normative information about a client's individual alcohol and other drug use status as compared to relevant groups (e.g., 16-year-old girls in Miami-Dade county). Each client receives personalized graphs comparing his or her use to relevant groups across four domains: (1) past month and past six-month reports of alcohol use, (2) past month reports of marijuana use, (3) lifetime cocaine use, and (4) past year reports of substance use and co-occurring risk behaviors.

The Personalized Feedback exercise (see Figures 2.6 and 2.7) allows clients, often for the first time, to examine their substance use vis-à-vis normative data gathered from relevant groups. This corrects common erroneous perceptions such as "most 15-year-olds smoke marijuana," or that "most seniors get drunk every weekend." It is suggested that the clinician introduce the

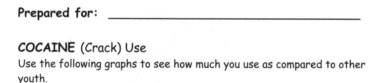

Prepared for: _____

COCAINE (Crack) Use
Use the following graphs to see how much you use as compared to other youth.

Lifetime COCAINE use among youth (15-24 years old)

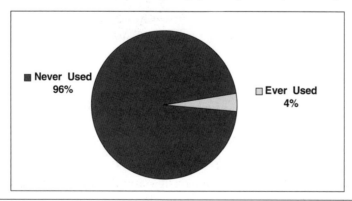

Figure 2.6   Personalized Feedback Summary: Where Does Your Lifetime Cocaine Use Fit In?

Prepared for: _____

Use the following graph to see how your behavior is compared to other youth.

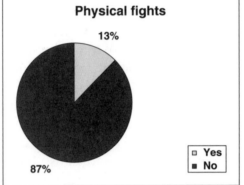

The proportion of seniors who reported getting in fights and breaking the law was greater among alcohol and drug users than nonusers in the past year.

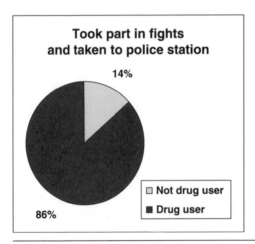 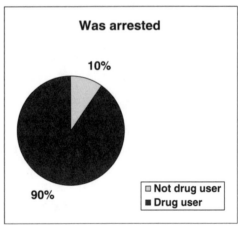

Figure 2.7   Personalized Feedback Summary: Where Do Your Substance Abuse and Risk Behaviors Fit In?

exercise by stating the following: *"Now, what I would like to do is to give you a sense of where your substance use fits in with other teenagers. The goal of this feedback is to provide you with information you can use to make better and more informed decisions about changing your alcohol or other drug use. We've found that feedback helps people identify behaviors they want to change."* Based on the data collected at the intake TLFB, the clinician and client then work together to identify where the client's drinking, substance use, or other risk behaviors stand out compared to other relevant groups.

A CASE EXAMPLE OF THE SESSION CHECK-IN

CLINICIAN: Now we are going to move on to something called the "Session Check-In." This is an activity that we are going to do every week at the beginning of each session. The idea is that it will help us see how you are doing from week to week and what your alcohol and other drug use was like each week. The Session Check-In has four quadrants, and I will explain each one as we go along. The first quadrant examines which days of the past week you thought about using and which days you actually used. So, you may have thought about using on Monday but not used, while on Tuesday you may have thought about using and actually used. Additionally, there may be days that you neither thought about using nor used, so just leave those blank. Why don't you go ahead and complete this now? Since today is Thursday, start with yesterday, which was Wednesday and go back from there. Does that make sense?

CLIENT: Yeah. Do I just skip Friday, Saturday, and Sunday since they haven't come yet?

CLINICIAN: No, just go ahead and think back to last week. I know it looks out of order on this page but we just want to get an idea of your substance use for the entire last week. OK?

CLIENT: Uh huh. *(completes first section)*

CLINICIAN: OK, let's go over what you have put down, starting with today.

CLIENT: OK. So today I have not used but I thought about it.

CLINICIAN: Sorry for interrupting, but I forgot to mention that since you use both alcohol and weed, for each instance, I would like you to put down a little *a* for alcohol, *w* for weed, or an *a* and *w* if you thought about/used both. That way when you are looking back at your materials, it will be clear. So for today did you think about weed or alcohol?

CLIENT: Weed.

CLINICIAN: OK, go ahead with the rest.

CLIENT: Yesterday I thought about weed but didn't use; Tuesday I didn't really think about it or use; same with Monday; Sunday I didn't think about it or use; and then on Friday and Saturday I did use.

CLINICIAN: OK, so even though it looks like you thought about using a lot, you only actually used on Friday and Saturday. That means there were many instances that you were able to avoid using despite the fact that you were thinking about it. How do you think you managed that?

CLIENT: I don't know. I really didn't have any weed at home, and I was just working on my car all week. I was kind of busy because my uncle came over and was helping me with the starter.

CLINICIAN: OK, so it sounds like you had a lot of other things going on that kind of distracted you from using this week.

CLIENT: Pretty much.

CLINICIAN: Let's move to the next quadrant, which says, "I wanted to use . . .". Here, we basically want you to think about the types of things that were happening on the days that you either thought about using or used. Did you feel like using because you felt the need to cope with something difficult, when you just wanted to have fun, when you were angry or upset, or was something else going on? You can check as many or as few of the choices as apply to you.

CLIENT: *(Completes section)*

CLINICIAN: OK, so what did you put down?

CLIENT: I put when I just wanted to have fun and I put when I was bored. Like on Friday and Saturday I just smoked 'cause I was at parties with my friends and we were all just hanging out and having fun. But like on the other days I was just bored, so I wanted to smoke.

CLINICIAN: This is important because it gives an idea of the times or situations when you are probably more likely to think about using and actually use. This brings us to the next quadrant, which says: "When I thought about using, I . . ." We can tell already that there were many instances that you didn't use, when you thought about it so this question just wants you to take a closer look to see how you managed to avoid using. So go ahead and complete it and then we'll discuss it.

CLIENT: *(Completes the section)* Um, I put "used," "did something else," and "avoided using."

CLINICIAN: Perfect, so as you mentioned earlier, working on your car and spending time with your uncle seemed to help you out. What about the other times, when you did use? What might help you to avoid using in those instances?

CLIENT: Maybe not going to parties, I guess.

CLINICIAN: OK, so what might you do instead?

CLIENT: Go to my girlfriend's house or just stay home and chill.

CLINICIAN: Sure, that makes sense. So keep those ideas in mind for this coming week. Those are just a couple of other options that may help you meet your goals. As you can see in the next quadrant, we would like you to select a goal for the next session. Basically, it's like a little experiment. What we want you to do is find some way of reducing your use over the next week. Ideally, it would be best if you did not smoke at all. If you decide to set a goal to reduce rather than stop, it is important to make a change that will reduce some of the associated risks of using. For example, you might want to set a goal not to use if you will have to drive. As you can see on the worksheet, there are a variety of options: use fewer days of the week, which for you might be one versus two; use fewer substances; or use smaller amounts when you use. So why don't you go ahead and decide what goal you would like to set for this week?

CLIENT: Do I just pick one?

CLINICIAN: Good question. Actually, you can pick more than one because some of these work together.

CLIENT: I put use fewer days of the week and use smaller amounts when I use.

CLINICIAN: Sounds good. Let's go ahead and be real specific so you really know what you are working on. By fewer days, do you mean one instead of two?

CLIENT: Yeah, one or zero.

CLINICIAN: Great, so you are giving yourself the option to not use at all but also having a backup plan of using one day versus two. What does using a "smaller amount" mean for you?

CLIENT: Maybe if I'm with my friends, like only smoking one blunt instead of two.

CLINICIAN: Good, so if you do use, not only will you be using fewer days, but you will be smoking less. By the way, do you think there is one day that you will be better able to avoid smoking than another? Like are Fridays easier than Saturdays or vice versa?

CLIENT: Fridays are probably easier because I can usually go to my girlfriend's house right after school.

CLINICIAN: OK, so just keep that in mind when the weekend rolls around, and you are trying to stick to your goal. The last thing we have to do is the weekly rating. I would like you to go ahead and rate the past week overall on a scale of 0 (lousy) to 10 (fantastic), and then write down a couple reasons why you rated the week like you did.

CLIENT: *(Completes section)* I put a 7.

CLINICIAN: Better than usual, OK. What were the reasons that you put a 7 down?

CLIENT: Got my starter fixed and no problems with my mom.

CLINICIAN: Sounds like a pretty good week overall. Is that unusual?

CLIENT: Kind of. Usually I'd be fighting with my mom all the time but I was hardly inside so we really didn't fight at all.

CLINICIAN: So, it seems like working on your car is a pretty helpful hobby. It keeps you busy so you don't fight with your mom and so you don't really have time to smoke. Plus, you ended up with a car that starts.

Session 2   Session 2 begins with the session check-in and a brief review of the topics covered in the initial session. The clinician then moves on to the primary topic of the second session: effective problem-solving strategies for coping with triggers for AOD use and violent/aggressive behaviors. This session is devoted to teaching clients problem-solving skills and self-control skills like those shown effective in studies with aggressive youth and adults (D'Zurilla, 1986; D'Zurilla & Goldfried, 1971; Kendall & Braswell, 1985, 1987) and youth with co-occurring substance use and conduct disorders (Azrin et al., 2001). The "triggers" and "options and action" are designed to teach clients the following problem-solving steps: (1) "stop and think," (2) "state the problem," (3) "identify all of my choices—brainstorm everything I can think of," (4) "identify the possible positive and negative consequences associated with each choice," and (5) "selecting the 'best' solution."

In addition, clinicians work with clients to identify the specific "actions" necessary to implement the "choice" identified as optimal. In GAPS, clients are first taught what a "trigger" for alcohol and drug use is (see Figure 2.8). Before moving on to the "My Triggers for Alcohol and Drug Use" worksheet (see Figure 2.9)," the clinician explains that this exercise is intended to teach three things: (1) how to solve problems in ways other than using substances, (2) how to handle high-risk drug-use situations (i.e., triggers) by doing things other than using alcohol and/or other drugs, and (3) among several options, how to decide which option is the best approach for managing a high-risk situation.

Clinicians work with clients in a nondirective, supportive fashion to help clients identify current "triggers" for AOD use (e.g., fight with girlfriend), the specific behaviors in which clients engage when confronted with this trigger (e.g., smokes weed), and its consequences, both positive (e.g., the weed calmed me down) and negative (e.g., I got too stoned to study for the midterm). The companion worksheet is the "Options and Actions Plan" (see Figure 2.10), which is designed to teach problem-solving steps needed to cope with triggers for AOD use. Clients are first instructed to identify the trigger (i.e., "the problem"). Next, clients are encouraged to brainstorm and list all possible "options" for dealing with this trigger. Clients then weigh the pros and cons associated with each option in order to identify the "best" option. In order to help clients understand what it will take to carry out this option in the real world, an action plan is developed whereby clients list the specific steps they will take in pursuing the option. For example, if the selected option is to "avoid AOD-using peers after school," then a possible action plan may be as follows: (1) Take the bus home instead of walking home with peers, (2) go to the gym or girlfriend's home instead of going out with AOD-using peers, (3) avoid areas typically frequented by AOD-using peers, and (4) avoid being home at times when you know AOD-using peers

A trigger is a situation, a behavior, a thought, or a feeling that is commonly associated with using alcohol or drugs, so that the trigger might bring on the urge to use substances.

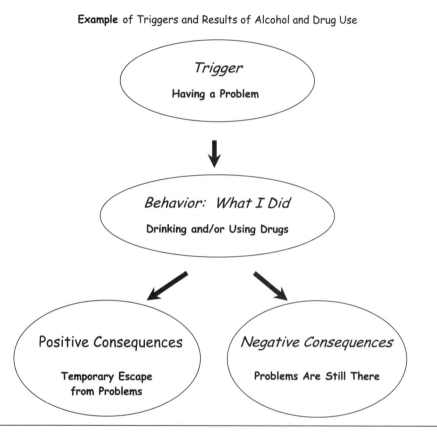

Example of Triggers and Results of Alcohol and Drug Use

Trigger

Having a Problem

Behavior: What I Did

Drinking and/or Using Drugs

Positive Consequences

Temporary Escape
from Problems

Negative Consequences

Problems Are Still There

Figure 2.8 Triggers for Alcohol and Drug Use

will come looking for you. The final step is to help clients examine the likely ramifications, social and otherwise, for implementing the selected option. These activities are then completed in the same manner for the client's triggers for violence and aggression. Clinicians emphasize that by understanding and utilizing the problem-solving strategies learned in this session, clients will be able to effectively (e.g., without the use of AOD or violence) cope with future trigger situations.

The final activity in session 2 involves a graphic of a mountain climber scaling a mountain (see Figure 2.11). "Mount Success" is used to remind clients that the skills developed through the course of the program (e.g., problem-solving steps) are the "tools" to help them achieve success. Clients

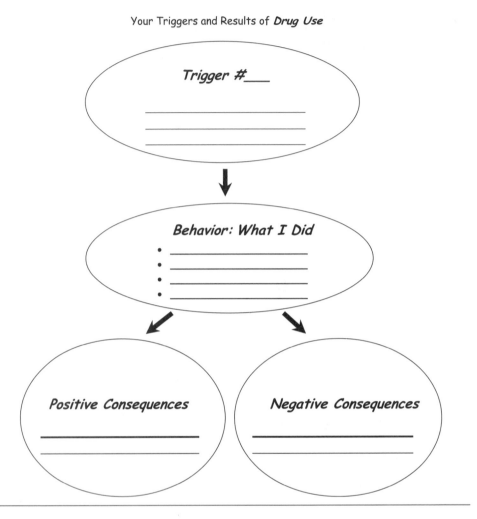

Figure 2.9 My Triggers for Alcohol and Drug Use

are told that, like the mountain climber in the picture, they can, with the right tools, energy, determination, and patience, conquer Mount Success.

A CASE EXAMPLE OF TRIGGERS AND OPTIONS/ACTIONS

CLINICIAN: OK, now that we understand what "triggers" are and how they often bring on the urge to use alcohol or other drugs, why don't we work on identifying your specific triggers. Thinking back on your experiences, what do you think is your biggest trigger for substance use? In your case that means marijuana, right?

CLIENT: Yeah. I would say my biggest trigger is just having nothing to do, like just sitting around the house being bored.

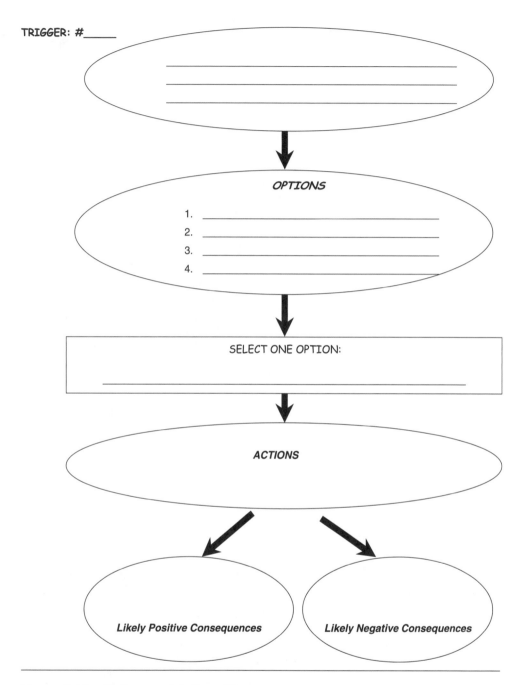

TRIGGER: #_____

OPTIONS

1. _____
2. _____
3. _____
4. _____

SELECT ONE OPTION:

_____

ACTIONS

Likely Positive Consequences

Likely Negative Consequences

Figure 2.10 Options and Actions Plan

CLINICIAN: So, when you're feeling bored, you usually feel the urge to smoke.

CLIENT: Yeah.

CLINICIAN: So when you feel the urge to smoke, what do you usually do?

Where I Want to Go

Where I Started

Figure 2.11   Climbing Mount Success

CLIENT: If I have weed, I just smoke. If I don't, then sometimes I go get it and smoke and sometimes I don't.

CLINICIAN: So, if you have it in the house or on you, it's pretty much a sure thing that you'll smoke; but if you don't have some on you, then it could go either way. Is that right?

CLIENT: It depends if I have money or not.

CLINICIAN: Oh, so if you have money, you will usually spend it on weed.

CLIENT: Yeah. Well, not always. I've been trying to fix up my car, so I have been trying to save my money for speakers or if I need new clothes or shoes.

CLINICIAN: OK, that makes sense. So, let's move on to the next step where we look at the potential consequences, positive and negative, of your typical response to the trigger situation, which in this case is to smoke weed. What would you say are the positive consequences associated with this choice?

CLIENT: I get high.

CLINICIAN: Right, and for you what is so "good" about being high? What are you really getting from the experience?

CLIENT: Well, I'm not bored anymore, and the time passes by kind of fast, and I don't really think about any annoying things like school or my mom pissing me off.

CLINICIAN: OK, so you like the fact that you can kind of "escape" from your current situation, which is feeling bored and thinking about stressful things like the problems you are having in school and your arguments with your mom.

CLIENT: Uh huh. But I just like being high anyways.

CLINICIAN: OK, so now let's look at the negative consequences of your choice to smoke. What not so good things often happen when you smoke weed?

CLIENT: Well, if I have to go buy it, then I am spending my money that is supposed to be for my speakers.

CLINICIAN: Anything else you can think of?

CLIENT: Yeah, I usually fall asleep and don't do my homework, and that's gonna end up screwing me because the only way I can pass math for the year is if I do the homework because I already failed two tests. Plus, if I don't turn in a science project, I fail the class for sure.

CLINICIAN: So, even though smoking weed after school seems to help you feel less bored and puts you in a better mood for the day, it sounds like there are some pretty serious consequences that aren't too good. It is interfering with your plans to get your speakers and to get on top of your homework so you can graduate this year.

CLIENT: Yep, that's about right.

CLINICIAN: Well, the next activity we are going to do will teach you the problem-solving steps you will need to deal with "trigger" situations in a way that helps you better meet your goals, which in this case are to smoke only once a week at the most, and to pass all your classes, right?

CLIENT: Uh huh.

CLINICIAN: OK, so you can see at the top of the page, we return to your trigger for drug use, which you have identified as "having nothing to do, just sitting around the house being bored." The next step is to come up with as many options, other than using substances, that you can do when your trigger situation, being bored, brings on the urge to smoke. What I want you to do is brainstorm, which means think of as many choices as you can and write them all down. We will go over the consequences associated with each choice later. What I want you to do now is think of as many options as possible.

CLINICIAN: OK, it looks like you've thought of quite a few. Great job. Why don't you tell me what you have come up with?

CLIENT: Play Grand Theft Auto, go to my girlfriend's house, work on my car, go to sleep, and play basketball.

CLINICIAN: Nice work. It sounds like you have come up with a variety of realistic options. What I would like you to do now is think about the pros and cons, good things and bad things associated with each option, and select what you think is your "best" option.

CLIENT: OK. I think going to my girlfriend's house or working on my car are the best options.

CLINICIAN: All right, so how did you make that decision?

CLIENT: Because I can play Grand Theft Auto without smoking but usually it's more fun when I smoke, and if I go to the park to play basketball, usually my friends have weed, and we smoke after we play or sometimes before.

CLINICIAN: OK, so it sounds like those two choices might make it a little more challenging to stick to your goal of reducing your weed smoking. What about the other two options, do you have a favorite?

CLIENT: Well, working on my car is good because I don't like to smoke when I'm fixing it up. It keeps me really busy because I'm focused on all the work I have to do. It's like my favorite thing to do. But I think maybe going to my girlfriend's is the best because I never smoke with her because she doesn't like it, and she does her homework every day and wants me to do it, too, so I can graduate.

CLINICIAN: OK, so you have selected "going to your girlfriend's house" as the primary option for this activity, but it sounds like working on your car is another great alternative. What we are going to do now is identify the specific "actions" you will need to take to ensure that you follow through with this option. So, what will it take for you to be able to go to your girlfriend's house after school?

CLIENT: Nothing. I just have take the bus to her house instead of walking home.

CLINICIAN: So, there are no issues with her parents or your mom about going over there?

CLIENT: No, my mom loves for me to go there, and her parents are cool.

CLINICIAN: If that's the case, then it sounds like the main thing you need to do is just plan ahead so you have bus fare so you can head straight there after school. I'm wondering if it would help you follow through if you sort of committed ahead of time, for example, made a plan with her the night before?

CLIENT: Yeah, probably, because then she will nag me if I try not to come over.

CLINICIAN: OK, so the action plan consists of: setting the plan with your girlfriend ahead of time, remembering your bus fare, and sticking to your plan to go to her house instead of your own. If this becomes your new plan, what do you think the likely positive and negative consequences will be?

CLIENT: The positive consequences will be that I will probably do my homework and probably pass math and science so I can most likely graduate.

CLINICIAN: Anything else?

CLIENT: Yeah, probably fight less with my girlfriend because she hates when I smoke, and she doesn't like me hanging out with my smoking friends. I will for sure smoke less because I never smoke with her.

CLINICIAN: OK, it sounds like there are a lot of positives associated with your plan. Can you think of any negative consequences of going to your girlfriend's house every day after school?

CLIENT: No. Well, yeah. My friends will probably call me a bitch for hanging out with a chick 24/7 instead of with them.

CLINICIAN: OK, so you might catch a lot of grief from your friends for implementing this new plan. How do you think you will deal with that?

CLIENT: I don't care. I'll just laugh and tell them at least I'm getting some.

CLINICIAN: I know this has been a lot of information, so how do you feel about the plan overall? Is it something you are ready to try?

CLIENT: Oh, I like the plan. I know I can do it.

Session 3 The session begins with the weekly check-in and a brief review of the problem-solving strategies learned in the previous week's session. If the client is successful in meeting the weekly goals, the clinician and client can explore the specific problem-solving strategies utilized to help him or her meet identified goals. If the client reports that he or she was *not* successful in meeting the weekly goals, then the clinician and client engage in a brief review of the problem-solving steps and the client's self-selected options for dealing with triggers for AOD use and/or violence. The clinician and client then move on to the primary focus of this session, social skills training, which includes skill development in the areas of effective refusal skills and assertive communication practices.

Clients are informed that one of the key components in being able to make and maintain changes in their AOD use is their ability to "refuse," or turn down, AOD use in situations where it is available. Clinicians work with clients to complete the "Refusal Skills" worksheet (see Figure 2.12). Clients identify the strategies they are currently using to refuse substances, as well as situations in which they have had trouble refusing. The clinician helps the client recognize how the problem-solving strategies learned in session 2 can be applied to situations that call for the use of "refusal skills." For example, if

A great way to change your substance use and achieve your goals is to improve your Refusal Skills so you will be able to refuse or turn down substances.

What are you currently doing to turn down drugs or alcohol when it is available?

_____

_____

_____

_____

What are some situations where you have trouble turning down drugs or alcohol?

_____

_____

_____

_____

How to develop good refusal skills

- Leave the situation/place where there is a possibility of using.
- Take a "time-out"—wait 10 minutes and think about your choice (e.g., Why do you want to use? What else can you do? What are the consequences?).
- Remind yourself of the reasons for making substance use changes and share them with others who are encouraging you to use.
- Ask for help.
- Stand up for your rights. Some issues are not negotiable. Knowing which issues are nonnegotiable for you (e.g., doing drugs or drinking alcohol). You ALWAYS have the option of saying "no" and you do not always have to have a clear reason.

Clear Reasons:	Unclear Reasons:
Illegal	My intuition tells me "no"
Inappropriate	I'm not sure
May hurt yourself or others	I've changed my mind
May get in trouble	It's not the right option

*****Develop and practice effective communication skills.**

Figure 2.12 Refusal Skills

a client finds her- or himself at a party where marijuana is available, in order to avoid using she or he can "Stop," take a 10-minute "time-out" to think about options (Why do I want to use? What can I do instead? What will the likely consequences be if I use? . . . if I don't use?), and then decide whether she or her will use. Modeling the appropriate use of refusal skills and role-playing with corrective feedback are two integral strategies used to facilitate the acquisition of effective refusal skills during this session.

The next aspect of social skills training addressed during session 3 is assertive communication. Clinicians explain to clients that another way to improve refusal skills is to develop effective communication skills that will allow you to assertively say no in risky situations. The clinician and client read and discuss the "Communication Skills" worksheet (see Figure 2.13), which describes (1) the importance of developing communication skills, (2) the difference between assertiveness and aggressiveness, and (3) basic

---

Why work on communication skills?
An important way to manage your mood is by improving specific communication skills that allow you to feel better about your interactions with others. Effective communication includes expressing yourself well *and* being a good listener.

Assertiveness Versus Aggressiveness:

- **Assertiveness** is the ability to express your thoughts and feelings honestly, openly, directly, and respectfully.
- **Aggressiveness** is when you use forceful and hostile actions and words to express yourself. When you are aggressive, others tend to get defensive and fight back.

Good Communication Is: The ability to interact with other people in a pleasant, successful, and assertive way that allows people to express themselves and to be understood. Assertiveness is the ability to express your thoughts and feelings honestly and directly while you respect both yourself and others. Good communication is especially necessary for resolving disagreements.

Effective communicators know their rights and respect the rights of others. These rights include:

- The right to make feelings and opinions known in a way that does not hurt others.
- The right to request that another person change behavior that affects them.
- The right to be treated with respect.
- The right to express oneself without interruption.

Figure 2.13 Communication Skills

"rights" associated with effective communication. The clinician focuses on helping clients understand good communication as a tool to solve problems, manage relationships, and increase positive feelings.

The next activity, "Steps Toward Better Communication" (see Figure 2.14), identifies the following seven practices for communicating effectively: (1) Speak from the "I" perspective, (2) Avoid using "put downs," (3) Focus only on current issues, (4) Deal with one issue at a time, (5) Avoid interrupting,

1. **Speak from the "I" perspective.**

   Effective: "I am angry when . . . "
   Ineffective: "You make me angry when . . . "

2. **Avoid using "put downs."**

   Effective: "I love you."
   Ineffective: "Of course I love you, stupid."

3. **Focus only on current issues.**

   Effective: "Right now, our relationship . . . "
   Ineffective: "Remember how you treated me two years ago when . . . "

4. **Deal with one issue at a time.**

   Effective: "I feel that it's important that we discuss this one issue."
   Ineffective: "Not only that; but you always nag, and don't let me go out with my friends, and I can never use the car when I want to and . . . and . . . "

5. **Avoid interrupting.**

   Effective: "Now that I've had a chance to hear you, let me tell you what I think."
   Ineffective: "Hey wait a minute . . . I think that. . . . "

6. **Avoid mind-reading.**

   Effective: "How do you feel about what happened yesterday?"
   Ineffective: "I know you're mad at me about yesterday!"

7. **Avoid avoiding issues.**

   Effective: "I feel it's important to discuss this."
   Ineffective: "I don't want to talk about it."

   > **NOTE: Better communication provides a basis upon which problem solving can occur and change can be experienced.**

Figure 2.14   Steps Toward Better Communication

(6) Avoid mind-reading, and (7) Avoid *avoiding* issues. For each communication step, the effective method is contrasted with an ineffective method of communication, and the likely consequences of each approach are discussed. For example, for strategy 4, "Deal with one issue at a time," the clinician and client will compare "I feel it's important that we discuss this one issue, extending my curfew" (effective communication) with "Not only is my curfew too early, but you always nag, and don't let me go out with my friends, and I can never use the car . . . " (ineffective strategy). In our experience, clients relate well to the examples and are readily able to identify the negative consequences associated with the ineffective approach (e.g., the argument got worse, nothing got fixed, I got grounded). After clients understand the differences between the effective and ineffective strategies, they engage in a role-play activity aimed at practicing these skills (see Figure 2.15). The role-play focuses on either (1) a real-life interpersonal problem chosen by the client or (2) a scenario from the "Practicing Better Communication" worksheet (e.g., Your teacher blames you for something you didn't do, and this makes you

---

Communication Skills Reminders

Speak from the "I" perspective
Avoid using "put downs"
Focus on current issues
Deal with one issue at a time
Avoid interrupting
Avoid mind-reading
Avoid avoiding issues

---

1. Your boyfriend/girlfriend seems more interested in another person than you.
2. You suspect your friend told someone else one of your personal secrets.
3. You and your friend are going to a party, but your parents want you home earlier than anyone else.
4. Your teacher blames you for something you didn't do, and this makes you really angry.

Figure 2.15   Practicing Better Communication

1.　The changes I want to make are:

2.　The most important reason I want to make these changes is:

3.　The steps I plan to make in changing are:

4.　The ways people can help me are:
　　　　Person　　　　　　　　　　Possible ways to help

5.　I will know that my plan is working if:

6.　The things that could interfere with my plans are:

Figure 2.16　Change Plan Worksheet

really angry). Clinicians use modeling as well as corrective feedback to foster and bolster effective communication skills.

The final activity associated with session 3 is the "Change Plan Worksheet" (see Figure 2.16). Clients are instructed to identify an aspect of their lives they are interested in changing and explain why making this change is personally important (e.g., do better in school). Next, clients are asked to identify the steps they plan to take to make this change (e.g., do my homework every day, get to school on time, not smoke weed so I can focus). Clients are asked to identify primary sources of social support, and the way(s) these supports may help them make this change (e.g., my girlfriend, because she always does her homework, and I can do it with her; my mom, because she can take me to school when she goes to work and I will be on time). Finally, clients are encouraged to identify factors that may interfere with making this change (e.g., hanging out with friends who smoke weed every day after school), as well as how they will know if they have been successful in making a change (e.g., will pass the tenth grade, mom will nag me less, will have less stress). The primary aim of this activity is to incorporate and apply the multiple skills clients have been taught by this point in the program.

A CASE EXAMPLE OF AN EXCERPT FROM SESSION 3: THE REFUSAL SKILLS ACTIVITY

Clinician: One of the main activities of today's session is to learn about something called "refusal skills." Refusal skills are basically the strategies that you use to turn down drugs or alcohol when they are around or when they are offered to you. The ability to turn down or avoid using drugs or alcohol—in your case we are pretty much talking about weed—is one of the best ways to make your changes stick. What we are going to do first is look at some of the refusal skills that you have already been using. Go ahead and complete the first part that asks what you are currently doing to turn down drugs or alcohol when it is available.

[Pauses]

CLINICIAN: OK, what did you put down?

CLIENT: That I think about the consequences.

CLINICIAN: Can you give me an example? What are some of the consequences that you think about?

CLIENT: That my girlfriend will get pissed off if she finds out.

CLINICIAN: Anything else?

CLIENT: That I won't have any money.

CLINICIAN: So thinking about how your girlfriend will react and the fact that you don't want to be spending your money on weed helps you turn it down when it is available for you to smoke or to buy.

CLIENT: Yeah, most of the time.

CLINICIAN: Well, the next question asks you to identify some situations where you have trouble turning down drugs or alcohol. Can you go ahead and answer that one now?

[Client Writes Down Answer]

CLINICIAN: OK, so what did you write?

CLIENT: When I'm around new people or like at a party with a bunch of people who are smoking.

CLINICIAN: For you, then, being around new people or in places where nearly everyone is smoking makes turning down or avoiding weed a big challenge.

CLIENT: Yeah.

CLINICIAN: What we are going to do is try to identify some additional refusal skills that you might be able to use in some of these more challenging situations. The idea here is that the more options you have in your "bag of tricks," the more likely you will be successful in turning down weed or avoiding it all together. Make sense?

CLIENT: Yeah.

CLINICIAN: All right then, let's go over the examples of refusals skills we have on the worksheet.

[Clinician and Client Read Through the Examples Listed]

CLINICIAN: Is there one of these that seems like it might be the most useful for you?

CLIENT: Yeah, the first one, "Leaving the situation/place where there is a possibility of using."

CLINICIAN: That makes sense since you seem to have the most trouble when you are in a party situation with new people and other users. Leaving the situation can certainly help you avoid using. Do you think that will be hard to do—to leave a party once you are there?

CLIENT: Maybe.

CLINICIAN: Can you think of any things that might make it easier?

CLIENT: Maybe going to my girlfriend's house or to the movies or something.

CLINICIAN: Exactly, great. You have identified a couple of alternative places that you can go and still have fun that don't include being at a party where you have a high risk of smoking weed when you don't want to. Another thing that might help is to really think about your options and develop an action plan, to make the option of leaving a little easier and more realistic. Do you remember how we learned to develop an action plan in last week's session?

CLIENT: Yeah, you thought of your options and picked one and then made up a plan of how to do it.

CLINICIAN: Exactly, and in the case of this refusal skills activity, the second refusal skill example on the worksheet suggests that you can "take a 10-minute time-out to think about your choice" (e.g., Why do you want to use? What else can you do? What are the consequences?) The idea is that instead of going ahead and smoking weed right away, you stop and give yourself a little time out to see if smoking is really what you want to do. You briefly remove yourself from the situation and really think about whether you want to use and how you will feel after you use. Will you be really disappointed in yourself? Will you have some serious consequences? If you decide you really don't want to use, then think about other things you can do instead. Do you see how this works? We are just applying the skills we learned last week to this specific situation.

CLIENT: Yeah. I think the time-out thing is good because sometimes I smoke without even thinking about it and then I'm pissed off at myself but it's too late.

CLINICIAN: Good, so it's making sense to you. And by the way, this worksheet just provides examples of refusal skills. There are many others that are not listed or that you might come up with on your own that apply to your specific situation. Can you think of any other good strategies for turning down or avoiding alcohol or drugs that are not listed?

CLIENT: Um, I could tell my friends that I can't smoke because of basketball.

CLINICIAN: So for you, turning down marijuana because of basketball seems like a comfortable option, like something you can do without feeling like a "punk" as you mentioned before.

CLIENT: Yep, I just tell my friends that I'm getting healthy so I can school their asses on the court.

CLINICIAN: Super, that's the idea, to think of options that are comfortable and realistic for you to use in a variety of high-risk situations where there may be pressure or the opportunity to use weed.

Session 4 This session is devoted to helping clients recognize stressors, understand how stressors may impact substance use and aggressive/violent behavior, and develop skills to cope with stress on a daily basis. Before working on the specific activities associated with stress, the clinician and client briefly review social skills content from session 3. Specifically, the clinician asks the client if he or she had a chance to practice any of the refusal skills over the previous week. The clinician and client explore the situations that are presented, the specific refusal skills employed, and what was or was not successful. At this point, clinicians will also refer back to the communication skills material and review alternate skills that can be utilized as needed. At this point, clients are asked to complete a second Brief Situational Confidence Questionnaire that will be used during the subsequent (and final) session (see Figure 2.17). During the weekly check-in activity, clients are encouraged to identify if and how the problem-solving and social skills learned in earlier sessions have facilitated success with specific goals related to weekly AOD use.

The next activity, "Feeling Badly if You Slip" (see Figure 2.18), is aimed at helping clients adopt a realistic, long-term perspective on changing their AOD use. This activity acknowledges that for many people, making changes in AOD use is a slow process that may include "slips." A "slip" is described as a brief return to previous patterns of substance use. Clients are informed that if they do "slip," such situations are best viewed as learning experiences rather than as failure experiences. Clinicians discuss the importance of distinguishing a "slip" from "failure." The thrust of this activity is to help clients learn how to prevent a slip from becoming a longer-lived return to problematic patterns of use. Clients are educated about the negative emotions that often follow a "slip" (e.g., guilt, weakness, failure, depression) and the strategies that can be used to combat these negative and potentially destructive thoughts and feelings. Specifically, clients are encouraged to conceptualize the "slip" as a mistake and to use their problem-solving skills to figure out

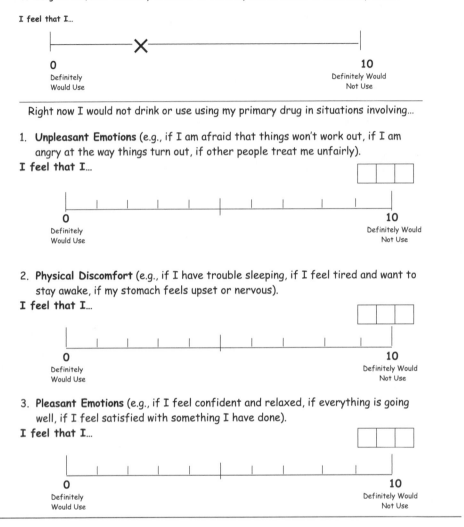

Figure 2.17   Brief Situational Confidence Questionnaire (BSCQ)

what went wrong and how to avoid making the same mistake in the future. Clients are also reminded that one slip is not the same as a permanent change to previous AOD use patterns (a "slip" is not a "fall"). Clients are encouraged to focus not simply on the "slip," but on their reasons for changing and all of the *effort* they have put into changing. Finally, clients are reminded that they do not have to "slip" again; rather, they can utilize their skills for dealing with high-risk situations to prevent future slips.

Clinicians then segue to the topic of stress by explaining to clients that one way to decrease the likelihood of having a "slip" in the first place is to learn to

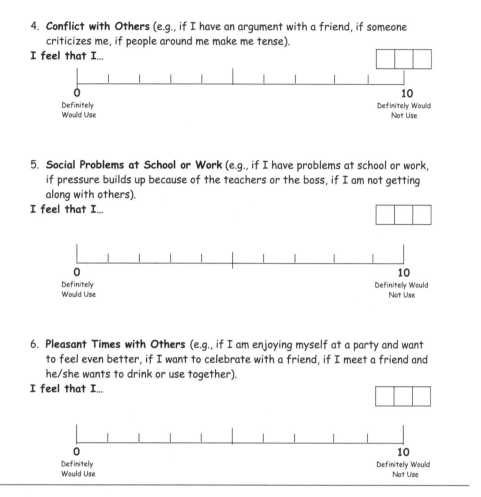

Right now I would not drink or use my primary drug in situations involving...

4. **Conflict with Others** (e.g., if I have an argument with a friend, if someone criticizes me, if people around me make me tense).
   I feel that I...

   0
   Definitely
   Would Use

   10
   Definitely Would
   Not Use

5. **Social Problems at School or Work** (e.g., if I have problems at school or work, if pressure builds up because of the teachers or the boss, if I am not getting along with others).
   I feel that I...

   0
   Definitely
   Would Use

   10
   Definitely Would
   Not Use

6. **Pleasant Times with Others** (e.g., if I am enjoying myself at a party and want to feel even better, if I want to celebrate with a friend, if I meet a friend and he/she wants to drink or use together).
   I feel that I...

   0
   Definitely
   Would Use

   10
   Definitely Would
   Not Use

Figure 2.17   (Continued)

manage stressors in a positive and effective manner. Clients are encouraged to share their thoughts on stress and how it is impacting their lives. Clinicians help clients to explore the idea of stress by asking questions such as *"What is stress?"*, *"What kinds of things cause stress?"* and *"How do you know when you are under stress?"* Clients are then asked to complete the "General Causes of Stress" checklist (see Figure 2.19), which is designed to help clients identify the specific sources of stress in their own lives. Clients are informed that this is a general list; any stressors important to the client not listed on the worksheet can be added on the sides or back of the page.

The clinician then explores with the client the identified stressors. The role that the specific stressors play in the client's AOD use and/or aggressive/violent behavior is examined, and the need for appropriate coping skills and

Despite your best effort to cope with high-risk situations, it is possible that you won't be successful every time. If you slip back, you will most likely experience a powerful negative emotional reaction (this reaction is known as "Slip Back Effect" or SBE).

If you slip, you are likely to:

- Feel that change is too hard and not worth the effort.
- Feel guilty, even somewhat depressed.
- Think of yourself as a weak person or a failure.
- Think that this slip makes you a problem user.

These are **natural reactions to a slip**. In order to get back on track, fight off these negative reactions in the following ways:

1. Think of the slip as a **mistake**: Everyone makes mistakes. Just like other mistakes, figure out what you did wrong and how to correct it or avoid doing it again.

2. Realize that **one slip** does not mean you are back to your old patterns of use.

3. Remind yourself of all your **hard work**. Review your reasons for changing and stick with it.

4. **Don't slip the next time!** Just because you slipped once does not mean you must return to previous use patterns. Negative feelings will decrease with each passing day.

NOTE: Do not interpret this as "permission" to have a slip. Remember—the surest way to quit using alcohol/drugs is not to use at all.

Figure 2.18   Feeling Badly if You Slip

---

stress prevention skills is discussed (see Figure 2.20). Clients are informed about the importance of learning and utilizing strategies to cope with stress that do not involve AOD use or aggressive/violent behaviors. Several safe, effective, nonviolent, non-substance-using strategies for coping with stressful situations are explored, including taking time-outs and learning to talk about stressors with trusted friends or family members. In addition, clients are reminded how to use their problem-solving skills to cope with a variety of stressors: (1) Stop, don't act immediately; (2) give yourself time to think about your options first; (3) weigh your options first; and (4) develop a plan. In order to prevent stress from building up over time to problematic levels, clients are taught to incorporate the following strategies into their daily lives:

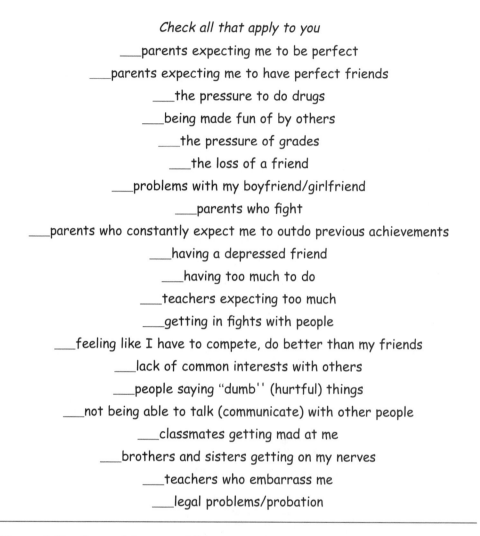

Check all that apply to you

___parents expecting me to be perfect

___parents expecting me to have perfect friends

___the pressure to do drugs

___being made fun of by others

___the pressure of grades

___the loss of a friend

___problems with my boyfriend/girlfriend

___parents who fight

___parents who constantly expect me to outdo previous achievements

___having a depressed friend

___having too much to do

___teachers expecting too much

___getting in fights with people

___feeling like I have to compete, do better than my friends

___lack of common interests with others

___people saying "dumb" (hurtful) things

___not being able to talk (communicate) with other people

___classmates getting mad at me

___brothers and sisters getting on my nerves

___teachers who embarrass me

___legal problems/probation

Figure 2.19   General Causes of Stress

learning to relax, exercising regularly, and goal setting. It is explained to clients that learning to set explicit, manageable goals is one way to manage some of the stress associated with making changes in AOD use and/or aggressive/violent behaviors.

The final activity, "Future Goals" (see Figure 2.21), asks clients to set specific short-term (one month) and long-term (one-year and five-year) goals related to AOD use and other areas (e.g., interpersonal relationships, school performance). This activity helps provide benchmarks for clients to evaluate their progress in attaining substance-related and personal goals and provides an opportunity to discuss how substance-related and personal goals may impact one another over time.

1. **Take a break.**
    - Take a deep breath.
    - Time out, even briefly, can do wonders.

2. **Talk it out.**
    - Discuss a problem with the source and/or a friend.

3. **Think it through.**
    - Don't act immediately! Give yourself time to think first!
    - Weigh your options.
    - Develop a plan.

Stress Prevention

1. **Learn to relax.**
    - As a daily routine, relaxation will make worlds of difference in your stress level.

2. **Exercise regularly.**
    - Moderately vigorous, enjoyable exercise is a great release.

3. **Set goals.**
    - Be realistic and don't try to change everything at once.

Figure 2.20 Coping with Stress

A CASE EXAMPLE OF AN EXCERPT FROM SESSION 4: GENERAL CAUSES OF STRESS AND COPING WITH STRESS

CLINICIAN: As we just mentioned during the last activity ("Feeling Badly if You Slip"), stressful situations or events often lead to "slips." That is because stressful situations or stressors often bring about difficult or negative emotions that can trigger the urge to use substances. So, one way to avoid slips and stay on track with your alcohol and drug use changes is to learn to prevent stress whenever

One Month

Alcohol and Other Drugs

_____
_____
_____
_____

Other Areas

_____
_____
_____
_____

One Year

Alcohol and Other Drugs

_____
_____
_____
_____

Other Areas

_____
_____
_____
_____

Five Years

Alcohol and Other Drugs

_____
_____
_____
_____

Other Areas

_____
_____
_____
_____

Figure 2.21 Future Goals

possible and cope effectively with stressors when they do arise. The first step in dealing effectively with stress is to be aware of the different sources of stress in your life. So, what I would like you to do is to look at the "General Causes of Stress" checklist that you have in front of you and to check off any of the stressors that apply to you. This checklist is by no means exhaustive, and you may have some stressors that are not listed, so please go ahead and jot down any other stressors you are experiencing either on the sides or back of the worksheet. When you are done just let me know and we will go over your list.

[Client Proceeds to Complete Worksheet]

CLINICIAN: You all set? OK, great, why don't you let me know what you checked off?

CLIENT: OK. I put parents expecting me to be perfect, parents expecting me to have perfect friends, the pressure to do drugs, the pressure of grades, problems with my girlfriend, having too much to do, teachers expecting too much, getting in fights with people, and people saying dumb (hurtful) things. And I added not having enough money and needing to find a job.

CLINICIAN: So, you were able to identify many different sources of stress in your life. Are there times that you feel pretty stressed out?

CLIENT: Yeah, like pretty much every day.

CLINICIAN: OK, so that's a lot—a lot of stressors and a lot of stress. I bet that can feel pretty overwhelming at times.

CLIENT: Yep.

CLINICIAN: Are there some things that are particularly stressful for you, like the things that seem to be your main sources of stress?

CLIENT: Probably my parents expecting me to be perfect and to have perfect friends. Mostly all my mom does is bitch at me and bitch at me about my grades and where I've been at and who I've been with and talking shit about my friends and it just gets on my nerves. I just wanna get the fuck out of there.

CLINICIAN: So the pressure at home can really get to you at times and you just want to escape from it all.

CLIENT: Yep, and then I just go to my room and smoke a big spliff, and it's all good.

CLINICIAN: So you can really see how stress, and in particular the stress from the conflicts you are having with your mom, really triggers the urge to smoke for you.

CLIENT: Yep, it's fucked up.

CLINICIAN: Because stress is a huge trigger for a lot of people and it is impossible to completely eliminate stress from our lives, the idea of this session is to identify and practice some strategies for coping with stress without relying on drugs or alcohol. To be honest, in order for you to reach and maintain your alcohol and drug use goals, it is really important to use good coping skills to deal with stress. Does that make sense to you?

CLIENT: Yep, sure does.

CLINICIAN: Then let's turn to the next page and look at the first step for coping with stress: (1) Taking a break, taking a deep breath, a time-out, even briefly, can do wonders. The idea of this is for you to get away from the stressful situation, at least temporarily, so that you give yourself a chance to calm down. Calming down will help you to make decisions that you will not regret later. Can you think of an example from your own life where you were either successful in taking a "time-out" from a stressful situation? Or a situation where you should have taken a time out?

CLIENT: Yeah, like if me and my girlfriend are fighting and I just leave the house and take a walk or play basketball or something then the fight is usually over that night. She usually ends up calling me crying and saying how she's all sorry and shit.

CLINICIAN: And what happens if you don't take a break from the situation?

CLIENT: Then I usually end up calling her a fucking bitch and the fight lasts for a week or something. Or I break her phone, and then I have to get her a new one.

CLINICIAN: So, not too good, huh?

CLIENT: Nope, it pretty much sucks.

CLINICIAN: OK, so from your own experiences, you can see the benefits of learning to use good coping skills in these types of stressful situations. Another important strategy for coping with stress is to "talk it out." This is pretty self-explanatory; it means you can discuss the problem with the source, whoever is causing it or a part of it, or with someone you trust who is not involved. Can you think of any instances where this has worked for you?

CLIENT: When me and my girlfriend are fighting, I usually talk to my cousin. He's already married, and he's been through all this crap.

CLINICIAN: So you've actually used this strategy before and it was successful for you?

CLIENT: Yeah.

CLINICIAN: What did you find useful about it?

CLIENT: Once I talk with my cousin, we just end up hanging out and watching the game or something, and I don't even think about her anymore.

CLINICIANS: Great, that's the idea. You are getting out all those frustrated or angry emotions in a safe and healthy way by "venting" or "letting it all out" to your cousin instead of in a way that is not so healthy, either getting high or getting into a screaming match with your girlfriend. If you learned to rely on these strategies, how might things be different in your life?

CLIENT: I'd probably have a lot less stress. I'm already stressed when I fight with my girlfriend, then if I end up breaking her phone or something, I have a bunch more stress because she's all pissed off, and I'm pissed off because I have to spend money on her stupid phone instead of some new [Nike AIR] Jordans or something. Or if I smoke, then she's more pissed 'cause she hates when I smoke.

CLINICIAN: Well, it sounds like you can really see how important stress-coping skills are, especially when you are trying to use less weed and fight less. The last example we have for this section, to "think it through," basically reminds you to apply the problem-solving skills you learned in session 2 to deal with the different stressors and conflicts that arise in your life. This strategy reminds you to think before you act, weigh all your options, and develop a plan. The idea is that once you have mastered these problem-solving steps, you can apply them to any situation that comes your way. If you do this successfully, then your stress will decrease, and you will be better able to stick to your goals. Can you see how these three coping strategies work together?

CLIENT: *(After a minute of thinking)* Like if my mom is bitching at me, then I can go play basketball instead of arguing with her, and I can talk with some of my boys about all the shit she's talking, and by the time I come home I'll be all calm because I just schooled some punks, and I won't even care what she says, so I'll just go to my room and go to sleep.

CLINICIAN: Right, it sounds like you get it. You use your break or "time-out" to either talk things out with a friend or to think about your options and develop a plan that will have the best outcome for you. In this case, the best outcome for you would be avoiding a fight with your mom so you don't get grounded or have your car taken, right?

CLIENT: Sure enough.

Session 5 Session 5 is the final session of the GAPS intervention. The primary focus of this session is to help clients recognize the progress they have made on their goals, as well as develop a plan to maintain success after treatment is over. The way this is approached is to have clients compare past and present (1) thoughts and feelings about their alcohol and drug use, (2) motivation to change or maintain changes in alcohol and drug use behaviors, and (3) confidence about making and maintaining changes. As clients complete the weekly check-in, the clinician prepares information from previous sessions in order to review changes and successes over the course of therapy. For example, if a client indicates that she or he has only "thought about using" on two days of the week but never actually "used," that might be compared to the session 2 check-in on which the client reported "thinking about using" every day of the week and actually "using" on three occasions. This information should be processed with the client in an effort to help the client understand what skills they have been implementing each week in order to meet his or her substance use goals. Because this is the last weekly check-in, the clinician reminds the client that the client will now be on his or her own when it comes to monitoring weekly progress and making adjustments in weekly goals when necessary.

At this point in the session, the clinician reviews with the client some of the specific changes made since entering treatment. The clinician presents the two Brief Situational Confidence Questionnaire (BSCQ) graphs (pre-treatment vs. session 4; see Figure 2.17) for the client to compare. To assist the client's recognition and understanding of the changes that have taken place, the clinician might ask, *"What changes have you noticed in the situations that you previously identified as high risk?"* or *"What actions or events do you think led to your increase in confidence that you would not use in this situation?"* In the typical case, client confidence to refuse alcohol or other drugs has dramatically increased across the majority of situational domains. However, it is likely that clients will continue to identify at least one situational domain in which they have limited confidence in their ability to avoid alcohol or drug use. In these instances, it is important to emphasize any progress that has been made, while at the same time helping the client recognize (1) the risk associated with these situations (e.g., a party or hanging out with friends on weekends) and (2) possible options (e.g., leaving the situation, taking a time out to think about choices). In order to facilitate such a discussion, the clinician might ask, *"What do you think might have to happen to increase your confidence in _____ situation, which you still see as challenging for you to avoid using?"*

For the next activity, clients are asked to complete their second "Decision to Change" worksheet (see Figure 2.2). Clients are reminded that they completed this worksheet in session 1 and are now completing it to see how they may have changed in their decision to change. As was done in session 1, once the client completes the worksheet, the client's feelings about making alcohol and drug use changes, especially any ambivalence, are explored and examined. In addition, the clinician asks the client to pull out the "Decision to Change" worksheet from session 1 so that the client and clinician can identify any shifts that have been made since the beginning of treatment. It is quite common for clients who, in session 1, had trouble identifying "less good things about using" to generate multiple "less good things about using" by session 5. Similarly, clients who had trouble identifying "good things about reducing or stopping" often check off the majority of the listed options by the final session. When there are changes from session 1 to session 5, a clinician might say the following: *"I notice that you think that one of the 'good things about stopping or reducing' is that 'it will make it easier to achieve life goals.' That was not something you felt to be true in session 1. What do you think has changed for you since then?"*

During the final session, the client also is asked to complete a second "Goals for Change" activity (see Figure 2.3). The clinician and client compare and contrast current and previous client ratings (0–100) of (1) the importance of making or maintaining alcohol and drug use changes and (2) confidence (0–100) that alcohol and drug use goals will be met. To facilitate this discussion, the clinician might ask some of the following questions: *"How has your substance use goal changed since the beginning of treatment?"*; *"What do you think led to this change?"*; *"How consistent is your current alcohol/drug use with your new goal statement?"*

A final paper-and-pencil task in session 5 is completing the client's third "Where are you now?" scale, which is compared to ratings from earlier time points (i.e., intake assessment and session 2). If the clinician determines that the client has changed (i.e., increased ratings since earlier sessions), then the clinician should help the client focus on maintaining progress after treatment. To do so, the clinician and client should engage in an exploration of possible strategies the client can use to "move a little further on this scale" (e.g., from an 8 now to a 9 or a 10). In addition, it is important to facilitate the identification of potential high-risk situations (e.g., spring break, brother getting released from jail) and develop a preliminary plan for managing these situations. If comparisons of the "Where are you now?" ratings indicate that the client has not changed or has lower ratings (e.g., a higher level of use), then it is important to work with clients to identify barriers impeding their progress and options for overcoming these barriers. At this point, it can be helpful to revisit some of the materials from previous sessions (e.g., options and actions, refusal skills).

The final objective of session 5 is to emphasize the important role of support systems in maintaining changes and continuing to make further changes. Clients are asked to complete the "Support Strategy" worksheet, where they identify the sources of support in their own lives, including people, groups, and organizations (see Figure 2.22). If clients have trouble generating supports, the clinician may remind them of persons or organizations they have identified as supportive during previous sessions. The clinician should discuss the need for support ebbs and flows based on circumstances clients might be experiencing, with high-stress times being times when clients may need to rely more heavily on their support systems. Finally, clinicians provide clients with the list of community support resources and phone numbers for substance use prevention and treatment services (see Figure 2.23), explaining that these resources can be useful if clients feel the need for a greater level of support in making/maintaining substance use changes.

Support is 100 percent necessary. Human beings need the emotional and psychological understanding and encouragement that can only be provided by other people.

Identify below the people, groups, and organizations that lend you support.

1. _____
2. _____
3. _____
4. _____
5. _____
6. _____
7. _____
8. _____
9. _____
10. _____

Figure 2.22   Support Strategy

GAPS Program	305-348-XXXX
Alcoholics Anonymous	305-371-XXXX
Addiction Counseling Hotline (24-hour hotline)	800-762-XXXX
Citrus Community Mental Health Center	305-888-XXXX
Children's Psychiatric Center (Markenson Unit – Hialeah)	305-558-XXXX
Children's Psychiatric Center (Sunset Unit)	305-274-XXXX
Here's Help	305-685-XXXX
Switchboard of Miami	305-358-XXXX
Community Health of South Dade	305-252-XXXX

Figure 2.23   GAPS Support Directory

The session ends with the client being presented a Certificate of Program Completion and his or her personalized Client Manual. It is important that the clinician emphasize that the manual represents the client's hard work and is something that has information that may be helpful for him or her in the future.

A CASE EXAMPLE OF AN EXCERPT FROM SESSION 5: REVIEW OF THE BRIEF SITUATIONAL CONFIDENCE QUESTIONNAIRE

CLINICIAN: So last week you completed the Brief Situational Confidence Questionnaire for the second time. Remember, this is the scale that measures how confident you are that you would not use weed or alcohol in six different situations: (1) when you are having bad or unpleasant feelings; (2) when you have physical discomfort, like a headache or trouble falling asleep; (3) when you are having good feelings, like peaceful, happy, confident in yourself; (4) when you are having a conflict with others, an argument or someone puts you down, those kinds of things; (5) when you have problems at school or work, like with a boss or a teacher or with other kids at school; and (6) when you are having a good time with other people, parties, celebrations, just hanging out, that kind of thing. What I have done is created a graph that shows your confidence level last week compared with your confidence level at the start of treatment. What we are going to do now is take a look and see how you might have changed as well as see if there are any situations that are still kind of tricky for you. Sound good?

CLIENT: Yeah.

CLINICIAN: OK, so let's take a look at your most recent graph first. What was your confidence level for situations involving unpleasant emotions?

CLIENT: High, a 9.

CLINICIAN: OK, so that's pretty close to definitely *would not* use. How does that compare with what you put down on the first one?

CLIENT: A lot different, the first one I put "0" definitely would use.

CLINICIAN: OK, so what do you think has changed for you since then?

CLIENT: Like I've been pissed a lot of times since then, and I still don't smoke, so I pretty much know I won't.

CLINICIAN: So what do you think it would take for you to reach a 10, to be all the way confident that you would not use?

CLIENT: Just staying away from it longer, like for three or four more weeks, and then I'll say for sure that I won't use.

CLINICIAN: So you just want a little more time to prove things to yourself. Makes sense. What did you put for the next one, when you feel physical discomfort?

CLIENT: I put a 6 this time and a 5 the first time.

CLINICIAN: It looks like you are still not too sure how you would handle feelings of discomfort. Were you thinking of a specific kind of physical issue?

CLIENT: Yeah, not being able to go to sleep. I can't handle that shit, and whenever I smoke I can just fall straight to sleep, no problem.

CLINICIAN: Sounds like you're not too sure that you would be able to avoid smoking weed if you couldn't fall asleep.

CLIENT: Yeah, because it hasn't come up lately so I don't really know what I would do because all I ever did was smoke before, and it worked.

CLINICIAN: This is important because it lets you identify a high-risk situation, not being able to sleep, that could sabotage the goals you've been working on. The idea is to come up with some strategies to help you deal with this situation in a way that does not interfere with your substance use goals. Can you think of anything besides weed that relaxes you and makes it easier to fall asleep?

CLIENT: Uh, basketball.

CLINICIAN: Great, so if you can somehow shoot some hoops before going to bed that may help you avoid this situation. However, if it's not possible to play basketball, is there some other type of exercise that you can do in the house or in your room that might help?

CLIENT: Maybe like sit-ups and push-ups, 100 each.

CLINICIAN: Good, so now you've already come up with some possible ways to stay on track even if you are faced with a situation that's tricky for you, like not being able to sleep. Let's move on to the next one.

CLIENT: For "Pleasant Emotions," I put 10 this time and 10 last time, too.

CLINICIAN: OK, so situations in which you are feeling pretty happy or relaxed were not really high-risk situations for you at the beginning of treatment and they still aren't, right?

CLIENT: Nope. I barely ever smoke when things are all good. What's the point?

CLINICIAN: The next one is "Conflict with Others"—what did you put for that?

CLIENT: I put a 10 this time, and a 4 last time.

CLINICIAN: Another big difference since the beginning of treatment; what do you think has changed for you?

CLIENT: Basically I'm not gonna let anybody else mess me up, so like if somebody's trying me or my mom is trippin,' I'm just gonna leave or whatever.

CLINICIAN: OK, so you've decided that rather than give up your own personal goals, which have been not to use, you are going to deal with the conflict in some other way like leaving or taking a time-out.

CLIENT: Basically, yep. If I decide to smoke, it's because I just want to relax, have fun or whatever, but not because somebody is trying to mess with me. I don't even care enough about all that.

CLINICIAN: Well, good for you. It seems you're now really confident that you won't smoke in a situation that used to be pretty risky for you just a few weeks ago. Let's go on to number 5, "Social Problems at School or Work."

CLIENT: I put a 10 now and a 9 before.

CLINICIAN: OK, so it wasn't too risky for you before, but you have moved all the way to "Definitely Won't Use." Why did this change?

CLIENT: I really never would smoke at work or school, so by the time I had weed I wasn't even thinking about it anymore; but now I know that I definitely wouldn't use because I really don't even have weed at my house, either.

CLINICIAN: OK, so by not having weed around, it really decreases the likelihood that you will use.

CLIENT: Yeah.

CLINICIAN: That's a really good thing for you to recognize; you can see how doing simple things, like not keeping it around, can really help you stick to your goals and make the decisions you want to make. Let's go ahead and take a look at the last category, "Pleasant Times with Others."

CLIENT: I put a 7 now, and a 2 in the beginning.

CLINICIAN: OK, so a big change here, too. What do you think is going on?

CLIENT: Before I would just go to parties or go hang out with my friends for the main purpose of smoking and chilling. Now I only go if it's going to be something fun, like a party with good music or like a football game or something, and don't really even think about smoking.

CLINICIAN: Wow, so that's a pretty big deal. What has helped you make that shift?

CLIENT: Usually I'm with my girlfriend, or I'm with my boys who don't even smoke. Before, I didn't really even think of it, it was just automatic that I would smoke. Now I try to not really be around it, or if I am I just try to do something else like pay attention to the game or something.

CLINICIAN: It sounds like you are really using some of the strategies you came up with in our other sessions. You still aren't completely confident that you won't use—what do you think it will take for you to get to a 9 or 10 for these types of situations?

CLIENT: Probably just testing myself more, like being in these situations more and knowing that I won't give in even if a lot of people are smoking or whatever. Probably just a longer time of me not doing it.

CLINICIAN: That makes sense. It sounds like you are still being cautious because you know these can be tricky situations. Great, it's important that you recognize that.

CONCLUSION

A variety of treatments based on social modeling, social problem-solving, or social skills training currently exist for treating substance use and related problems among adolescents and young adults. There is good evidence supporting the effectiveness of many of these treatments, which typically focus on the following goals: (1) increasing knowledge about the consequences of substance use; (2) fostering social and self-regulative skills for resisting substance use; (3) providing guided practice and corrective feedback to build self-efficacy; (4) expanding non-user social support; (5) addressing social norms favoring alcohol and other drug use; (6) improving problem-solving skills, particularly in the social arena; and/or (7) building motivation to engage in competent problem-solving strategies. Guided Adolescent Problem Solving (GAPS) is a brief treatment focusing on problem-solving and social skills training for adolescents struggling with substance use and related behavior problems. GAPS also incorporates Motivational Interviewing (MI) strategies in order to maximize client therapeutic engagement. In this chapter, we used examples from GAPS to illustrate how therapeutic techniques emphasizing problem-solving and social skills may be effectively employed in the treatment of substance-abusing youth and young adults. We hope that these examples are helpful to clinicians working with substance-abusing adolescents, and encourage clinicians and researchers to pursue a professional agenda related to problem-solving and social skills interventions.

RESOURCES

WEB-BASED RESOURCES

National Institute on Alcohol Abuse and Alcoholism: www.niaaa.nih.gov/
National Institute on Drug Abuse: www.nida.nih.gov/
Community-Based Intervention Research Group: http://cbirg.fiu.edu/
Parents Resource Center: www.drugfree.org/Parent/#

REFERENCES

Allen, J. P., Aber, J. L., & Leadbeater, B. J. (1990). Adolescent problem behaviors: The influence of attachment and autonomy. *Psychiatric Clinics of North America, 13,* 455–467.

Allen, J. P., Leadbeater, B. J., & Aber, J. L. (1994). The development of problem behavior syndromes in at-risk adolescents. *Development and Psychopathology, 6,* 323–342.

Azrin, A. H., Donohue, B., Teichner, G. A., Crum, T., Howell, J., & DeCato, L. A. (2001). A controlled evaluation and description of individual-cognitive problem-solving and family-behavior therapies in dually-diagnosed conduct-disordered and substance-dependent youth. *Journal of Child and Adolescent Substance Abuse, 11,* 1–43.

Barkin, S. L., Smith, K. S., & Durant, R. (2002) Social skills and attitudes associated with substance use behaviors among young adolescents *Journal of Adolescent Health, 30,* 448–454.

Borsari, B., & Carey, K. B. (2003) Are social norms the best predictor of outcomes among heavy-drinking college students? *Journal of Studies on Alcohol, 64,* 331–341.

D'Zurilla, T. J. (1986). *Problem-solving therapy: A social competence approach to clinical intervention.* New York: Springer.

D'Zurilla, T. J., & Goldfried, M. R. (1971). Problem solving and behavior modification. *Journal of Abnormal Psychology, 78,* 107–126.

D'Zurilla, T. J., & Nezu, A. M. (1999). *Problem-solving therapy: A social competence approach to clinical intervention* (2nd ed.). New York: Springer.

Fodor, I. G. (1992), *Adolescent assertiveness and social skills training: A clinical handbook.* New York: Springer.

Freedman, B. J., Rosenthal, L., Donahue, L. P., Schlundt, D. G., & McFall, R. M. (1978). A social-behavioral analysis of skills deficits in delinquent and non-delinquent adolescent boys. *Journal of Clinical and Consulting Psychology, 46,* 1448–1462.

Jaffee, W. B., & D'Zurilla, T. J. (2003) Adolescent problem-solving, parent problem-solving, and externalizing behavior in adolescents. *Behavior Therapy, 34,* 295–311.

Kendall, P. C., & Braswell, L. (1985). *Cognitive-behavioral therapy for impulsive children.* New York: Guilford Press.

Kendall, P. C., & Braswell, L (1987). Treating impulsive children via cognitive-behavioral therapy. In N. Jacobson (Ed.), *Psychotherapist in clinical practice.* New York: Guilford Press.

Kendall, P. C., Padawer, W., Zupan, B., & Braswell, L. (1985). Developing self control in children: The manual. In P.C. Kendall & L. Braswell (Eds.), *Cognitive-behavioral therapy for impulsive children* (pp. 179–209). New York: Guilford Press.

Kuperminc G. P., & Allen, J. P. (2001). Social orientation: Problem behavior and motivations toward interpersonal problem-solving among high risk adolescents. *Journal of Youth and Adolescence, 30*(5), 597–622.

Leadbeater, B. J., Hellner, I., Allen, J. P., & Aber, J. L. (1989). Assessment of interpersonal negotiation strategies in youth engaged in problem behaviors. *Developmental Psychology, 25,* 465–472.

Michelson, L. K., Kazdin, A. E., Sugai, D. P., & Wood, R. P. (2007). *Social skills assessment and training with children: An empirically based handbook*. New York: Springer.

Miller, W., & Rollnick, S. (2002). *Motivational interviewing: Preparing people for change, Second Edition*. New York: Guilford Press.

Rinn, R. C., & Markle, A. (1979). Modification of social skill deficits in children. In A. S. Bellack & M. Heren (Eds.), *Research and practice in social skills training* (pp. 107–129). New York: Plenum Press.

Sobell, L. C., & Sobell, M. B. (Eds.). (1992). *Timeline Followback: A technique for assessing self-reported alcohol consumption*. Totowa, NJ: Humana Press.

Sobell, L. C., & Sobell, M. B. (1996). *Timeline Followback users' manual for alcohol use*. Toronto, Canada: Addiction Research Foundation.

Spivack, G., Platt, J. J., & Shure, M. B. (1976). *The problem-solving approach to adjustment*. San Francisco: Jossey-Bass.

Winters, K. C., Leitten, W., Wagner, E., & O'Leary Tevyaw, T. (2007). Use of brief interventions in a middle and high school setting. *Journal of School Health, 77*, 196–206.

CHAPTER 3

Adolescent Community Reinforcement Approach (A-CRA)*

SUSAN H. GODLEY, JANE ELLEN SMITH, ROBERT J. MEYERS, and MARK D. GODLEY

T HE ADOLESCENT COMMUNITY Reinforcement Approach (A-CRA) is an intervention that has been developed and tested over a number of years. It has been replicated by over fifty agencies providing adolescent treatment in at least twenty states. In this chapter, we review how the Community Reinforcement Approach was developed and how it was adapted for adolescents. We specify the adolescents for whom the approach is appropriate, any contraindications, the general session flow, and the content of sessions. We also provide a description of A-CRA procedures, including sample dialogues for many of the procedures, discuss the use of the intervention for different settings and populations, and offer training recommendations.

HISTORY OF CRA

The Community Reinforcement Approach (CRA) was originally developed and tested with adults who had such severe problems with alcohol that they were admitted to a state-run hospital for inpatient treatment. This was during the time when people were admitted to state hospitals because they provided

*We wish to acknowledge support for this work from a Center for Substance Abuse Treatment (CSAT), Substance Abuse and Mental Health Services Administration contract (HHSS 270200700004C) and grants from the National Institute on Drug Abuse (RO1 DA 018183) and the National Institute on Alcohol Abuse and Alcoholism (2RO1 AA010368 and RO1 AA017625). The interpretations and conclusions are solely those of the authors and do not represent official positions of our funders. We also wish to thank Randy Muck, Jutta Butler, Brandi Barnes, Michael L. Dennis, Luis Flores, Bryan R. Garner, Courtney Hupp, Julie Macpherson, Vickie McGinley, Karen Mertig, Brian Serna, and Kelli Wright for their contributions to this work.

one of the few treatment options for those with alcohol problems and limited financial resources. The first studies (Azrin, 1976; Hunt & Azrin, 1973) were done during the early 1970s, and at that time, the predominant treatment method was based on the twelve steps of Alcoholics Anonymous (AA). A group of researchers, who had been trained in operant conditioning methods, thought it was worthwhile to investigate the application of these methods to help individuals with severe alcohol use disorders find a rewarding life with their families and in their communities without the use of alcohol and, thus, be able to make healthy lifestyle changes.

CRA Adaptation for Adolescents

In October 1997, a three-year study (known as the CYT study) began to evaluate different outpatient treatments for adolescents who used marijuana and had problems associated with this use. This study was funded by a U.S. federal agency (Center for Substance Abuse Treatment; CSAT) because annual survey data showed that in 1996, marijuana use among adolescents 12 to 18 years old had reached the highest levels in twelve years. Even though these data showed that marijuana use was very high among the nation's youth, there were no interventions that had been designed or evaluated specifically for use with adolescents. Other data indicated that most adolescents entering treatment related to marijuana use attended outpatient rather than residential treatment programs. Thus, five different outpatient interventions were evaluated in an experiment across four different sites in the United States (see Appendix A for a summary on the effectiveness of A-CRA).

The research group leading the study decided an adaptation for adolescents of CRA would be one of the interventions evaluated in this study. An existing book had already outlined CRA procedures and forms for the treatment of adults with alcohol disorders (Meyers & Smith, 1995), and this book served as the basis for adapting the approach for adolescents. A manual that described the adaptation of CRA for adolescents, so that it was developmentally appropriate, was written, and clinical staff working in the research study were trained and supervised to the manual (Godley, Meyers, et al., 2001). Many of the procedures in the book and manual drew upon other research related to behavioral skill training and were adapted for adolescents with little revision, such as skill training in problem solving and communication skills. Adaptations included using examples in the manual and during training that emphasized how these skills might often be used with adolescents, for example, in communicating with parents, school authority or juvenile justice figures. Other procedures needed more adaptation. For example, CRA has had a long history of addressing marital relationships, and for the adolescent version, these procedures were revised to address relationship skills between adolescents and their parents. CRA used a goal planning procedure based on the participant's response to a clinical "happiness" or "satisfaction" scale. In A-CRA, the Happiness Scale was revised to reflect life areas that are relevant for adolescents.

WIDE-SCALE IMPLEMENTATION OF A-CRA

Study findings demonstrating the effectiveness of A-CRA (see Appendix A), coupled with an increased interest among funders in evidence-based approaches, led to substance abuse treatment agencies and funders wanting to implement A-CRA. Early replications relied on two- to three-day training sessions with limited follow-up with the trainees. These attempts at replication were found to be insufficient, as trainees often did not incorporate the treatment procedures and components into their everyday practice. A more systematic training and certification approach was developed to support a wide-scale implementation effort funded by the U.S. federal government. In September 2006, Center for Substance Abuse Treatment (CSAT) awarded fifteen grants to local agencies across the United States to implement A-CRA and its continuing care adaptation, Assertive Continuing Care (ACC), under an initiative titled Assertive Adolescent and Family Treatment. An additional seventeen grants were awarded under the same initiative in September 2007. The grants to these thirty-two organizations totaled almost $27.5 million over three years to provide treatment services to adolescents with substance abuse problems. Approximately 6,700 adolescents will participate in these replications. Based on data supplied by the sites, the race/ethnicity of the adolescents is expected to be 32 percent Caucasian, 25 percent Hispanic, 19 percent African American, 15 percent Native American, and 9 percent Mixed/Other. Most (69 percent) participants will be male. Another advantage of this implementation is that important demographic, clinical characteristic, and outcome data are being collected from the participants at their admission into services and during follow-up interviews at three, six, and twelve months after their admission. In addition, data that describes the A-CRA procedures delivered to each participant are also being collected, so that this data set will provide a tremendous opportunity for further research on this intervention, its mechanisms of change, and its outcomes across a large number of adolescents.

The training model designed for the federally funded replications was based on a synthesis of the literature on implementation research (Fixsen, Naoom, Blasé, Friedman, & Wallace, 2005) and two randomized clinical trials that evaluated therapist training methods for Motivational Interviewing (Miller, Yahne, Moyers, Martinez, & Pittitano, 2004) and Cognitive Behavior Therapy (Sholomskas et al., 2005). It includes an initial three-and-a-half-day centralized training and the use of a website for uploading therapy session digital recordings. Once these recordings are reviewed by intervention experts who have been trained to rate A-CRA procedures and provide feedback, written feedback is given to the therapists on the website. Ongoing coaching calls are also provided to review some of the session feedback, answer questions, and review procedures. When therapists have demonstrated a satisfactory level of competency across nine procedures, they receive basic A-CRA certification. They receive full A-CRA certification when they demonstrate competency across all A-CRA procedures. In order to help foster sustainability at the agency level, there is also a supervisor certification process. Training recommendations are described in more detail below.

INDICATIONS

To illustrate when the use of A-CRA may be indicated, we review the characteristics of the adolescents who have participated in one of the randomized clinical trials of this intervention or in the large CSAT-funded replication. A-CRA has been evaluated with adolescents who have presented for outpatient treatment at community-based treatment agencies and with homeless adolescents in the Southwest who made contact with a drop-in center. Increasingly, A-CRA procedures are being implemented in residential treatment programs as well, and these programs are more likely to be designed to treat adolescents who have a higher level of severity, both in terms of their substance use severity and the presence of comorbid problems.

SUBSTANCE USE AND READINESS FOR TREATMENT

The majority of adolescents who have participated in randomized clinical trials of A-CRA during outpatient treatment or in ACC after residential treatment have symptoms of alcohol or marijuana abuse and dependence. Often, they have problems with both alcohol and marijuana. This is not surprising, since alcohol and marijuana are the most commonly reported substances for adolescents who present for treatment in the United States. While in the homeless study, 26 percent of the adolescents were involved with IV drug use; in general, the percentages of adolescents in treatment who report weekly crack/cocaine, heroin/opioid, or other drug use besides marijuana are much lower than those who report use of alcohol and marijuana. Most use alcohol and/or drugs weekly and most began using alcohol or drugs between the ages of 10 and 14. With regard to their readiness for treatment, less than 25 percent of adolescents perceive that their alcohol or drug use is a problem. In contrast to adults, who may have experienced more physical consequences due to decades of substance use, adolescents typically do not have physical symptoms. Most enter treatment because of pressure from juvenile justice (over 80 percent) or because their school or parents strongly encourage that they attend treatment. Thus, the A-CRA approach acknowledges that most adolescents are not motivated to quit alcohol or drug use at the time they enter treatment.

PRIOR TREATMENT AND A-CRA TREATMENT SETTINGS

When adolescents enter treatment for A-CRA, they come from a variety of previous treatment experiences. However, the majority of adolescent participants report that they have not been in substance abuse treatment before. To date, most adolescents have entered treatment in outpatient or intensive outpatient treatment settings. This might even be considered the case for adolescents who participated in the homeless study and who were recruited at a drop-in center. In many places in the United States, assignment to treatment level (i.e., school-based, outpatient, intensive outpatient, or residential) is based on their substance use severity and the presence of additional comorbid disorders. Increasingly, A-CRA treatment procedures also are being incorporated into residential treatment programs. The advantage of this trend is that adolescents have ample opportunity to practice many of the skills they learn in A-CRA and thus should be more likely to use these skills when they return to their natural environment. When used in continuing care following discharge from residential or other type of treatment, A-CRA procedures are used in combination with assertive case management procedures.

COMORBID ISSUES

One of the important findings from the CYT study is that adolescents who present for substance abuse outpatient treatment typically have additional problems. This was evident with the 600 adolescents in this study, and this finding has continued to be validated with subsequent studies and implementations of this approach. Based on over 750 adolescents who have participated in the CSAT replication of A-CRA, we know that approximately 70 percent report symptoms of co-occurring disorders. These include internalizing disorders like major depression (40 percent), generalized anxiety (14 percent), and posttraumatic stress disorder (28 percent). It is very common for adolescents with substance use disorders to report a history of victimization, and this will be even more pronounced with adolescents who have higher substance abuse severity or who are homeless. Furthermore, suicidal thoughts or actions are quite prevalent (24 percent). Additionally, externalizing disorders like conduct disorder (51 percent) and attention deficit-hyperactivity disorder (50 percent) are common. We also know that approximately 80 percent are involved in the juvenile justice system. This involvement could be in a diversion or probation program or could follow incarceration. Adolescent drug courts are becoming more common across the country, but as far as we know, A-CRA has not been evaluated in a juvenile drug treatment court setting.

SUMMARY

A-CRA has been successfully used with adolescents who have several substance abuse diagnoses and with adolescents with co-occurring disorders. It is important that therapists who work with adolescents have thorough assessment information so that they understand both the level of substance use severity and the presence of other comorbid disorders. For example, it may be important for certain adolescents to be referred for a psychiatric evaluation or for another evidence-based intervention, like a trauma-focused intervention.

CONTRAINDICATIONS

It is difficult to specify a population for whom A-CRA is contraindicated, as no studies have been done to establish this. In the absence of such data, one might examine the exclusion criteria for A-CRA and CRA clinical trials and identify the populations for which the Community Reinforcement Approach has not been tested. For example, actively psychotic people and those with cognitive deficits that would interfere with participation in therapy typically have been excluded from studies (e.g., Smith, Meyers, & Delaney, 1998).

As noted in the comorbidity section of this chapter, it is extremely common to see adolescent substance abusers with multiple psychiatric diagnoses. These include various anxiety and mood disorders, as well as attention deficit-hyperactivity disorder and conduct disorder. Future research will need to determine whether diagnoses such as these either interfere with or perhaps lengthen A-CRA treatment. Furthermore, the issue of how to best offer the empirically supported treatments that are indicated for the comorbid conditions requires additional investigation for these adolescents. Finally, the fact that various components of A-CRA (e.g., functional analyses, problem solving, communication skills) appear well suited for treating at least some of the symptoms of these other disorders also is worthy of study.

OVERVIEW OF SESSION FLOW AND CONTENT

A-CRA Is Flexible and Procedure-Based

Some evidence-based approaches are designed so that therapists are directed to finish certain activities in particular sessions. That is, the corresponding treatment manual describes what the therapist is going to do in session 1, session 2, and so on. The therapist goes into the session knowing exactly what will be discussed that day or what forms will be completed. Other therapy approaches are very nondirective, and the therapist is skillful in asking questions that help individuals, for example, understand what their motivations for change are and how they might go about changing. A-CRA is somewhere in between these two types of approaches. It is more directed than the latter approach, but still a very flexible therapy. The framework is behavioral and procedure-based. A-CRA has a menu of seventeen procedures, and therapists learn how to introduce a given procedure at the appropriate time during a session depending on their interactions with an adolescent. There is some logical sequencing of the procedures that are described below, but the therapist has great leeway in the order they are introduced. It can be more difficult to learn A-CRA than a session-based approach, but during qualitative interviews, therapists have indicated that they liked its flexibility and the fact that the procedures can be individualized for each adolescent (Godley, White, Diamond, Passetti, & Titus, 2001).

Begin (and End) with Reinforcers

The most important aspect of A-CRA delivery is that the therapist is constantly listening for information or clues about what reinforces or motivates the adolescent. The therapist approaches each adolescent with the understanding that alcohol or drug use is serving a reinforcing function in the adolescent's life, and that it is important to help the adolescent find positive activities and goals that can replace the function that alcohol and drugs are serving. When we talk about reinforcers, we include a broad range of desires and activities that could be immediate or long-term. For example, some adolescents would like to graduate high school, others might want to spend more enjoyable time with their parents, and still others just want to "get off" probation. It is often obvious to therapists what the consequences are for an adolescent's substance use behavior, and there may be a desire to clarify the connections for the adolescent. However, the A-CRA approach is to help facilitate the adolescent's discussions so that he or she sees those connections, rather than requiring that the therapist confront the adolescent on the consequences of behavior. There are many ways to discover what an adolescent's reinforcers are, including asking open-ended questions about what each individual likes or hopes to do. Several of the A-CRA tools also provide opportunities to learn more about an adolescent's reinforcers, as is illustrated from the therapy dialogue examples below.

BASIC SESSION GUIDELINES

There are general expectations about how an A-CRA session should be conducted. The overall style is behavioral or cognitive behavioral. As noted above, there is an emphasis on discerning the adolescent's reinforcers and providing verbal reinforcement when possible. Therapists also are expected to project a positive approach that is upbeat and supportive. In most sessions, therapists are expected to use A-CRA procedures appropriately during a significant portion of the session. Throughout the session, the therapist's general clinical skills are important, as with any approach. That is, the therapist demonstrates warmth, understanding, and is nonjudgmental. The therapist is expected to maintain the session focus so that small talk is minimized and to ensure that procedures are completed. Also, there is a logical progression from one procedure to another. Finally, A-CRA therapists skillfully guide the session so there is an appropriate balance between the amounts of time the therapist and the adolescent talk.

CONTACT FREQUENCY AND DURATION OF TREATMENT

The A-CRA manual, which was based on how the intervention was implemented during CYT, describes a fixed length intervention. Approximately ten 1-hour sessions are conducted individually with adolescents, two 1-hour sessions are conducted with parent(s), and two generally longer than 1-hour sessions are held with the adolescents and parents together. The manual describes a twelve- to fourteen-week duration for treatment. Since the model has been tested based on this number of sessions and duration, these parameters might be considered the minimal acceptable for faithful implementation of the model. However, individual therapists and programs might add additional sessions based on adolescent and family needs.

A-CRA PROCEDURES

OVERVIEW OF A-CRA

The first session with an adolescent provides the opportunity for engagement and an explanation about how participation in the approach can be helpful. There are certain expectations about basic information to be covered in this session. The therapist describes the basic objective of the counseling sessions, including that the goal is to help the adolescent find healthy and fun activities that he or she enjoys doing that can replace the substance-using behavior. Several procedures are previewed to provide the adolescent with more detail about what is going to happen during therapy. The therapist sets positive expectations that the approach will be helpful for the participant by noting its scientific base. It is also important that the therapist describes the duration of treatment and begins the very important task of identifying reinforcers for the particular adolescent.

Below is an illustration of how a therapist covers the basic components of an overview session with a male participant. This adolescent lives with his mom and attends a regular school. He wants to be a game designer. His mom wants him to stop using marijuana. It illustrates that the necessary overview components can be completed in a relatively short period of time and leave additional time for rapport building.

A CASE EXAMPLE: IDENTIFICATION OF REINFORCERS AND INTRODUCTION TO SEVERAL PROCEDURES

THERAPIST: Thanks again for doing that assessment last week. You did a great job. Glad you were able to sit through it.

ADOLESCENT: It was long.

THERAPIST: It sure was. But you did it. That information will be very helpful. Today, we're going to move on and talk about the treatment that I'm going to be offering you. I'll give you an overview of the program, like how long it is and the different skills you can learn. But before I get into that, I want to hear from you in terms of what's important to you. What are your goals here? What do *you* want to do?

ADOLESCENT: I kind of want to make it in life.

THERAPIST: Make it in life? Good. Go ahead. Can you tell me a little more about that?

ADOLESCENT: My parents and everyone are telling me to look around me, to look at the friends I'm hanging out with and see where they're headed. So I'm trying to plan ahead and do what's right.

THERAPIST: Good for you. So, it sounds like you're saying that you want to work on making some positive decisions and doing the right thing, like staying away from the crowd that keeps getting into trouble. Is that it? So what do you see as being the right thing? What's your definition of the right thing? What does it look like for you?

ADOLESCENT: Getting good grades, finishing school, definitely getting a good job.

THERAPIST: Those are all really good goals.

ADOLESCENT: This is my opportunity to do things right. But the thing is, I know I have a problem saying "no" to drugs. My mom is thinking about signing me out of school this year and maybe putting me in detox, because school is where all my problems start. So I have to be able to say "no."

THERAPIST: We can definitely work on skills to refuse drugs and alcohol from people. And we can work on the other things you mentioned, too, like getting good grades and getting a good job. We can set some longer-term goals in those areas and then set some weekly goals, too. And it will all be stuff that *you* want to work on. I'm not going to tell you what you have to do.

ADOLESCENT: That's cool.

The therapist wisely started the session by asking the adolescent what *he* wanted to get out of treatment. The therapist then illustrated how the treatment could offer skills training in areas that would allow the adolescent to make progress toward achieving his goals.

DESCRIPTION OF TREATMENT FORMAT AND ADDITIONAL PROCEDURES

THERAPIST: That's how programs work the best anyway. But I'll start just by talking about the time length. The program lasts for three months. There will be fourteen sessions. Ten sessions will be me and you meeting individually, usually once a week for about an hour. Now if something's going on where there's a crisis or something and you really need to talk about it, you can come in another day, too. Also, there will be two sessions that I meet with you and your mom together, and two more when I meet just with your mom. That will give her a chance to talk about some of her concerns and to say what she'd like to see happen. For the two family sessions that involve the three of us, we'll be talking about your relationship with your mom and how to make it better. So, we'll work on how the two of you communicate. I'll teach you both communication skills for you to try out. For example, maybe you'll want help telling your mom that you'd like her to recognize some of your accomplishments more, right? How does this sound so far?

ADOLESCENT: OK. I guess I have trouble with my communication skills sometimes.

THERAPIST: Being able to communicate is important for the other thing you mentioned, too: being able to say "no" to drugs to your friends. Now I know that's kind of hard when they put that stuff in your face and you're supposed to say, "Hey dude, no thanks," right? So we'll be working on drug refusal skills to help you with that. We'll also talk about problem-solving skills. Those are great skills because you can use them for any kind of problem, whether it's a problem with a girlfriend, or at school, whatever. You told me when we were doing the assessment that your anger sometimes gets you into trouble and then things don't go so well, right? Well, we can talk about anger management skills. These are ways you can recognize your anger coming on, and ways you can help yourself. And we're also going to do this thing with a fancy name, a functional analysis. Basically, it means we're going to look at what's going on before you're using drugs or alcohol. And then besides just talking about the negative consequences of using drugs and alcohol, we're going to talk about what are some of the reasons why you do it, right? There are some positive reasons why you do it, because if it didn't make you feel good, you wouldn't keep doing it, right?

ADOLESCENT: Yeah. That's a lot of stuff.

The therapist informed the adolescent that their time together would be limited, and that the parent would be receiving skills training, too. An area of considerable concern to the adolescent, being able to turn down drugs from his friends, was highlighted as an area on which they could focus.

EXPLANATION OF BASIC OBJECTIVE OF TREATMENT

THERAPIST: Yeah, it is a lot of stuff. But we'll move at your pace. If you want to move fast, we will. If you want to slow down, we will. Remember that the main goal of this program is to help you live a lifestyle without drugs or alcohol, but it has to be a lifestyle that *you're* cool with. If your life sucks without drugs, then we know you'll eventually go back to the drugs, right? As part of this, I can help you identify things that are satisfying and enjoyable to you that aren't drug- and alcohol-related. And so then you'll feel less stress and be happier. We have to make sure you get the kind of life you want. And you already have some good ideas about what you want out of life. That's what this program is about. What do you think?

ADOLESCENT: Sounds OK to me.

The therapist explained the basic A-CRA objective: to help adolescents find a healthy, enjoyable, fulfilling lifestyle that does not involve alcohol or drugs.

Positive Expectations Set

THERAPIST: Excellent! Once you're done with the treatment, you'll have these skills for the rest of your life. And you know, I'm not just making this stuff up. There's been a lot of research done, studies and stuff, on these methods and different interventions that are effective, like the drug refusal skills. These interventions that I'm telling you about have been successful with lots of different kinds of kids; kids who have been using various types of drugs and various different levels of drugs and alcohol. Kids from all different kinds of backgrounds, too. It's not like we're saying, "Let's try this stuff and see if it works." No—it's actually been tested already and we *know* that it works. So, I think I covered all the bases. Do you have any questions?

ADOLESCENT: Not really.

The scientific foundation of A-CRA was stressed as a means to instill confidence and increase motivation.

Further Discussion of Reinforcers and Description of Homework Assignments

THERAPIST: OK. Since we have a few minutes left, let's go back to that "good job" you were talking about wanting. Can you tell me if you've thought at all about the *type* of job you're thinking about getting someday?

ADOLESCENT: I want to be a game designer.

THERAPIST: That's cool.

ADOLESCENT: Yeah, I could make video games, or something along that level.

THERAPIST: Great! So you'd design computer games or video games? That's cool. Do you know of any places around here where you could learn how to do that?

ADOLESCENT: Yeah. I signed up for some information from a college.

THERAPIST: Wow. That's one of the things, too, that I can help you with, whether it's looking for a job or looking into schools and stuff like that. Terrific! I'm glad you're so motivated to get a good job. And I can help with some of the things that will need to happen before you can get to that college, like helping you figure out how to get the good grades you want in high school.

ADOLESCENT: Yeah. I might need some help with that.

THERAPIST: No problem. Part of it will involve our coming up with some type of assignment for you to work on each week, because there's a lot of time between sessions, and there's lots of work to do, right? It can be something like going to a teacher and asking for extra help. And we'd practice what you'd say to the teacher before you went and did it. You'd be prepared.

ADOLESCENT: I'm not sure I want to go ask for extra help. Not yet anyway. I want to see if I can fix the problem on my own.

THERAPIST: No problem. The assignment definitely has to be something that *you* want to work on. Period.

ADOLESCENT: OK. That's good then.

THERAPIST: Great. So before we finish up today, I'll ask you to pick something specific you want to work on this week that will move you one step closer to becoming a game designer someday. Cool?

ADOLESCENT: Cool.

The therapist identified a long-term reinforcer (i.e., becoming a game designer), broke it down into a short-term goal (improving grades), and then discussed appropriate homework assignments. The specific goal and the assignment would be spelled out clearly before the session ended.

Functional Analysis of Substance Use

A common procedure to use within the first two or three sessions with an adolescent is the Functional Analysis of Substance Use (see Figure 3.1). The adolescent is asked to describe a common substance use episode. The therapist helps participants make the connections between behaviors and feelings that lead up to the substance use, then identifies both the positive and negative consequences of that use. This information can be used in many ways. For example, it can help adolescents learn to recognize their triggers and change risky behaviors or situations or to find healthier ways to attain the positive consequences they associate with substance use. As with all procedures, the therapist begins by providing a rationale that explains why it is important to spend session time completing the procedure. The therapist then asks the adolescent to think of a "common" using episode to serve as a basis for examining what comes before and after substance use. The next step is for the adolescent to describe both internal and external triggers. The therapist asks details about the behavior, including who else was with the adolescent, how much was used, where the use occurred, and how long the use period was. They discuss both the positive and negative consequences of the use. Finally, the therapist clarifies how the information from the functional

External Triggers	Internal Triggers	Using Behavior	Short-Term + Consequences Good Things (rewards)	Long-Term − Consequences Not So Good Things
1. *Who* are you usually with when you use?	1. *What* are you usually *thinking* about right before you use?	1. *What* do you usually use?	1. What do you like about using with (*who*)?	1. What are the negative results of your using in each of these areas:
A friend	I'm going to get high	Marijuana	Conversation, jokes	**a) Family:** Mom doesn't trust me
			2. What do you like about using (*where*)? Nobody bothers us; can do what we want	**b) Friends:**
2. *Where* do you usually use?	2. What are you usually *feeling physically* right before you use?	2. *How much* do you usually use?		—
Friend's house	Relaxed	Five blunts (shared)	3. What do you like about using (*when*)? Helps me sleep	**c) Physical:** —
			4. What are the pleasant *thoughts* you have while using?	**d) Emotional** —
			It's fun to be high	**e) Legal:** Thinks about a friend who got arrested for drugs

122

3. *When* do you usually use?	3. What are you usually feeling *emotionally* right before you use?	3. Over *how long* a period of time do you usually use?	5. What are the pleasant *physical feelings* you have while using?	6. What are the pleasant *emotions* you have while using?	f) School:
Evenings (start at 7:00)	Excited, relaxed	Five hours (7:00–midnight)	Not tense	Excited	Late for class after smoking the night before (?)

g) Job:
—

h) Financial:
Spend about $105/week on weed

Figure 3.1 Functional Analysis For Substance Use Behavior

From *Clinical Guide to Alcohol Treatment: The Community Reinforcement Approach* (pp. 34–35), by R.J. Meyers & J.E. Smith (1995), New York: Guilford Press. Adapted with permission.

analysis can be helpful to the adolescent. The latter can be as simple as pointing out what the adolescent's particular triggers are or how they can work together to learn other ways to find the positive reinforcers that come from the adolescent's drug use. The following example illustrates how this procedure might be implemented with the same adolescent described above.

A CASE EXAMPLE: FUNCTIONAL ANALYSIS OF SUBSTANCE ABUSE

Rationale and Overview of Common Episode

THERAPIST: Today I'd like to look at some of your drug use so that I can learn a little bit more about how you view it. Do you think we can do that today?

ADOLESCENT: Yeah.

THERAPIST: OK. Here's a chart that will help us (See "Functional Analysis for Substance Use"). We're going to go through this together. The technical name for this is a functional analysis. I know that probably sounds kind of strange, but all it really means is that we're going to look at the function, the *purpose* of your substance use. We're going to just talk about the type of things that lead you to marijuana use in the first place. OK? There might be things that happen in your environment or things that you feel inside. And then we can talk about the consequences of your drug use, both the negative and the positive consequences. When we're done, we can see how this might help us come up with a treatment plan that you're OK with. So how does that sound?

ADOLESCENT: Good, I guess.

THERAPIST: OK, great. First, I'd like to see if you can tell me about a typical time when you use marijuana.

ADOLESCENT: I just smoke at nighttime.

THERAPIST: You mostly smoke at nighttime. OK. Can you describe the situation a little more so that I can get a clear picture of what's going on when you smoke? In other words, what leads up to it and what happens afterwards?

ADOLESCENT: I don't know. I just want to smoke, so I smoke. If I'm at a friend's house, I go home then and go to sleep.

THERAPIST: And it's pretty much the same pattern every night?

ADOLESCENT: Yup.

After providing a rationale for the functional analysis exercise, the therapist attempted to get the adolescent to describe a common using episode. Since the adolescent was not particularly forthcoming with the details, it simply means that the therapist will have to follow up by asking more of the specific questions on the A-CRA Functional Analysis form.

Triggers: External and Internal

THERAPIST: Fair enough. Let me just ask you a few specific questions about those evenings when you smoke. Here, I'll show you where the questions are coming from on the chart. For example, do you see the first column? It asks who you're usually with when you smoke.

ADOLESCENT: I'm by myself, or like I said, I might be with a friend.

THERAPIST: Would you say it's more common for you to smoke by yourself or with a friend?

ADOLESCENT: Probably somebody is usually with me.

THERAPIST: And where do you usually use?

ADOLESCENT: Huh?

THERAPIST: Where do you usually smoke in the evening?

ADOLESCENT: In the neighborhood.

THERAPIST: OK. But can you be a little more specific about where in the neighborhood? Is it at someone's house, or in the park maybe?

ADOLESCENT: Someone's house.

THERAPIST: You mentioned being with a friend. So you're at a friend's house, or somebody else's house?

ADOLESCENT: A friend's.

THERAPIST: OK, thanks. And when you say you smoke in the evening, can you give me a ballpark idea of the time that you start? For example, do you go to your friend's house and start at around 7:00? 10:00?

ADOLESCENT: Probably around 7:00, usually.

THERAPIST: Thank you. So, now I'm just wondering if you know what a trigger is? Do you know what that refers to?

ADOLESCENT: It means that you go back to the person that triggers the use.

THERAPIST: Right. A trigger is something that leads to a behavior. Something happens and that triggers you to do a certain kind of behavior. We've been looking at your external triggers, what happens in your environment. We're also going to look at some internal triggers, what happens inside yourself, like your thoughts and feelings. Do you know what some of your *internal* triggers are?

ADOLESCENT: No.

THERAPIST: No? You said that you're usually with a friend when you smoke, right? So when you're around certain friends does it make you want to smoke?

ADOLESCENT: If I feel like just getting high.

THERAPIST: OK. What are you usually thinking about right before you use?

ADOLESCENT: That I'm going to get high.

THERAPIST: That you're going to get high. OK. And can you tell me what you're feeling physically in your body right as you're saying to yourself, "I'm going to get high"?

ADOLESCENT: Excited.

THERAPIST: And how about how you feel emotionally right before you use?

ADOLESCENT: I don't know. I guess nothing.

THERAPIST: You actually said excited a minute ago. I guess that's more of an emotion, isn't it? So back to maybe the physical feelings right before you use; something you feel in your body, like a tightness or looseness or anxiety or something like that? In other words, how do you know that you're feeling excited?

ADOLESCENT: I don't know. I just feel excited.

THERAPIST: I know these are odd questions, so I appreciate your willingness to answer them. I've got another one. You said that you feel excited as you think about smoking. See if you can answer this, "I feel excited as I think about smoking because . . ."

ADOLESCENT: I like how it makes me feel.

THERAPIST: Good! And it makes you feel . . . ?

ADOLESCENT: Relaxed, I guess.

THERAPIST: Relaxed. Boy, that could be an emotion or a physical feeling. I think I'll put it in both categories. Excellent job!

It is not unusual for adolescents to have difficulty identifying internal triggers. The therapist probed for details and backed off appropriately, so as not to unnecessarily annoy the adolescent.

SUBSTANCE USE BEHAVIOR

THERAPIST: OK. Let's just spend a few more minutes going over that typical time when you use in the evening, so that I can get a few details about how much you're using.

ADOLESCENT: What do you want to know?

THERAPIST: How much do you usually use?

ADOLESCENT: A day? No more than five.

THERAPIST: Five blunts?

ADOLESCENT: Yeah.

THERAPIST: But since you're doing this with a friend, are you sharing the five blunts with this friend?

ADOLESCENT: Usually.

THERAPIST: And are the five blunts all at night, or are some of them in the daytime, too?

ADOLESCENT: Night.

THERAPIST: And over what period of time do you use? I know you said you started around 7:00.

ADOLESCENT: Several hours.

THERAPIST: So what would you say several hours is? How many hours about?

ADOLESCENT: Six.

THERAPIST: Six hours? OK. So that would be from about 7:00 to 2:00 in the morning. Does that sound about right?

ADOLESCENT: No. Maybe four hours.

THERAPIST: OK. I'm glad you're telling me all this. It's helpful to go through this process to sort out your pattern of use.

It is worthwhile for therapists to question some of the information being offered by the adolescent if it does not seem feasible. Of course, this should be done in a nonaccusatory manner.

SHORT-TERM POSITIVE CONSEQUENCES

THERAPIST: Now, I want to talk about some of the positive consequences of getting high. I know that you're being really open with me and I appreciate that. I think it's great that you're willing to tell me exactly how you use, who you use with, how much, and so on. Now it's important for us to look at all the things you like about smoking marijuana. Can you tell me, for example, what you like about using with your friend?

ADOLESCENT: Conversation.

THERAPIST: Conversation?

ADOLESCENT: And jokes.

THERAPIST: Jokes, OK. And what do you like about using at your friend's house?

ADOLESCENT: The same thing.

THERAPIST: Which is?

ADOLESCENT: Conversation and jokes.

THERAPIST: How about specific to the location? Why your friend's house? What do you like about using at that place?

ADOLESCENT: Nobody bothers you there.

THERAPIST: So you can do what you want?

ADOLESCENT: Yup.

THERAPIST: OK. And what do you like about using at nighttime?

ADOLESCENT: So I can sleep.

THERAPIST: So you can go to sleep. OK. And what are some of the pleasant thoughts you have while using?

ADOLESCENT: I don't know what you mean. My thoughts?

THERAPIST: Yes. Picture back to a time when you've been smoking. What are you thinking about? I know there have to be some pleasant thoughts, or you wouldn't keep doing it—right?

ADOLESCENT: I guess.

THERAPIST: But you can't recall? Again, let's go back to an evening at your friend's house when you're using. You're smoking some marijuana with a friend. What would you guess you're thinking about?

ADOLESCENT: I don't know. We're laughing, so I guess I'm thinking that it's fun to be high.

THERAPIST: Good. And how about some pleasant emotions you might have while you're using?

ADOLESCENT: Just excited.

THERAPIST: OK. Any pleasant physical sensations? You said earlier that you look forward to getting relaxed when you smoke. What does this feel like?

ADOLESCENT: I don't know. I never think about it. I just feel all relaxed. Not tense.

THERAPIST: That's a good one. Not tense. So these are a list of the things you like about smoking pot. Anything else you want to add?

ADOLESCENT: No.

THERAPIST: Well, thanks for sharing all of that with me.

The therapist obtained a reasonable list of positive consequences. This important information eventually will be revisited, since one major purpose of the exercise is to identify the factors that are maintaining the substance use so that they can be replaced with healthy alternatives. The therapist begins with the positive consequences for use because there are immediate reinforcers for substance use that are maintaining the adolescent's behavior. It helps build rapport to acknowledge that there are reasons that an individual wants to use substances and helps identify possible reinforcers that can be sought through other ways than substance use. Then, the therapist finishes the functional analysis with a discussion of the long-term negative consequences. Adolescents in treatment typically have had negative consequences from their use (that is why they are in treatment), and ending the exercise this way helps the adolescent see the connection between use and negative consequences. It is preferable that the adolescent leaves the treatment sessions thinking about the negative rather than the positive consequences of his use.

LONG-TERM NEGATIVE CONSEQUENCES

THERAPIST: Now we move on to the last column of the functional analysis chart. What do you think are some of the negative results of using? We just went over some of the positive things, the things you like about smoking pot. Do you think there are some bad consequences about using?

ADOLESCENT: Probably.

THERAPIST: Do you want to try to tell me more about that, or should I go ahead and ask you about a bunch of different areas that might have been affected by your use?

ADOLESCENT: Ask away!

THERAPIST: Fair enough. Like, for example, does getting high have a negative impact on your relationship with your mom?

ADOLESCENT: She don't like it.

THERAPIST: So your mom doesn't like it. How has that impacted your relationship with her?

ADOLESCENT: She thinks I'm not trustworthy.

THERAPIST: So it sounds like your mom is having some difficulties trusting you as a result of your getting high.

ADOLESCENT: Yeah.

THERAPIST: And how does it affect some of your friendships? Any problems there?

ADOLESCENT: If they don't like my smoking, then they don't need to be my friend.

THERAPIST: How about any negative physical affects from using? Like getting tired, or getting dry mouth, or forgetting things? Anything like that?

ADOLESCENT: No, not really. It makes me sleepy, but that's a good thing.

THERAPIST: Right. So it doesn't make you tired the next day at a time when you don't want to be tired?

Adolescent: Nope.

Therapist: And I know you mentioned several positive things that you feel when you use. Are there any *unpleasant* feelings afterwards? Like some people say they don't like how it feels to come down off the high.

Adolescent: I don't think so.

Therapist: OK. You can see on the chart that the next area is called "legal situations." Would you say that you've had some negative legal things happen that are related to your smoking?

Adolescent: A friend of mine was arrested for drug possession, but nothing's happened to me.

Therapist: Are you worried that something could happen to you?

Adolescent: I wouldn't say that I'm worried, but I think about it.

Therapist: I'll put that down then. What about school?

Adolescent: I've had some problems in school, but I don't think it's because of my smoking.

Therapist: What kind of problems?

Adolescent: I have to go to detention a lot because I'm late in the morning.

Therapist: That's an interesting one. Well, you're right, it's not directly related to your pot smoking, but I wonder if it's indirectly related?

Adolescent: What do you mean?

Therapist: Do you have more trouble getting up in the morning and getting to school on time if you've stayed up late smoking the night before?

Adolescent: Maybe. Probably.

Therapist: That's what I'm thinking. Is it OK for me to put that on the chart then? We could take it off later if we find out it's not true.

Adolescent: I don't care. Sure.

Therapist: About how much money do you think you spend on marijuana?

Adolescent: About $15.

Therapist: $15 a day?

Adolescent: Yeah.

Therapist: So how much do you spend each week then on marijuana?

Adolescent: $105.

Therapist: Yes, $105. You're quick. Quicker than me. So at $105 a week, how much do you spend each month on marijuana? I have to write this one down because I'm not that good. Can you do it in your head? $105 times four?

Adolescent: 105 times four is 420.

THERAPIST: Wow, you're really good at math, aren't you? Do you like math at school? That's great. That's a chunk of money, isn't it? Let's figure out a year. To make it easier, let's just figure out 10 months. What would that be? $4200, right? If we add in another two months . . .

ADOLESCENT: It's over $5000.

THERAPIST: So, what do you think you might spend that money on instead of marijuana?

ADOLESCENT: Clothes.

THERAPIST: Clothes. Yeah, what else?

ADOLESCENT: Shoes.

THERAPIST: Shoes. So you'd have a lot of use for that money, huh?

ADOLESCENT: Yeah.

THERAPIST: Yeah, you would. What else do you like?

ADOLESCENT: That's really it.

THERAPIST: Well, there's a lot of things you could use that money on, so if you stopped smoking, would you have more money?

ADOLESCENT: Yeah.

THERAPIST: That's a financial kind of thing that you're facing smoking on a daily basis. It's got a big cost associated with it. Boy, just imagine all the money you'd have for clothes . . . and shoes.

ADOLESCENT: Yes.

THERAPIST: So not smoking weed actually could save you some money, is that right?

ADOLESCENT: Yeah.

THERAPIST: I wonder what you could buy with $420 a month?

ADOLESCENT: A lot of stuff.

THERAPIST: Yeah. Like what?

ADOLESCENT: Probably two pairs of shoes and two outfits.

THERAPIST: Wow. Just imagine every month you could get that. So, if you didn't smoke, then you wouldn't have to buy it and you'd save all that money to buy two pairs of shoes and two outfits every month. Do you like to go shopping?

ADOLESCENT: Yeah.

THERAPIST: Who do you go with?

ADOLESCENT: Nobody usually. Or maybe a friend.

THERAPIST: How about we finish up this analysis of your use, and then we take a look at your saving some of the pot money?

ADOLESCENT: OK.

In discussing the negative consequences, the therapist recognized that the most powerful motivator for the adolescent was the money he would have available to him if he stopped smoking. The therapist will incorporate this finding into the treatment plan and homework.

Treatment Implications and Homework

Therapist: I'd like to review what we found here today and then show you how we might use this information. Is that all right with you?

Adolescent: Yes.

Therapist: Good. And thanks again for doing all of this. It looks like your biggest external trigger is going over to your friend's house where you smoke. As far as internal triggers, looks like you think about getting high when you're in the mood to relax. But you also said that you look forward to joking around and having fun. As far as the things you really like about smoking, it's the good conversation you have with your friend when you're high, and the fact that you can get to sleep better after smoking. Is this right so far?

Adolescent: Sounds right to me.

Therapist: The not-so-good parts of smoking include not having your mom trust you, thinking about getting in legal trouble like your friend did, and maybe being late for school. We haven't decided for sure about that one. But the biggest drawback seems to be all the money you spend on marijuana that you could be spending on clothes and shoes instead.

Adolescent: That's right.

Therapist: Now I know that you're working hard to stop smoking. I wonder if it might be an incentive to start keeping track of all the money you'd be saving if you didn't smoke? Are you interested in saving some money?

Adolescent: Yeah.

Therapist: And should we use some of our time to work on that together here?

Adolescent: Yeah, OK. I've got a bank account.

Therapist: Oh yeah? Great! Should we come up with a plan for putting some money into that account?

Adolescent: Sure.

Therapist: What if you were to jot down every day the amount of money you spend buying marijuana? I know that you said you spent about $15 a day, but it might motivate you to skip smoking a day here and there if you wrote it down right as it happened. What do you think?

Adolescent: I could do that.

THERAPIST: Can you think of anything else that would help motivate you to put that money aside for clothes and shoes?

ADOLESCENT: I could go to the mall and see what I could buy for $105 this week.

THERAPIST: Excellent idea! You're good at this. OK, so are you going to need a little note pad to write it down on?

ADOLESCENT: No, I can put it on my phone.

THERAPIST: Oh, smart. You have a little thing on your phone. So, when do you think you'll start?

ADOLESCENT: Tomorrow.

THERAPIST: That's what I like to hear. Now whenever we come up with a plan for the week, it's always a good idea to try to figure out obstacles, things that might get in the way of carrying out the plan. What could get in the way of you keeping track of the money you're spending on marijuana, and getting to the mall to see what $105 can buy?

ADOLESCENT: I might forget. But I can set an alarm on my phone to remind me.

THERAPIST: Not bad. It's best to keep track of the money right as you're spending it, but this will work as a backup. What else might get in the way?

ADOLESCENT: I might not have a ride to the mall.

THERAPIST: Good point. What will you do then?

ADOLESCENT: I'll go online to see what I could buy for the money.

THERAPIST: Impressive! Great. Sounds like you're all set. Hey—thanks so much for doing this with me. Maybe next week we can decide what to do with some of the other information you gave me. For example, we can try to figure out other ways for you to relax and joke, if you'd like. And we can definitely look into other ways to help you sleep at night. Of course, we'll only do these things if you're up for it. All right?

ADOLESCENT: Yes.

THERAPIST: Great. So, do you have any other questions before we close today?

ADOLESCENT: No.

THERAPIST: Well, thanks for coming in and working so hard today. We'll start off our next session by reviewing how your assignment went.

The therapist determined that the best area for an assignment was the area in which the adolescent appeared the most motivated: saving money. The therapist worked together with the adolescent to generate a reasonable, specific assignment, then spent time identifying and addressing potential obstacles.

Many adolescents use one drug (e.g., marijuana) with other substances (e.g., alcohol). It would be appropriate during one Functional Analysis, if it is typical, to include how the client is using substances together. For example, the adolescent could say, "I smoke some marijuana and drink some beers." The therapist could find out about the quantity of both substances that are used. It is not necessary to do a functional analysis for every drug used, unless there are different triggers and consequences for these drugs and the adolescent does not seem to be able to generalize information gained from the first functional analysis. If additional functional analyses seem necessary, it is preferable to space them out in order to maintain engagement.

FUNCTIONAL ANALYSIS OF PROSOCIAL BEHAVIOR

The use of some type of functional analysis of substance use may be fairly common in treatment programs that are evidence-informed; however, the use of a functional analysis to examine prosocial behavior is rather unique (see Figure 3.2). This prosocial functional analysis might be used in an early session to reinforce the need to increase positive behaviors and to plan approaches for doing so. This procedure helps clarify antecedents and consequences of engaging in healthy behaviors. The therapist also can learn more about a particular adolescent's reinforcers and what might serve as barriers to increasing an activity that an adolescent enjoys. One of the therapist's tasks is to help an adolescent identify and problem solve how best to overcome barriers that might get in the way of spending more time in a positive activity. The steps of a Functional Analysis of Prosocial Behavior are exactly the same as for the Functional Analysis of Substance Use. The form used is also similar, except the last two columns are reversed, with the FA of Prosocial Behavior ending with the positive consequences of engaging in the behavior, so that adolescents leave the exercise with thoughts about how increasing prosocial behaviors can increase the experience of positive consequences. In the following example, the adolescent is in a residential treatment program. Like most adolescents in inpatient treatment, he has used multiple substances and has had serious legal issues. Recall that there is no particular session or order in which a therapist is required to introduce procedures; however, it would make sense to complete the FA of Prosocial Behavior procedure during one of the first four sessions since an emphasis in A-CRA is on increasing participation in prosocial behaviors.

External Triggers	Internal Triggers	Behavior	Short-Term – Consequences Not So Good Things	Long-Term + Consequences Good things (rewards)
1. **Who** are you usually with when you (*garden*)?	1. What are you usually *thinking* about right before you (*garden*)?	1. *What* is the nonusing activity?	1. **What do you dislike about** (*gardening*) with (*who*)?	1. **What are the positive results of** (*gardening*) **in each of these areas:** **a) Family:**
		Gardening	Nothing	
Fruit lady, another staff, 5–6 clients	Eating stuff, going outside, fresh air, see what's going on		2. **What do you dislike about** (*gardening*) (*where*)? Wish it were somewhere else; other clients are a bother sometimes	Mom likes flowers; fruits/vegetables will save $$ **b) Friends:**
				Can talk more with friends when gardening
		2. *How often do you engage in it?*	3. **What do you dislike about** (*gardening*) (*when*)?	**c) Physical:**
2. *Where* do you usually (*garden*)?	2. **What are you usually *feeling* physically right before you** (*garden*)?		Gets hot sometimes	It's exercise
		Every Sunday afternoon		**d) Emotional:**
Big garden out behind facility	Antsy		4. **What are the unpleasant *thoughts* you have while** (*gardening*)? I don't like to pull weeds; wish it could last longer	Happy, relaxed, less angry & anxious **e) Legal:**
		3. *How long does it usually last?*		Not getting in trouble

(continued)

135

External Triggers	Internal Triggers	Behavior	Short-Term – Consequences Not So Good Things	Long-Term + Consequences Good things (rewards)
3. When do you usually (garden)?	**3. What are you usually feeling emotionally right before you (garden)?**	1–2 hours	**5. What are the unpleasant physical feelings you have while (gardening)?**	**f) School:**
				Preparing for botany class
Sunday afternoon	Happy, "good"		Back hurts	**g) Job:**
				Getting ready for job at Bargain-Mart Garden Center
			6. What are the unpleasant emotions you have while (gardening)?	**h) Financial:**
			Unhappy when it's time to stop and have to go back inside	Save $$ on food
	Pro-Social		Long-Term + Consequences Good things (rewards)	

Figure 3.2 Functional Analysis for Pro-Social Behavior (Gardening)

From Clinical Guide to Alcohol Treatment: The Community Reinforcement Approach (pp. 38–39), by R.J. Meyers & J.E. Smith (1995), New York: Guilford Press. Adapted with permission.

A CASE EXAMPLE: FUNCTIONAL ANALYSIS
OF PROSOCIAL BEHAVIOR

RATIONALE AND OVERVIEW OF PLEASANT BEHAVIOR

THERAPIST: Remember last session we did something called a Functional Analysis of Substance Using Behavior? We looked at your use of weed, right?

ADOLESCENT: Yeah.

THERAPIST: Today, we're going to do something called a Functional Analysis of Prosocial Behavior. And a prosocial behavior is a non-using behavior that's fun. When we looked at your substance use, the idea was to help you stop using. We broke it down and looked at your different triggers for substance use. Today, we're going to look at the things you like to do that *don't* involve drugs or alcohol and kind of break that down and see what the effects are of that.

ADOLESCENT: OK.

THERAPIST: Sound good? So, I'll start off by asking you to tell me about a couple of things that you like to do that don't involve drugs or alcohol. Just some different hobbies.

ADOLESCENT: Riding my bike, swimming, gardening. Did you see the big garden we have over there?

THERAPIST: Oh, yeah. You work on the weekends, right?

ADOLESCENT: The staff says they're going to give me the green thumb award.

THERAPIST: Oh, what's that?

ADOLESCENT: It's a prize. I think it's just a piece of paper with the name of the prize on it. And my name. I'll hang it up on my wall.

THERAPIST: That's great. You must be really good at gardening.

ADOLESCENT: My mom got me started on it. We mostly had indoor plants, though. I like the big garden we have here.

THERAPIST: It *is* a nice one. Now, do you remember a few weeks back we were talking about reinforcers, the things that reinforce our positive behaviors and keep us away from drugs and alcohol?

ADOLESCENT: I kind of remember.

THERAPIST: It's the things that we value that keep us on that good path of not using alcohol and drugs. For example, I know that you and your mom talk about your church community all the time.

ADOLESCENT: Yeah. They're nice people. I like going to church with my mom now when I have a weekend pass. We hang out after the service for coffeecake.

THERAPIST: And so we'd say that those nice people, and maybe the coffeecake, are reinforcers, because they make you want to keep going to church. And anything positive like going to church is real important, because you'll be less likely to use drugs when you leave here if you keep doing fun activities like that. So out of these four things you just mentioned, riding your bike, swimming, gardening, and going to church, what is the one thing you'd like to break down and look at so that we can figure out a way for you to do more of it?

ADOLESCENT: Gardening.

THERAPIST: Gardening? OK. And how many days each week are you gardening right now?

ADOLESCENT: Just on Sundays.

THERAPIST: And since the purpose of this exercise today is to help you figure out a way to do the fun activity more, I feel like I need to ask if it's possible for you to be allowed to garden more than just the one time each week.

ADOLESCENT: Yeah. They already asked me if I wanted to. I just haven't gotten around to it yet. But I've been thinking about it.

THERAPIST: Oh, good. That's perfect then. So take one day, one Sunday of gardening, and tell me more about it. Like paint me a picture.

ADOLESCENT: We go out there and we pull the weeds, we plant stuff every once in a while, we water, we pick the fruit and vegetables, and sometimes we play around and throw stuff at each other. That's really fun. And the staff doesn't even get mad. Sometimes we pick flowers.

THERAPIST: Good. Anything else you can tell me about it? Like when or who you're with?

ADOLESCENT: We're with one staff member and the Fruit Lady and about five other clients. I volunteer to show the new kids the ropes, and the rest of the people are inside watching movies when we're out there. I don't really care, though. I'd rather be out there in the fresh air and stuff. The Fruit Lady tells us a bunch of stuff about plants and how to take care of them. Sometimes we feed the plants with garden pellet things.

THERAPIST: Oh, are they sort of like vitamins or something?

ADOLESCENT: Yeah, they're vitamins. I was going to tell the Fruit Lady we should start growing some pumpkins.

THERAPIST: Oh, you like pumpkins, huh?

ADOLESCENT: Yeah. Well, they remind me of Halloween.

THERAPIST: Have you ever eaten fresh pumpkin? Have you ever had a homemade pumpkin pie? Yum!

ADOLESCENT: My auntie made us one once. It was really good.

THERAPIST: That's great. Thank you for telling me about that. That's a lot of good info.

It was important for the therapist to identify a healthy activity that the adolescent really enjoyed and one that could realistically be increased. Also, given the format of the functional analysis, it only is appropriate if the activity is ongoing.

TRIGGERS: EXTERNAL AND INTERNAL

THERAPIST: So, we're just going to go through this and the different columns are the same as the functional analysis from last week—except that the last two columns are switched. But don't worry about that for now. I'll explain it when we get to it. So, the external triggers are the things that are going on around us. They are external to us: who we're with, where we are, and when we are doing something. The prosocial or the nonusing behavior is the gardening. Now you already said who you're usually with; you said one staff member. I'm just going to jot down little notes on this chart (See Functional Analysis for Prosocial Behavior), if that's OK. The Fruit Lady, is that what she's called?

ADOLESCENT: Yeah. That's what everybody calls her. Nobody knows her name. I think it's Melanie, or something.

THERAPIST: Yeah? That's kind of like a nickname? Fruit Lady?

ADOLESCENT: I guess. I don't know why we don't call her the Vegetable Lady. Or the Fruit and Vegetable and Flower Lady.

THERAPIST: That's funny. Too much of a mouthful, I guess. And other clients are there, too, right? A pretty sizable group?

ADOLESCENT: Yeah, about five or six. But there's usually another staff person nearby, too.

THERAPIST: Oh, good. Thanks for clearing that up. And as far as where you usually do this, I would guess that it's the big garden you showed me out back?

ADOLESCENT: Yup. Right over there.

THERAPIST: And you said that you do this on Sundays?

ADOLESCENT: Sundays. Sunday afternoon.

THERAPIST: Great. Now the internal triggers are the things that are going on inside of us. Like the things that we're thinking about or feeling, and what our body is experiencing when we're getting ready to do this activity. So what are you usually thinking about right before you start gardening?

Adolescent: Nothing really. Just thinking about gardening.

Therapist: Yeah?

Adolescent: Thinking about going outside and eating stuff that's out there.

Therapist: Oh, so you get to eat the stuff right then?

Adolescent: Yeah. Fresh strawberries and we got a plum tree. The plums aren't good yet. I wish. I love plums. The peas, carrots; I eat all that stuff.

Therapist: So, you look forward to being outside and eating the fruit. All right. And you said there are vegetables, too?

Adolescent: Peas and carrots mostly. We've got a few tomato plants, too. They said we don't need a lot, because each plant will give us lots of tomatoes. I'm not sure about that though.

Therapist: So, you'll believe it when you see it, right?

Adolescent: Sort of. But the Fruit Lady knows a lot about plants, so maybe she's right.

Therapist: Ok. Now you said that you're thinking about being outside. What else comes to mind as you think about just being outside?

Adolescent: Fresh air. I like being out in the fresh air. I like to see what's going on outside, too.

Therapist: I'm going to add them to our list, too, then. Can you describe what you're feeling physically, what's going on inside your body, as you think about going outside to garden?

Adolescent: I feel happy. Good.

Therapist: And when you say "good," do you mean anything specific? Like do you feel it in a specific part of your body, maybe?

Adolescent: Not really. My brain, I guess. The staff says I get antsy before I go outside. Maybe I do.

Therapist: Antsy. Like fidgety? Do you have trouble sitting still in anticipation of going outside?

Adolescent: Something like that.

Therapist: Thanks. That's very descriptive. And you just answered the next question. The next question is how do you feel emotionally? And you said happy and good. Any other emotions? Any other emotions or feelings that you have going on?

Adolescent: Not really.

The therapist gathered information about factors that normally set the stage for the pleasant activity. These triggers can be referred to at a later point when the adolescent is learning to make a decision to choose a prosocial activity over drugs.

THE PROSOCIAL BEHAVIOR

THERAPIST: The middle column is the behavior. That's where I list the actual doing of the activity. I think we've already answered most of these. Let's see—it's gardening, and it's once a week, on Sunday afternoon. Did you already tell me how long you stay outside and garden?

ADOLESCENT: At least an hour. Sometimes two, though.

THERAPIST: That was an easy column. We're done with it.

The therapist already had obtained much of the necessary information about the prosocial behavior. Many therapists actually start the Functional Analysis of Prosocial Behavior by completing the middle column (the behavior) first, as a means of determining whether the selected behavior is an appropriate one for the exercise.

SHORT-TERM NEGATIVE CONSEQUENCES

THERAPIST: The next column asks about short-term negative consequences. Last week when we were talking about your using behavior, we wrote down on the chart the immediate effect of the using that made you want to use more. Remember? So it's the same thing this week, but it's the immediate effect of gardening instead. But this time I want to ask you first about the immediate effects that you *don't* like about gardening. So, is there anything you dislike about gardening? Maybe with the Fruit Lady, the staff, the other clients?

ADOLESCENT: Pulling the weeds.

THERAPIST: That's not the fun part, huh?

ADOLESCENT: It makes my back kind of hurt. It's pretty fun, though. I don't really mind the hard labor.

THERAPIST: Now, what do you dislike about where the garden is?

ADOLESCENT: I wish it were out of here. Away from here, that'd be cool.

THERAPIST: So, like if you had a garden at home rather than here at the facility?

ADOLESCENT: Yeah. That'd be nice.

THERAPIST: Maybe that's something we can talk about as far as a long-term goal. What do you dislike about the people you garden with?

ADOLESCENT: Nothing. I don't like it when the stupid people come out here and bother us when we're trying to work.

THERAPIST: And who are the stupid people. The clients?

ADOLESCENT: Yeah, some clients are stupid. They don't like to do no work.

THERAPIST: I'll be sure to add that. Is there anything about gardening on Sunday afternoons that you don't like?

ADOLESCENT: Sometimes it gets a little hot. I don't mind that much, though.

THERAPIST: And what are some unpleasant thoughts you have while you're gardening?

ADOLESCENT: I don't have any unpleasant thoughts while I'm gardening.

THERAPIST: How about right as you're finishing?

ADOLESCENT: I'm just thinking I wish it could last longer.

THERAPIST: OK. How about unpleasant physical feelings?

ADOLESCENT: My back pain.

THERAPIST: And that's been a constant thing. It seems that isn't just from the weed pulling. I remember you mentioned having back pain before.

ADOLESCENT: Yeah, it's been like this for a long time. I don't think these crummy beds here help either.

THERAPIST: Are you and your mom going to see a specialist about your back?

ADOLESCENT: Eventually. I think we have an appointment in a month.

THERAPIST: It's hard to wait for these appointments with specialists, isn't it?

ADOLESCENT: You better believe it!

THERAPIST: How about unpleasant emotional feelings either during or right after gardening?

ADOLESCENT: Like the first time, I went off kind of depressed because it was the first week I was here. I came in here on a Friday and went out there on Sunday. I was like homesick and all that.

THERAPIST: How about every Sunday after that?

ADOLESCENT: Not really.

THERAPIST: Let me make sure I have this straight. The first time you worked in the garden you were homesick and depressed, but since that first time you haven't had any unpleasant emotions. Is that right?

ADOLESCENT: Pretty much. Well, I don't feel happy when they tell us we have to go back inside.

THERAPIST: Thanks. I'll add that.

The therapist attempted to discern whether there were any noteworthy unpleasant aspects to the gardening that might prevent the adolescent from choosing to do it more often. Since the adolescent had reported at the outset that the staff already had offered more opportunities to garden, it was important to gather information as to the possible roadblocks so they could be addressed eventually.

LONG-TERM POSITIVE CONSEQUENCES

THERAPIST: The last column asks about the long-term positive consequences. These are the good things about gardening. I'm thinking mostly about the good things that happen over time. And remember when we were doing the using behavior we talked about how your relationships have changed with family, how your friendships have changed, and the legal situations with probation, school, all those things. But here we're talking about a healthy activity, gardening, and so we're going to look at the positive things that come from it in these important areas I just mentioned. What do you think are some of the positive consequences, the good things that happen when you garden? How about in terms of your family?

ADOLESCENT: Positive results? I don't really know. I never garden with them anymore.

THERAPIST: That's OK. You don't have to be gardening with your family for there to be a payoff for your relationship with them. How about reaping the rewards of the gardening? The fruits and the vegetables. How do you think that would affect your family?

ADOLESCENT: In a good way. My mom likes the flowers I bring her.

THERAPIST: Wow. So they have fruits, vegetables, and flowers out there? Wow.

ADOLESCENT: Hollyhocks, daisies, and poppies.

THERAPIST: Now, did you know all those words, all the names of the flowers before this?

ADOLESCENT: Some of them. But now I know a lot more.

THERAPIST: I'm so impressed. I don't know that many names of flowers. That'd be neat to learn all that different stuff. It's beautiful from here just looking in the distance and seeing the pretty flowers. Do you know what those tall ones are?

ADOLESCENT: Hollyhocks.

THERAPIST: Really? Those are beautiful.

ADOLESCENT: I've known that since I was little.

THERAPIST: Really?

ADOLESCENT: They have red ones, pink ones, burgundy ones, white ones, yellow ones, orange ones. All kinds of different colors. I've never seen a blue hollyhock before. That would be awesome.

THERAPIST: Oh, wow, you should ask the Fruit Lady if they come in blue. And how about if you were to start growing fruits and vegetables for your family?

ADOLESCENT: My mom would be happy because it would save her some money.

THERAPIST: I'll add that to our chart then. Can you think of any positive consequences with friends that would come from gardening?

ADOLESCENT: From gardening? Not really. They aren't into gardening.

THERAPIST: What if you talked one of your friends into trying it with you? It would give you something healthy to do together.

ADOLESCENT: My friends would probably end up killing the plants. They aren't very patient.

THERAPIST: Well, it's probably true that some of your friends wouldn't like gardening, or wouldn't be good at it. But look at the folks your age here who like it. I know it's a small group when you consider how many teenagers are here, but that would be like having one friend of yours like gardening out of all your friends. It could happen.

ADOLESCENT: Maybe. I guess I could ask somebody when I get out.

THERAPIST: I know it's kind of hard to imagine something new if you've never done it with a friend. But I was thinking that sometimes it's easier to talk to a friend if you're doing an activity together. Lots of times if you're sitting in front of the TV together, you're just watching TV, and you're not really talking. But maybe being outside together you'd be able to talk.

ADOLESCENT: I guess we do some of that here.

THERAPIST: Should I add that to our chart or not? I'd be saying that one positive consequence of gardening is that it allows you to talk more with your friends.

ADOLESCENT: You can put it down. I just never thought of it that way. I *do* talk to the other clients out in the garden about all sorts of things.

THERAPIST: OK. I'll add it then. How about physical feelings; stuff in your body? Has gardening had a positive effect on that?

ADOLESCENT: I don't think so. It makes my back hurt. I gotta crouch down real low.

THERAPIST: You're right. That's definitely not a positive thing then. What do you think about your body getting exercise? Do you think gardening involves doing good things to your body?

ADOLESCENT: Yeah. It makes you sweat.

THERAPIST: That's a good one. Yeah, it takes a lot of hard work, like you were saying before about hard labor. But you said you don't mind the hard labor, so the sweat is a good thing, right?

ADOLESCENT: I think it must be a pretty good workout for my body.

THERAPIST: How about positive emotional feelings from gardening?

ADOLESCENT: I feel happy. I always want to learn more.

THERAPIST: Yeah. And before you were saying that it helps you relax, too. Let's see. I know that in our past sessions we talked about anxiousness and anger a lot. Do you think it has an effect on those two emotions that you have?

ADOLESCENT: Anger? I can't really get angry over there. I don't really get angry at all.

THERAPIST: Yeah? OK, so you feel less anger. Or you don't really feel the anger that sometimes you would feel. Being out in the garden is relaxing, so that's good for your anxiousness. How about legal situations? Is there any consequence to gardening?

ADOLESCENT: Not really. But I'm not getting into trouble if I'm in the garden.

THERAPIST: True. How about school situations? Do you think there's a positive consequence of gardening that involves school?

ADOLESCENT: Not really. I don't know any schools that have a garden class. Wait, there's botany, isn't there?

THERAPIST: Yeah.

ADOLESCENT: That's flowers. I know of one high school that has a real good botany class. They have watermelons, strawberries, all kinds of stuff over there.

THERAPIST: Wow.

ADOLESCENT: They have a greenhouse. It's huge. It must be like two of these things long and wide. Awesome. I remember that from like eight years ago.

THERAPIST: I know that you and your mom were going to look into schools again when you get out of here. If you're really interested in botany, it would be worth looking into that school. You know? How about job situations? How do you think that gardening would help you with a job situation?

ADOLESCENT: I doubt it would. Well, maybe. Like at the garden section at Bargain-Mart. I could probably get a job there.

THERAPIST: Hey.

ADOLESCENT: I never thought about that.

THERAPIST: I hadn't either. That's great. Those places like workers with a certain expertise. You have to know your stuff, and it sounds like from a young age you and your mom have been learning about this stuff, and now you've got experience from here. That's great. How about financial situations? How could gardening help with that?

ADOLESCENT: Like we said before, my mom wouldn't have to spend so much money on food if I grew it. I could grow potatoes and carrots, peas and lettuce, tomatoes. I wouldn't have to buy any of that.

THERAPIST: You are so creative. I would not have thought about saving money to grow your own food.

ADOLESCENT: You can pick up seeds for 97 cents a packet and have a bundle of food.

THERAPIST: Awesome.

The therapist appropriately spent a fair amount of time helping the adolescent identify a long list of positive consequences associated with gardening. The main objective is to motivate the adolescent to make the decision to choose gardening over drug use.

TREATMENT IMPLICATIONS AND HOMEWORK

THERAPIST: Look at all these different things here. Wow. What do you make of all this? Did you learn anything about yourself?

ADOLESCENT: I like how we talked about gardening making me feel less angry. I hadn't thought about that before.

THERAPIST: That's a good one, isn't it? It will come in real handy. Anything else?

ADOLESCENT: I like how we figured out that maybe all this gardening stuff I'm learning can help me get a job at Bargain-Mart's garden center.

THERAPIST: I bet you'll be way more qualified than most people who apply for jobs there. Can you tell me some of the other good things that can come from the gardening? Here. Look at the chart that I filled in.

ADOLESCENT: Oh, yeah. The physical stuff. I'm sweating and getting some good exercise. Oh right—school. I can maybe take a botany class at school. Maybe I could even do something online if I can't go to a school with an actual botany class.

THERAPIST: Good for you! You're full of creative ideas today! How about financial?

ADOLESCENT: I'll save my mom money if I grow our own fruits and vegetables. She'll like that. Heck, she'll just be happy if I'm staying out of trouble, even if nothing grows!

THERAPIST: I bet you're right. So if anything grows and you save her money, that's icing on the cake. Real impressive. All this stuff came from your brain. I especially like the insight about less anger. OK. But one of the things we have to think about is what's getting in the way of you gardening more if it's so great—right?

And they've even offered you the chance to do it more than just Sundays. We came up with a few things that are sort of the negative side to gardening. We have to figure out how to address these obstacles so that you feel like doing it more. Does that make sense?

ADOLESCENT: Yup. Sometimes I'm just lazy and don't want to get up off my butt.

THERAPIST: Would it help if you had a regular time arranged to garden, like you do on Sundays?

ADOLESCENT: Probably. I can ask them to set me up. They will.

THERAPIST: Shall we make that part of your assignment then for the week? Can you describe what you'll do?

ADOLESCENT: I'll go to Harry. He's the one who asked me a few weeks ago if I wanted to work in the garden an extra day each week. I'll tell him I'm ready for it.

THERAPIST: Excellent. Before we finish up today, we'll practice that conversation just so that it goes smoothly. OK. When is a good time to talk to him? Let's get that nailed down.

ADOLESCENT: I will see him at dinner tonight. I'll ask him if I can talk to him when we're done.

THERAPIST: Good. Let's talk about obstacles again for a minute, but this time in terms of doing this assignment. What might get in the way of you talking to Harry after dinner tonight?

ADOLESCENT: If somebody is acting up at dinner, he won't be able to talk. But I'll see him after lunch tomorrow, too.

THERAPIST: Good. So you have a backup plan. Any other obstacles?

ADOLESCENT: Not that I can think of.

THERAPIST: OK. Let's say Harry gives you the extra day. So we can add that part of your assignment, too, to work in the garden two days this week instead of one. How does that sound?

ADOLESCENT: Good. I want to.

THERAPIST: Now, let's pretend that Harry says you can't start the extra day this week for some reason. Is there some other assignment you want to do in that case? Remember, we're still working toward getting you to garden more.

ADOLESCENT: They give us time on the Internet here. I could look to see if Bargain-Mart has any openings in the garden center.

THERAPIST: Sounds good. Of course, you're going to be here a while yet . . .

ADOLESCENT: I know. But I can at least get an idea of what the requirements are for jobs like that. I could check out other plant places, too.

THERAPIST: Now you're talking! Yes, check out nurseries and garden centers. Let me think a minute. Obstacles. OK. What if Harry says you *can* start the extra day this week, but then you run up against one of the negative things about gardening. Like maybe you start thinking, "I don't feel like it. I just want to sit and watch TV." Or, maybe you think about your back hurting, or how you're only going to be pulling lots of weeds. How can you talk yourself into doing it anyway?

ADOLESCENT: If I get scheduled for the day, I'll do it. Or I could talk a friend into doing it with me. Then I'll have somebody to talk to.

THERAPIST: You're a pro at this! Hey, you know what's interesting? I remember when we did your Functional Analysis for Substance Use last week, you said that when you looked forward to using pot you were happy and relaxed. Do those feelings sound familiar?

ADOLESCENT: Didn't I say something like that for gardening?

THERAPIST: You sure did. Kinda cool. But the best part is that gardening has lots of other good things about it, too, and you don't get into trouble for it! Right?

ADOLESCENT: Right.

THERAPIST: I'll check on how your assignment went when I see you next week. And then we can try to come up with more activities that make you feel good, relaxed, happy, and not angry. And we'll figure out a way for you to do them more. Because we want to figure out the triggers for drug use and then replace them with positive stuff. Does that sound good?

ADOLESCENT: Yeah.

THERAPIST: That's great. Hey—thank you. I appreciate your hard work here. You're a sharp kid. You give me such good information that you make my job really easy.

ADOLESCENT: Thanks.

THERAPIST: Oh, wait! We forgot to practice the conversation you're going to have with Harry. Let's do it really quick.

Since the point of the Functional Analysis for Prosocial Behavior is to increase an ongoing pleasant activity, it was important for the therapist to make sure the assignment for the week was a step toward that goal. As with all assignments, it needed to follow the basic requirements of being brief, positive, specific, reasonable, and under the adolescent's control. Obstacles were carefully noted and addressed.

HAPPINESS SCALE AND GOALS OF COUNSELING

An important feature of A-CRA is that the therapist emphasizes his or her interest in all areas of the adolescent's life, not just the substance use. The emphasis on multiple areas of an adolescent's life helps enhance engagement and is a recognition that substance use does not occur in a vacuum. One of the procedures that illustrates the therapist's interest in multiple areas of the adolescent's life is the Happiness Scale (see Figure 3.3). This tool helps the

Name: Susie Adolescent _____ **Adolescent ID:** _____ **Date:** _____

This scale is intended to estimate your *current* happiness with your life in each of the 16 areas listed below. You are to circle one of the numbers (1 to 10) beside each area. Numbers toward the left side of the 10-unit scale indicate various degrees of unhappiness, whereas numbers toward the right side of the scale reflect increasing levels of happiness. Ask yourself this question as you rate each area of life: *"How happy am I today with this area of my life?"* In other words, state according to the numerical scale (1 to 10) exactly how you feel today. Try to exclude yesterday's feelings and concentrate only on today's feelings in each of the life areas. Also, try *not* to allow one category to influence the results of the other categories.

	Completely Unhappy								Completely Happy	
1. Marijuana use/nonuse	1	2	3	4	5	(6)	7	8	9	10
2. Alcohol use/nonuse	1	2	3	4	5	(6)	7	8	9	10
3. Other drug use/nonuse	1	2	3	4	5	6	7	8	(9)	10
4. Relationship with boyfriend or girlfriend	1	2	3	4	5	6	7	8	9	(10)
5. Relationships with friends	1	2	3	(4)	5	6	7	8	9	10
6. Relationships with parents or caregivers	1	2	3	4	5	6	7	(8)	9	10
7. School	1	2	3	4	5	6	7	(8)	9	10
8. Social activities	1	2	3	4	5	6	7	(8)	9	10
9. Recreational activities	1	2	3	4	5	6	7	8	(9)	10
10. Personal habits (e.g., getting up in the morning, being on time, finishing tasks)	1	2	3	4	5	6	7	(8)	9	10
11. Legal issues	1	2	3	(4)	5	6	7	8	9	10
12. Money management	1	2	3	4	5	6	7	(8)	9	10
13. Emotional life (feelings)	1	2	3	4	5	6	7	(8)	9	10
14. Communication	1	2	3	4	5	6	7	(8)	9	10
15. General happiness	1	2	3	4	5	6	7	(8)	9	10
16. Other	1	2	3	4	5	6	7	(8)	9	10

Figure 3.3 Happiness Scale

therapist and adolescent work together to identify those areas of the adolescent's life where good things are occurring and to identify areas of the adolescent's life where improvements might be made. Therapists also have found this tool helpful with adolescents who are less verbal because after it is completed, it provides many opportunities to ask open-ended questions about what is going well or not so well in the adolescents' lives. The therapist has flexibility regarding the frequency of administering the Happiness Scale. Generally, it is used in one of the first sessions to establish a baseline of satisfaction/dissatisfaction across these life areas. After the initial Happiness Scale, it makes sense to complete others at least monthly, or whenever the adolescent seems uncertain as to what he or she wants to work on next. A Happiness Scale is also routinely administered during a final session, at which time the therapist will show adolescents the Happiness Scales they completed during treatment so they can see the progress they have made.

See Figure 3.3 for an example of a completed Happiness Scale. When introducing this tool to the adolescent, as the instructions indicate, adolescents are asked to circle on a 1 to 10 scale, with 10 being the best, how they feel right now. After the scale is completed, the therapist begins by talking about those areas that are rated highest and asks open-ended questions to learn why those areas are rated high. This process provides opportunities to reinforce the adolescent for areas of life that are going well. Then they might discuss areas rated low. Eventually, they will work toward developing goals in one or

Name: Susie Adolescent, _____ **Date:** _____

Problem Areas/Goals "In. the area of ___ I would like:"	Intervention	Time Frame
1. Marijuana use/nonuse		
2. Alcohol use/nonuse		
3. Other drug use/nonuse		
4. Relationship with boyfriend/girlfriend		
5. Relationships with friends; make one new nonusing friend	1. Attend church youth group this week.	1 month
6. Relationships with parents/caregivers		
7. School		
8. School activities		

Figure 3.4 Goals of Counseling – I

Note: These would *not* all be assigned at once!

two areas of the Happiness Scale, focusing on goal areas of most interest to the adolescent (not the therapist). From the completed example, it is possible to see that the adolescent is very happy about his relationship with his girl-friend, but less happy about his relationship with friends and legal issues.

The Goals of Counseling Form has been designed to map directly onto the Happiness Scale (see Figures 3.4 and 3.5) and is a type of treatment plan that can be reviewed and changed weekly as needed. The completed Happiness Scale is used to select goal categories. Guidelines for writing goal statements are that they are (a) brief, (b) stated positively, (c) specific and measurable, (d) reasonable, (e) under the adolescent's control, and (f) based on skills that the adolescent already has. Therapists ask about obstacles that might interfere with accomplishing goals and help the adolescent brainstorm solutions to these obstacles. Most important, in follow-up sessions, the therapist checks

Name: Susie Adolescent, _____   **Date:** _____

Problem Areas/Goals "In the area of ___ I would like:"	Intervention	Time Frame
9. Recreational activities		
10. Personal habits (e.g., getting up in the morning, being on time, finishing tasks)		
11. Legal issues. **Make it through the month with no new charges**	*1. Play video games after school with my two nonusing friends (Sam and Pete).*	
	2. Use refusal skills whenever offered alcohol or drugs.	1 month
12. Money management		
13. Emotional life (my feelings)		
14. Communication		
15. General happiness		
16. Other		

(Participant Signature   (Date)   (Counselor Signature)   (Date)

(Guardian Signature, Optional)   (Date)   (Supervisor Signature)   (Date)

Figure 3.5 Goals of Counseling – II

Note: These would *not* all be assigned at once!

back in with the adolescent to see if he or she has followed through with the specific action plan that was outlined to help achieve the goal.

Sobriety Sampling

As we have noted earlier, most adolescents who enter treatment are not convinced that they need to completely quit using alcohol or other drugs. They enter treatment because they are pressured and may not have made a commitment to change their behavior. By the time they enter treatment, adolescents often have been regularly using alcohol or other drugs for years and cannot remember what it was like to enjoy life without substance use. The rationale that underlies sobriety sampling is that it provides an opportunity for the adolescent to commit to and have success with a shorter period of abstinence, rather than requiring an unrealistic commitment to permanent abstinence. This period of sobriety helps the adolescent build new coping skills or strengthen nonsubstance related skills, enables the adolescent to see what it is like to have even brief periods of sobriety, and shows parents or others that he or she is making an effort to be substance-free. The following are the components of sobriety sampling:

- As with any procedure, begin by providing the rationale for the procedure.
- Negotiate with the adolescent for a reasonable period of sobriety.
- Develop a specific plan for maintaining sobriety for a relatively short period of time.
- Develop a backup plan with the adolescent.
- Remind the adolescent of reinforcers he or she has identified for sobriety.

The following example illustrates these components with an adolescent who is going to have a pass to go home from residential treatment, but the same components work well for an adolescent who is in outpatient treatment. In a residential setting, the therapist would work towards negotiating a time period that matches the length of his or her pass. Working with an adolescent in outpatient treatment presents a different situation, since these adolescents do not have the "forced abstinence" common in residential settings. When working with an adolescent in outpatient treatment, the therapist would usually start by proposing a longer period of sobriety (e.g., two weeks) and negotiate with the adolescent until they agree on a shorter period (e.g., one week). In both settings, in a subsequent session, the therapist would negotiate for a longer or shorter period of sobriety depending on how the adolescent responded to the initial sobriety sampling period.

A CASE EXAMPLE: SOBRIETY SAMPLING

RATIONALE

THERAPIST: Sounds like you're concerned about the pass this weekend, correct? And I know that the last time you were home you had a lot of anxiety, right?

ADOLESCENT: Yeah. Like on my last pass. Maybe it was because I was back in the same area where I use. I don't know. That anxiety really gets me.

THERAPIST: Yes, anxiety is one of your main triggers. And this is for an overnight pass again. I know it's been a while since you had one.

ADOLESCENT: That's because I messed up bad when I had my last overnight.

THERAPIST: Are overnight passes harder in some way?

ADOLESCENT: I don't know. Seems like it. I think it's just because I get more nervous if I'm home for a while. I guess I know that I have more time to get into trouble. But I have to learn how to be OK with being home.

THERAPIST: That's true. So, I'm wondering if it would make sense to come up with some agreement about you staying clean and sober while on your pass. I know you don't want to keep getting into trouble, right?

ADOLESCENT: I can't afford to!

THERAPIST: And what would be some of the other benefits for staying sober for a period of time?

ADOLESCENT: I don't know how to put this in words. If I go home on a pass and I stay sober, it can help me. It can help me during that pass, because instead of getting high I can do positive things, positive things that I can do when I go home for good. If I get high on a pass, I'm not really spending time with my family. I'm not really doing positive things that I can do when I go home for real.

THERAPIST: It's kind of like learning how to adjust to being at home, learning new coping skills at home, and that kind of thing. Learning to do positive things around your family. Makes sense. OK. Can you think of any other benefits to staying clean while you are on your weekend pass?

ADOLESCENT: I guess it would prove to folks here that I can handle an overnight pass again. That would be good, because I'd like to be home more when it gets to be the holidays.

THERAPIST: That's something good to shoot for.

The therapist worked with the adolescent to identify a number of advantages to sampling a period of being clean and sober during his visit home. The next step involves negotiating the length of time for this period.

NEGOTIATION

THERAPIST: So, if we had to come up with an agreement about a reasonable period of time for you to be clean and sober while at home, what do you think that would be?

ADOLESCENT: Just for today?

THERAPIST: Today is a start. I was thinking more like this whole weekend and next weekend, since you will get to go home again next weekend, if you stay clean this pass. Do you think you could say that you could be clean and sober for both weekends?

ADOLESCENT: I guess I could say it, but I don't know if I could do it.

THERAPIST: Well, I have always appreciated your honesty. It's best not to commit to something if you're not pretty sure you can do it. What do you think would be more reasonable? And keep in mind all the incentives for staying sober that we just discussed: earning longer passes as it gets close to the holidays, spending some real time with your family without being high, and finding new ways to cope so that you'll be prepared for when you go home for good. What do you think? Do you think you can commit to being clean and sober both weekends—for the reasons we just discussed?

ADOLESCENT: I don't know. I'd like to, but . . .

THERAPIST: But you're still not sure. I can dig that. Tell me what you're comfortable with.

ADOLESCENT: How about I say that I can do it for the time I'm on the pass this weekend: Friday night, all day Saturday, and until I get back here on Sunday?

THERAPIST: Again, thanks for searching your soul and trying to come up with something you really think you can do. You know yourself pretty well, so if you say you want to try it this weekend only, I'm going to go along with that. We can talk about next weekend when we meet next week.

As is commonly done, the therapist started the negotiation process by proposing a relatively long period of sobriety, knowing full well that the adolescent probably would opt for something shorter. This is fine, as the adolescent typically is still selecting a reasonable period for sampling sobriety. The benefits to staying clean and sober were reviewed. The third and final phase of sobriety sampling entails developing a plan for successfully achieving the sobriety goal.

THE SOBRIETY PLAN

THERAPIST: Excellent. And now the crucial part: How are you going to maintain sobriety during your weekend pass?

ADOLESCENT: Stay away from old using friends.

THERAPIST: Easier said than done, though, I bet. So if we were to take a look at the biggest triggers that you'll face there, should we start with those friends?

ADOLESCENT: Definitely. My old using friends, for sure. That's what happened last time I had the overnight.

THERAPIST: Right. I remember. Let's review how you ended up being with those friends in the first place. Because I know that we'd talked about trying to stay away from them.

ADOLESCENT: I had it all planned out. I was going shooting with my mom that time.

THERAPIST: Shooting?

ADOLESCENT: Sharp shooting.

THERAPIST: OK. What happened?

ADOLESCENT: The gun club is right across from the sportsmen's club, and I had a friend who lived in the sportsmen's club that I used with. She saw me drive up with my mom, and she gave me a signal to meet her out back. So I did. I made up some excuse to my mom, like I had to use the bathroom. Anyway, it was stupid.

THERAPIST: Did you return and shoot then when you were high?

ADOLESCENT: Yeah. Not too smart. My mom knew right away that something was up.

THERAPIST: Are you likely to run into this friend on this weekend?

ADOLESCENT: Not if I stay away from the gun club. I don't have any plans to go there this time.

THERAPIST: Phew! I'm glad to hear that. We'll practice your drug refusal skills again before you leave on the pass, though, just in case you run into her or some of your other using friends. Where are you likely to see some of these other friends, and what's your plan for dealing with them?

ADOLESCENT: The word gets out pretty fast when I'm home for a visit. So they'll know. A couple of my friends won't bother me, though. They know I was really having a hard time before I left for rehab. They don't want to see me all messed up again.

THERAPIST: Sounds like these friends have some good qualities. How about the friends, though, who might want you to use while you're home? Where are you most likely to run into them?

Adolescent: At the mall. Or at one of the fast food joints. So I'll only go to those places if I have my sister or my mom with me. They won't come over and offer me anything then.

Therapist: What if one of them gives you the signal to meet her in the bathroom or somewhere? Couldn't that happen again?

Adolescent: I guess. But I think I'll be OK this time.

Therapist: What else could you do so that you're *sure* you'll be OK this time? We don't want to leave anything to chance.

Adolescent: I'll have my cell phone with me. I could call my sponsor.

Therapist: Good for you! What about a backup plan in case your sponsor doesn't answer?

Adolescent: I actually have several sponsors, and I have them all programmed into my phone.

Therapist: Impressive! Now your main emotional trigger, as we've been discussing, is your anxiety. When are you most likely to feel anxious while on your pass, and what's a good plan for dealing with it?

Adolescent: I know I'm probably going to get anxious because it's happened every time I've gone home on a pass. That's not the only time, of course.

Therapist: Maybe you can do something to prevent yourself from getting anxious in the first place. What's helped you with that in the past?

Adolescent: I'm not sure. All I know is that lots of times I get nervous when I'm around people who are using. I think I get nervous because I'm trying to figure out whether I should use or not.

Therapist: Maybe it will help if you go into the weekend saying to yourself that you're not going to use. Because we've just made this agreement, right? And we're working out the details. Then supposedly you wouldn't have to be anxious about making a decision; the decision will already have been made.

Adolescent: I think that would help.

Therapist: But that's probably not enough. Let's say you go into the weekend saying you aren't going to use, but then you have urges to use after all. Then what?

Adolescent: I'm planning on spending most of the time with my mom, so she'll be a good distraction.

Therapist: Good. And if the distraction doesn't work and you get an urge?

Adolescent: Geez! You don't let up!

Therapist: I'm just trying to help you think this all through so that you can meet *your* goal of being clean and sober the whole weekend.

ADOLESCENT: I know. You're right. I'd say to my sister, "Come on! We need to go to a dollar movie right now!" She'd go.

THERAPIST: You could rely on her to do that? Excellent. And if she wasn't available?

ADOLESCENT: I have one nonusing friend who I could go with. I *do* need to make some more nonusing friends eventually, though.

THERAPIST: We can definitely work on that in here. In the meantime, would it be a good idea to have a meeting all lined up for you while you're home? Do you remember the times?

ADOLESCENT: Yes. They are in the community center on Friday and Saturday nights at 5:00. I'll go to the Friday night one with my mom.

THERAPIST: If your mom is busy, who could take you?

ADOLESCENT: I have a sponsor at home, too. I could call her.

THERAPIST: Why don't we go ahead and call her right now, just to be sure she'd be available to take you if necessary? We can practice the call first.

ADOLESCENT: Sure.

THERAPIST: And then after the call we'll review drug refusal skills.

Plans were developed for dealing with several of the highest-risk triggers for the adolescent. Each plan had a backup as well.

COMMUNICATION SKILLS

Many adolescents have difficulty with communication skills, and adolescents with substance use problems are no different. Oftentimes problems at school, with the law, or with parents can be caused or at least exacerbated by poor communication skills. Adolescents frequently say that having a fight with parents or others can be triggers for substance use, and good communication can help prevent altercations. Learning positive communication skills can enhance the quality of adolescents' relationships with their peers, parents, and other adults. Adolescents will be more likely to get what they want from authority figures or their peers and more likely to receive positive communication in return. During A-CRA, adolescents are taught the basics of good communication in an individual session, parents are taught these same skills in one of their sessions with the therapist, and then the adolescent and parent practice these skills together in a joint session.

The therapist begins this procedure by talking about why good communication is important and helpful. Next, the therapist describes the three elements of good communication, which include (a) making an understanding

The goal of using communication skills is to be able to get your message across to another person to help you get what you want. Using these communication skills should enable individuals to compromise or agree on a solution to a problem. When everyone agrees on a solution, compliance by both sides and contentment with the solution are more likely. It is important to stay positive during the communication skills training and avoid blaming.

Understanding statement. The goal of the understanding statement is to open up communication and show that you are aware of another person's thoughts on a problem. That is:

- ❑ **Come from the other person's perspective.**
  Example: "Mom, I understand you would like my room cleaned because it is a real mess, and you would like the house to be clean when friends come over."
- ❑ **Come from your perspective.**
  Example: "But Jimmy is having a birthday party at his house, and I have not seen Jimmy for a while, so I would really like to go."
- ❑ **Make a request (a request should be brief, positive, and specific).**
  Example: "I would really appreciate it if you would let me clean my room later tonight, maybe around 8 pm when I get home."

Partial responsibility. The goal of the statement of partial responsibility is to avoid blaming the other person. Remember to state how you or the other person see yourselves, fitting into the problem or solution. That is:

- ❑ **How do you fit into the problem?**
  Example: "I know I made a real mess by not putting my clothes away, and I have not always followed through with cleaning my room, and I am sorry about that."
- ❑ **Repeat the request (optional).**
  Example: "But I would really appreciate it if you would let me clean my room around 8 pm tonight after I get home from Jimmy's party."

Offer to help. The offer to help is used to show that you are willing to work on a solution that works for everyone and that you would like input from others on possible solutions. That is:

- ❑ **Offer several possible solutions**.
  Example: "If there is anything I can do to help make that happen—help out with another chore around the house, help out with dinner, or just do a quick 10-minute cleaning for now and do the rest later—I would really appreciate it."
- ❑ **State your openness to listen to and consider the other person's ideas**.
  Example: "Or if there is anything that you can think of, I would be willing to listen."

Following the offer to help, individuals may try to compromise on a solution or do some problem solving. It may be necessary to go through the communication skills again to state your point.

Figure 3.6   Communication Skills

statement, (b) accepting partial responsibility, and (c) offering to help. See Figure 3.6, which is a handout on communication that the therapist can provide to the adolescent while reviewing it. To help the adolescent understand these elements, the therapist provides examples of each component. Next, the therapist would engage the adolescent in a role-play so that the adolescent has the opportunity to practice these skills. Sometimes it is worthwhile to start with a "reverse role-play," in which the adolescent plays the person with whom he or she is having difficulty communicating. This helps the therapist see how that person might act, and it affords the adolescent an opportunity to develop empathy for that person's position. And since the therapist is playing the part of the adolescent in a reverse role-play, it also gives the therapist the chance to model an appropriate communication style. All A-CRA sessions end with a mutually agreed upon homework assignment, and communication skill training provides material that can easily translate into such an assignment. The following example is based on another male adolescent living with his mom. He has had legal trouble and has been diagnosed with alcohol abuse and marijuana dependence.

A CASE EXAMPLE: COMMUNICATION SKILLS TRAINING

Introduction and rationale

Therapist: You seem really upset today.

Adolescent: My mom's a jerk! I've been doing really good lately, but she still won't let me go hang out with my friends this weekend. I might as well be in jail!

Therapist: You sound frustrated and angry with your mom because it doesn't feel like she recognizes how hard you have been working at staying clean.

Adolescent: Well, wouldn't *you* be? What do I have to do to show her that she doesn't have to worry about me all the time? One screw-up and you're branded for life!

Therapist: That *is* upsetting, isn't it? And I bet it would be useful to take a look at how a typical conversation about stuff like this goes between you and your mom. Maybe we can work on it a little so that your mom is more ready to listen to you.

Adolescent: What good does it do for her to listen if she still says "no"?

Therapist: I can't guarantee that she'll say "yes," but there's definitely a better chance that she will at least listen and negotiate if she doesn't get defensive right from the start. Do you know what I mean by getting defensive?

ADOLESCENT: Yes. It's like you're ready for a fight.

THERAPIST: That's right. And if Mom is ready for a fight the moment you open your mouth and ask for something, then what are the chances she's going to agree to *anything* you want?

ADOLESCENT: Zero.

THERAPIST: That's right. So if we work on how you talk to her, I bet we can improve upon zero. Plus, I'd also bet that if you start talking nicer to your mom, she'll start talking nicer back. Can you see how that might work? Are you game?

The therapist introduced the notion of working on communication skills at a time when it was relevant to the adolescent. A basic rationale was provided as an incentive.

ASSESSMENT OF CURRENT QUALITY OF COMMUNICATION

THERAPIST: It would help if I could first get a better idea of how the conversation went between you and your mom. Can you show me what you started off with?

ADOLESCENT: I said something like, "Mom, I've had clean UAs for a month now, so I want to go hang out with Keira and Michelle Friday night. OK?"

THERAPIST: Good. And your mom said what?

ADOLESCENT: She said, "Don't start bothering me all the time about going out. Just because you haven't smoked for a few weeks, it doesn't mean that everything is back to normal."

THERAPIST: Thank you. And then what happened?

ADOLESCENT: I told her that I hated how she treated me. Then I said a few things under my breath and stomped out.

THERAPIST: Thanks. That helps me see how I'll play your mom when we practice in a few minutes. And it also gives me an idea of how to take the positive parts of your current communication style and incorporate them into the positive style that I'd like to show you now. What do you think? Are you up for trying to change how the conversations go between you and your mom? I know you marked "communication" as an area of low happiness on your Happiness Scale last week. Is that something you'd like to work on? We haven't talked about it specifically as a goal yet.

ADOLESCENT: I guess we can look at it, especially if I'm more likely to get what I want.

This assessment of the current communication style does not need to entail an actual role-play, since the purpose is to simply gather basic information to use later. Note that the therapist does not assume that the adolescent wants to work on improving communication with his mother, but instead probes to see if that is a goal area.

A-CRA's Communication Components with Examples and a Reverse Role-Play

THERAPIST: I'm going to start by giving you a handout that contains information about communicating in a positive way [see Figure 3.6, Communication Skills]. You can take it home with you. I'll go over the important points here. There are three basic parts to good communication that we like to emphasize as part of this treatment program. The first one is to use an understanding statement. An understanding statement is a way of putting yourself in the other person's shoes. It helps you see things the way they do. Do you have any idea of why it's helpful to try to see the problem from the other person's point of view? In your case, it would be from your mom's perspective.

ADOLESCENT: Not really.

THERAPIST: Fair enough. Maybe it would help if we made it more "real." Think back to the conversation you just had with your mom about wanting permission to hang out with your friends Friday night. Try to think like your mom for a minute. Why might she be reluctant to give you permission to hang out with your friends?

ADOLESCENT: Because she always says "no" without even thinking?

THERAPIST: That might be what's going on now. But how did she get to that point?

ADOLESCENT: I started getting into trouble, I guess. Now she won't let me do *anything* fun.

THERAPIST: And she won't let you do anything fun because . . . ?

ADOLESCENT: Because she's afraid I might get into more trouble.

THERAPIST: Good for you. I think you're right. Your mom is afraid. I'm suggesting that you start your conversation with your mom by saying exactly what you just said here, that you understand she's afraid that you might get into trouble.

ADOLESCENT: Why would I want to remind her of that?

THERAPIST: Good question. I'll demonstrate it on you, and you can tell me whether you think it's helpful. This is what we call a reverse role-play, because you're playing your mom and I'm playing you. Just pretend that we're having the beginning of the conversation you had with your mom earlier this morning. Make believe you're your mom. I'd say something like, "Hi, Mom. Can I talk to you a minute?"

ADOLESCENT (*playing mom*): "I'm kind of busy. What do you want?"

THERAPIST (*playing adolescent's part*): "Mom, I understand that you worry about me a lot. But I'd really love to be able to go hang out with Keira and Michelle Friday night. You know that neither of them use."

ADOLESCENT (*playing mom*): "But how do I know that *you* won't use again?"

THERAPIST (*playing adolescent's part*): "I can understand why you don't trust me."

ADOLESCENT: Oh, I see. It sounds nicer if you say, "I understand."

THERAPIST: That's right. Can you say more about how it made you feel when I said, "I understand"?

ADOLESCENT: Like I'd probably listen to more of what you had to say.

THERAPIST: Excellent! We're definitely trying to keep the lines of communication open so that you and your mom can talk in a positive way, and so that you're more likely to get what you want.

ADOLESCENT: This might freak my mom out because she's always saying that I never think about how my behavior affects her.

THERAPIST: Well, then you'll definitely get her attention with an understanding statement! But we'll practice it so that you can say it in your own words. You don't even have to say, "I understand" if that sounds too strange.

ADOLESCENT: It sounds strange, but it's easy to remember.

THERAPIST: That's fine then. OK. Now before we go on to the other two main parts of a good communication, let's look at how you make your request. It's helpful to make your request in a way that's brief, positive, and specific. Again, the whole point of bothering with these "rules" is because they help us get something that we want. Let's work on this together with an example. Let's take your request to "hang out with your two friends on Friday night." It's already brief, so that's good. And you're letting your mom know what you'd like to do as opposed to what you *don't* want to do anymore. In other words, it's great that you're saying that you want to hang out with two of your nonusing friends because that's considered a positive statement. A negative statement would be saying that you *won't* hang out with your using friends. The problem with the negative statement is that it doesn't say who you *will* be hanging out with—and I'm sure Mom would want to know. Does that sound too confusing?

ADOLESCENT: No, I get it. I can do that.

THERAPIST: Great. Let's see now if we can make your request more specific. I bet your mom will be less worried about you if she knows exactly what you want to do with your friends. So how could you make your request to hang out with your friends on Friday night more specific?

ADOLESCENT: Before she got into the habit of just saying "no," she used to ask me those annoying questions like, "Where are you going? Who are you going to be with? When will you be back? Will there be any adults there?" Do you mean I should tell her stuff like that?

THERAPIST: Actually, we encourage parents to ask those annoying questions, so you might be hearing more of that again soon! But to answer your question, I think it *would* help to tell her some of that information. Wouldn't she have less to worry about if she knew your whereabouts and knew you were safe? And then wouldn't she be more likely to agree to let you go?

ADOLESCENT: Maybe.

THERAPIST: You're right; there's no guarantee. But I bet your chances are better. With that in mind, what should we change about your request to "hang out with Keira and Michelle on Friday night"? What would Mom like to know?

ADOLESCENT: I could tell her that I want to go to Michelle's house to listen to music and watch movies.

THERAPIST: Good. And can I assume that this is what you *will* actually be doing if your mom agrees to let you go Friday night?

ADOLESCENT: Of course! I can't afford to get into any more trouble.

THERAPIST: I apologize. I just felt like I needed to get that question out in the open.

ADOLESCENT: No big deal.

THERAPIST: All right. The only things I might add to make your request more specific are the times and the transportation.

ADOLESCENT: I've already got the transportation figured out. Keira's mom said she'd stop at my house on her way to drop off Keira at Michelle's. I think she's going to bring her there around 7:00.

THERAPIST: I bet it would help if you told your mom these details. Then she'd know exactly what you'd be doing and where . . . and who you'd be with. I'd also suggest that you mention what time you'd be getting home—and how, as well as whether any adults will be there. Can you put that all together and talk to me like I'm your mom?

ADOLESCENT (*in role-play*): "Mom, I understand that you worry about me a lot, but I haven't gotten into any trouble in over a month now. So, could I please go to Michelle's house Friday night? I could get a ride with Keira's mom. She said she'd bring me back home at 11:00."

THERAPIST (*playing mom*): "That sounds kind of late. And will either of Michelle's parents be there?"

ADOLESCENT (*in role-play*): "Her mom will be there for sure. I don't know about her dad."

THERAPIST (*playing mom*): "Maybe. I need to think about it a little."

ADOLESCENT (*in role-play*): "OK. Thanks."

THERAPIST: Good job! What did you like about your conversation?

ADOLESCENT: I didn't get upset. And I knew what I wanted to say, so it wasn't too hard.

THERAPIST: You made it look easy! And you included a number of the things we talked about adding. Can you tell me some of those things?

ADOLESCENT: I was specific; I told her that I had transportation, and when I'd get home.

THERAPIST: Yes. That was excellent. And you were brief and positive. There was just one part that could have been a little more specific. I didn't hear you mention what you'd be doing that night with your friends.

ADOLESCENT: Oh, right.

THERAPIST: You also started off with an understanding statement. Do you know what you said?

ADOLESCENT: I think I said the same thing I did before, something about her worrying about me.

THERAPIST: Good. That's right. Now let's try it again. Based on the feedback I've given you, what would you like to add or change this time?

ADOLESCENT: I'm going to tell her what I'll be doing with my friends.

THERAPIST: Take it away!

ADOLESCENT (*in role-play*): "Mom, can I talk to you a minute? I understand that you worry about me a lot, but I've been doing really good lately. So is it ok if I go over to Michelle's house Friday night until about 11:00? Keira's mom said she could give me a ride both ways. Oh—and Michelle's mom will be there the whole time. And we're going to just listen to music and watch a movie."

THERAPIST (*playing mom*): "Well, I don't know. I guess you *have* been doing good. I like those two friends. You said Michelle's mom is going to be there?"

ADOLESCENT (*in role-play*): "Yes. Do you want to call her?"

THERAPIST: Wow! You get better and better each time. I like how you even went ahead and suggested that your mom call Michelle's mom. This is getting into another part of positive communication that I was planning on talking about shortly: offering to help. I'll get back to that in a minute, though. First—tell me what you liked about your conversation.

ADOLESCENT: I remembered to tell her what I was going to be doing at Michelle's. I think I did everything else, too. I was real specific and positive, and I said, "I understand."

THERAPIST: You sure did! Let's move on then. The next part of a positive communication is called "accepting partial responsibility." Typically, this means letting the other person know that you played some part in creating the problem. Just like with the understanding statement, the partial responsibility statement makes it easier for the other person to listen to you. And that's half the battle. Can you think of something that you could accept partial responsibility for in this situation?

ADOLESCENT: I'm not sure what you mean. Am I supposed to take partial responsibility for not being able to get to Michelle's house? No, that doesn't sound right. I'm not sure what to say.

THERAPIST: It *is* a tough one to sort out at first. I'll illustrate with an example in a minute. But as far as what you're supposed to accept partial responsibility for, usually it's for part of the original problem. In this situation, the problem is that your mom won't let you go to your friend's house. Can you see what role you played in that? What could you accept responsibility for?

ADOLESCENT: She used to let me go over to Michelle's before I got into trouble for smoking pot. Maybe I could accept responsibility for her not trusting me?

THERAPIST: If you're comfortable doing that, it would be perfect. You could say something like, "Mom, I know that one of the reasons you don't want me to go to Michelle's is because of my pot smoking. But I'm not doing that anymore, so . . . "

ADOLESCENT: It's OK to accept some responsibility and then explain why she doesn't need to worry anymore?

THERAPIST: Yes. It's good to reassure her.

ADOLESCENT: I can do that.

THERAPIST: As long as you're on a roll, let me go ahead and explain the last part of a positive communication, which is an "offer to help." You actually did something quite similar to this earlier when you suggested that your mom call Michelle's mother to make sure the mother was going to be there. An even better offer would be to say, "Mom, do you want to call Michelle's mom so you can make sure she's going to be at home Friday night? Here—I'll give you her phone number." Besides being a nice thing to do, an offer to help makes it easier for the other person to give you what you want. But I don't want to put words in your mouth. What other types of offers to help could you make in this situation?

ADOLESCENT: Sometimes my mom likes it when I call her a couple of times while I'm at a friend's house; I guess so that she knows I'm OK.

THERAPIST: Excellent idea. You could offer to call her from Michelle's a couple of times Friday night. I should also add that sometimes a good offer to help is simply, "How can I help?" The other person might have some clear idea of what they need from you.

When presenting the basic guidelines for positive communication, it is helpful to involve the adolescent in the discussion so as to avoid "lecturing." Typically, this entails having the adolescent offer relevant and comfortable examples of the improved communication. Abbreviated role-plays are sometimes included as part of this presentation, as are reverse role-plays in which the therapist plays the adolescent and the adolescent plays the other person (e.g., the mom). Regardless, complete role-plays that enact a more natural conversation follow.

STANDARD ROLE-PLAY

THERAPIST: Let's review the basic parts of positive communication before we practice again. There are three things we ask you to use.

ADOLESCENT: I'm supposed to say, "I understand" and to accept partial responsibility.

THERAPIST: Yes. And the third one—the one where you told your mom you'd give her the phone number for Michelle's mom?

ADOLESCENT: Right. An offer to help. But what was that other stuff we did? You had me being specific, positive . . .

THERAPIST: Good for you! Yes, it's also good if you can make your request in a way that's brief, positive, and specific. Although we don't consider these the three main components, they're still very useful.

ADOLESCENT: So, should I use them?

THERAPIST: Well, considering how good you seem to be at this, I'd say to go for it! We'll practice using all of the pieces here, but don't worry if you miss some of them when you're having a conversation out in the real world. Before we get started though, can you tell me when would be a good time to have this conversation with your mom? When are the two of you likely to be in good moods?

ADOLESCENT: She's *never* in a good mood anymore.

THERAPIST: OK. So what's the *best* of the bad-mood times for her?

ADOLESCENT: Huh?

THERAPIST: Even if she's in a bad mood all of the time, there are different degrees of "bad."

ADOLESCENT: I get it. And maybe she's not *always* in a bad mood. Anyway, I have the best luck talking to her after dinner.

THERAPIST: How about tonight then? Would after dinner tonight work?

ADOLESCENT: Sure.

THERAPIST: Now if something unexpected happens and one of you is in a bad mood tonight, it's better to abort the plan and wait until tomorrow night. Does that make sense?

ADOLESCENT: Yup.

THERAPIST: Good. Let's do it! Let's pretend that we've just finished dinner.

ADOLESCENT (*in role-play*): "Mom, I've got something to ask you. I understand that you worry about me a lot, because of the trouble I've gotten in. But I haven't been in any trouble for a long time now. So is it OK for me to go to Michelle's Friday night? I've got a ride with Keira's mother. And she can bring me home at 11:00, too. Here's the phone number for Michelle's mom in case you want to talk to her."

THERAPIST (*playing mom*): "Just because you haven't been in trouble for a month doesn't mean that I have nothing to worry about."

ADOLESCENT (*in role-play*): "I know. It doesn't help that I went behind your back and did those things. But I'm not hanging around with those kids anymore."

THERAPIST (*playing mom*): "If you *were* still hanging out with them you'd never get any privileges anymore. Let me think about it. I'll see what your dad says."

ADOLESCENT (*in role-play*): "I guess I'll check back with you later then."

THERAPIST: Good job! Tell me what you liked about your conversation.

ADOLESCENT: I used an understanding statement and I offered to help by giving her the phone number. I think I accepted partial responsibility, didn't I?

THERAPIST: Yes. You said you knew it didn't help the situation by going behind your mom's back. That was really good. What about the brief, positive, and specific guidelines?

ADOLESCENT: I think I did those when I talked about the time and the transportation, and when I said what I was going to be doing, and . . . oh wait! I didn't say what we were going to be doing that night. I keep forgetting that!

THERAPIST: It might not be necessary. Your mom might agree to let you go anyway. The partial responsibility and the understanding statements themselves are very powerful. And remember that you don't have to use *all* of these pieces of a positive communication.

ADOLESCENT: But if I can't remember to say it in here, how am I going to remember to do it with my mom?

THERAPIST: That's why we keep practicing here, so that you're more likely to remember to say what you want to with your mom. Let's do it again, and how about you add that piece this time? Also, I'm going to give you a little bit of a harder time, just in case your mom does. This will be a good test. You've been doing such a good job of *not* getting upset that I know you'll be able to handle this.

Brief role-plays are repeated several times so that the adolescent can get more comfortable with the conversation and incorporate feedback. Additionally, it gives the therapist the opportunity to increase the difficulty of the communication by playing a more resistant person. Finally, it is important for the therapist to discuss the possibility that the adolescent will not have the request honored despite using positive communication skills. Typically, the session ends with the homework assignment (i.e., to have the conversation at the preplanned time) being made explicit, and with potential obstacles raised and addressed.

CAREGIVER ONLY AND COMBINED CAREGIVER/ADOLESCENT SESSIONS

Most adolescents who enter substance abuse treatment live at home with their parents. Often, the relationship has become strained because the adolescent has gotten into a lot of trouble related to his or her alcohol and drug use. While some families have severe problems, including parental addiction that interferes with parenting, adolescent substance use disorders can occur in any family. Best practice guidelines recommend that it is important to include parents when working with their children. Thus, in designing A-CRA, we thought it was important to provide assistance to parents and help teach both parents and their adolescent skills to improve their relationship. At a minimum, the manual suggests two sessions with the parents or designated caregivers individually, and two sessions that include both the adolescent and the caregivers together. More of these sessions are possible if needed and within the scope of a local treatment provider. Since many substance abuse treatment professionals are not trained in family interventions and a fair number are apprehensive about conducting sessions with parents, these sessions are highly structured. Many therapists benefit from practicing these sessions with their supervisor or another therapist before they have the sessions with parents. We do recommend that the therapist begin to work with parents as soon as possible during the adolescent's treatment episode to ensure that all four sessions are completed.

Often during the first session with an adolescent, the therapist invites the parent into the session for around 15 minutes in order to provide an orientation to the treatment and to answer any questions. However, there are two full Caregiver Only sessions. The two individual caregiver sessions are to (a) motivate the parents to participate in treatment, (b) build rapport with parents, and (c) provide parents with information about effective parenting. Prevention research has suggested that there are several parenting practices that can help decrease adolescent substance use, and these are reviewed with parents in the context of what might help their adolescent, while being careful not to accuse parents of any poor behaviors. These practices are (a) being a good role model by refraining from alcohol and drug use themselves; (b) increasing positive communication with their adolescent; (c) monitoring their adolescent's whereabouts by knowing where they are and who they are with; and (d) becoming involved with their adolescent's life outside the home by encouraging and participating with them in positive activities. After discussing positive parenting practices with the parents, the therapist teaches and practices both communication and problem-solving skills with them. They will also work to prepare them for the session with their adolescent by priming them, for example, to think of three positive things they can say about their adolescent during the first combined session.

There are also two sessions with the adolescent and caregivers together. It is important that both the adolescent and the caregiver are primed for these sessions to maximize their effectiveness and limit negativity. The session begins with each party saying three positive things about the other to help set a positive tone. The therapist asks the adolescent and parent to face and speak to each other and is liberal with praise about their efforts. The therapist also asks the recipient of the positive comments to talk about what he or she heard the other person saying, so as to reinforce the good feelings that accompany hearing the praise. Next, each party completes a tool similar to the Happiness Scale, which is called the Relationship Happiness Scale. These have items specific to parents and adolescents, and each completes the scale based on how they feel about the other person (see Figures 3.7 and 3.8). After completing the scales, the ratings are discussed, and using the communication and problem solving skills that each have already been taught and practiced, the therapist helps the adolescent and caregivers address an area that one or the other would like to see changed. The therapist also introduces

Name:_____ ID:_____ Date:_____

This scale is intended to estimate your current happiness with your relationship with your adolescent in each of the eight areas listed below. You are to circle one of the numbers (1 to 10) beside each area. Numbers toward the left end of the 10-unit scale indicate various degrees of unhappiness, whereas numbers toward the right end of the scale reflect increasing levels of happiness. Ask yourself this question as you rate each area: "How happy am I today with my adolescent in this area?" In other words, indicate according to the numerical scale (1 to 10) exactly how you feel today. Try to exclude feelings of yesterday and concentrate only on the feelings of today in each of the life areas. Also, try not to allow one category influence the results of the other categories.

	Completely Unhappy									Completely Happy
1. Household responsibilities	1	2	3	4	5	6	(7)	8	9	10
2. Communication	1	2	3	4	(5)	6	7	8	9	10
3. Affection	1	2	3	4	5	6	7	(8)	9	10
4. Job or school	1	2	3	(4)	5	6	7	8	9	10
5. Emotional support	1	2	3	4	5	6	(7)	8	9	10
6. General happiness	1	2	3	4	5	(6)	7	8	9	10
7. Time spent with adolescent	1	2	3	4	5	6	7	(8)	9	10
8. General home atmosphere	1	2	3	4	5	6	(7)	8	9	10

Figure 3.7 Relationship Happiness Scale (Caregiver Version)

and explains how to use a tool called the "Daily Reminder to Be Nice" (see Figure 3.9). The tool was used in relationship counseling with adults, but is equally useful for relationship counseling for parents and their adolescents. An example of a caregiver and adolescent session follows.

OTHER A-CRA PROCEDURES

There are a number of other procedures that are usually a part of A-CRA. These procedures are not less important than the ones described above, but space does not allow the detailed description and examples for each of them. All are described in detail in either the CRA book by Meyers and Smith (1995) or the A-CRA manual (Godley, Meyers, et al., 2001). The following provides a listing and basic description of each.

Name:_____ ID: _____ Date: _____

This scale is intended to estimate your current happiness with your relationship with your parent or caregiver in each of the areas listed below. You are to circle one of the numbers (1 to 10) beside each area. Numbers toward the left end of the 10-unit scale indicate various degrees of unhappiness, whereas numbers toward the right end of the scale reflect increasing levels of happiness. Ask yourself this question as you rate each life area: "How happy am I today with my parent in this area?" In other words, indicate according to the numerical scale (1 to 10) exactly how you feel today. Try to exclude feelings of yesterday and concentrate only on the feelings of today in each of the life areas. Also, try not to allow one category influence the results of the other categories.

	Completely Unhappy									Completely Happy
1. Time spent with me	1	2	3	4	5	(6)	7	8	9	10
2. Allowance	1	2	3	4	(5)	6	7	8	9	10
3. Communication	1	2	3	4	5	(6)	7	8	9	10
4. Affection	1	2	3	4	5	(6)	7	8	9	10
5. Support of school/work	1	2	3	4	5	(6)	7	8	9	10
6. Emotional support	1	2	3	4	5	6	(7)	8	9	10
7. General happiness	1	2	3	4	5	(6)	7	8	9	10
8. General home activities	1	2	3	4	5	(6)	7	8	9	10

Figure 3.8 Relationship Happiness Scale (Adolescent Version)

A CASE EXAMPLE: CAREGIVER AND ADOLESCENT SESSION

OVERVIEW AND THREE POSITIVE STATEMENTS

THERAPIST: I'm glad everybody made it here today. It sure says that this family cares about each other. OK. Now normally we start off a session checking in on your assignment, but since this is a family session, I'm going to hold off on that for the most part. Sam, we'll be meeting again later this week, so we can go over your assignment then. And Mom and Dad, since we've finished our separate sessions, I'll call you later this week to see how your assignment went. Does that sound OK to everyone? And let me know if you don't remember what you were working on for the week.

MOTHER: I think we're good.

ADOLESCENT: Me, too.

THERAPIST: Good. Then I'll start by giving you an overview of what we're going to do today. Oh—but first, I want to see if anything major happened during the week that we need to make sure we set aside time to address today. Anything?

ADOLESCENT: Nope. Pretty boring week.

FATHER: Nothing out of the ordinary happened.

THERAPIST: Fair enough. So, I'll go ahead with the agenda then. As we discussed in our sessions last week, we're going to start by having you each say three positive things about each other. Then we'll do what's called the Relationship Happiness Scale, so that we can see how everybody is thinking things are going in the home and where you'd like to see some changes. Sam, you've done the regular Happiness Scale already, so this will look pretty familiar to you.

ADOLESCENT: Yeah, I remember that. It's short.

THERAPIST: Yeah, it's not like some of those long forms, is it? Next, we'll try to negotiate some of the changes you'd like to see—using our best communication skills, of course! If we have time we'll do some problem solving, too. We'll finish up with an assignment to do an exercise called the Daily Reminder to Be Nice. Interesting name, isn't it?

MOTHER: I guess it wouldn't hurt us to be reminded to be nice now and then.

THERAPIST: I think that would probably hold for most people. Let's start with the three positive things exercise. I know you've all had time to think about this.

MOTHER: Do you want me to go?

THERAPIST: Sure. If you're ready. Three positive things about Sam. And Dad can help with these, too.

MOTHER: Sam is polite. And he's smart.

THERAPIST: These are terrific! Now, can you look right at Sam and tell him those two positive things?

MOTHER: Sam, you're smart and polite. I like that about you.

THERAPIST: Excellent. How about another one? Dad?

FATHER: Sam, for the most part, you have good common sense.

THERAPIST: OK. Not bad. But maybe you could fix it a little, make it a little more positive? Because when you say "for the most part," it takes some of the compliment away. Do you see what I mean?

FATHER: Yeah. OK. Then I'll just say, Sam, you have good common sense.

THERAPIST: Great! Now Sam, can you look at your parents and repeat the three positive things they said about you?

ADOLESCENT: They said I'm smart and have common sense. Oh, and I'm polite.

THERAPIST: And how does that make you feel to hear your parents say that about you?

ADOLESCENT: It feels good. I'm surprised.

THERAPIST: You're surprised?

ADOLESCENT: Well, they don't act like they think those things about me.

FATHER: Well, sometimes you don't act like you have common sense. So we have to see it first.

THERAPIST: OK. Let's hold off here. We can get back to that discussion later if you'd like. But we're sticking with the three positive things for now. So, Sam it's your turn. Three positive things about your mom or your dad. And look right at them when you say it.

ADOLESCENT: Mom and Dad, you are both very caring.

THERAPIST: OK.

MOTHER: It's tough when you're on the spot, isn't it?

ADOLESCENT: Sort of. Mom, you're a very good cook.

THERAPIST: Very good. One more.

ADOLESCENT: Dad, you're very good about getting stuff done around the house.

THERAPIST: Well, that's certainly a compliment. Mom and Dad, can you repeat back the positive things Sam said about you both?

MOTHER: It was nice. He said we were caring and that I'm a good cook, a very good cook.

FATHER: And he said that I got stuff done around the house. I do. He's right.

THERAPIST: And how does it feel to hear Sam say these things about you?

MOTHER: Like he cares, and he notices some of the things we do for him. It feels good.

THERAPIST: Dad?

FATHER: It feels real good to hear it.

Since the main point of the Three Positive Statements exercise is to set a positive stage for the remainder of the session, it is important for the therapist to prevent the discussion from deteriorating into a series of arguments and accusations. Furthermore, the therapist should make sure that family members are actually listening to each other during the exercise and are offering their own feelings in response.

RELATIONSHIP HAPPINESS SCALE

THERAPIST: Nice job, everybody. Let's move on now to the Relationship Happiness Scale (see Figures 3.7 and 3.8, Relationship Happiness Scales). Here. I'll give you each a copy. Sam, do you want to start off with the instructions? You've done a slightly different version of this before. But I'll let your parents know what is different with this version in a minute.

ADOLESCENT: See these numbers from 1 to 10 here on this chart? You're supposed to circle how you feel right now in each of these areas. And see how it goes from "completely unhappy" on one end to "completely happy" on the other end. Is that right?

THERAPIST: Excellent job. Now here's the part that's different. Instead of indicating how happy you are with *yourself* in each area, you'll be saying how happy you are with somebody else in the family. Mom and Dad, you'll be saying how happy you are with Sam in these areas on the sheet. Work together on it and try to come up with a rating that you both think fits. Sam, you'll be marking off how happy you are with your mom and dad. Try to do just one rating for your parents. If they are really different in a category here and there, though, you can rate them separately and write it in to clarify. What do you think of that?

ADOLESCENT: And it's OK to be honest?

THERAPIST: Absolutely. Of course, we should agree before starting that anything that comes up in this session is not going to be used against anybody. Otherwise, it won't be safe, and people will feel like they can't talk, right?

FATHER: Agreed.

THERAPIST: Good. And when you fill this out, try to rate each category independently. Don't let your feelings about one category influence how you rate another. I know that's hard sometimes, but do the best you can. And just so you know, when you're done, we can take a look at the ratings and decide what areas you all want to work on.

MOTHER: Getting us all to agree on something isn't going to be easy.

THERAPIST: But that's OK, because you can pick different areas to work on. You don't have to agree. So here you are. This should only take a few minutes. Rate how you feel *today*. Let me know if you have questions. [*Five minutes pass.*] Let's see what you've got here. Mom and Dad, looks like you gave some nice high ratings for your relationship with Sam in several areas, like "time spent with adolescent" and "affection." You rated those each an "8." Can you tell us how you arrived at those ratings?

MOTHER: Sam has always been an affectionate child. And when he's in a good mood he can be a lot of fun.

THERAPIST: Sam, how do you feel about hearing these positive things from your parents?

ADOLESCENT: Good. I like when they tell me I'm fun to hang out with.

THERAPIST: Looks like they mean it. What kind of things do you all do together that's fun?

FATHER: Sometimes we go fishing together. And we all like going to the movies. And eating out.

MOTHER: I still wish we'd do it more, though.

THERAPIST: Right. So a rating of "8" seems pretty accurate, because it allows a little room for improvement. Sam, let's see what areas you rated high for your parents. Your highest was a "7" for "emotional support." Can you tell me a little about that? Why did that get your highest rating?

ADOLESCENT: Because if I need something, they're there. Like when I got into trouble. They were mad, but they tried to help.

THERAPIST: Mom and Dad, what do you make of that?

MOTHER: I like hearing it. And I think he's right.

FATHER: We do try, but sometimes he makes it hard.

ADOLESCENT: Well, sometimes it isn't easy talking to you guys about some problems.

THERAPIST: It's important for us to steer clear of blaming each other for problems. Instead, let's put it on the list of problems we can address. OK, back to the Relationship Happiness Scale. Let's take a look now at a few categories that you each rated a little lower, like somewhere in the middle of the scale. And these are often the best categories to start working on, so be thinking about which one you might like to ask the other person for a change in. Mom and Dad, you rated communication a "5." Can you tell me about why you rated it that way?

MOTHER: Because we *do* talk, but lots of times we're either yelling at Sam or he's yelling at us.

FATHER: Yes, there's lots of room for improvement there—for all of us.

THERAPIST: I like how you're using good positive communication skills as you talk about it. I know we only went over it quickly in an earlier session, but do you remember the three positive parts of a good communication? One of them was to "accept partial responsibility." And I think you've done that when you say that *everybody* in the family could benefit from some communication skills training. Good for you, Dad!

Father: Look at that—I'm a pro!

Therapist: Well, let's say you're in the "advanced class." Next stop is the pros. You also rated "job or school" somewhere in the middle of the scale, a "4." Can you tell me how you settled on that rating?

Father: He's late for school all the time because he won't get up in the morning. We make ourselves nuts trying to get him out of bed. I'm really sick and tired of the battle each morning.

Adolescent: I can't help it! I'm tired.

Father: Well, you wouldn't be so tired if you went to bed at a decent hour.

Therapist: This sounds like an excellent category to make a request in. Can we mark that one for yours, Mom and Dad?

Father: I'd like to.

Mother: Yes, it would be a good one. We've tried everything.

Therapist: Good. And I think we'll be able to practice our communication skills as we work on it, so you'll get that category partially addressed as well. We might even get to practice problem solving with it, too. OK. Sam, it's your turn. In looking at your Relationship Happiness Scale, I see that you rated "allowance" a "5." Can you explain why you rated it a "5"?

Adolescent: Because I don't get enough money. I do a lot of chores and don't get paid much. Most of my friends get more.

Mother: But some of them get less, too.

Adolescent: Who?

Mother: Well, I talked to Ben's mom, and I know . . .

Adolescent: But they're giving him more now, and besides . . .

Therapist: Let's just hold off on this discussion for a minute, OK? Sam, do you want to select the "allowance" category, then? This would mean that you get to make a request in it this week. It doesn't mean that your parents have to agree, but we'll at least try some negotiation on it. What do you think?

Adolescent: Yeah. I pick "allowance."

Therapist: Good. The next thing we'll do then is use our positive communication skills to make requests of each other in these categories.

The therapist started the review of the Relationship Happiness Scale by highlighting several of the categories that received high ratings. This was done to foster a positive tone in the session, to remind the family members that there were aspects of each other that they truly liked and appreciated. The therapist then helped the family select reasonable categories on which to work.

COMMUNICATION SKILLS

THERAPIST: We've already talked today about one of the components of positive communication, accepting partial responsibility. Does anyone remember the other two?

ADOLESCENT: An understanding statement and an offer to help.

THERAPIST: Perfect! Good for you, Sam. All we have to do now is put these into practice. Not so easy sometimes, though. So before we try to put them all together into a real conversation, let's try to come up with some examples of each of these components. Mom and Dad, let's start with your request for Sam. You said he's late for school because he gets up late in the morning. Tell me what you'd ideally like to see. Remember, you can ask for anything you want, but then I imagine we'll probably negotiate. And it's always best to make your request in a way that's brief, specific, and said in a positive way, which means that you ask for what you'd *like* to see happen.

MOTHER: I'd like to have Sam get up after I've asked him once.

ADOLESCENT: But what if I don't hear you because I'm asleep?

THERAPIST: Thanks, Sam, for identifying an obstacle. That's always important to do. But let's just let your parents work on asking for what they want in a real positive way. We can sort out the problems later.

MOTHER: Yeah, like the problem of him having to rush out the door without any breakfast.

FATHER: And whose fault is it if he doesn't have time for breakfast?

ADOLESCENT: I'm not hungry in the morning anyway!

THERAPIST: OK. Let's remember that we're going to try to use only positive communication today. I know that it's easy to fall back into old habits. Hey—look at the kind of statement I just used. Did anybody catch it?

ADOLESCENT: Which statement?

THERAPIST: When I said that I knew it was easy to fall back into old communication habits.

ADOLESCENT: That's easy. It's an understanding statement.

THERAPIST: You sure know your stuff, Sam!

FATHER: How come we never hear that kind of stuff at home?

THERAPIST: Well, as I said before, this different way of communicating takes a lot of practice. And that's part of what we're here to work on today. So Mom, how about we take your basic request for Sam to get out of bed after you've only called him once, and we add an understanding statement to it. First of all, what's something you could show empathy for when it comes to Sam not wanting to get out of bed? Because an understanding statement is a way of showing empathy.

FATHER: We shouldn't have to show empathy. He needs to get up. How's he ever going to make it at basic training someday?

THERAPIST: But I think the real issue right now is that the two of you wanted to work on the problem of Sam having trouble getting out of bed in the morning. And we're trying something different; we're going the positive communication route. Now, we might have to do some problem solving around the issue, too, but that can come later.

MOTHER: I can say that I realize it's early and the bed feels really good, but he needs to get up and get going so he's not late.

THERAPIST: Excellent! How about a partial responsibility statement? Can you add that?

MOTHER: Do I have this right? Am I supposed to accept partial responsibility for Sam not getting up?

THERAPIST: Yes. And even though you may not feel particularly responsible, a partial responsibility statement sure helps to get the other person to listen.

MOTHER: I could take responsibility for not sending him to bed earlier, and he could then take responsibility for not going to bed. How about that?

FATHER: Why don't we do this? Why don't we decide right here and now what time is the proper time to get out of the bed in the morning?

THERAPIST: I think it probably *is* a good idea to negotiate that. But let's hold off on that for a few minutes and just stick with our communication practice, if that's OK. Mom, the last piece is an offer to help. What do you think?

MOTHER: I could offer to set an earlier bedtime for him, but I'm not sure he'd like it.

ADOLESCENT: You're right. I wouldn't.

THERAPIST: An offer to help is usually best when it really feels like something helpful to the other person. So you're wise, Mom, to see that Sam wouldn't experience an earlier bedtime as something welcome. Got anything else?

MOTHER: I could offer to remind him to set his alarm. He forgets to do that a lot.

THERAPIST: Good. Let's go with that for now.

FATHER (*teasing*): I could offer to say, "Sam, get up. Your legs work fine."

THERAPIST: You certainly could, but again, we're trying to improve the situation, so I'm not sure . . .

FATHER: I know. I'm just kidding around.

THERAPIST: Fair enough. Mom, can you put it all together and make your request? And make the request directly to Sam. Don't answer yet, Sam. We have to work on *your* end of the positive communication next.

MOTHER: Sam, I know you don't want to get up in the morning, especially when it's cold out and the bed feels really good. And I probably should have done something to help you get into the habit of going to bed earlier. Your sister used to stay up late, too, and she had trouble getting up on time. How about if I remind you to set your alarm each night?

THERAPIST: Wow! You are *good* at this! You actually used all three components of positive communication. I loved the part about Sam's sister. A great start! All right. Sam, it's your turn. An understanding statement.

ADOLESCENT: Same topic?

THERAPIST: Yes. About getting up.

ADOLESCENT: Look, Mom and Dad, I understand you want me to get up out of bed on time, but 6:00 is too early. I've got a whole hour and 30 minutes to get up and get ready. Once I'm up, I'm ready.

THERAPIST: All right, Sam, what about partial responsibility? What can you say to show that you're accepting responsibility for the problem?

ADOLESCENT: I don't know. I should go to bed a little bit earlier so I can get up.

THERAPIST: Excellent. You're accepting responsibility for it, right? OK. The offer to help is just that: offer to help solve the problem. What's that going to be?

ADOLESCENT: I will try.

MOTHER: No, no, no, no. I *will*.

THERAPIST: Don't worry, Mom. We will negotiate the details in a minute. We're just getting started.

ADOLESCENT: I will try to get to bed earlier every night. I'm not saying it will work, but I'll try.

THERAPIST: Excellent. Very good. Can you put it all together and use all three components?

ADOLESCENT: Mom and Dad, I know it bugs you when I don't get up on time in the morning, and maybe I should go to bed earlier. I'll try harder.

FATHER: That doesn't sound very convincing. It sounds like what we've heard before.

THERAPIST: Interesting. Did all of it sound the same? Let's try this again, but this time, Mom, you start it off, and Sam, you respond. Go ahead and say it the way you both just practiced.

MOTHER: Sam, I'd really appreciate it if you'd get up after I've only called you once. I know it's hard to get out of that warm bed, but I hate to see you late for school. I know your sister had the same problem. I probably should have gotten the two of you into the habit of going to bed earlier. How about if I remind you to set your alarm each night?

ADOLESCENT: Mom, I understand that you get bugged when I don't get up right away. And I know that you worry about me being late for school. I'll try harder to go to bed earlier. The alarm should help. Wait—is that all? I can't remember the rest.

THERAPIST: Don't worry about it. Let's take a minute to discuss what it feels like to have somebody talk to you this way. Sam, what was it like to have your mom talk to you like this?

ADOLESCENT: It made me want to try to get up on time.

THERAPIST: That's what I'd guess. And Mom, what was it like to have Sam respond to you like he did?

MOTHER: I liked it. It felt like he respected me and that he was really going to try harder.

THERAPIST: I want to commend both of you. You're both really good at this. And don't worry if you don't include all three components. Lots of times it helps to just add one or two of these statements.

FATHER: But is anything going to change?

THERAPIST: That's the key question, isn't it? We've got two people who are listening to each other, which is half the battle, but what has to happen next? Let's start the negotiation, but still use positive communication. What are you all in agreement about so far?

FATHER: Looks like everybody agrees Sam should get up after just being called once. Right, Sam?

ADOLESCENT: Yeah, I'm cool with that.

THERAPIST: And your mom offered to remind you about setting your alarm. How's that?

ADOLESCENT: That's good, too.

THERAPIST: Your mom also accepted responsibility for not setting an earlier bedtime. How about we have the two of you discuss that?

MOTHER: Sam, instead of having a 10:00 bedtime, how about we make it 9:00? I know it would be hard to adjust to it at first, but maybe we could cut it back gradually, like make it 9:30 for the first week.

THERAPIST: Look at you getting fancy with your communication skills! Both an understanding statement and an offer to help! Sam?

ADOLESCENT: I really don't want an earlier bedtime. I mean, I *understand* that you think an earlier bedtime would help me get up earlier, but I'd like to try something else instead.

MOTHER: Like what?

ADOLESCENT: I don't know. But I don't want an earlier bedtime.

THERAPIST: This might be the perfect time for us to practice our problem solving exercise then. You've all done a great job making the request, and responding, but we're still left with a problem. Maybe the reminder to set the alarm will make all the difference, but we could go ahead and come up with another solution as well. What do you think?

ADOLESCENT: Sounds good to me.

MOTHER: Sure.

If the session had been running late, the therapist probably would have simply continued the negotiation process instead of completing the problem-solving exercise. Problem solving could have been saved for the second Caregiver–Adolescent session in that case. Regarding the communication skills training, since both of the caregivers were present at the session, the therapist normally would have made sure that each of them had an opportunity to practice.

PROBLEM SOLVING

THERAPIST: I know we've all done problem solving before, so let's just go right into it. What's the first step?

ADOLESCENT: You've got to say what the problem is.

THERAPIST: Exactly. That's really important. So, what is the problem we're talking about? Let's be very specific, because then we'll be able to come up with more helpful ideas during brainstorming.

FATHER: The problem is that Sam doesn't get up when he's called in the morning.

THERAPIST: Good. Anybody care to modify that slightly, given what we've already agreed upon as part of our communication skills work?

MOTHER: I'd say that the problem is that Sam needs to get up after being called just once.

FATHER: Well, we already agreed on the alarm reminder, too.

THERAPIST: We could go either way with that one. In some ways, that sounds like more of the solution, though. How about we list that as one of the brainstorming ideas that we pick? Maybe we'll end up changing it a little bit in the process as we discuss the problem more. And speaking of brainstorming . . .

Assume that the problem-solving exercise continues based on the A-CRA problem-solving procedure. When problem solving is conducted during the Caregiver–Adolescent session, the procedure is modified slightly to accommodate the additional participants. All family members (and sometimes the therapist) offer potential solutions for the brainstorming step. Since typically all of the family members are invested in the problem, they all must agree on the preferred solution. Thus, each individual participates fully in the remaining steps of problem solving. The selected solution, which often involves some type of action from each family member, becomes the assignment.

The therapist would next return to the Relationship Happiness Scale so that the adolescent could have his turn making a specific request. Sam had chosen "allowance" as the category in which he wanted to see some change. His request would be shaped so that it ultimately was brief, specific, and positive. For example, assume that Sam started off saying simply that he needed "more money." The next iteration could be a request for a $5 per week raise in his allowance. The therapist would remind Sam to use his positive communication skills in making his request. With assistance and practice, the final request might be: "Mom and Dad, I understand that you don't think I do much around the house (*understanding statement*), and maybe I don't right now (*partial responsibility*), but I am willing to do more. So if I start doing extra chores, like cleaning out the shed (*offer to help*), can I get another $5 each week in my allowance?" The parents would then negotiate with Sam. For instance, they might only agree to the increase in pay if a specific additional chore is identified and completed each day. Alternatively, they might only agree to a $3 raise. The therapist would remind each family member to use positive communication skills throughout.

DAILY REMINDER TO BE NICE

THERAPIST: You guys are doing a terrific job today. Unbelievable!

FATHER: That's because we're all working together like a team. That's how it should always be.

THERAPIST: And hopefully it *will* happen more often, since you can now use both your problem-solving and communication skills. We have one thing yet to do today. I mentioned it earlier. It's called the Daily Reminder to Be Nice. I think you folks are ready for this type of exercise. I'll explain it now and we'll practice a little, but it's something you'll also do as an assignment, if you think it makes sense for you all.

MOTHER: We need all the help we can get, so I'm sure it will make sense.

THERAPIST: Good. Basically, we use the Daily Reminder to Be Nice. Look at this handout (see Figure 3.9) as a way to make sure there are some positive interactions going on in the home every day . . . even when people might not feel like being particularly nice to each other. It's a way to "jump-start" the pleasant interactions. Although they might feel a little artificial at first, over time they feel very natural. And when one person is saying and doing nice things, it's contagious! The rest of the family tends to automatically join in.

FATHER: What kinds of things are you talking about? We're all so busy . . .

THERAPIST: Good question. They're little things: inexpensive and not very time-consuming. Let's go over a few examples. Take a look at the form. Sam, can you read the first item?

ADOLESCENT: "Did you express appreciation to the other person today?" Appreciation for what?

THERAPIST: That's the beauty of it. It can be appreciation for anything. Take a moment to think. What's some little thing you can express appreciation to either your mom or dad for?

ADOLESCENT: Mom and Dad, I appreciate you coming to my session today.

MOTHER: You're welcome, honey.

THERAPIST: Dad, how did that sound to you?

FATHER: It sounded good. But if we *have* to do these, how do I know whether he's just saying these things because he's supposed to?

THERAPIST: Actually, it might start off that Sam is just saying these things because he's supposed to, but eventually they naturally become sincere because the atmosphere in your home will be getting better. And as all of you start to get along better, you'll all feel like saying and doing nice things for the rest of the family.

FATHER: I guess so.

THERAPIST: Well, also remember that you each get to choose which of these items you want to do each day and *how* you want to satisfy it. So, I would guess that there will be underlying truth to what you

Date _____ Session # _____ Therapist Init. _____

Name: _____ Adolescent ID _____ Week Starting: _____

Activity	Day						
	Sun	Mon	Tue	Wed	Thu	Fri	Sat
Did you express appreciation to the other person today?							
Did you compliment the other person on something?							
Did you give the other person a pleasant surprise?							
Did you express affection?							
Did you initiate pleasant conversation?							
Did you offer to help?							

Figure 3.9 A-CRA Daily Reminder to Be Nice

From *Clinical Guide to Alcohol Treatment: The Community Reinforcement Approach* (pp. 179), by R.J. Meyers & J.E. Smith (1995), New York: Guilford Press. Adapted with permission.

choose to say. Anyway, is it worth a try? You can always drop it if it doesn't seem to help.

MOTHER: I definitely think it's worth a try.

FATHER: Yeah, you're right.

THERAPIST: Sam?

ADOLESCENT: Sure. How many are we supposed to do each day?

THERAPIST: Good question. Just one. You *can* do more than one if you want to, but one is enough. And Sam, technically you only have to do one of these things for *one* of your parents each day, but if you're up for a challenge you could try to do one for *each* of your parents each day. What do you think?

ADOLESCENT: I think it depends on how hard they are to do. And if I remember.

THERAPIST: Good points. Forgetting to do stuff can always be an obstacle for any kind of assignment, can't it? Let's get to that in a minute. Anyway, you just did the first item. You expressed appreciation to both of your parents for coming today. How would you rate how hard that was to do?

ADOLESCENT: It was pretty easy.

THERAPIST: Glad to hear that. Let me ask your parents to try that one out before we continue. Hopefully, we'll address your concerns as we go along. Mom and Dad, can you express appreciation to Sam for something?

MOTHER: Sam, I appreciate the fact that you are coming to therapy every week, even though you didn't want to at first.

ADOLESCENT: Sure, Mom.

THERAPIST: How did that feel, Sam? Can you tell your mom?

ADOLESCENT: It was nice, Mom.

THERAPIST: Good job. Dad?

FATHER: Sam, I appreciate that you're being more honest with us.

ADOLESCENT: Thanks, Dad.

THERAPIST: Excellent. Let's skip down to the third one: "Did you give the other person a pleasant surprise?" What do you think about that one? Who wants to go first? Just tell us what you could do for that.

ADOLESCENT: I could clean up my room without my mom getting after me for it.

MOTHER: That would be a great surprise!

ADOLESCENT: But now I can't do it because it wouldn't be a surprise (*teasing*).

MOTHER: You can still surprise me because I won't know which day you're going to do it.

THERAPIST: Good for you, Mom. An excellent idea, Sam. Who's next for the surprise?

FATHER: And you said we don't have to do each of these every day, right? So maybe I'd be doing the surprise once a week?

THERAPIST: That would be perfectly fine. Actually, you wouldn't *ever* have to pick the surprise one if you didn't want to. You could do just the others. But I'd really encourage you to try them all out. Mix it up a bit, you know?

FATHER: No, that's fine. I was just thinking that I could take everyone out to a movie some night for my surprise, but I didn't want to be expected to do something like that all the time.

THERAPIST: That's totally reasonable to only do a surprise of that size now and then. But who knows? I'm hoping that eventually your family will want to do activities like the movies together on a regular basis. But that's down the road a ways. Sam, what would that be like if your dad took you and your mom to a movie for a surprise?

ADOLESCENT: That would be fun. Oh wait—would I get to pick the movie?

FATHER: We'd all get some say in it. We'd discuss it using our communication skills (*teasing*).

MOTHER: Or we'd problem solve how to pick one (*teasing*).

THERAPIST: You guys are too much! I've created a monster! Mom, what about your surprise?

MOTHER: I could make their favorite dessert, gator pie.

ADOLESCENT: That's a great surprise!

FATHER: I second that.

THERAPIST: It's settled then. OK. You all get the idea. And I should also mention that it's important to go ahead and do one of these items each day, even if you're not sure whether the rest of the family is doing them. You might just have missed what they did. And then the whole thing will fall apart if everyone waits for the other person to do something. Agreed?

FATHER: Agreed.

THERAPIST: Good. Sam raised an important issue earlier when he said that he might forget to do this. So, what's a good way to address this potential obstacle?

MOTHER: We could use a magnet and put it on the refrigerator.

ADOLESCENT: We could buy a small bulletin board and hang it on it. My friends have those in their kitchens.

FATHER: I could make us a small bulletin board so we don't have to buy one.

> **THERAPIST:** Now that's what I call teamwork again!
>
> The session would end with the therapist asking the family to state what the assignments are for the week. The next caregiver–adolescent session would be scheduled as well.

Increasing Prosocial Recreation   Since one of the proposed changes that underlies A-CRA effectiveness is an increase in prosocial activities, this procedure is an important one and might be used often during A-CRA and accompanied with homework assignments. It begins with a discussion about why it is important for the adolescent to have a satisfying social life: what role that would play in his or her life. Next, the therapist can choose from various tools to help identify a reasonable activity to try before the next session. These tools include one that has already been described, the Functional Analysis for Prosocial Behavior, but can also include problem solving, completing leisure checklists, or helping the adolescent complete a two-by-two chart of activities that can be done with/without money, or with/without other people. The final step in the procedure is to help the adolescent develop a specific plan to sample the new enjoyable activity. The therapist reviews with the adolescent how the plan was implemented and how well he or she liked the activity in the next session. If the adolescent did not follow through with the activity, the therapist would help the adolescent discuss barriers, problem-solve how to address them, and make a new plan.

Systematic Encouragement   Often individuals are too intimidated to attempt working on a goal that might be a multistep process and might lack the skills needed to figure out all the steps required. Systematic Encouragement involves leaving nothing to chance, making sure the first step in this multistep process occurs during the session. It then provides support for the adolescent to complete the remaining steps. For example, an adolescent may decide that he wants to lift weights at a local YMCA, but does not know anything about what is available, what it costs, or what time the facility is open. During a session, the therapist can help him identify appropriate questions, role-play a call to the local YMCA, and then actually have him make the call and gather the information while in the therapy session. Homework would be related to the goal and might include a visit to the facility, which would be planned at some time prior to the next session. Additional steps would be addressed in a similar fashion until the adolescent reached his goal of lifting weights on a regular basis.

Drink/Drug Refusal Skills Many substance abuse treatment approaches include teaching drug refusal skills because it is so common for adolescents to be approached by friends with whom they have used substances in the past. The components of A-CRA refusal training are: (a) enlisting social support; that is, helping the adolescent identify people who would support the adolescent's abstinence; (b) reviewing high-risk situations; and (c) reviewing options for assertive refusal, including saying "No, thanks" assertively, demonstrating assertiveness through body language, suggesting alternatives, changing the subject, directly addressing the aggressor, or leaving the situation. After reviewing the approaches, the therapist and adolescent practice them in brief role-plays with the therapist providing reinforcement where appropriate and specific feedback.

Problem Solving The A-CRA problem-solving procedure is frequently used during sessions as adolescents talk about the challenges that they are encountering in their daily lives. It includes a review of six different steps including defining the problem, brainstorming, eliminating undesired suggestions, selecting a potential solution for trying in the next week, generating possible obstacles, addressing the obstacles, and deciding on a related task for the following week. After reviewing the specific components of the procedure, the therapist helps the adolescent work through them with a specific problem in his or her life. For a more detailed exposition on problem solving, see Chapter 2.

Relapse Prevention Relapse prevention is another skill that is frequently taught in substance abuse treatment programs, and the therapist can use several different A-CRA procedures for this purpose. In the event that a relapse has occurred between treatment sessions, the therapist can use a relapse version of the Functional Analysis of Substance Use. This allows the adolescent to examine the internal and external triggers that preceded the substance use and the positive and negative consequences that followed the substance use. Another procedure that can be used is the construction of a behavioral chain of events or triggers that led up to use. The behavioral chain is usually diagrammed by going backwards from the point of relapse. It lists each small event/decision that preceded the relapse, ending with the first behavior of the day that ultimately played a role in the relapse. The therapist helps the adolescent decide where in the chain he or she could have made another response that would have changed the outcome. The chain of events can be illustrated on paper or on a white board, with arrows linking each action that led up to the substance use. A final relapse prevention procedure entails setting up an early warning system. Basically, an individual who would support the adolescent's abstinence would be identified and invited to attend a session. This monitor would help the adolescent set up an early warning system plan such that specific steps would be agreed upon should the adolescent find him- or herself in a high-risk situation again. Typically, the monitor plays a role in this plan (e.g., could agree to call the adolescent's therapist or sponsor).

Job-Seeking Skills It is very common for adolescents who participate in treatment to want a job so that they can get more (or any) spending money. If finding a job is an obvious reinforcer for an adolescent, then the therapist will want to help the adolescent learn the skills that will help with successful job finding. The A-CRA components of this procedure include providing an overview of what is involved in job finding, helping the adolescents generate lists of job categories that interest them, developing a list of possible job leads or places to apply, rehearsing how to make phone calls to potential employers, and actually making those phone calls during sessions. The therapist helps the adolescent learn to complete applications and rehearse for job interviews; the therapist also discusses how to maintain a job after one is found. It is important to remember that once adolescents find jobs, they have more disposable income and have co-workers who may invite them to use alcohol or other drugs, so it is also important that these topics be discussed with the adolescent. If there are potential triggers for substance use in the work place, the therapist can use relapse prevention procedures with the adolescent.

Anger Management Many of the adolescents who have alcohol or substance abuse problems also have difficulty managing their anger, which has exacerbated problems in other areas of their life either at school, home, or in other settings. By assisting the adolescent learn how to better manage his or her anger, the therapist is helping with an important skill that can help reduce stress and potential triggers for alcohol and substance use. Within the A-CRA approach, the steps for anger management include (a) identifying reinforcers to manage anger by helping adolescents articulate how their lives will be better if they control their anger; (b) helping the adolescent learn to recognize high-risk situations for anger and early warning signs; and (c) teaching the adolescent strategies (like how to "cool down" or "empathy") to use in situations when anger occurs. Some therapists like to complete a Functional Analysis based on a typical situation in which an adolescent gets angry to help the adolescent understand triggers and consequences for this behavior.

Alcohol and Drug Testing During the CYT studies, monthly random urine tests were a part of the A-CRA intervention that was tested. Most adolescent substance abuse treatment programs in the country use some type of drug testing, so this aspect of a comprehensive treatment approach is important to consider. When we conduct trainings with programs around the country, we have a discussion about drug testing and how this tool is used in local programs. There has been a trend in adolescent substance abuse treatment to become closely aligned with juvenile justice programs, a major referral source. Drug tests are often conducted by the treatment agency and shared with juvenile justice, and this information can be used by the courts to sanction adolescents for continued use. We think that it is preferable if court officers conduct the drug tests and use the information from them for their own purposes, while therapists use drug test results in a therapeutic manner. Others, particularly researchers, have used drug testing to provide opportunities for rewards for clean tests, and there is some data to support this approach. However, our current read of research does not provide definitive evidence whether more drug testing or a particular way of handling drug testing is more effective, although we do think this is an important question for future research. It is important that programs and individual therapists carefully consider how drug test information will be used in their setting and how it will be shared with those who might make decisions that impact an adolescent's life. At a minimum, in a program using the A-CRA model, we generally recommend some level of drug testing and that this information is used within an A-CRA framework. That is, adolescents should receive verbal reinforcement when these tests suggest that they are abstinent. If the tests indicate substance use has occurred, this information is discussed in a nonconfrontational manner and viewed as an opportunity for appropriate A-CRA procedures like relapse prevention or problem solving.

A-CRA IN DIFFERENT SETTINGS AND WITH DIFFERENT POPULATIONS

GROUP DELIVERY OF A-CRA

Although the delivery of A-CRA in a group format has not been studied, the adult version of CRA has been tested in a group format. Smith and colleagues (1998) conducted a trial with homeless alcohol-dependent adults in which all of the skills training components of CRA were offered in groups. Alcohol outcomes up to a year clearly favored the CRA condition when contrasted with the homeless day shelter's standard treatment program (e.g., onsite Alcoholics Anonymous meetings, individual twelve-step counselors).

The cost-effectiveness of therapy is a critical issue for treatment agencies and is certainly one of the main reasons that substance abuse programs offer much of their treatment in a group format. Furthermore, many individuals have great difficulty paying for substance abuse treatment, and consequently the more affordable groups are a welcome option for clients. Still, future studies are needed in order to test the effectiveness of group versions of various empirically supported treatments, including A-CRA. Given the over-all efficacy and cost-effectiveness of both A-CRA (Dennis et al., 2004; Slesnick, Prestopnik, Meyers, & Glassman, 2007) and CRA (Finney & Monahan, 1996; Miller et al., 2004; Miller, Zweben, & Johnson, 2005), it seems to be an excellent choice for further study.

Conceivably, there are advantages to offering A-CRA in a group format aside from the financial benefits to the adolescent and the provider. For example, adolescents often report that they appreciate the support they receive from peers within the context of group treatment because they believe that adolescents can more strongly identify with the issues than can many therapists. Honest feedback from an adolescent's peers also is valued highly, and at times, seems to carry more weight than the same words coming from a therapist. In terms of treatments that offer skills training, such as A-CRA, therapists often report that the role-plays are much more natural (and consequently more useful) when adolescents are playing the other "roles" in the role-play. Furthermore, this "practice arena" affords multiple oppor-tunities for adolescents to model their preliminary attempts at new skills and for group members to become optimistic as they observe other individuals with similar problems improve (Foote & Knapp Manuel, in press).

The specific A-CRA procedures that appear to lend themselves most readily to a group format include: (a) Problem Solving, (b) Communication Skills, (c) Drink/Drug Refusal, (d) Anger Management, and (e) Relapse Prevention. Additional A-CRA procedures have been delivered in groups with some minor modifications. For the most part, the modifications include using a volunteer from the group to demonstrate the technique, then encour-aging the remaining group members to attempt the procedure on their own. If possible, the therapist then spends individual time with each adolescent, ensuring that everyone is following the proper protocol and assisting when necessary. An attempt is made to individualize the resulting homework assignments as well. These modified procedures include: (a) Happiness Scale, (b) Goals of Counseling (treatment plan), (c) Functional Analyses (both Substance Use and Prosocial Behavior), and (d) Job-Seeking Skills.

RESIDENTIAL TREATMENT SETTINGS

In recent years, A-CRA has been adapted for residential treatment settings. In most places in the United States, residential treatment is reserved for those adolescents who have the most severe problems with substance use and who have co-occurring problems. Often, these are adolescents who have not responded well to outpatient treatment. A positive aspect of residential treatment is that it provides the opportunity for adolescents to be in an alcohol- and drug-free setting while they learn new and better coping skills.

However, at some point, adolescents are discharged from residential treatment and return to their natural environment and peer groups where they encounter many triggers for renewing alcohol and drug use.

Residential programs are located both in locked or unlocked facilities. Whatever the setting, an approach that enhances therapeutic engagement is expected to help adolescents make changes in their thought patterns and behavior and increase retention. We know that the nonconfrontational style of A-CRA, which emphasizes an adolescent's reinforcers, helps promote alliance and engagement, so this is one reason it works well in residential settings. A-CRA also appears to work well alongside other interventions that address co-occurring problems, including pharmacological interventions. In this setting, adolescents are constantly interacting with several different adult staff members and peers in close quarters, and they often are attending school at the program site. Thus, they have many opportunities to practice new skills under the guidance of staff who can coach them. These programs are typically staffed with paraprofessional staff members during the evenings and at night who can be trained to help the adolescent with certain skills they are learning in A-CRA. For example, on a daily basis, adolescents would have the opportunity to practice communication and problem solving as they are interacting with their peers and dealing with new situations. Many adolescents need practice with anger management, and ample opportunities to practice these skills present themselves as well. Rather than having situations escalate so that, for example, privileges are taken away as a consequence, it is preferable to help the adolescent practice positive skills. The skill training can be done in groups, which often works well for residential settings. Certain procedures, like sobriety sampling, are especially appropriate prior to an adolescent going on a home visit so that the therapist and adolescent can plan what activities will replace those associated with using substances. Other adaptations that sites have used include using the functional analysis for many other behaviors, and targeting the Functional Analysis of Prosocial Behavior on activities that are available in the residential setting. Some programs have paired contingency management approaches and rewarded appropriate use of skills in the residential setting. After discharge, the Assertive Continuing Care (ACC) approach, which combines A-CRA and case management during home visits, helps the adolescent generalize what has been learned in the residential setting to the natural environment.

CONTINUING CARE

Background   The Community Reinforcement Approach was adapted to serve outpatient adolescents in 1997, for the Cannabis Youth Treatment (CYT) study (Dennis et al., 2004). A few years earlier, S. Godley and her colleagues at

Chestnut Health Systems were studying case management approaches to supporting recovery among adolescents returning home after residential treatment. An exploratory study of Chestnut's case management work as a continuing care intervention demonstrated that case managers could engage adolescents post-discharge, provide support, and help them access needed services (Godley, Godley, Pratt, & Wallace, 1994). However, these case managers asked for additional clinical training to improve the quality of the time they spent with adolescents and their families when they met with them in their home, transported them to a needed service, or provided other services. Because A-CRA is a flexible, procedure-based treatment, Chestnut researchers soon began to realize that it might be useful imbedded in a continuing care case management model. About the same time in 1997, Chestnut Health Systems researchers began studying A-CRA in the CYT trial funded by CSAT and the ACC randomized trial funded by the National Institute on Alcoholism and Alcohol Abuse. The ACC study thus incorporated A-CRA into the now established case management protocol. The research design did not assess the separate effects of A-CRA procedures from case management, but the overall findings showed significantly more abstinence from alcohol and other drugs for the A-CRA plus case management condition (known as ACC) when compared to usual continuing care (Godley, Godley, Dennis, Funk, & Passetti, 2002, 2007). Encouraged by these findings, Chestnut is now studying the ACC combination of A-CRA and case management following outpatient treatment in a randomized trial funded by the National Institute on Drug Abuse (Godley, 2004; RO1 DA018183).

Natural Suitability   As a continuing care intervention, A-CRA follows another intervention, especially residential or intensive outpatient treatment, that often includes multiple components such as individual, group, or twelve-step approaches. While A-CRA is based on operant learning principles or reinforcement, the approach is easily compatible and can build upon progress made in more medical, disease model treatment. The major underlying theory of A-CRA is to increase prosocial activity in order to compete with and replace time spent using drugs. Thus, increasing twelve-step attendance, or participation in religious or secular prosocial activities, is congruent with A-CRA philosophy.

Another feature of A-CRA that makes it ideally suited to follow a primary treatment (as in continuing care) is its flexible approach. Thus, if adolescents discharged from residential treatment have already spent time examining their triggers and consequences sufficiently, therapists would not do a functional analysis of substance use, although they might ask adolescents to educate them about what they learned in the process. The range of A-CRA procedures is sufficiently broad that it is not difficult to stay within the model during the session, and it is possible to draw upon one or more procedures to structure the session. Weekly homework assignments to implement what they learned in session, to sample a new prosocial activity, or to use one or more of the relapse prevention procedures are particularly useful during continuing care.

Continuing Care Adaptations   Because of the natural suitability of A-CRA to serve as a continuing care intervention, there are no specific adaptations to the procedures. Just as in any A-CRA treatment setting (primary or continuing care), it is the therapist's responsibility to weave procedures into the session in accordance with the information the adolescent provides in terms of his or her reinforcers, strengths, and needs. Since A-CRA is added to case management in continuing care to form the ACC model, there are additional procedures tailored to the unique experience of an extended continuing care intervention. These procedures are detailed below.

1. *Linkage to ACC*—Adolescents discharged from a primary treatment episode will not always (a) receive a referral to continuing care; or (b) initiate continuing care services if they do receive a referral. In U.S. treatment programs today, fewer than 50 percent of adolescents complete a primary treatment episode as planned. According to the definition of continuing care offered by the American Society of Addiction Medicine (2001), this does not mean they should be denied additional services, but rather assisted to access and obtain a service that may benefit them. Accordingly, ACC seeks to enlist the consent of the adolescent and his or her parent/guardian early in the primary treatment program. Once this is accomplished, the continuing care therapist can follow up to initiate services regardless of the type of discharge or lack of a referral by the primary treatment provider.

2. *Home/Community Sessions*—Research has also shown that referral recommendations are not usually followed, even by adolescents who successfully complete primary treatment, when the adolescent has to initiate services at a different provider organization. ACC overcomes these problems by asking the therapist to "assertively" initiate continuing care sessions with the adolescent in his or her home, school, or other community setting. By conducting sessions in the community, the ACC therapist overcomes most of the barriers that inevitably occur when trying to retain adolescents in extended treatment (e.g., transportation, motivation). Conducting A-CRA in adolescents' homes can present unique challenges to confidentiality and session continuity, but these can usually be overcome through careful scheduling, changing locations upon arriving at the home, or other methods. Similarly, caregivers often

find it easier to participate in the caregiver and family sessions when these are conducted at the home.

3. *Midweek Telephone Calls*—While not every adolescent has a cell phone or a landline, the majority have access to one. We have found that it is possible to reach adolescents about 60 percent of the weeks they are in continuing care. The purpose of the midweek phone call is twofold. First, it serves to remind adolescents or caregivers of the upcoming appointment to increase the likelihood that the therapist's efforts to see them at home, school, or elsewhere are not in vain. Second, it provides the opportunity to check in with adolescents regarding progress or obstacles encountered in accomplishing their homework between sessions. Thus, the midweek call provides an excellent opportunity to praise work accomplished, relapse triggers avoided, twelve-step meetings attended, or other prosocial activities they engaged in while also helping them work through or solve any barriers they encountered to homework completion. If adolescents have been putting off the homework or forgotten to do it, then the midweek call serves as a friendly reminder.

4. *Case Management Activities*—Most adolescents in treatment are also involved in one or more additional societal institutions like juvenile justice, school, child welfare, or in mental or physical healthcare services. Case management activities are especially important to many adolescents struggling to fulfill requirements of juvenile probation or high school or GED completion. Several of the A-CRA procedures (e.g., communication skills, problem solving, systematic encouragement) have proven helpful in coaching adolescents to better comply with probation or school requirements. The therapist may also provide advocacy, linkage, and transportation assistance to assist adolescents in accessing needed services, complying with court orders, or complying with some other requirement.

Working with Homeless and Runaway Adolescents

Adolescents and young adults who are homeless are difficult to engage in treatment because they rarely have family members or probation officers requiring them to attend. They tend to be distrustful and have a history of negative relationships with adults. Many adolescents run away from home due to negative relationships with a parent or caregiver. All of the individuals (ages 14 to 22) who participated in the homeless study (Slesnick et al., 2007) did so without external pressure. The location for the study was a treatment center that was a safe haven where they could get free meals and snacks, use computers, do laundry, take showers, and simply visit with friends and staff members. Therapists had to be patient during the engagement process, as the study demonstrated that adolescents visited the treatment center for weeks before asking to see a therapist. Once adolescents engaged with the therapist, they often missed many of their scheduled appointments. Thus, project therapists learned to keep open appointments on their schedule so they could see interested individuals as soon as possible. Once a therapeutic alliance was established, it was easier to rely on scheduled appointments.

Procedures that were used frequently with this population were the Happiness Scale and the Functional Analyses. For example, if an adolescent endorsed all low scores on the Happiness Scale, the therapist knew there was an opportunity to work toward gaining the young person's trust and helping to build self-esteem. For example, one young man indicated that he had health problems, specifically, a bad toothache. The therapist put on his "case manager" hat and arranged for the tooth to be repaired by a dentist. The adolescent was extremely grateful and was ready to work with the therapist. Therapists frequently helped identify goals and plans related to survival, food, shelter, and clothing. Many of the adolescents who attended treatment looked forward to completing the Happiness Scale and Goals of Counseling so that they could have help addressing these critical issues. The Functional Analysis usually took two sessions to complete and mainly focused on alternative ways for the adolescents to improve their current situation. For example, one behavior that was a common focus of the Functional Analysis was street fighting. As with any Functional Analysis, the objective was to clarify the conditions that triggered the behavior (street fighting) and the positive and negative consequences associated with it. Then a plan was developed that helped the adolescent reduce involvement in street fights.

Just as with adolescents who live at home, when therapists work with homeless and runaway youth, they seek to discover what prosocial activities are available in the adolescents' natural environment and help them learn to link with these activities. Given that these individuals' social lives revolved around drugs and gangs, it was necessary to spend considerable time working with them to find meaningful and enjoyable replacements whenever possible. The treatment plans that outlined the desired changes were always developed jointly between the adolescent and therapist, and weekly assignments were standard. Given the negative connotation associated with homework, the adolescents tended to prefer the term weekly "experiments." Therapists had to be persistent, as well as supportive and caring, when they worked with the teens to complete these experiments.

The adolescent runaway study was unique because there were no caregivers available to participate in sessions. An adaptation that was made for this population was to establish external social support for the adolescents with other participants in the program, who acted as partners to help with homework assignments (experiments) and other prosocial tasks. This peer support seemed very helpful.

Use with Different Cultural Groups

Due to the CSAT-funded replications at thirty-two sites across the United States, the intervention has been replicated with large numbers of youth from various cultural groups. All A-CRA forms have been translated into Spanish for use with individuals who only speak Spanish or are more comfortable speaking Spanish. (These forms are downloadable from www.chestnut. org/LI/ downloads/forms/A-CRA_Forms_Spanish_0808.pdf). The intervention is also being implemented in various settings, including *"colonia"* along the Texas–Mexico border, urban areas, rural areas, and in all parts of the country. Since A-CRA is an intervention designed around addressing individuals' needs identified through the Happiness Scale and tools like the Functional Analysis, we believe that it is easily adapted to the needs of different cultural groups. There is recognition that an individual adolescent's and parent's culture is important, and there is a committee from the CSAT initiative that is currently working to identify how A-CRA can be even more culturally responsive to different cultural groups.

TRAINING RECOMMENDATIONS

It is clear from existing implementation research that it is challenging for programs or individuals to implement evidence-based interventions with fidelity. Adequate implementation is based on a number of different factors. For example, therapists working within treatment programs need the support of their supervisors and management staff to implement a particular model. Financial resources are needed for initial training, monitoring, and feedback to ensure that therapists are incorporating the new practices in their therapy work. In prior attempts of our group and other groups who have provided training on evidence-based treatment approaches, we have learned that therapists attend two- to three-day training seminars and often are not able to incorporate changes into their therapeutic approach if there is no follow-up monitoring, feedback, and assistance. To address these implementation challenges, a multiple-step process has been developed for training and certifying therapists and supervisors in A-CRA. There are dual certification processes: one for clinical supervisors and one for therapists. We recommend that supervisors attend training and begin the certification either with therapists they supervise or prior to therapists beginning the process. This approach helps shape an environment that supports adoption of the model by the therapist and helps to provide model sustainability.

An individual who wants to learn A-CRA will attend a multiday training to become familiar with the A-CRA procedures and general clinical approach. Prior to attending the training, attendees are asked to read the A-CRA manual and take an A-CRA knowledge test until they are able to achieve a score of 80 percent or better. The multiday training provides an overview of the research supporting the model and A-CRA procedures, includes demonstrations of the procedures, allows an opportunity to role-play different procedures, and provides background information on the Assertive Continuing Care approach. After training, therapists are asked to record therapy sessions with a digital recorder as they begin to implement the procedures they have learned. These recordings are uploaded to a website and expert raters listen to and provide quantitative ratings based on a comprehensive rating manual (Smith, Lundy, & Gianini, 2007). See Garner, Barnes, and Godley's (in press) description of the training process for A-CRA expert raters. Narrative comments that highlight what was done well and what needs improvement are also provided for every session reviewed. Therapists also participate in coaching calls led by model experts with other sites or with other trainees at their site, so that they have an opportunity to ask questions and learn from session reviews of other therapists. Basic A-CRA certification is achieved after a therapist demonstrates competence based on expert ratings across nine specific A-CRA procedures. This process can take between six and nine months, depending on how often the therapist uploads session recordings for review. After certification in the nine procedures, therapists are encouraged to continue the certification process and to demonstrate competence in all A-CRA procedures.

CONCLUSION

A-CRA builds on research from the adult-oriented CRA approach and its adaptation for adolescents has been supported by rigorous randomized clinical trials. Therapists like A-CRA because it is flexible and can be individualized based on each adolescent's strengths, motivators, and environment (Godley, White, et al., 2001). Its nonconfrontational approach helps promote engagement with adolescents who are in a developmental stage marked by the need to assert their independence. A-CRA has a large menu of procedures, which provide the trained A-CRA therapist with a full toolbox, and it is becoming a widely implemented evidence-based practice for adolescents with substance use problems by community-based treatment providers across the United States.

Studies are helping us learn more about A-CRA mechanisms of change, how to increase its effectiveness, and how to implement it with greater fidelity. Our analyses suggest, for example, that exposure to A-CRA procedures is positively related to treatment retention and outcomes (Garner et al.,

2009). We also have learned that greater adherence to continuing care after residential treatment is associated with reductions in environmental risks, and a reduction in these risks is then related to reduced substance use among adolescents nine months after discharge (Garner, Godley, Funk, Dennis, & Godley, 2007). One current study is examining if contingency management paired with A-CRA can help improve outcomes for adolescents who participate in ACC after residential treatment (Godley, 2003; 2R01 AA010368). Additionally, data collected from over 4,000 adolescents during the CSAT-funded A-CRA replications at thirty-two community-based organizations will be analyzed to help identify mechanisms of change by examining which A-CRA procedures adolescents received and how they were related to outcomes. The CSAT initiative is also helping inform how best to train and certify therapists and their supervisors in A-CRA in order to promote sustainability after grant funds end. Additionally, we are blending research funds with the CSAT initiative to support a randomized controlled trial that examines if providing therapists with incentives for how well they implement A-CRA helps improve their implementation of the model and adolescent outcomes (Garner, 2008; R01 AA017625). Finally, an important area for further research is how to successfully integrate best practices for adolescents with multiple problems, since multiple problems are the norm for adolescents entering community-based treatment.

RESOURCES

WEB-BASED RESOURCES

ACC Manual: www.chestnut.org/LI/bookstore/Blurbs/Manuals/K107-Assertive_ Continuing_Care.html

A-CRA/ACC informational website: www.chestnut.org/LI/acra-acc/index.html

A-CRA Manual: www.chestnut.org/LI/bookstore/Blurbs/Manuals/CYT/CYT-v4-ACRA.html

Dr. Robert Meyers website: www.robertjmeyersphd.com

SAMHSA's National Registry of Evidence-Based Programs and Practices (NREPP) website: www.nrepp.samhsa.gov/programfulldetails.asp?PROGRAM_ID=149

For further assistance, readers can also contact ebtxquestions@chestnut.org; Lighthouse Institute, Chestnut Health Systems, 448 Wylie Drive, Normal, IL 61761; phone: (309) 451–7700; fax: (309) 451–7761.

REFERENCES

American Society of Addiction Medicine (ASAM). (2001). *Patient placement criteria for the treatment for substance-related disorders* (2nd ed.). Chevy Chase, MD: Author.

Azrin, N. H. (1976). Improvements in the community reinforcement approach to alcoholism. *Behavior Research and Therapy, 14*, 339–348.

Dennis, M. L., Godley, S. H., Diamond, G., Tims, F. M., Babor, T., Donaldson, J., Liddle, H., Titus, J. C., Kaminer, Y., Webb, C., Hamilton, N., & Funk, R. R. (2004). The Cannabis Youth Treatment (CYT) Study: Main findings from two randomized trials. *Journal of Substance Abuse Treatment, 27*, 197–213.

Finney, J. W., & Monahan, S. C. (1996). The cost-effectiveness of treatment for alcoholism: A second approximation. *Journal of Study of Alcohol, 57*, 229–243.

Fixsen, D. L., Naoom, S. F., Blasé, K. A., Friedman, R. M., & Wallace, F. (2005). *Implementation research: A synthesis of the literature.* Tampa, FL: National Implementation Research Network.

Foote, J., & Knapp Manuel, J. (in press). CRAFT in groups. *Journal of Behavior Analysis in Health, Sports, Fitness, and Medicine.*

Garner, B. R. (2008). *Reinforcing therapist performance study* (NIAAA R01 AA017625). Bloomington, IL: Chestnut Health Systems.

Garner, B. R., Barnes, B, & Godley, S. H. (in press). Monitoring fidelity in the Adolescent Community Reinforcement Approach (A-CRA): The training process for A-CRA Raters. *The Journal of Behavior Analysis in Health, Sports, Fitness, and Medicine.*

Garner, B. R., Godley, M. D., Funk, R. R., Dennis, M. L., & Godley, S. H. (2007). The impact of continuing care adherence on environmental risks, substance use and substance-related problems following adolescent residential treatment. *Psychology of Addictive Behaviors, 21*, 488–497.

Garner, B. R., Godley, S. H., Funk, R. R., Dennis, M. L., Smith, J. E., & Godley, M. D. (2009). Exposure to Adolescent Community Reinforcement Approach (A-CRA) treatment procedures as a mediator of the relationship between adolescent substance abuse treatment retention and outcome. *Journal of Substance Abuse Treatment, 36*, 252–264.

Godley, M. D. (2003). *Effectiveness of assertive continuing care and contingency management with adolescents* (NIAAA 2 R01 AA010368). Bloomington, IL: Chestnut Health Systems.

Godley, M. D., Godley, S. H., Dennis, M. L., Funk, R. R., & Passetti, L. L. (2002). Preliminary outcomes from the assertive continuing care experiment for adolescents discharged from residential treatment. *Journal of Substance Abuse Treatment, 23*, 21–32.

Godley, M. D., Godley, S. H., Dennis, M. L., Funk, R. R., & Passetti, L. L. (2007). The effect of Assertive Continuing Care on continuing care linkage, adherence, and abstinence following residential treatment for adolescents with substance use disorders. *Addiction, 102*, 81–93.

Godley, S. H. (2004). *Adolescent outpatient and continuing care study.* Funded by National Institutes on Diseases of Addiction (NIDA, R01 DA018183). Bloomington, IL: Chestnut Health Systems.

Godley, S. H., Godley, M. D., Pratt, A., & Wallace, J. L. (1994). Case management services for adolescent substance abusers: A program description. *Journal of Substance Abuse Treatment, 11*, 309–317.

Godley, S. H., Meyers, R. J., Smith, J. E., Godley, M. D., Titus, J. C., Karvinen, T., Dent, G., Passetti, L. L., & Kelberg, P. (2001). *The Adolescent Community Reinforcement*

Approach (A-CRA) for adolescent cannabis users (DHHS Publication No. (SMA) 01-3489, Cannabis Youth Treatment (CYT) Manual Series, Volume 4). Rockville, MD: Center for Substance Abuse Treatment, Substance Abuse and Mental Health Services Administration. Retrieved from www.chestnut.org/li/cyt/products/acra_cyt_v4.pdf.

Godley, S. H., White, W. L., Diamond, G., Passetti, L., & Titus, J. (2001). Therapist reactions to manual-guided therapies for the treatment of adolescent marijuana users. *Clinical Psychology: Science and Practice, 8*, 405–417.

Hunt, G. M., & Azrin, N. H. (1973). A community-reinforcement approach to alcoholism. *Behavior Research and Therapy, 11*, 91–104.

Meyers, R. J., & Smith, J. E. (1995). *Clinical guide to alcohol treatment: The Community Reinforcement Approach.* New York: Guilford Press.

Miller, W. R., Yahne, C. E., Moyers, T. B., Martinez, J., & Pittitano, M. (2004). A randomized trial of methods to help clinicians learn motivational interviewing. *Journal of Consulting and Clinical Psychology, 72*, 1050–1062.

Miller, W. R., Zweben, J., & Johnson, W. R. (2005). Evidence-based treatment: Why, what, where, when, and how? *Journal of Substance Abuse Treatment, 29*, 267–276.

Sholomskas, D. E., Syracuse-Stewart, G., Rounsaville, B. J., Ball, S. A., Nuro, K. F., & Carroll, K. M. (2005). We don't train in vain: A dissemination trial of three strategies of training clinicians in cognitive-behavioral therapy. *Journal of Consulting and Clinical Psychology, 73*, 106–115.

Slesnick, N., Prestopnik, J. L., Meyers, R. J., & Glassman, M. (2007). Treatment outcome for street-living, homeless youth. *Addictive Behaviors, 32*, 1237–1251.

Smith, J. E., Lundy, S. L., & Gianini, L. (2007). *Community Reinforcement Approach (CRA) and Adolescent Community Reinforcement Approach (A-CRA) therapist coding manual.* Bloomington, IL: Author and Lighthouse Institute Publications.

Smith, J. E., Meyers, R. J., & Delaney, H. D. (1998). The community reinforcement approach with homeless alcohol-dependent individuals. *Journal of Consulting and Clinical Psychology, 66*, 541–548.

PART 3

FAMILIES

CHAPTER 4

Family Behavior Therapy for Substance Abuse and Associated Problems*

BRAD DONOHUE, DANIEL N. ALLEN, and HOLLY B. LaPOTA

FAMILY BEHAVIOR THERAPY (FBT) as applied to the treatment of substance abuse and dependence is a comprehensive intervention that was initially developed in the early 1990s by Nathan Azrin, Brad Donohue, and their colleagues. In this model, substance use is conceptualized to be a strong inherent positive reinforcer, whereby substance use brings about pleasurable physiological symptoms and support from others. However, it is also negatively reinforcing, as it may be used to relieve aversive feelings, thoughts, and physical pain. Although negative consequences resulting from substance use (e.g., arguments, hangovers) may occur, persons who are addicted to drugs often suppress, distort, or delay the occurrence of these consequences, thus weakening their association. Therefore, FBT is focused on altering the environment and skill set of those affected by drug abuse and dependence to effectively manage drug-associated stimuli, weaken positive associations between drug use and its inherent reinforcers, and reinforce behaviors associated with abstinence.

As immediately apparent in reading the other treatment approaches in this book, substance disorders require multifaceted treatments that have consistently demonstrated positive outcomes in controlled trials, are capable of ameliorating problem behaviors that co-exist with substance disorders, include empirically validated methods of assessing treatment integrity,

*This chapter was supported by a grant from the National Institute on Drug Abuse (1R01DA020548–01A1).

and are readily transportable to community settings. Along these lines, the development of FBT is relatively young, but its course is practically and empirically guided. Indeed, as will be indicated below, its interventions are robust, effective, and exciting to implement. We begin with an overview of FBT to provide a context in which to understand the integration of its components. We then examine the clinical applications of FBT, and present a comprehensive battery of assessment methods that may be selected to assist in treatment planning and evaluation of treatment outcomes. Finally, the treatment components of FBT are emphasized, including rationales for their inclusion. (An examination of the empirical support for FBT can be found in Appendix A.)

OVERVIEW OF FAMILY BEHAVIOR THERAPY

Family Structure

The family structure in FBT sessions usually includes the primary client who has been identified to evidence problems with illicit drugs, and at least one adult significant other from this person's social ecology who cares about this person. Primary clients are adults or adolescents. Adults are usually referred by criminal justice and child welfare systems. Although some adults are self-referred, adolescents are almost exclusively referred by parents, public schools, and juvenile justice systems (i.e., probation, parole, judges). Adult significant others are utilized to assist in supporting clients throughout assessment and treatment. These persons ideally have no current history of problems due to substance use and are in a position to positively influence the addicted individual's behavioral patterns through contingency management (e.g., parents, spouses). They have an extended history living with the addicted individual and are committed to attending treatment sessions, assisting in the treatment plan and therapy assignments, and restricting primary clients from accessing substances. Optimum significant others are often absent or hard to enlist in drug abuse populations for various reasons (e.g., upset with the primary client, poor social skills, distrust therapists, physically/emotionally abusive, frequently move, caustic in their approach to conflict resolution). Therefore, if an ideal significant other is unavailable, efforts are made to recruit the "best" adult significant other available. When adult significant others abuse drugs, they are treated concurrently with the primary client. Significant others may also be children and adolescents. However, their participation is limited to family exercises and skill-building exercises that do not explicitly address substance use. Their treatment is focused on keeping them safe, improving their conduct, and enhancing their relationship with the primary client.

FBT programs usually last six months and include administration of pre-treatment, post-treatment, and sometimes follow-up assessment batteries. Administration may also occur during treatment, such as urinalysis to assess illicit drug use, breathalyzers to assess alcohol use, and self- and significant other-reports of the number of days per respective time period the primary client engaged in behaviors that are relevant to presenting concerns (e.g., substance use, employment, attended school, domestic violence). There are sixteen to twenty-five treatment sessions ranging from 1 to 2 hours. In outpatient settings, one therapist implements FBT. However, when problem behavior is especially severe or children are involved in therapy, it is highly recommended that two therapists implement FBT in the primary client's home. When children are involved in therapy, the entire family is seen together when treatments do not explicitly address drug use. However, during drug-explicit interventions, one therapist assumes primary responsibilities with adults, while another therapist or family member concurrently provides therapy with the children.

Assessment   A large battery of methods may be used to assess problem areas typically targeted in FBT. These methods are implemented to examine the effects of treatment and guide treatment implementation. Most measures are standardized, evidence good psychometric support, require minimal training, and are quick and easy to administer, score, and interpret. When FBT is conducted in community settings, the particular assessment measures that are recommended for administration vary to accommodate the unique aspects of program referrals. However, it is generally recommended to include self- and significant other reports of the primary client's use of substances, urinalysis testing to objectively determine the presence of substance use, a semi-structured interview to obtain diagnostic information, a measure of the family's functioning, relationship satisfaction between the primary client and significant other, satisfaction with factors relevant to treatment, service utilization, and risk of contracting HIV. When the primary client is a parent, additional assessment methods are administered to determine factors that impede effective parenting, the extent of parental stress, and home safety. As might be expected, when primary clients are adolescents, it is particularly important to assess their conduct and life satisfaction with standardized questionnaires.

Treatment   FBT includes more than twenty behavioral interventions capable of addressing a wide array of problem behaviors associated with, and including, substance abuse and dependence. Along these lines, FBT treatment plans often target co-existing mood, anxiety and conduct disorders, as well as poor family relationships, child maltreatment, domestic violence, unemployment, poor academic performance, and HIV prevention. There are foundation treatments that are implemented with all families and secondary treatments that are implemented when indicated. Foundation treatments are implemented in a set order at the beginning of therapy, whereas secondary interventions are initially implemented based on the priority rankings of the family, and subsequently reviewed in the remaining sessions to a progressively lesser extent based on their contemporaneous importance.

Each treatment session is initiated with an agenda listing target interventions and estimated administration times. Family consumers and therapists can modify agendas based on extenuating circumstances. Primary clients then complete a Basic Necessities checklist to assist in identifying potential emergency situations that may soon occur or have already occurred (e.g., no electricity due to unpaid bills, relapse, violence). Attempts are made to ameliorate these concerns utilizing components of our Self-Control intervention. These components include thought stopping, negative rehearsal of consequences, problem-solving steps, and imagining successful implementation of the selected solutions during practice trials. The Self-Control method is also used spontaneously throughout therapy when drug use antecedent "triggers" are identified.

In the first two treatment sessions, a structured Program Orientation is completed, and clients establish Behavioral Goals that are complemented with our Contingency Management system. Goals are primarily focused on the elimination and management of antecedent stimuli (i.e., cues) to substance use, prevention of HIV risk behaviors, and, when primary clients are parents, the acquisition of parenting and home safety skills training. Once established, behavioral goals are reviewed at the start of each treatment session, and significant others are encouraged in providing contingent rewards for completed goals.

Stimulus Control is utilized to teach primary clients to avoid and escape from stimuli that precede substance use and other problem behaviors, and facilitate time with stimuli that are incompatible with substance use and other problem behaviors. When problem behaviors are identified during the Stimulus Control intervention, secondary treatments are implemented (e.g., communication skills training, child management) in their immediate amelioration, and the respective problem behaviors are converted into the Goals Worksheet and targeted in Contingency Management. Thus, FBT is comprehensive and flexible.

Generalization of skill acquisition to the home environment is enhanced in several ways. First, treatment rationales are provided prior to implementing each major intervention for the first time. These rationales help family consumers appreciate how the treatments are conceptualized to be of assistance, and thus peak interest and motivation in attempting to learn the respective interventions. Therapists also model all intervention skills and effectively engage family consumers in rehearsing these skills. Therapists model easy scenarios first and subsequently increase difficulty of the scenarios based on role-play performance of family consumers. Therapists utilize checklists during treatment sessions to assist in maintaining strict adherence to prescribed protocols. These protocol checklists indicate the specific therapeutic operations involved in the implementation of treatments. Although therapists are encouraged to stick to the prescribed protocols, they are encouraged to do nonprescribed procedures between prescribed operations when indicated. The therapies are implemented in the homes of primary clients whenever feasible to adapt intervention plans to better accommodate their social ecology, and therapy assignments facilitate in vivo practice and subsequent review in the natural environment. Thus, FBT is organized to maintain high levels of fidelity while balancing flexibility.

FBT ASSESSMENTS

An important component of FBT is the formal assessment process that occurs prior to initiation of treatment and then after treatment is completed. Information obtained in the initial assessment helps guide the implementation of the FBT interventions. A second assessment conducted after completion of FBT provides information that demonstrates the effectiveness of the treatment. Measures included in the assessments are designed to provide information regarding substance use and other related problems, and selection of measures to include in the assessment may vary substantially based on the unique needs of the client populations and the treatment programs. However, substance use measures are always included as a part of the assessment process given FBT's focus on treatment of substance use disorders.

FBT ASSESSMENT PROCEDURES

In most cases, it is recommended that FBT assessments be conducted in the client's home. Two assessors ideally conduct these home-based assessments. In addition to the client, an adult significant other is queried in the assessment so that collateral information regarding the client's alcohol and drug use can be obtained. Using two assessors has a number of advantages, including increasing efficiency of the assessment, managing issues that might interrupt the assessment procedures, and providing increased safety for the assessors. If two assessors are used, the one who has the most assessment experience serves as the primary assessor and implements the major components of the assessment, starting with obtaining informed consent and then administering the majority of assessment measures. The second assessor is responsible for managing ancillary issues, such as childcare, so that the assessment progresses efficiently. The secondary assessor may also assist by preparing assessment forms for the primary assessor and interacting with significant others when they are not directly involved in the assessment, which helps to prevent the significant other from listening to confidential information the identified client is discussing with the primary assessor. The secondary assessor may also enlist the support of older family members to assist with child management. When possible, the assessment team is composed of a male and female because some assessment procedures (e.g., urine drug screening) necessitate that the assessor is the same gender as the client. Also, participation of young children in the assessment process is limited because they are unable to provide reliable information (although later they will be actively engaged in therapy). Rather, adult and adolescent clients are relied upon as the chief informants, with adult significant others serving as collateral informants.

There are often safety concerns associated with home-based assessments and the safety of the assessors can be enhanced in a number of ways. For example, assessments are typically scheduled prior to dusk. Furthermore, when the assessment is scheduled, clients are asked if there are any dangerous areas that the assessor might travel though on the way to the client's home. Clients are also asked to verify directions to the home and to meet the assessor at the car when the assessor arrives at their home. When leaving the client's home, assessors can call clinic staff to let them know that the assessment is completed and provide an estimated time that they will be arriving back at the clinic. Assessors may also call clinical staff periodically throughout the assessment, to let them know how the assessment is progressing. These calls are made with the client present. In order to protect the completed assessment materials, assessors transport all assessment materials and client information in a locked waterproof carrying case.

Assessment conducted in the home requires that the assessors take special care in being sensitive and adapting to the family's culture (e.g., the therapist may ask if he or she should remove shoes if it is noticed that the family is not wearing them). It is also critical that the assessor review formal guidelines with the family that ensure the assessment can be conducted efficiently and validly. These guidelines may vary but generally include such things as no telephone use or television watching, no alcohol use, and no visitors during the assessment. Evaluation time varies from 2 to 5 hours depending on the number of measures that are selected and structured agendas that are used to guide the administration of assessment measures.

When the assessment begins, a description of FBT is provided to the referred client and the significant other. Questions are answered and if the client is agreeable to participating in FBT, formal written consent to participate is obtained. The consent form includes information regarding potential risks, costs, program duration and session length, and contact information for program staff. It is also explained that participation is voluntary and limits of confidentiality are described. Finally, because audiotapes are used to evaluate therapist compliance with treatment protocols, clients also consent to be audiotaped during treatment sessions. The consent form is read aloud to the client, who is provided a copy of the form and encouraged to silently read along with the examiner. When the client is less than 18 years old, consent is obtained from the legal guardian to allow the minor child to participate in treatment, and an additional informed "assent" is obtained from the minor child. The assent includes all of the aforementioned treatment information contained in the adult consent form. Clients are then given copies of all forms for their records.

During the consent or assessment process, it may become apparent that clients are hesitant to disclose negative information because they fear that disclosure could result in legal consequences such as having a child removed from the home for physical abuse or prosecution for drug-related activities. These fears may cause a failure to report relevant information or the clients to present an unrealistically positive image of themselves and their families. These tendencies can be countered by assuring the clients of the limits of confidentiality at regular intervals during the assessment, drawing a clear distinction between the assessor and referral agencies such as the court or family services, clarifying how the results of the assessments will be used (i.e., to guide treatment and assess outcomes), assuring that the assessors understand extenuating circumstances that might contribute to undesirable behaviors, projecting a nonjudgmental and empathetic style, and reviewing the therapist's response to court subpoenas and the low probability of a subpoena being issued. In some cases, the opposite situation may occur in which clients provided extensive details in response to the assessment questions. This type of response style can negatively impact the assessment process by extending the assessment time beyond what was originally scheduled, thus precluding the completion of all assessment procedures. In these cases, clients are thanked for their openness but are informed that they do not need to provide detailed responses and that the assessor will prompt for more information if it is needed.

Because of the nature of home-based assessments, it is often necessary to accommodate to situations that are not present when assessments are conducted in an office setting. Clients may need to perform ancillary duties such as cooking while being assessed, particularly if the assessment is long. The challenge for the assessor is to continue to administer the assessment measures in a standardized manner while accommodating for these situations. For example, the assessor may allow clients to cook lunch for their children while answering some of the assessment questions. It may also be necessary to simplify difficult vocabulary words or read the assessment questions to the client in order to accommodate lower reading abilities. Finally, the order of the assessment procedures may need to be changed to accommodate the schedule of the adult significant other.

FBT ASSESSMENT DOMAINS AND MEASURES

FBT utilizes a wide variety of measures to assess not only substance abuse, but also problem behaviors that commonly occur in populations that abuse substances. The latter measures are only administered to clients who evidence the particular problem behavior and include procedures to assess family functioning, risk for child maltreatment, mental health diagnosis, HIV and sexually transmitted disease (STD) risk behaviors, as well as the antecedent stimuli that lead to these undesired behaviors. Given that substance use has a high potential to negatively influence effective parenting, when clients have children, measures that assess child management skills, child abuse potential, child conduct, and home safety are routinely administered. Assessment of supplementary services provided by other professional organizations is assessed, as is the client's satisfaction across a number of domains. In the following sections, descriptions of the assessments and their target behaviors are provided.

Background Information   A structured interview (administration time 3 to 5 minutes) is used to collect background information that is directly relevant to FBT. Substance abuse history is of particular importance (e.g., treatment, legal involvement, medical complications), but other relevant areas are also assessed, such as basic demographic information (e.g., gender, age, ethnicity), vocation and educational experience, family demographics and dynamics (e.g., number of children and adults living in the home), medical and mental health history, and details relevant to the presenting substance abuse problem. Other information required by specific referral or funding agencies is also collected. This background information provides the context in which assessment results are interpreted and may assist in determining program needs. For instance, if families with fathers in the home are more likely to complete treatment than families where the father is not living with the family, treatment may need to be adjusted to address the unique needs of single mothers, and engagement strategies may also be implemented to increase session attendance.

Literacy Screen   Because clients with substance use disorders and co-occurring problem behaviors frequently have limited educational experiences and higher rates of learning disabilities, the Wide Range Achievement Test—Reading Comprehension subtest (WRAT-4; Wilkinson & Robertson, 2006; administration time 5 to 10 minutes) is used at the start of the assessment to determine if clients can read and comprehend at a sixth-grade level, because this level is a requirement for completion of many paper and pencil self-report measures. If the client is unable to read at this level, then the assessor reads all of the items to the client in order to ensure that limited reading abilities do not invalidate the results of the tests. Some clients who are able to read at or above the sixth-grade level also prefer to have the questions read to them, so we offer this option to all clients regardless of reading level. Reliability coefficients reported in the WRAT-4 test manual indicate alternate form reliability coefficients ranging from .82 to .90 (immediate) and from .68 to .91 (delayed), with internal consistency reliability coefficients from .87 to .96 (Wilkinson & Robertson, 2006). The WRAT-4 also has acceptable concurrent validity and moderately high convergent validity (Wilkinson & Robertson, 2006).

More extensive assessment of neurocognitive function is not a standard part of FBT assessment, but may be important to consider as neurocognitive deficits can interfere with substance abuse treatment (Allen, Goldstein, & Seaton, 1997; Burgard, Donohue, Azrin, & Teichner, 2000). For instance, deficits in memory may reduce a client's ability to learn and retain treatment relevant information, while deficits in executive function may impede successful application of problem-solving skills and strategies to real-world situations and thus hinder achievement of behavioral goals (e.g., gainful employment). Because substance use is associated with increased risk for neurocognitive deficits, neurocognitive functioning is important to consider in treatment planning for individuals with substance use disorders. When the results of the WRAT-4 suggest the client may have a significant limitation comprehending the evaluation procedures, it is also likely that similar difficulties will interfere with comprehension of information presented in therapy. In these instances, referral for more extensive neuropsychological evaluation may be warranted. Also, if difficulties with comprehension result in frustration, therapists will need to assist the client in understanding the material, provide opportunities for breaks in the assessment, or complete assessment procedures across multiple sessions. WRAT-4 results may also assist in determining if referrals to educational and vocational programs are necessary. When this is the case, involvement in educational or vocational programs can be recorded in Behavioral Goals and rewarded in Contingency Management. Reading may also be scheduled as an enjoyable family activity, or be assigned as a "safe" item during the Stimulus Control intervention (see Stimulus Control section later in this chapter).

Substance Use Assessments   Assessment of substance use involves both self-reports measures that are administered to the client and significant other (as a collateral informant), as well as objective drug testing. The Timeline Follow-Back assessment interview is used to obtain self-reports of the client's substance use (TLFB; Sobell, Sobell, Klajner, Pavan, & Basian, 1986; administration time approximately 15 minutes). The TLFB utilizes month-by-month calendars to assess substance use over the four months immediately preceding the assessment, although shorter time periods (i.e., one or two months) may also be assessed depending on the needs of the program and clientele. (For an example TLFB calendar, see Nova Southeastern University's helpful website at www.nova.edu/gsc/online_files.html. Also note that additional information can be found on most of the instruments reviewed in the following sections through a simple Google search.) In fact, modifying the time period assessed does not negatively impact the psychometric properties of the TLFB with better reliabilities reported for shorter time periods (Donohue, et al., 2004; Donohue, Hill, Azrin, Cross, & Strada, 2007). The TLFB uses memory anchor points such as birthdays, anniversaries, holidays, family events, and paydays to improve the reliability of substance use self-reports. These memory anchor points are marked on the calendars by the assessor after which the client is prompted to indicate on which days alcohol and drug use occurred. The adult significant other also completes the TLFB to provide a collateral report of the client's alcohol and drug use, and these reports are obtained separately from the client (Babor, Cooney, & Lauerman, 1987). Significant others are also taught to indentify signs of drug use (e.g., smell of marijuana, dilation of pupils, unsteady gait) during the FBT Behavioral Goal Setting and Contracting intervention (described below), which enhances accuracy of these collateral reports. Accuracy of self-reports is further enhanced when information regarding drug use available from caseworkers or probation officers is recorded on the TLFB calendars prior to administration with the client, as these events also act as memory anchor points. Self-reports obtained using the TLFB correspond closely to official records and reports of substance use (Ehrman & Robbins, 1984; Sobell et al., 1986; Sobell, Sobell, & VanderSpek, 1979) and its test–retest reliability coefficients range from .93 to .64 from one to six months preceding the day of assessment (Carey, 1997; Sacks, Drake, Williams, Banks, & Herrell, 2003). Furthermore, the TLFB and Addiction Severity Index have excellent agreement (Carey, 1997), and significant correlations are present among youth and caregiver TLFB reports of marijuana, hard drugs, and alcohol use with results of urine screen results (Donohue et al., 2007).

In addition to providing documentation regarding the frequency and types of drugs used, the TLFB results are also used to guide treatment. Accordingly, during the FBT Program Orientation that occurs in the first treatment session, the TLFB results are reviewed with the client, and the client is queried regarding antecedent stimuli that consistently led to substance use indicated on the TLFB calendar. The therapist also points out specific days in the week or time periods associated with increased or decreased frequency of substance use, and the client is asked to indicate environmental influences that contributed to substance use and nonuse. This procedure helps the client gain an understanding of factors that are likely to maintain substance use in the future as well as aid in efforts to decrease substance use. The TLFB may also be used for the ongoing assessment of substance use between treatment sessions, although the calendar and memory anchors are not typically necessary when the time period between sessions is relatively short and the client has intact memory functioning. Finally, the TLFB method may be useful in increasing the accuracy of other self-report information, such as days attending school and work, frequency of domestic violence or child maltreatment, number of days incarcerated or hospitalized, and frequency of HIV risk behaviors.

Because of the sensitive nature of this information, it is not uncommon for clients and significant others to be uncomfortable disclosing alcohol and drug use history. If it appears that significant others are withholding information, they are reminded the information is important for developing a treatment plan that will best meet the needs of the clients and that the clients have provided consent for the significant others to share this information with the assessor. Additionally, during treatment, clients who use multiple substances may disclose marijuana or alcohol use but deny "hard" drug use (e.g., cocaine, opiates). Thus, if contingent rewards will be provided as a part of treatment, it is important to specify if the rewards will be provided for abstinence from all substances or all drugs other than alcohol.

Because there is an inherent bias for clients and at times, significant others, to deny substance use it is important to perform urine testing in addition to self-reports. Urine testing provides objective information regarding substance use (Olmeztoprak, Donohue, & Allen, 2009) and is appealing because samples can be reliably and inexpensively tested onsite using enzyme immunoassay. Positive immunoassay screens can be verified using gas chromatography for alcohol and thin layer chromatography for all other substances, although we do not find this necessary. Substances tested vary from one screen to the next, but screening typically includes marijuana, amphetamines, cocaine, opiates, barbiturates, benzodiazepines, PCP, and methaqualone. Alcohol use can be tested using a portable handheld breathalyzer (Allen & Holman, 2009).

Given the sensitive nature of urine testing, a set of standardized procedures is necessary in order to assure the privacy of the client while at the same time ensuring that the testing is performed in a valid manner. Assessors conducting urine testing should be certified by the toxicology lab providing the drug screen materials, which includes training in the standardized administration of the tests. When in the client's home, the client is initially informed that a urine drug test is required and that the test will be observed by an assessor in order to ensure it is completed correctly. The assessor is the same sex as the client and the client is observed through a partially open bathroom door. Clients are then informed that the test results are used to guide their treatment, when obtained before or during treatment, or to assist in determining the effectiveness of FBT, if obtained after treatment. They are instructed to leave excess clothing such as coats or heavy sweaters outside the bathroom (because bulky clothing is sometimes used to hide bogus urine samples). They are then instructed to wash their hands, fill the cup at least one-third with urine, and refrain from flushing the toilet or washing their hands until the sample is given to the assessor. The assessor marks the specimen cup with the date of the assessment before giving it to the clients, and subsequently checks that the date is correct after receiving it back from the client. The assessor wears latex gloves when handling the urine specimen. A temperature strip attached to the specimen cup allows the assessor to determine if the specimen temperature is within normal limits, and once this is verified, the test pad is dipped into the sample and the results are recorded. When the test has been completed, the urine is poured in the toilet, and all testing supplies are discarded in the trash. Urinalysis results are not disclosed to the client prior to completing the TLFB because of the tendency for some clients to deny drug use if they know that the UA results are negative, or underreport use when they know the specific substances for which the test results were positive.

A number of common problems may occur during urine testing. Often, clients will report that they are unable to urinate. When this occurs, they are informed that the testing must be completed before the end of the session and are instructed to drink juice or water during the remainder of the evaluation, with urinalysis then attempted later in the assessment. Some clients may also attempt to provide false urine samples in an attempt to conceal drug use. In addition to removing bulky clothing, it is also important to watch and listen for things that would permit a false urine sample, such as diluting the sample by dipping the specimen cup into the toilet, opening storage areas or cabinets in order to acquire adulterants, or switching specimen cups. At times, clients with a positive urine test deny drug use on the TLFB. Informing the clients that the urine test results were positive (although not disclosing the exact substances that were positive) and instructing the client and significant others to reexamine their TLFB reports can assist in obtaining more accurate self-reports.

Urinalysis may also be used to track drug use during treatment. When this occurs, a behavioral contract is specified in which each negative or "clean" urine test is reinforced. FBT sessions begin by first obtaining self-report data and then performing the urine testing. Obtaining self-report data first ensures that the client and significant other reports are not biased by the urine testing results, and the knowledge that the urine testing will occur motivates more accurate self-reporting. To assist in the contingency management process, clients and adult significant others are informed of the UA results (positive or negative) although clients are not typically informed about the results for each of the specific drugs. This is because knowledge of the results for specific substances may allow clients to determine the amount or frequency of drugs that may be used without being detected. Sometimes, the urinalysis is negative but the TLFB reports are positive. In these cases, the results of the urinalysis are deemphasized in order to prevent denial of substance use on future testing. When urine test results and TLFB reports are negative, the therapist leads a celebration with the client and significant other and makes sure that the positive consequences outlined in behavioral contracting take place. It is also important to mention that marijuana use is detectable for up to 3 or 4 weeks in some clients, so it is possible that marijuana will be detected in urine testing even though use did not occur since the last testing. If this happens, review of the THC level may help (i.e., if the level is lower than in the previous testing and the client denies substance use, then it may be assumed that use has not occurred). On the other hand, if the progressively lower levels are not demonstrated on repeated testing, it is likely that marijuana use is recurring.

Psychiatric Diagnosis Because of the increased incidence of mental disorders in populations that abuse substances, *DSM-IV-TR* Axis I mental disorders are diagnosed using the Structured Clinical Interview for DSM-IV diagnosis (SCID; First, Spitzer, Gibbon, & Williams, 2002; administration time 45 minutes to 120 minutes). The SCID can be used to establish diagnoses of substance abuse and dependence, as well as diagnose co-existing disorders that will need to be addressed during the course of therapy, such as major depressive disorder. The SCID-IV has good validity and reliability (Spitzer, Williams, Gibbon, & First, 1992), as well as demonstrated utility in outcome studies involving drug abuse treatment (e.g., Azrin et al., 2001) and in clinical settings. While considered by many to be the gold standard diagnostic interview for *DSM-IV-TR* Axis I diagnoses, the SCID can take as much as 2 hours to administer, and the assessor requires extensive training in order to complete it in a valid and reliable manner, which may limit its usefulness in some community settings.

Monitoring Ancillary Services Provided by Other Organizations   From a clinical services provision viewpoint, ongoing monitoring of services provided to clients by other agencies is a critical but often overlooked element in the assessment process, because it assists in demonstrating that FBT reduces costs associated with professional services that are provided outside of FBT. However, monitoring service provision is a complex task due to the wide range of services provided to these clients, unpredictability of the referral system, and differences in the quality and content of services provided by different agencies. Despite these complexities, some assessment methods are available to assist in this process, including methods that code services into distinct categories (e.g., individual psychotherapy, psychiatric medicine) (Chaffin et al., 2004). Service categories can also be quantified using the Local Use of Services Instrument (LUSI; Kolko, Selelyo, & Brown, 1999). These procedures require clients to rate if services were received, and a frequency score is computed. Clients also provide ratings of their satisfaction with services received. It is most effective to combine service information from these measures (Chaffin et al., 2004; Kolko et al., 1999) in order to adequately characterize the diverse needs and services evidence by FBT clients.

Also, since FBT includes a Basic Necessities intervention (see Assurance of Basic Necessities section, later in this chapter), this intervention may be used to assist in monitoring the services received by clients. For example, if clients who receive a high frequency of services as indicated by the assessment, but continue to have difficulty in ensuring that the basic needs are being met (e.g., housing, food, utilities) as indicated by the Basic Necessities intervention, it is apparent that the services are inappropriate, insufficient, or both. The Basic Necessities intervention teaches the client to evaluate positive and negative aspects of current issues, such as services received, and to generate solutions to resolve these issues. Thus, evaluation of existing services not only provides an indication of the effectiveness of FBT, but allows for an examination of the usefulness of current services and decreased duplication of services and permits FBT therapists to help clients develop effective strategies to ensure that their basic needs are met.

Satisfaction Measures   FBT incorporates measures to assess the client's' satisfaction across a number of domains including satisfaction with their own life, their relationship with others, their children, and the FBT intervention itself.

Client Satisfaction with Services.   In order to assess client satisfaction with the services they receive, the Client Satisfaction Questionnaire is used (CSQ-8; Larsen, Attkisson, Hargreaves, & Nguyen, 1979; administration time < 5 minutes). The CSQ-8 is composed of eight items and has been used in outcome studies to assess clients' overall satisfaction with the treatment methods and process (see Fals-Stewart, O'Farrell, & Birchler, 2001), and is designed to be administered following completion of treatment. Internal consistency estimates for the CSQ range from .87 to .93, and CSQ-8 satisfaction ratings correlate significantly with treatment outcomes and session attendance (Attkisson & Zwick, 1982). The CSQ-8 may be used at the end of the assessment in order to judge the client's satisfaction with the assessment process, but is more typically used at the end of treatment to provide feedback to the FBT therapists. In addition, clients are asked to rate their satisfaction with each FBT intervention on a 7-point Likert-type scale (1 = extremely unhelpful, 7 = unhelpful). Low helpfulness ratings are queried to help the therapist enhance the effectiveness of the intervention. As such, these ratings provide structured ongoing opportunities for therapists to receive feedback from clients and adapt interventions so they better meet the unique needs, circumstances, and motivational sets of each client.

Life Satisfaction.   Overall life satisfaction is assessed using the Life Satisfaction Scale (LSS; Donohue et al., 2003; administration time < 2 minutes). The LSS is composed of twelve content items, with an additional item that is used to assess "overall life satisfaction." Content items assess friendships, family, school, employment/work, fun activities, appearance, sex life/dating, drug use, alcohol use, money/material possessions, transportation, and control over one's own life. Clients rate each of these areas using a 0 to 100 percent scale of happiness. Scale scores may be derived by averaging scores of the twelve content areas, although this average score may not be consistent with "overall life satisfaction" rating, because very low satisfaction in one content area may cause low satisfaction with life in general. The LSS has excellent reliability and validity (Donohue et al., 2003) and its simplicity allows it to be easily understood by clients. Content areas in which the client is least and most happy can be used in the treatment planning process by asking the client to identify behavior changes that would lead to 100 percent happiness in the identified content area. While used in the initial assessment, this scale can be completed during treatment sessions to guide intervention. It can also be administered after treatment is completed as an indicator of treatment effectiveness.

Youth Satisfaction.   Because FBT has been used effectively to treat adolescents with substance use disorders and conduct disorders, satisfaction measures are also used to assess youth satisfaction when appropriate, including satisfaction with parents and general life satisfaction. *Parental Satisfaction* is assessed with the Youth Satisfaction with Parent Scale (YSPS; Donohue, De Cato, Azrin, & Teichner, 2001; administration time 3 to 5 minutes). The YSPS is composed of eleven content items that assess youths' degree of satisfaction with their parent in the areas of Communication, Friends and Activities, Curfew, Household Rules, School, Response to Rewards, Response to Discipline, Chores, Alcohol Use, Drug Use, and Illicit Behavior. Youth rate their happiness with each area using a scale of 0 to 100 percent happiness. Their general happiness is assessed with an additional item "Overall Happiness," with the parent utilizing the same scale. Averaging across the eleven items yields a Total Scale score. Donohue and colleagues (2001) report that the reliability and validity of this measure is adequate. General *Life Satisfaction* is assessed with the Life Satisfaction Scale for Drug Abusing and Conduct Disordered Youth (LSS-A; Donohue, De Cato, Azrin, & Teichner, 2001; administration time 3 to 5 minutes). The LSS-A consists of twelve content items and an additional item that requires the youth to rate "overall life satisfaction." Content items assess happiness in twelve aspects of his or her life, including Friendships, Family, School, Employment/Work, Fun Activities, Appearance, Sex Life/Dating, Drug Use, Alcohol Use, Money/Material Possessions, Transportation, and Control Over One's Own Life. Each area is rated using a 0 to 100 percent scale of happiness, and a Total Scale score may be calculated by averaging across the scores from the twelve content domains. Donohue et al. (2001) report adequate reliability and validity for this measure.

Assessment of Co-occurring Problems   While FBT has been demonstrated to improve outcomes with regard to substance abuse, it is also well known that individuals with substance use disorders frequently have co-occurring problems that may be a direct result of their substance use, or that are substantially influenced by it. Examples of three co-occurring problems that can be addressed in the FBT assessment and treatment include child maltreatment, domestic violence, and increase risk for contracting HIV. Measures in this section are discussed briefly, although more in-depth descriptions are provided in Allen, Donohue, Sutton, Haderlie, and LaPota (unpublished manuscript) and in the referenced sources.

Child Maltreatment.   Substance abuse increases the risk of child maltreatment, including both child physical abuse and child neglect. Indeed, it is estimated that approximately 50 percent of caregivers involved in the Child Protective Service system also have illicit drug use. Because of this, FBT has been adapted to address issues relevant to child maltreatment and also includes measures that assess outcomes in these domains including interpersonal, intrapersonal, and environmental factors that increase the risk for child maltreatment. These assessment measures may be used in cases where the client with substance use also is identified for child maltreatment, when there is suspicion of child maltreatment, or when it is apparent that the substance use behaviors of the parents put the child at increased risk for child maltreatment.

Potential for Child Maltreatment. The potential for child maltreatment is assessed using the Child Abuse Potential Inventory (CAPI; Milner, 1986; administration time 20 to 25 minutes). The CAPI consists of 160 items and has been used extensively in both clinical and research settings. The CAPI yields an overall Abuse scale as well as a number of factor scores associated with abuse including Distress, Rigidity, Unhappiness, Loneliness, Problems with Others, Problems with Child, Problems with Self, and Problems with Family. Also, the CAPI has three validity scales that allow for detection of response biases. Internal consistency estimates for the Physical Abuse scale are high and test–retest reliabilities are very good (Heinz & Grisso, 1996). Changes in CAPI scores have been noted as a result of treatment (e.g., Donohue & Van Hasselt, 1999) and differentiate mothers who maltreat their children from those who do not (Milner, 1986). Neglectful behaviors can be assessed with the Short Form of Mother Child Neglect Scale (MCNS-Short; Lounds, Borkowski, & Whitman, 2004). The MCNS-Short is an eight-item, four-point Likert-type scale that measures mothers' perceptions of neglectful behaviors in four areas (Emotional, Cognitive, Supervision, Physical). The MCNS-Short has good internal consistency and demonstrates significant correlations with a number of important variables including maternal histories of neglect (Lounds et al., 2004).

Family Functioning Assessment of family functioning focuses on family conflict and cohesion, family support, as well as problem behaviors exhibited by children in the family. The Family Environment Scale (FES; Moos & Moos, 1984; administration time 5 to 10 minutes) is used to measure family conflict and family cohesion. The family conflict and family cohesions scales have been widely used to examine family relationships in homes where child maltreatment has occurred (see Donohue & Van Hasselt, 1999; Santisteban et al., 2003). The FES Cohesion scale measures the extent to which the family perceives itself as harmonious and "close," while the FES Conflict scale measures the extent to which the family perceived its members argumentative and disagreeable. Psychometric properties are good in parents with no current child maltreatment (Haskett, Ahern, Ward, & Allaire, 2006), in mothers with children involved in Head Start programs (Reitman, Currier, & Stickle, 2002; Whiteside-Mansell et al., 2007), and in child maltreatment populations (Abidin, 1995). Family support is assessed with the Family Support Scale (FSS; Dunst, Jenkins, & Trivette, 1984; also see Cherniss & Herzog, 1996; administration time 4 minutes). The FSS contains eighteen items that assess the mother's perception of the helpfulness of sources of support in raising her children, such as support provided by significant others and organizations. The FSS has adequate to moderately high reliability and validity (Cherniss & Herzog, 1996; Hanley, Tassé, Aman, & Pace, 1998). Youth problem behaviors are assessed using the Youth Self Report (YSR;

Achenbach, 1991; administration time 15 to 20 minutes). For the YSR, youth provide ratings on a three-point response scale for how true each item was in the past six months. The YSR includes subtests assessing competence, somatic complaints, anxiety/depression, social problems, thought problems, attention problems, delinquent rule-breaking behaviors, aggression, internalizing, externalizing, and scales assessing DSM disorders.

Home Safety and Beautification   Because substance abuse leading to child neglect is associated with home environments that are non-nurturing and dangerous, inspections of the clients' homes are a standard part of the evaluation for families with these co-occurring problems. Home inspections are completed using a modified version of the Home Safety and Beautification Assessment Tour (HS-BAT; see Donohue & Van Hasselt, 1999; administration time 20 to 25 minutes), which assists in determining severity of home hazards (e.g., toxins, electrical hazards) and the extent to which the home facilitates social and personal development of the child (e.g., developmentally appropriate toys, books, and clothing). Using the HS-BAT, a room-by-room tour of the home is conducted with the family. For each room, HS-BAT items are rated on a five-point scale ("0" = home hazard is absent, "4" = high priority for treatment) and the client and assessor also independently provide overall "safety" and "appearance" ratings for each room. Items with rating of "4" are considered imminent threats to children in the home, and require immediate intervention to correct the hazard, while items rated "2" or "3" are targeted for intervention later in therapy.

Child Management and Parenting   The FBT assessment includes an evaluation of the extent that significant stressors distract parents from caretaking responsibilities, as well as parental skills and attitudes that are relevant to child management. Parental stress levels are assessed with the Parenting Stress Index Short Form (PSI-SF; Abidin, 1995; administration time 5 to 10 minutes). The PSI-SF is composed of thirty-six items that assess stress in the parent–child system. Scores reflecting Total Stress, Parental Distress, Parent–Child Dysfunctional Interaction, and Difficult Child are calculated and reliability and validity are generally good (Ethier & LaFreniere, 1993). When high scores are obtained, behavioral goals are set that are aimed at decreasing stressors, stopping intrusive stress-related thoughts, and increasing communication skills. Parents' attitudes and beliefs are evaluated using the Adult–Adolescent Parenting Inventory-2 (AAPI-2; Bavolek & Keene, 2001; administration time 5 to 10 minutes). The AAPI-2 is made up of forty self-report items that assess parents' inappropriate expectations of children, lack of empathy toward the child's needs, and reversal of parent–child role responsibilities. AAPI-2 scales discriminate between parenting behaviors of parents who maltreat their children and parents who do not (see Bavolek & Keene,

2001). AAPI-2 scales correlate significantly with other instruments measuring similar constructs with adequate internal consistency estimates (Conners, Whiteside-Mansell, Deere, Ledet, & Edwards, 2006). Elevated AAPI-S scores are reviewed with clients during the FBT Program Orientation and methods to address expressed concerns are included in the Treatment Plan. Parental satisfaction with their child is assessed with Parent Satisfaction with Child Scale–Revised (PSCS-R; Donohue et al., 2001). The PSCS-R has eleven content items and an "overall happiness with child" item that are rated by the client on a happiness scale ranging from 0 to 100 percent happy. The original version of the PSCS-R was found to have adequate reliability and validity (Donohue et al., 2001).

Domestic Violence   Incidences of domestic violence, including child abuse and adult-to-adult aggression, are assessed using a TLFB procedure. Thus, for the prior four months the significant other and client are asked to recall a number of relevant events, such as the number of days children were taken out of the home and the number of days the client was reported for child maltreatment. Because of the sensitive nature of this information and the tendency for questions regarding family violence to be met with defensiveness and at times hostility, a rationale is provided to minimize these negative reactions and increase the likelihood of open and honest reporting. Specifically, we have followed the approach developed by William O'Farrell and colleagues in which the following is stated, *"The next questions are about family aggression. All families disagree and argue. Sometimes, these disagreements can build from a calm discussion to a more heated exchange, which may include yelling, swearing, sulking, and so forth. In some instances or for some families, when the families disagree, they may engage in what is often referred to as angry touching."* Clients and significant others are then separately presented with a list of behaviors ranging in severity from "throwing something" to "threatening with a knife," and asked to indicate on the TLFB calendar days on which any of these behaviors have occurred. It is of vital importance to avoid an insinuation of blame when conducting these interviews in order to increase the likelihood of honest reporting.

HIV Risk Behaviors   Drug use and sexual behaviors that increase risk for HIV are assessed using the HIV Risk Assessment Battery (RAB; Navaline et al., 1994; administration time 5 to 10 minutes) as well as a TLFB procedure. The RAB is available in several versions and we have used a seventeen-item form that includes nine items assessing risky sexual behaviors (e.g., exchanging sex for drugs, multiple male partners) and eight items assessing risky drug use behaviors (e.g., intraveneous drug use, sharing needles). The RAB was developed for use in longitudinal studies of HIV transmission and increased scores are predictive of increased risk for HIV seroconversion. Information from the RAB is used in the Behavioral Goals intervention (see Behavioral Goals and Contingency Management in the following section) to develop behavioral goals that are incompatible with HIV risk behaviors. The TLFB is also used to collect information regarding sexual behaviors that increase risk HIV seroconversion. Unlike the other TLFB procedures previously described, collateral reports are not collected for sexual behaviors because of the sensitive nature of information about sexual behaviors and practices. The TLFB method defines HIV risk days as those days on which clients engaged in unprotected sex (Stein, Anderson, Charuvastra, & Friedmann, 2001; administration time 10 to 15 minutes). Because TLFB information is collected for alcohol and drug use, the TLFB method of recording HIV risk days allows for documentation of the temporal relationship between risky sexual behavior and drug use, including days on which risky sexual behaviors were associated with alcohol and drug use.

BEHAVIOR INTERVENTION COMPONENTS

PROGRAM ORIENTATION

The Program Orientation is the first FBT intervention implemented. As with all FBT interventions, therapists utilize a protocol checklist to guide them in the initiation of therapeutic steps. Figure 4.1 shows what the structure of protocol checklists looks like utilizing the Program Orientation method as an example.

As can be seen, this form includes all materials that will be required in order to implement the Program Orientation. In this case, the results of several questionnaires, a blank case report form, and guidelines for communication are needed. There is a spot to indicate the time the intervention is implemented and later in the checklist a spot to indicate when the intervention is terminated. This assists supervisors in determining if therapists spend too much, or too little, time performing the particular treatments. After the start time is recorded, therapists refer to the particular steps necessary to implement the respective therapy. For the Program Orientation protocol, the first topic area to be addressed is to delineate the various "program policies." Therefore, as an example, the first few program policies are listed in Figure 4.1. As can be seen, each step is limited to one sentence, abbreviating terms (e.g., mins. instead of minutes) and deleting words (e.g., elimination of "the") that are unnecessary, whenever possible. This permits therapists to quickly scan the protocol. Therapists need not interpret therapeutic steps. Rather, they quickly comply with the prescribed "actions" to be performed. At first intuition, this may appear to limit therapeutic flexibility. However, therapists are taught extensively in role-plays to manage issues that sometimes interfere

Client ID#: _____   Clinician: _____   Session #: _____ Date of Session: _____

MATERIALS REQUIRED:
- Client Results of Timeline Follow-Back
- Completed pretreatment Life Satisfaction Scale
- Completed pretreatment Parent Satisfaction Scale
- Monthly Caseworker Progress Report
- Standard Treatment Session Progress Note
- Communication Guidelines Handout (2 copies)

Begin Time:_____

PROGRAM POLICIES

_____a. Explain tx. sessions will be audio-tape recorded so supervisor can examine therapist performance

_____b. State lots to cover in upcoming sessions, so important nobody talks > than a min. w/out feedback

_____c. Explain 1st 2 sessions are 2 hours, and remaining sessions are 90 mins., occurring 1/wk.

    _____1. 20 sessions must be completed within a 6-month time frame.

    _____2. If all sessions are completed as scheduled, program can be completed in 5 months.

Rating of Client's Compliance
- Rate client compliance on a 7-point scale (1 = extremely noncompliant, 7 = extremely compliant)
- Factors that contribute to compliance ratings are:

    1. Attendance (Client & Sig. Others)
    2. Participation & Conduct in session (Client & Sig. Others)
    3. Homework completion (Client & Sig. Others)

- Compliance Rating:_____

__1. Disclose client's compliance rating and factors that influenced this rating.

Conduct Client's Assessment of Program Orientation

_____a. Ask client how helpful the Program Orientation was on a 1-to-7 scale and inform client not to feel obligated to provide high scores, as honest assessment helps therapists better address client's needs. (1 = extremely unhelpful, 2 = very unhelpful, 3 = somewhat unhelpful, 4 = don't know, 5 = somewhat helpful, 6 = very helpful, 7 = extremely helpful).

Client's Rating: _____

Figure 4.1   Program Orientation

*Note: The remaining protocol is not included, as the aforementioned steps are included to provide a sense of what the protocol checklists look like.

with protocol adherence, and in doing so, have a "green light" to spontane-ously insert their own therapeutic methods between prescribed protocol.

The remaining prescribed protocol for Program Orientation not listed in Figure 4.1 includes statements about the importance of maintaining confidentiality, as well as its limitations. There is an explicit attempt to differentiate FBT therapists from third parties, such as criminal justice and child protective service systems. These statements usually result in clients feeling more comfortable permitting therapists to acknowledge their attendance and efforts in therapy to the referral agent. The reason for referral is extensively examined, including problems that may have been experienced with the referral agency and each family member's motivation for therapy. Clients are queried about their experience in the assessment process, including their expectations for treatment. An attempt is made to assess factors that influenced relatively high and low rates of substance use during the past few months as per the Timeline Follow-Back reports. The desired and undesired consequences of illicit drugs and alcohol are also reviewed to assist in understanding motivational factors necessary in developing the treatment plan, and an attempt is made to obtain a commitment to reduce illicit drug and alcohol use. This is very important, even if it is a reduction from seven to six days per week because it permits therapists to refer to the primary client's goal to reduce substances throughout therapy. The results of the relationship and life satisfaction scales are reviewed to determine activities that are likely to bring about immediate reinforcement (i.e., high satisfaction areas), and assist in understanding circumstances that need to be changed to bring about 100 percent happiness in each of the assessed areas (e.g., curfew, chores). The therapist also mentions potential reinforcers for outstanding therapy participation, including letters to probation officers and attempts to determine how the primary client and significant other(s) will be able to accomplish therapy goals. Commitments are also obtained from all family members to comply with various communication guidelines during therapy sessions.

The bottom of Figure 4.1 includes brief directions relevant to recording, and subsequently disclosing, the therapist's rating of compliance for the primary client and significant other during, in this case, the Program Orientation. This seven-point rating reflects compliance that is relevant to factors we have found to be necessary in the effective administration of therapies, including attendance of all relevant family members, extent of participation (e.g., role-plays) and conduct (e.g., paying attention, asking questions) in session, and completion of homework (if relevant). Quite fortuitously we discovered immediate disclosure of these ratings appears to be a tremendous motivator, particularly when releases are obtained to provide these scores to referral agents (e.g., court). Figure 4.1 also shows how the primary client is queried to provide an assessment of how "helpful" the intervention was in accomplishing the client's treatment needs. Of course, clients are queried how treatment can be enhanced when low scores are obtained. Thus, therapists are prompted to receive immediate feedback from clients about their performance, thus assisting in recognition of problems that often lead to dropout.

BEHAVIORAL GOALS AND CONTINGENCY MANAGEMENT (BGCM)

Since FBT is a skill-based therapy, therapists emphasize the importance of establishing goals that are specific to the presenting problems of primary clients and their families. In BGCM, the primary client reviews a list of stimuli with the therapist that have been reported by others to be common antecedents to drug use (more than twenty stimuli), and the therapist queries how often these stimuli occur prior to the client's own drug use utilizing a Likert-type scale (see Figure 4.2).

For each stimulus that is endorsed "sometimes" or "a lot," the therapist indicates a generic goal that has assisted others in effectively managing the stimulus and queries if the client would like to target the goal. When goals are endorsed, the primary client is prompted to identify potential obstacles that may inhibit goal accomplishment, and generic goals are customized, whenever necessary. This general format is utilized to establish goals relevant to the prevention of HIV and, when primary clients are parents, to assist in generating goals relevant to effectively performing caretaking responsibilities (see Figures 4.3 and 4.4).

All goals are transferred to a written contract (i.e., Goals Worksheet). Figure 4.5 shows a sampling of several program goals that are automatically included in the contract and not generated from primary clients (lowercase), as well as goals that are generated from the client (UPPERCASE). There are sometimes more goals listed in these contracts than clients can effectively manage on a daily basis. Moreover, applicability of particular goals may fluctuate from week to week. Therefore, although clients are encouraged to do behaviors that are consistent with all goals that they initially set for themselves, they are also prompted to indicate which goals will be a focus of attention during each upcoming week. Adult significant others are prompted to reward primary clients when all goals that were a focus of their attention during the week are accomplished. In doing so, each week significant others review the Goals Worksheet and examine how many overall goals were endorsed to be a focus during the upcoming week. Significant others then indicate what reward will be provided to the primary client for accomplishing goals that are listed as foci. Thus, focus goals and commensurate rewards may change from week to week, and these weekly contingencies (if sessions occur on a weekly schedule) are determined a priori. In this way, primary clients know they will receive greater rewards when greater effort is demonstrated.

• **Review Drug Incompatible Goals Rationale before completing the Drug Incompatible Goals Worksheet**

HOW OFTEN DO YOU (POTENTIAL DRUG TRIGGER BELOW) BEFORE YOU USE DRUGS?	"WOULD YOU LIKE TO (DRUG IN-COMPATIBLE BEHAVIOR BELOW) AS A GOAL?"	"WHAT WOULD MAKE IT EASIER FOR YOU TO (DRUG INCOMPATI-BLEBEHAVIOR)?" (Empathize, solicit info, volunteer help)	ASSIST IN DEFINING GOALS BEHAVIORALLY/SPECIFICALLY
Drink alcohol ☐ almost never (proceed to next trigger) ☒ sometimes? ☐ almost always	**Avoid alcohol use** ☐ no (proceed to next trigger) ☒ yes	STAY AWAY FROM JOHN AND HIS HOUSE	TELL JOHN NOT TO COME AROUND

Figure 4.2 Drug Incompatible Goals

228

• Review Positive Parenting Goals Rationale before preceding to the Positive Parenting Goal Worksheet

How often have you been able to (positive parenting behavior)?	Would you like to set this as a goal?	What would make it easier for you to (positive parenting behavior)? (Empathize, solicit info, volunteer help)	Assist in defining goals behaviorally/specifically
Make sure your children avoid junk food. ☐ almost never ☒ sometimes ☐ almost always (proceed to next positive parenting behavior)	☐ no (proceed to next positive parenting behavior) ☒ yes	WRITE A SHOPPING LIST WITHOUT JUNK FOOD	DON'T BUY KIDS JUNK FOOD BY MAKING NON–JUNK FOOD SHOPPING LIST

Figure 4.3 Positive Parenting Goals Worksheet

• **Review HIV incompatible behavioral rationale before preceding to HIV Incompatible goals worksheet**

Please let me know if you have experienced any of the following in your lifetime. Even if it happened a very long time ago or it wasn't your choice to experience it	KNOWING THAT (HIV RISK BEHAVIOR IN FIRST COLUMN) IS A RISK FACTOR FOR HIV/AIDS, WOULD YOU LIKE TO (RESPECTIVE HIV INCOMPATIBLE BEHAVIOR) AS A GOAL:	WHAT WOULD MAKE IT EASIER FOR YOU TO (RESPECTIVE HIV INCOMPATIBLE BEHAVIOR)? (Empathize, solicit info, volunteer help)	ASSIST IN DEFINING GOALS BEHAVIORALLY/SPECIFICALLY
Sharing needles that have been used by drug users. □ no ⊠ yes	**Avoid using needles that have been used by others** □ no (proceed to next HIV risk behavior) ⊠ yes	AVOID DOWNTOWN	AVOID NEEDLES BY STAYING AWAY FROM DOWNTOWN

Figure 4.4 HIV Incompatible Goals Worksheet

GOAL	FOCUS FOR THE WEEK	INDICATE HOW GOAL WAS COMPLETED	GOAL	FOCUS FOR THE WEEK	INDICATE HOW GOAL WAS COMPLETED
Attend treatment sessions. (1)	X	ON TIME	Ensure an adult significant other attends treatment sessions. (2)	X	GAVE REMINDER CALL
Stay clean from drugs. (3)	X	FOCUSED ON WORK AND KIDS	Maintain contact with client service representative (4)	X	SCHEDULED APPT. AFTER WORK
Avoid using needles that have been used by others. (5)	X	STAYED AWAY FROM DOWNTOWN	Talk, play, and read with your children each day. (6)	X	BASKETBALL OR CHESS OCCURRED AFTER SCHOOL
Assist your children with homework. (7)		SUMMER SO NO SCHOOL FOR 2 MORE WEEKS	Praise your child every day. (8)	X	COMPLIMENTED HIM DURING PLAY TIME
Effectively manage anxiety by taking dance class. (9)		EVEN THOUGH NOT A FOCUS STILL CALLED DANCE PLACES	Stay busy doing things that do not involve drugs. (10)	X	FOLLOWED SCHEDULE THROUGHOUT DAY, AND WHEN BORED, TALKED WITH SOMEONE ON PHONE OR IN PERSON

Reward for client from significant other if all focus goals are completed: GO TO MUSEUM.
Reward for significant other from client if significant other supports client: COOK DINNER EACH DAY.
I agree to complete all my focus goals for the week and reward my significant other if I receive support:

_____

Client's Signature

I agree to support client in focus goals and provide a reward if they are completed

_____

Significant Other's Signature

Figure 4.5 Goals Worksheet

231

STANDARDIZED TREATMENT PLAN

The process of determining the treatment plan involves a structured process that is consumer driven. First, the therapist briefly describes each FBT intervention to the primary client and adult significant others following a semi-structured interview and handout. After each intervention is described, the therapist indicates that two interventions (Assurance of Basic Necessities and Stimulus Control) will be implemented immediately to assist in monitoring that the primary client's basic needs are being maintained. The therapist then prompts the primary client and significant other (whenever appropriate) to rank order the extent to which each intervention is perceived to be helpful. Their scores are averaged, and this rank ordering determines the order in which these interventions will be initiated during treatment.

ASSURANCE OF BASIC NECESSITIES

Illicit drug and alcohol abuse are often associated with domestic-related emergencies (e.g., child abuse, illness, and domestic violence; Amaro, Fried, Cabral, & Zuckerman, 1990; Hunkeler, Hung, Rice, Weisner, & Hu, 2001). Indeed, parental substance abuse has been found to be associated with being two times more likely to be exposed to physical and sexual abuse in childhood (Walsh, MacMillan, & Jamieson, 2003). Emergencies appear to occur suddenly, although warning signs are often present but not recognized. Of course, when emergencies occur they necessitate immediate intervention and disrupt therapists from adherence to the treatment plan. Therefore, in FBT an attempt is made to carefully monitor potential emergencies and systematically manage emergencies that do occur. In doing so, Assurance of Basic Necessities is implemented at the beginning of each treatment session. The primary client reviews a list of common emergency conditions and antecedents to emergency conditions (see Figure 4.6), and is prompted to subsequently indicate if these conditions are occurring or may soon occur.

The client is then taught to utilize a series of FBT Self-Control intervention components to either prevent the emergency from happening (if it was indicated that the emergency may soon occur) or manage the emergency (emergency endorsed as happening). Although the Self-Control intervention is described below in greater detail, within the context of Basic Necessities, clients imagine successful performance of several behavioral steps that have been shown to assist in the management of undesired behaviors associated with upset or impulsiveness. First, the primary client is prompted to imagine an antecedent stimulus to the trigger (e.g., being warned by a landlord that an eviction notice will occur if rent is not paid)

1. Adult-to-adult aggression/ violence	Not present	Present	May soon occur
2. Adult-to-child aggression/ violence	Not present	Present	May soon occur
3. Child-to-child aggression/ violence	Not present	Present	May soon occur
4. Aggression/violence to yourself	Not present	Present	May soon occur
5. Not having enough food	Not present	Present	May soon occur
6. Illness or need for medical attention	Not present	Present	May soon occur
7. Bills are due (e.g., water, power, rent, car payments/ insurance, etc. . .)	Not present	Present	May soon occur
8. Unsanitary/unclean conditions in home	Not present	Present	May soon occur
9. Difficulty getting basic needs from caseworker	Not present	Present	May soon occur
10. Difficulty getting basic needs from FBT team	Not present	Present	May soon occur
11. Sexual assault	Not present	Present	May soon occur
12. Custody issues	Not present	Present	May soon occur
13. Court hearing	Not present	Present	May soon occur
14. Plans to move	Not present	Present	May soon occur
15. Substance use	Not present	Present	May soon occur
16. Exposed to potential HIV risk behavior	Not present	Present	May soon occur

Figure 4.6 Basic Necessities and Safety Checklist

and consequently utilize thought-stopping aloud to terminate the scenario. The client then reports one negative consequence for self and one negative consequence for someone else if the emergency is permitted to occur without intervention. Negative consequences are reported to bring about strong motivation, as clients often feel overwhelmed and sometimes "give up" without effort. The client then attempts relaxation exercises (e.g., deep breathing, imagining a calm beach scenario), initiates generation of solutions, and considers positive and negative consequences of each solution. Clients pick a solution and subsequently imagine themselves being reinforced for implementing the desired solution. Last, clients imagine telling someone they love how they were able to solve the problem. Of course, throughout the trial, therapists assist in prompting effective solutions. Solutions are transferred to the BGCM Goals Worksheet (Figure 4.5) and targeted as goals during each remaining treatment session until underlying issues maintaining the emergency are resolved.

Stimulus Control

The Stimulus Control intervention is utilized to effectively manage the primary client's environment to facilitate abstinence from drugs. Along these lines, all stimuli that have been associated with drug use and nondrug use are solicited through interviews with the primary client and adult significant others (i.e., people, places, and situations that client enjoys spending time with and has used drugs, as well as never having used drugs). Lists of commonly reported stimuli identified by others (see Figures 4.7 and 4.8 for abbreviated lists) are useful in this process.

These stimuli are then recorded in the Safe and At-Risk Associations List (see Figure 4.9 for abbreviated sample). Of course, "Safe" or non-drug-associated stimuli are recorded in one column and "At-Risk" or drug-associated stimuli are listed in another column. Safe stimuli include family members and friends who spend their time in non-drug-associated activities, such as exercising, attending classes, or church. Of course, it is important to avoid assumptions in determining if stimuli are "Safe" or "At-Risk." Indeed, stimuli that are safe for some people may put others at risk for substance use. Conversely, at-risk people use drugs and spend their time doing activities that are drug-related, such as sex for cash, selling drugs, and going to parties. Negative emotions and unpleasant circumstances are notorious triggers for drug use and include upset, anger, bad dates, various stressors, boredom, physical pain, excitement, and celebrations. However, it should be mentioned that these triggers are usually preceded by stimuli in the environment that may be more important in the management of drug abstinence (e.g., if an argument leads to anger, intervention should focus on preventing arguments). Many of the antecedents to HIV (e.g., using needles) and other undesired behaviors (e.g., violence) also act to trigger drug use. Therefore, antecedent stimuli to undesired behaviors should be assessed, and added to the At-Risk list. We separate primary clients and their significant others when developing this list, even when they wish to do otherwise (i.e., "We share everything.").

After the Safe and At-Risk lists are developed, the therapist reviews things that are liked and disliked about the solicited stimuli. This assessment assists in understanding potential obstacles that must be addressed later in therapy when reviewing listed stimuli. Such assessment also assists therapists in understanding potential reinforcers that may be utilized when attempting to restructure the environment to facilitate abstinence. The client and significant other monitor the client's time spent with safe and at-risk stimuli and complete the Safe and At-Risk Associations List during therapy sessions. In reviewing stimuli, therapists solicit behaviors that were performed to "stay clean" from illicit drugs and alcohol, and provide

Leisure Activities

- ☐ Going to parks
  - ○ Fishing in the local ponds
  - ○ Feeding the ducks
  - ○ Playing tennis/volleyball
- ☒ Going to restaurants
- ☐ Visiting museum/historical landmarks
- ☐ Visit Visitor Center for local lakes, state or federal parks
  - • Kids can become Jr. Rangers and earn badges
  - • Nature walks/hikes
  - • Guided tours or learning workshops
- ☒ Going to the movies or attending plays
  - • Free movies at local libraries
  - • Inexpensive plays at schools/universities
- ☐ Gardening
- ☐ Playing/Walking with a pet
- ☐ Doing arts/crafts
  - • See attached sheet for fun family craft ideas and resources
- ☐ Active Recreation: Participating in sport leagues, bicycling, dirt bike riding, ice skating, skateboarding
  - • Review newspaper for community events sponsoring these types of free or discounted events
  - • Community centers often have inexpensive swimming pools
  - • Community centers may have free dance classes

Figure 4.7 Things to Do And Places I Like to Visit

Note: This is a sampling of drug-incompatible activities in this handout.

Put a check mark next to each thing you like to do that does not involve drug use or HIV risk behaviors and benefits your family.

suggestions to assist in doing so, whenever appropriate. When clients indicate substance use, therapists reiterate that they are first interested in understanding what behaviors were performed in their attempts to maintain abstinence, and FBT skill-based intervention components are subsequently utilized to prevent similar relapses from occurring in the future. When positive actions are identified, they are recorded as goals in the BGCM Goals Worksheet. Throughout the intervention, therapists attempt to modify the environment to decrease the likelihood of substance

A. Things That Put You at Risk for Drug Use	
☐ Co-workers	☐ Family/Friends that cause anger/stress
☒ Friends who have used	☐ Drinking alcohol
☒ Smoking cigarettes	☐ Attending parties/get-togethers

B. Things That Do Not Benefit Your Children	
☐ Children regularly staying up late on weekends	☐ Not keeping alcohol/drugs away from kids
☒ Children not attending school	☒ Not saying "I love you" to children
☐ Children being left alone	☒ Not playing with children

C. Things That Put You at Risk for HIV	
☒ Boyfriend/Husband	☒ Sexual intercourse w/more than one person at a time
☒ Sharing needles	☐ Getting a tattoo/piercing with unclean equipment

Figure 4.8 Things That Put Clients at Risk

Please indicate if you have engaged in each of the following items that have been associated with increasing your risk of drug use, HIV risk behaviors, and/or prevents you from being the best parent you can be.

Note: This is only a sampling of risk items listed in actual handout.

use. For instance, a therapist might develop a plan to have paychecks directly deposited into a bank and have release of funds be contingent on the signature of a significant other.

SELF-CONTROL

As indicated in the Basic Necessities module above, Self-Control components may be utilized to assist in the identification and management of emergencies and prevention of potential emergencies. However, this intervention was originally developed to decrease urges for drug use and reduce problem behaviors associated with impulsiveness and upset. The Self-Control procedure is taught in highly structured trials during therapy

Safe List	Mo	Tue	We	Thu	Fri	Sat	Sun	At-Risk List	Mo	Tue	We	Thu	Fri	Sat	Sun
Caseworker:								DOWNTOWN							
Client services team member:								JOHN							
MOM								NOT SAYING I LOVE MY CHILDREN							
BOWLING								CIGARETTES							

Figure 4.9 Safe and At-Risk Association List

Note: Uppercase list items represent a sampling of client-generated stimuli, whereas lowercase list items represent a sampling of items that are *a priori* listed for all clients.

sessions. The individual is prompted to imagine a recent experience that involved risk of using drugs. This situation is usually identified when reviewing the Stimulus Control At-Risk List, or when clients spontaneously indicate drug use relapse. However, drug use thoughts, images, and cravings are not permitted to recur. Rather, the individual imagines the very first thought or image related to substance use in the situation being terminated early in the response chain, when cravings are likely to be relatively weak. That is, rather than imagining grabbing a crack pipe when physiological cravings are likely to be very strong and difficult to eliminate, the individual imagines the first very brief image of being paid after work. At this time, the craving is relatively weak, and the individual is more likely to engage in non-drug-associated behaviors (e.g., deposit money in bank). Indeed, as individuals are permitted to think of the reinforcing aspects of substance use, they are likely to become increasingly motivated to engage in behaviors that will facilitate substance use. In other words, it is easiest to terminate drug images, cravings, and thoughts when antecedent stimuli (triggers) are initially recognized, before feelings of excitement are permitted to intensify. This approach is different from Cautela's covert sensitization procedure, in which the individual imagines the last step in the behavioral response chain (i.e., raising a glass of alcohol to drink) and pairs this image with aversive thoughts or stimuli (e.g., bad smell, thought of running over a small child while intoxicated). In our earlier trials, we anecdotally discovered the physiological cravings of some drugs (e.g., crack cocaine) were too intense to be managed by associated aversive thoughts. Therefore, Self-Control was developed to teach clients to identify triggers to substance use early and effectively manage drug use antecedent stimuli by imagining negative consequences when desire is relatively low. As can be seen in Figure 4.10, clients are then instructed to engage in a relaxation exercise, state at least four prosocial alternatives to drug use in the imagined situation, imagine performance of one of the generated alternatives, telling a loved one how drug use was avoided, and reporting positive consequences that are likely to occur due to abstinence.

Clients are also taught to utilize these steps *in vivo* consequent to encountering antecedent triggers to drug use in their home environment. Of course, when performed *in vivo*, they are taught to imagine the steps rather than talking aloud. Therapists also guide clients in Self-Control trials and use the Self-Control Rating form (Figure 4.10) when performing feedback after trials. Along these lines, clients are rated on a scale from "0" (forgot step) to "100" (perfect performance). This form is also useful to monitoring urge levels, whereby "0" is equal to no thought, image, or craving relevant to drug use, and "100" matches drug use. Clients are taught to terminate the image, thought, or craving when it is low on the scale (i.e., ideally less than 5).

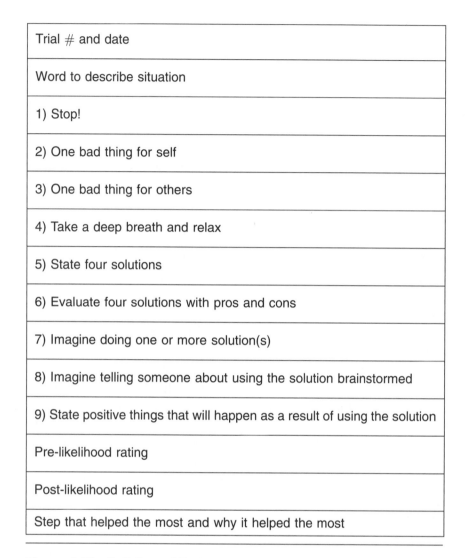

Trial # and date
Word to describe situation
1) Stop!
2) One bad thing for self
3) One bad thing for others
4) Take a deep breath and relax
5) State four solutions
6) Evaluate four solutions with pros and cons
7) Imagine doing one or more solution(s)
8) Imagine telling someone about using the solution brainstormed
9) State positive things that will happen as a result of using the solution
Pre-likelihood rating
Post-likelihood rating
Step that helped the most and why it helped the most

Figure 4.10   Self-Control Rating Form

The Self-Control steps may also be used to identify stimuli that precede HIV risk behaviors, negative emotions (e.g., anger), parenting cues that are often ignored, and other undesired behaviors that intensify as reinforcing thoughts and images are allowed to occur. Therapists must determine mutually with the client, whether adult significant others are permitted to watch the trials. In some cases, observation by others appears to motivate better performance, whereas for other clients observation appears to disinhibit performance.

COMMUNICATION SKILLS TRAINING (RECIPROCITY COUNSELING)
I've Got a Great Family (IGGF)   Poor communication and critical comments influence drug use because these things lead to various negative emotions

and stressors. Thus, effective positive communication is likely to assist in eliminating potential antecedent stimuli to drug use. The theoretical underpinnings of IGGF are grounded in the Community Reinforcement Approach (see Chapter 3) and based on the assumption that pleasurable relationships occur when there is reciprocity in the exchange of reinforcement between family members. Relationships are also conceptualized to be reinforcing when members in the relationship acknowledge their appreciation of one another. Indeed, in a population of caregivers of elderly parents, family satisfaction was related to the amount of positive affect and number of positive and negative exchanges from the elderly parents (Carruth, Tate, Moffett, & Hill, 1997). In IGGF, each family member is prompted to indicate "things" that are loved, admired, or respected about all other family members in the Things My Family Does to Support One Another form (see Figure 4.11). Family members are subsequently instructed to take turns exchanging these positive statements, including statements of appreciation. To eliminate negative affect and motivate conflict resolution, IGGF is performed toward the beginning of each session or spontaneously subsequent to family arguments.

The Positive Request (PR) procedure is borrowed from the Community Reinforcement Approach to substance abuse. In this intervention, family members are taught to solicit reinforcement from one another in a positive, nonaversive manner, thus preventing potential arguments that often lead to drug use. Therapists utilize behavioral rehearsal to teach family members how to briefly and politely state what, and when, behaviors are desired

In the top row of the form, list names of each of the family members, with one family member per column. Fill in the rows with things your family members do that you love, admire, or respect.

Things My Family Does to Support One Another					
Family Member 1 KARIANNON	Family Member 2 KENDRASUZ	Family Member 3 VALDIANA	Family Member 4 HEATHEROB	Family Member 5 KELSEYROO	Family Member 6
MASSAGES ME AFTER WORK	DOES HOMEWORK TO MAKE ME PROUD	READS ME BOOKS WHEN I'M BORED AND EYES HURT	GOOD HUGGER	SINGS WHEN I'M SAD	

Figure 4.11 Things My Family Does to Support One Another

(rather than what is not desired). They are also taught to indicate benefits that are likely to occur if the requested action is performed and why the requested action might be difficult or inconvenient to perform. The requestor is prompted to offer help in facilitating the request and offer to reciprocate reinforcement in some way. Last, family members are taught to generate alternative actions with the recipient of the request. In responding to positive requests, recipients are taught to never refuse requests, but rather attempt to perform at least some small part of what is being requested.

PR is usually implemented when family members are upset during sessions. The therapist provides a handout that lists the specific PR component steps and encourages the person to make a request while the recipient is encouraged to listen to the complete request. After the request is made, the recipient is prompted to either accept the request or make a positive request consistent with a compromise. After positive request components are effectively performed during session, family members are assigned to practice them at home, referring to the handout whenever needed.

Arousal Management (AM)   Illicit drug and alcohol abuse often exacerbates irritability and upset, and upset increases stressors that are known to influence future substance use. Therefore, it is important to assist clients and their significant others in arousal management. Along these lines, when family members get upset during a session, they are instructed to utilize AM. First, they are provided a handout that lists several procedural steps that are involved in AM. Family members are taught to identify antecedent triggers to upsetting thoughts and feelings, and upon first recognition of upset, engage in a relaxation exercise, state the problem in an objective manner that blames occurrence of the problem on environmental circumstances, and suggest how they may have contributed to the respective problem. When anger is perceived to be caused by others, as soon as AM is performed, individuals are instructed to initiate the Positive Request procedure to assist in resolving the underlying problems. Family members are also assigned to practice AM at home on a regular basis and to utilize this intervention in the home environment when antecedent triggers to upset are recognized.

Financial Management (FM)   Primary clients are often underemployed or unemployed, which may lead to stress, anxiety, boredom, or other antecedents to drug abuse. In fact, individuals consuming marijuana or cocaine are more likely to quit their current job more often than those individuals not using cocaine or marijuana (Hoffman, Dufur, & Huang, 2007). Therefore, FM was developed to assist clients in achieving greater income and decreasing expenses. In this procedure, they are taught to recognize problems that lead to financial deficits, prioritize their expenses, and brainstorm methods of creating additional methods of generating income. First, they are instructed to indicate their expenses in the Financial Management Expense Worksheet (see Figure 4.12), and these expenses are totaled.

Therapists then assist clients in brainstorming methods of decreasing expenses that are ranked low in priority, and projected savings are recorded in the last column of this worksheet. They are instructed to list their income in the Financial Management Income Worksheet (see Figure 4.13 worksheets), and therapists then assist clients in generating additional methods of earning extra income.

The lists of projected savings and income are then added together, and therapists reinforce clients for generating extra income. Financial goals are recorded in the Goals Worksheet to be targeted in therapy. This therapy is also valuable because clients are provided a clear appreciation of their financial deficit or surplus, which helps them effectively balance their budget. When deficits are determined, they learn to prioritize expenses from highest priority to lowest priority, and they are prompted to develop strategies to eliminate or reduce low-priority expenses. In cases where eliminating or reducing low-priority expenses are infeasible or undesirable, therapists teach clients to brainstorm methods of increasing their monthly income.

Job-Getting Skills Training As indicated above, individuals who abuse illicit drugs often have difficulties in achieving gainful employment and are sometimes employed in positions that facilitate substance use, such as working in nightclubs, topless bars, or other entertainment event venues. Although it is certainly true that primary clients generally lack technical or job-specific skills training relevant to non-substance-abusing peers, we have found employment in non-drug-associated environments is often restricted because these individuals have poor "job-getting skills." That is, they frequently lack confidence or skills necessary to assertively seek out gainful employment and sometimes perform relatively poorly during pre-employment interviews. Therefore, this intervention assists primary clients in obtaining job interviews with potential employers, as well as improving skills relevant to job interviewing. First, modeling, behavioral rehearsal, and handouts (e.g., see Figure 4.14) are utilized to teach primary clients how to solicit job interviews over the telephone. First, they are taught methods of getting in contact with prospective employers. During these initial contacts, they are taught to report their job-related skills and positive qualities to assist them in requesting formal meetings to discuss their professional aspirations. When meetings cannot be arranged, clients are taught to solicit job referrals. Along a different vein, they are taught how to present themselves for interviews, including what to wear, how to assertively perform basic introductions, and methods of keeping the job interview positive.

Rank	Monthly Expenses	Amount	Ways to Decrease Expenses	Projected Savings
	Rent/Mortgage	$850	TALK TO LANDLORD FOR REDUCTION DUE TO GOOD HX.	$25
	Average spent on food per week $___60__.___X 4 =	$240	CUT OUT JUNK FOOD	$15
	Electric bill	$90		$
	Gas bill	$70	WEAR SWEATERS IN WINTER, TAKE COLD SHOWER	$ 10
	Water bill	$30		$
	House phone	$		$
	Car payment	$		$
	Car insurance	$		$
	Car repair bills	$		$
	Cell phone	$35		$
	Cable	$35	TAKE OFF 1 MOVIE CHANNEL	$ 5
	Credit cards	$		$
	Medical	$40		$
	Home products and furniture	$		$
	Other: DIAPERS	$35		$
	Other:	$		$
	Total Monthly Expenses =	$1425	Total Projected Savings =	$55

Figure 4.12 Financial Expense Management Worksheet

Monthly Income	Amount	Ways to Increase Income	Projected Gains
Main Job	$1300	ASK FOR RAISE	$50
Part-time job(s)	$	SELL MAGAZINES	$95
Child support	$		$
Legal settlement awards	$		$
State and federal assistance	$200		$
Private or church-based assistance	$		$
Inheritance and/or investment income (e.g., stocks, bonds, real estate sales):	$		$
Assistance from family/friends	$		$
Other:	$		$
Total Monthly income:	$1500	Total Projected Gains:	$145

Total Monthly Income	1,500	Projected Savings	55
Total Monthly Expenses	−1,425	Projected Gains	+145
Remaining Balance	= (+/−) 75	Projected Extra Income	= 200

Figure 4.13 Financial Management Income Worksheet

Child Management Skills Training Most of the aforementioned therapies are exclusive to adult and adolescent primary clients and adult significant others. However, when primary clients are parents, they are encouraged to consider participation in child management skills training involving all family

Follow these steps when attempting to set up an interview with an employer over the phone.

1. **Introduce yourself.**
2. **Ask the name of the manager on shift.**

3. **Ask to speak with the manager.**
  • If asked why or what it is regarding, answer that it's personal.
  • If manager is unavailable, state that you will call back or leave a message to call back.

4. **When manager answers, do the following:**
  • Introduce self.
  • Thank the manager for taking the call.
  • List a few qualifications or personal strengths to the manager.
    a. _____
    b. _____
    c. _____
  • Ask to schedule an in-person interview to further discuss qualifications.
    a. If scheduled, state you're looking forward to the interview.
    b. If manager can't arrange interview, attempt to schedule a later time.
    c. If not scheduled, ask for a referral to other similar employers.
      • When contacting employers suggested by manager, be sure to state that the referring manager recommended you.

Figure 4.14 Job Club: Interviewing Skills Worksheet

members. These interventions are similar to the original parent training programs developed by Hanf, Forehand, Patterson, Azrin, and their colleagues. The initial instructional sets are exclusive to parents and, potentially, older siblings. However, all family members are encouraged to participate during practice exercises and reviews of therapy assignments while the therapists provide encouragement and descriptive praise. Child management treatments are usually implemented during home sessions or during outpatient sessions when significant others are able to watch the children while primary clients review drug-specific treatments.

Catching My Child Being Good (CMCBG).   Substance abuse and dependence often result in depressed mood, irritability, and lack of energy, which makes it difficult for parents to consistently provide positive attention to their children. Further, mothers who abuse drugs are generally unresponsive, disengaged, and inconsistent (Ridener & Thurman, 1994; Schuler, Nair, & Black 2002). Of course, when children are neglected, they may engage in a wide array of problem behaviors (e.g., whining, aggression, noncompliance) in search of social reinforcement, which may exacerbate already poor relationships between primary clients and their children. Parents are also more likely to use drugs to cope with children when they are perceived to be unmanageable. Therefore, CMCBG incorporates modeling, behavioral rehearsal, and homework assignments to assist parents in learning to increase the amount and quality of positive reinforcement provided to their children.

The parent is prompted to select an activity that both the identified child and parent enjoy doing together. The activity must be interactional and, ideally, educational. With the client pretending to be the child engaged in the respective activity, the therapist models a series of behavioral techniques, including immediate attention and descriptive praise for desired behaviors, tactile reinforcement (e.g., hugs), pleasant tone, queries, and avoiding criticism. The therapist also models incidental teaching (i.e., when children show interest in something, the parent provides information about the desired topic or object) and ignoring undesired behaviors that are not a threat to safety. As might be expected, the parent is encouraged to attempt these skills in a simulated role-play encounter with the therapist enacting the child. After the parent is able to sufficiently demonstrate the aforementioned parenting skills, the target child is engaged in the practiced activity, and the parent is prompted to practice the learned skills *in vivo*. Finally, the family is assigned to participate in family activities throughout the week. During these interactions, the parent practices CMCBG. These family activities are reviewed with the therapist in subsequent sessions. In doing so, therapists descriptively reinforce skill sets and positive affect demonstrated by family members in these interactions.

Positive Practice (PP). Parents who have evidenced problems due to substance abuse and dependence are sometimes critical and overly harsh in disciplining their children when they have performed undesired behaviors. They may also erroneously misinterpret the intentions of noncompliant children as malevolent. PP is utilized to assist parents in nonaversively managing undesired behaviors that cannot be ignored, because these behaviors would result in either property damage or persons being harmed. PP is a child management procedure that may be utilized by parents to nonaversively punish undesired behaviors that have occurred by first blaming undesired behaviors on situational factors that are outside the child's control and subsequently instructing the child to practice alternative desired behaviors.

The therapist first models PP with the parent enacting the role of a child who has just performed an undesired behavior (e.g., slamming door). The therapist blames the misbehavior on an environmental circumstance outside the child's control (e.g., *"I know you didn't mean to slam the door. The draft was a lot stronger than we thought."*) and instructs the child to practice the desired behavior (e.g., *"Go ahead and practice shutting this door so you can get comfortable with how to shut it without the wind catching it."*). The parent and therapist switch roles, and the parent practices PP in different scenarios until the steps are mastered. In all future sessions, the parent is instructed to utilize PP *in vivo* when the children perform undesired behaviors, while the therapist provides encouragement and support in the process. Parents are also instructed to practice PP at home and to record these experiences on an assignment worksheet so the experiences can be accurately reviewed during treatment sessions.

Child Compliance Training (CCT).   PP is the preferred discipline when undesired behaviors have already occurred. However, this intervention is not appropriate when children are noncompliant (at least initially). In CCT, therapists teach parents to clearly, succinctly, and politely direct their children to perform desired behaviors, provide warnings when their children are noncompliant, and punish continued noncompliance with relatively non-aversive consequences (e.g., time-out, withdrawal of privilege). First, therapists solicit potential benefits of corporal punishment, and potential unpleasant consequences. When the parent espouses corporal punishment, the therapist utilizes motivational interviewing techniques (e.g., open-ended questions, listens without judgment, empathize with concerns, points out discrepancies and faulty thinking patterns; see Chapter 1) and subsequently invites the parent to determine receptivity to CCC. Assuming the parent is motivated, the therapist models CCT with the parent enacting the role of a noncompliant child in a simulated role-play situation. The parent and therapist switch roles, and the parent practices CCT until the steps are mastered. In all future sessions, the parent is instructed to utilize CCT *in vivo* when the children are noncompliant, while the therapist provides encouragement and support. Parents are also instructed to practice CCT at home, and to record these experiences in a worksheet so these experiences can be reviewed during treatment sessions.

Home Safety and Beautification Tour (HSB)   The homes of primary clients are often unclean and evidence hazards and fixtures that need to be replaced or repaired due to years of neglect. These concerns are particularly warranted when children live in their home and during times when primary clients are intoxicated (e.g., may fall down unsteady stairs). Thus, it is important to determine the extent to which the homes of primary clients are safe and clean, particularly when children are involved.

During home tours, the therapist utilizes a standardized checklist of common home hazards and cleanliness issues to determine the extent to which the home is clean and safe and to monitor progress in therapy. Home and health hazards on the checklist include toxins, electrical hazards, problematic home access, inadequate food/nutrition, lack of maintenance of medical checkups, and unsatisfactory home cleanliness. There is also a section that may be used to prompt home equipment and materials that promote personal and social growth of children. During home tours, family members are prompted to identify hazards. They are praised for discovering and implementing solutions and assisted with the generation and implementation of solutions, whenever indicated.

Child-Focused Treatment Components   Along operant conditioning lines, if children are perceived by parents to be reinforcing to them, parents are more likely to reciprocate positive behaviors with their children in drug-incompatible activities. Similarly, positive relationships lower stress, making drug use less likely to occur. Therefore, the child-focused treatment components are utilized to teach children to reinforce their parents, and thus assist these parents in perceiving their positive qualities, thereby motivating these parents to engage in non-drug-associated pleasant activities with their children.

Catching My Parents Being Good (CMPBG).   This intervention involves first soliciting parental behaviors that have been appreciated by the identified child(ren). The therapist then shows the child how to descriptively praise his or her parents when they perform these behaviors, and subsequently instructs the child to role-play descriptive praise in similar scenarios with the therapist enacting the parent. Homework assignments are established for the child to practice descriptively praising the parent and to record these efforts in a practice book. Parents are taught to assist the child in this endeavor (e.g., *"Did you like how I cooked your soup?" "Would you like me to write how you liked my soup in your practice book?"*), and homework is assigned, and subsequently reviewed, in all remaining sessions.

Offering to Help My Parents (OHMP).   In this therapy, the child is provided an example in which it is appropriate to offer to assist the parent (e.g., bringing home groceries). The therapist then assists the child in generating ways the parent can be assisted in the presented scenario, and subsequently models the generated methods of "offering to help" the parent. The child subsequently role-plays similar offers and is assigned to practice spontaneous offers to help parents at home. Parents are taught to assist children in the completion of this assignment, and completed assignments are reviewed during all remaining treatment sessions.

Why I'm Special Show (WISS).   In WISS, therapists utilize a checklist to assist children in choosing activities that are fun, educational, developmentally appropriate, and skill-oriented. For instance, a child might learn to thumb wrestle, engage in singing a song, write a poem, or read a literary passage. The children practice these activities with the therapist and their siblings and later "show off" these skills in a "talent show" for their parents. Parents are instructed to praise their children for their participation in these activities and lead their children in learning similar activities at home.

Child Home Safety Skills.   This treatment incorporates results from the aforementioned home tour assessment, parental input, and behavioral role-plays with children to determine specific home hazards that will be a focus during the course of treatment. Once home hazards are prioritized according to their potential for harm, corresponding safety skill stories are read to the children. Throughout these stories, therapists model safety skills and prompt children to practice the modeled skills. Children are also taught to identify home hazards and determine skills that are relevant to decreasing each home hazard. Children demonstrate newly learned skills to other family members in the home, and family members are encouraged to praise and practice the safety skills with the children.

METHODS OF ENHANCING MOTIVATION FOR TREATMENT

In one of our controlled trials with adolescents who were diagnosed with both conduct and substance disorders, we developed a telephone intervention that significantly improved session attendance and promptness by almost 30 percent as compared with a less intense intervention (Donohue et al., 1998). These results were exciting and led our research team to explore other enlistment and retention procedures that were determined to be effective in controlled trials. Results of this literature review demonstrated that most enlistment and engagement programs conducted in samples affected by substance abuse consistently resulted in approximately 15 to 30 percent attendance improvement (see review by Lefforge, Donohue, & Strada, 2007). We combined many of these interventions into an overall enlistment and engagement program and discuss these methods below. It is important to understand that this intervention is evolving, and although it appears promising because it incorporates evidence-supported strategies, examination of this newly developed program has not yet occurred.

ENLISTMENT AND RETENTION TELEPHONE CALLS

The current FBT telephone intervention is scheduled to occur once per week and is implemented by either retention specialists or FBT therapists two or three days prior to each respective treatment session. The telephone calls include introductions, expressing congratulations for getting accepted into the program, indicating that the purpose of the client services team is to ensure clients are getting their needs met, requesting permission to speak with significant others openly unless requested to keep information confidential, and specifying that FBT is a model program. Clients are queried to briefly report their goals for therapy, their personal strengths, and family members who could be invited to participate in FBT as support systems. The clients are also asked to report if there's anything that can be done to strengthen their relationships with others. Positive qualities of the therapists are emphasized to build enthusiasm. Throughout treatment, clients are assessed for drug urges and the presence of other potential risk factors that may result in substance use. When clients are parents, they are queried to disclose difficulties with children and adult family members, and solutions are solicited to enhance these relationships. After treatment goals have been established, clients and adult significant others are queried about contingency management, including if rewards were provided when earned for the completion of goals. To assist in bringing about greater therapy assignment completion, practice assignments are reviewed, and the next scheduled appointment is verified. Brainstorming exercises are utilized to generate solutions to obstacles that may interfere with session attendance.

The retention call preceding the last therapy session emphasizes praise in completing the program, and the client is queried to indicate what was liked about the program and how the client will utilize acquired skills. There is an attempt to provide additional referrals, if needed. When clients do not have telephones, an attempt is made to call clients when they are at the homes of significant others, or they are mailed letters with content similar to the telephone calls. FBT clients may be provided cell phones, including paid minutes each time a session is attended. Similar telephone calls occur with the client's significant other, assuming informed consent/assent is provided by the client.

CONCLUSION

It is an exciting time in the development of substance abuse treatments. Whereas twenty years ago many substance abuse treatment providers debated whether to learn evidence-based treatments, today they argue the merits of one treatment over another. Indeed, there is now a menu of evidence-based treatment options in substance abuse, and treatment providers are careful to choose options that best match the needs of their consumers. With support from federal agencies (e.g., SAMHSA, NIDA), treatment providers have received more informed training and are more knowledgeable of issues affecting their clients, such as evidence-based identification, assessment and treatment of co-occurring disorders, and consideration of various diversity issues. Administrators of community-based treatment programs have become more hands-on and appreciative of the importance of science guiding practice. Similarly, applied researchers have become more appreciative of dissemination pitfalls identified by treatment providers and are now developing sophisticated methods of balancing treatment integrity in real-world settings. Mirroring the field of substance abuse treatment, FBT has grown in its application. For instance, its treatment protocols have been modified and developed to address comorbid problems, such as child maltreatment, internalizing and externalizing behavior problems, and risk of contracting HIV. Its methods of treatment integrity have been validated in controlled trials (Azrin et al., 2001) and community settings (Sheidow, Donohue, Hill, Henggeler, & Ford, 2008), and program forms and clinic procedures have been developed to assist in its dissemination (Donohue et al., in press). However, there is much work to be done. Our own work, for instance, is testing different FBT-oriented models of enlistment and engagement strategies in samples that have historically evidenced the poorest treatment completion rates of all substance-abusing populations (i.e., co-existing child maltreatment). We are also examining the relationship between patient compliance in therapy and consumer satisfaction across FBT modules. These studies will assist in determining which FBT intervention components are perceived to be most helpful, and are most predictive of successful treatment outcomes. Moreover, Stage III transportability studies are just now starting to be designed. Thus, the future of FBT and other evidence-supported treatments is bright, and with ongoing developments that will advance our field and improve outcomes for people with substance use disorders.

RESOURCES

WEB-BASED RESOURCES

Family Behavior Therapy website: www.unlv.edu/centers/achievement/index.html

REFERENCES

Abidin, R. (1995). *Parenting Stress Index* (3rd ed.). Psychological Assessment Resources, Inc., Lutz, FL.

Achenbach, T. M. (1991). *Manual for the Youth Self-Report and 1991 profile*. Burlington, VT: University of Vermont, Department of Psychiatry.

Allen, D. N., Goldstein, G., & Seaton, B. E. (1997). Cognitive rehabilitation of chronic alcohol abusers. *Neuropsychology Review, 7*, 21–39.

Allen, D. N., & Holman, C. (2009). Alcohol testing. In G. L. Fisher and N. A. Roget (Eds.), *Encyclopedia of substance abuse prevention, treatment, and recovery* (pp. 56–62). Thousand Oaks, CA: SAGE Publications.

Amaro, H., Fried, L. E., Cabral, H., & Zuckerman, B. (1990). Violence during pregnancy and substance use. *American Journal of Public Health, 80*, 575–579.

Attkisson, C. C., & Zwick, R. (1982). The client satisfaction questionnaire: Psychometric properties and correlations with service utilization and psychotherapy outcome. *Evaluation and Program Planning, 5*, 233–237.

Azrin, N. H., Donohue, B., Teichner, G. A., Crum, T., Howell, J., & DeCato, L. A. (2001). A controlled evaluation and description of individual-cognitive problem solving and family-behavioral therapies in dually-diagnosed conduct disordered and substance-dependent youth. *Journal of Child & Adolescent Substance Abuse, 11* (1), 1–22.

Babor, T. F., Cooney, N. L., & Lauerman, R. J. (1987). The dependence syndrome concept as a psychological theory of relapse behaviour: An empirical evaluation of alcoholic and opiate addicts. Special issue: Psychology and addiction. *British Journal of Addiction, 82*, 393–405.

Burgard, J., Donohue, B., Azrin, N. H., & Teichner, G. (2000). Prevalence and treatment of substance abuse in the mentally retarded population: An empirical review. *Journal of Psychoactive Drugs, 32*, 293–298.

Carey, K. B. (1997). Reliability and validity of the Time-Line Follow-Back interview among psychiatric outpatients: A preliminary report. *Psychology of Addictive Behaviors, 11*, 26–33.

Carruth, A. K., Tate, U. S., Moffett, B. S., & Hill, K. (1997). Reciprocity, emotional well-being, and family functioning as determinants of family satisfaction in caregivers of elderly parents. *Nursing Research, 46*, 93–100.

Chaffin, M., Silovsky, J. F., Funderburk, B., Valle, L. A., Brestan, E. V., Balachova, T., Jackson, S., Lensgraf, J., & Bonner, B. (2004). Parent–child interaction therapy with physically-abusive parents: Efficacy for reducing future abuse reports. *Journal of Consulting and Clinical Psychology, 72*, 500–510.

Cherniss, C., & Herzog, E. (1996). Impact of home-based therapy on maternal and child outcomes in disadvantaged adolescent mothers. *Family Relations, 45*, 72–79.

Conners, N. A., Whiteside-Mansell, L., Deere, D., Ledet, T., & Edwards, M. C. (2006). Measuring the potential for child maltreatment: The reliability and validity of the Adult Adolescent Parenting Inventory-2. *Child Abuse & Neglect, 30*, 39–53.

Donohue, B., Allen, D. N., Romero, V., Hill, H., Vasaeli, K., Lapota. H., Tracy, K., Gorney, S., Abdel-al, R., Caldas, D., Herdzik, K., Bradshaw, K., Valdez, R., & Van Hasselt, V. B. (in press). Description of a standardized treatment center that utilizes evidence-based clinic operations to facilitate implementation of an evidence-based treatment. *Behavior Modification*.

Donohue, B., Azrin, N. H., Lawson, H., Friedlander, J., Teichner, G., & Rindsberg, J. (1998). Improving initial session attendance of substance abusing and conduct disordered adolescents: A controlled study. *Journal of Child & Adolescent Substance Abuse, 8*(1), 2–13.

Donohue, B., Azrin, N. H., Strada, M. J., Silver, N. C., Teichner, G., & Murphy, H. (2004). Psychometric evaluation of self and collateral Timeline Follow-Back reports of drug and alcohol use in a sample of drug abusing and conduct disordered adolescents and their parents. *Psychology of Addictive Behaviors, 18*, 184–189.

Donohue, B., De Cato, L. A., Azrin, N. H., & Teichner, G. A. (2001). Satisfaction of parents with their conduct-disordered and substance-abusing youth. *Behavior Modification, 25,* 21–43.

Donohue, B., Hill, H. H., Azrin, N. H., Cross, C., & Strada, M. J. (2007). Psychometric support for contemporaneous and retrospective youth and parent reports of adolescent marijuana use frequency in an adolescent outpatient treatment population. *Addictive Behaviors, 32,* 1787–1797.

Dononhue, B., Teichner, G., Azrin, N. H., Weintraub, N., Crum, T. A., Murphy, L., & Silver, N. C. (2003). The initial reliability and validity of the Life Satisfaction Scale for Problem Youth in a sample of drug abusing and conduct disordered youth. *Journal of Child and Family Studies, 12,* 453–464.

Donohue, B., & Van Hasselt, V. B. (1999). Development of an ecobehavioral treatment program for child maltreatment. *Behavioral Interventions, 14,* 55–82.

Dunst, C. J., Jenkins, V., & Trivette, C. M. (1984). Family support scale: Reliability and validity. *Journal of Individual, Family, and Community Wellness, 1,* 42–52.

Ehrman, R. N., & Robbins, S. J. (1984). Reliability and validity of 6-month reports of cocaine and heroin use in a methadone population. *Journal of Consulting and Clinical Psychology, 62,* 843–850.

Ethier, L. S., & LaFreniere, P. J. (1993). Le stress des meres monoparentales en relation avec l'agressivite de l'enfant d'age prescolaire. *Journal International De Psychologie, 28,* 273–289.

Fals-Stewart, W., O'Farrell, T. J., & Birchler, G. R. (2001). Behavioral couples therapy for male methadone maintenance patients: Effects on drug-using behavior and relationship adjustment. *Behavioral Therapy, 32,* 391–411.

First, M. B., Spitzer, R. L., Gibbon, M., & Williams, J. B. W. (2002). *Structured Clinical Interview for DSM-IV-TR Axis I Disorders, Research Version, Non-patient Edition (SCID-I/NP).* New York: Biometrics Research, New York State Psychiatric Institute.

Hanley, B., Tassé, M. J., Aman, M. G., & Pace, P. (1998). Psychometric properties of the Family Support Scale with Head Start families. *Journal of Child and Family Studies, 7,* 69–77.

Haskett, M. E., Ahern, L. S., Ward, C. S., & Allaire, J. C. (2006). Factor structure and validity of the Parenting Stress Index-Short Form. *Journal of Clinical Child and Adolescent Psychology, 35,* 302–312.

Heinz, M. C., & Grisso, T. (1996). Review of instruments assessing parenting competencies used in child custody evaluations. *Behavioral Sciences and the Law, 14,* 293–313.

Hoffman, J. P., Dufur, M., & Huang, L. (2007). Drug use and job quits: A longitudinal analysis. *Journal of Drug Issues, 37,* 569–596.

Hunkeler, E. M., Hung, Y. Y., Rice, D. P., Weisner, C., & Hu, T. (2001). Alcohol consumption patterns and health care costs in an HMO. *Drug and Alcohol Dependence, 64,* 181–190.

Kolko, D. J., Selelyo, J., & Brown, E. J. (1999). The treatment histories and service involvement of physically and sexually abusive families: Description, correspondence, and clinical correlates. *Child Abuse and Neglect, 23,* 459–476.

Larsen, Attkisson, Hargreaves, & Nguyen. (1979). Assessment of client/patient satisfaction: Development of a general scale. *Evaluation of Program Planning, 2,* 197–207.

Lefforge, N. L., Donohue, B., & Strada, M. J. (2007). Improving session attendance in mental health and substance abuse setting: A review of controlled studies. *Behavior Therapy, 38,* 1–22.

Lounds, J. J., Borkowski, J. G., & Whitman, T. L., (2004). Reliability and validity of the Mother-Child Neglect Scale. *Child Maltreatment, 9,* 371–381.

Milner, J. S. (1986). *The Child Abuse Potential Inventory: Manual* (2nd ed.). Webster, NC: Psytec.

Moos, R., & Moos, B. (1984). *Family Environment Scale.* Palo Alto, CA: Consulting Psychologists Press.

Navaline, H. A., Snider, E. C., Petro, C. J., et al. (1994). An automated version of the Risk Assessment Battery (RAB): Enhancing the assessment of risk behaviors. *AIDS Research and Human Retroviruses, 10S,* 281–283.

Olmeztoprak, E., Donohue, B., & Allen, D. N. (2009). Urine testing. Client engagement. In G. L. Fisher & N. A. Roget (Eds.), *Encyclopedia of substance abuse prevention, treatment, and recovery* (pp. 982–985). Thousand Oaks, CA: SAGE Publications.

Reitman, D., Currier, R. O., & Stickle, T. R. (2002). A critical evaluation of the Parenting Stress Index-Short Form (PSI-SF) in a Head Start population. *Journal of Clinical Child and Adolescent Psychology, 31,* 384–392.

Ridener, G. S., & Thurman, S. K. (1994). The effects of prenatal cocaine exposure on mother-infant interaction and infant arousal in the newborn period. *Topics in Early Childhood Special Education, 14,* 217–231.

Sacks, J. A. Y., Drake, R. E., Williams, V. F., Banks, S. M., & Herrell, J. M. (2003). Utility of the Time-Line Follow-Back to assess substance use among homeless adults. *The Journal of Nervous and Mental Disease, 191,* 145–153.

Santisteban, D. A., Coatsworth, J. D., Perez-Vidal, A. P., Kurtines, W. M., Schwartz, S. J., LaPerriere, A., & Szapocznik, J. (2003). Efficacy of brief strategic family therapy in modifying Hispanic adolescent behavior problems and substance use. *Journal of Family Psychology, 1,* 121–133.

Schuler, M. E., Nair, P., & Black, M. M. (2002). Ongoing maternal drug use, parenting attitudes and a home intervention: Effects on mother–child interaction at 18 months. *Journal of Developmental and Behavioural Pediatrics, 23,* 87–94.

Sheidow, A. J., Donohue, B., Hill, H. H., Henggeler, S. W., & Ford, J. D. (2008). Development of an audio-tape review system for supporting adherence to an evidence-based practice. *Professional Psychology Research & Practice, 39,* 553–560.

Sobell, M. B., Sobell, L. C., Klajner, F., Pavan, D., & Basian, E. (1986). The reliability of the timeline method of assessing normal drinker college students' recent drinking history: Utility for alcohol research. *Addictive Behaviors, II,* 149–162.

Sobell, M. B., Sobell, L. C., & VanderSpek, R. (1979). Relationships among clinical judgment, self-report, and breath-analysis measures of intoxication in alcoholics. *Journal of Consulting Clinical Psychology, 47,* 204–206.

Spitzer, R. L., Williams, J. B., Gibbon, M., & First, M. B. (1992). The structured clinical interview for the DSM-III-R (SCID): I. History, rationale, and description. *Archives of General Psychiatry, 49,* 624–629.

Stein, M. D., Anderson, B., Charuvastra, A., & Friedmann, P. D. (2001). Alcohol use and sexual risk taking among hazardously drinking drug injectors who attend needle exchange. *Alcoholism: Clinical and Experimental Research, 25,* 1487–1493.

Walsh, C., MacMillan, H. L., & Jamieson, E. (2003). The relationship between parental substance abuse and child maltreatment: Findings from the Ontario health supplement. *Child Abuse & Neglect, 27,* 1409–1425.

Whiteside-Mansell, L., Ayoub, C., McKelvey, L., Faldowski, R. A., Hart, A., & Shears, J. (2007). Parenting stress of low-income parents of toddlers and preschoolers: Psychometric properties of a short form of the Parenting Stress Index. *Parenting: Science and Practice, 7,* 27–56.

Wilkinson, G., & Robertson, G. J. (2006). *Wide Range Achievement Test Professional Manual.* FL: Psychological Assessment Resources.

PART 4

ADULTS

CHAPTER 5

Cognitive Behavioral Coping Skills Therapy for Adults

DANIELLE E. PARRISH

T HE EFFORT TO obtain and maintain sobriety from drugs or alcohol often poses a daunting challenge as individuals must learn or relearn ways of living that will protect them from relapse—how to interact effectively with the people in their lives (including whether to rebuild or extinguish relationships); how to alter the way they think about themselves, others, challenging situations, and alcohol or drugs; and how to cope more effectively with life in general. Cognitive Behavioral Coping Skills Therapy (CBST) is an empirically supported treatment approach designed to meet this need by enhancing substance-abusing individuals' social and cognitive coping skills. This chapter is written for professionals who are interested in learning the "nuts and bolts" of the CBST approach for use with substance-abusing adults. The introductory section of this chapter provides an overview of CBST, including the history and theory that guides this approach; the indications and contraindications of CBST; and a discussion of the potential combination of CBST with other substance abuse treatment approaches. The large bulk of the chapter follows this introduction and focuses on CBST treatment issues, the overall structure of CBST treatment, and how to tailor CBST to individual or group treatment needs. Next, four sample CBST sessions are presented to further illustrate this approach. The chapter concludes with a brief description of resources to further support the implementation of CBST.

WHAT IS COGNITIVE BEHAVIORAL COPING SKILLS THERAPY?

CBST is a short-term, highly structured substance abuse treatment approach based upon a cognitive behavioral model. More specifically, CBST has been described as " . . . a family of related treatment approaches for alcohol dependence or other psychiatric disorders that aims to treat the patient by improving his or her cognitive and behavioral skills for changing problem behaviors" (Longabaugh & Morgenstern, 1999, p. 78). The theoretical rationale that guides this approach, similar to other cognitive behavioral approaches, is a cognitive-social learning perspective on substance abuse and use (Monti, Kadden, Rohsenow, Cooney, & Abrams, 2002). From this perspective, substance abuse (or any psychopathology for that matter) is viewed as a habitual, maladaptive learning process (Abrams & Niaura, 1987; Longabough & Morgenstern, 1999). The central tenet of this approach is that individuals can be taught, through various learning techniques (behavioral rehearsal, modeling, cognitive restructuring, didactic instruction, cue exposure with or without coping skills training), to find new and more adaptive ways of coping with life's demands without the use of addictive substances (Monti et al., 2002). To assist clients in meeting this goal, CBST utilizes a "broad-spectrum treatment approach" that not only focuses on a client's substance abuse, but addresses any life areas that may be meaningfully related to an individual client's substance abuse and relapse (Longabough & Morgenstern, 1999).

CBST has been developed for use in both group and individual settings, although it was originally designed for use with groups (Monti et al., 2002). Similarly, while this approach was originally developed for use with persons with an alcohol dependency, it has also been found to be effective with other substances of abuse (e.g., cocaine), less serious forms of alcohol use, and even in treating severe psychological disorders such as schizophrenia (Granholm et al., 2005; Monti, Rohsenow, Michalec, Martin, & Abrams, 1997; Monti et al., 2002). The CBST approach was initially guided by the seminal book *Relapse Prevention: Maintenance Strategies in the Treatment of Addictive Behaviors* by Marlatt and Gordon (1985). Since this time, variations on the CBST approach with regard to duration, modality, content and treatment setting have been developed to treat alcohol dependence (Longabaugh & Morgenstern, 1999). Despite these differences, all CBST approaches have the following in common:

- Reliance on social cognitive theory as applied to alcohol and substance abuse dependency to understand the cause and maintenance of substance misuse. The key tenet emphasized within this theory is that substance misuse is caused and maintained by an inadequate repertoire of coping skills when dealing with life stressors and substance-related cues.
- A focus on identifying and providing skills training (e.g., modeling, role play and behavioral rehearsal) to address each individual's unique coping deficits. (Longabaugh & Morgenstern, 1999)

The first training manual for CBST was published in 1989 by Monti and colleagues and is entitled *Treating Alcohol Dependence: A Coping Skills Training Guide.* A second manual on CBST, entitled the *Cognitive-Behavioral Coping Skills Therapy Manual,* was later developed and it represents a modified and shortened version of Monti and colleagues' (Monti, Abrams, Kadden, & Cooney, 1989) original text (from twenty-seven sessions to twelve sessions). One important modification was the adaptation of the NIAAA manual into an individual treatment format (as opposed to the original group CBST format from Monti and colleagues, 1989). A third manual utilizing the CBST approach was developed to treat cocaine addiction by Dr. Kathleen Carroll of Yale University in collaboration with the National Institute on Drug Abuse (NIDA). The most recent manual (Monti et al., 2002) is the second edition of the original Monti and colleagues' (1989) manual, and it incorporates many of the newer developments in alcohol treatment. While retaining a primary focus on group treatment, this newer manual also offers ideas for modifying the content for individual treatment. Further information regarding how to obtain these aforementioned manuals can be obtained at the end of this chapter. These treatment manuals, especially the more recent manual by Monti and colleagues (2002) and the Carroll (1998) manual published by NIDA, are heavily relied upon within this chapter to convey the CBST treatment model.

The authors of the aforementioned manuals and other proponents of CBST (Longabaugh & Morgenstern, 1999) suggest that this approach is flexible in terms of the total number of sessions, but all approaches have included the following core topics: Introduction to the CBST approach, Coping with Urges to Drink/Use, Managing Thoughts About Drinking or Using, Refusal Skills/ Assertiveness, Problem Solving, Coping with Emergencies, and Seemingly Irrelevant Decisions. In addition to these core topics are a wide variety of additional sessions focused on both interpersonal and intrapersonal skills that can be selected by the therapist to meet the individual needs of the client (or target population) within the constraints of a particular treatment setting. The developers of the CBST approach suggest that the most important factor in implementing CBST is that ample time and opportunities are provided to model, role-play, practice, discuss, and provide feedback regarding selected coping skills (Monti et al., 2002).

HISTORY, THEORY, AND RATIONALE FOR CBST

The CBST approach has not only been found to be one of the effective approaches for treating adult substance abuse, it also has a solid theoretical grounding. Based upon social learning theory (SLT), this approach considers the interaction of genetic influences, psychosocial factors, and environmental factors as salient in understanding whether a person will develop a substance abuse problem (Bandura, 1969; Monti et al., 2002). This perspective differs from theories of addiction that view the individual as primarily "passive" or that view "fixed person-factors" as largely explanatory of substance dependence (Abrams & Niaura, 1987). Bandura (1986), a key proponent of SLT, proposed the reciprocal causal nature of these factors, which have disparate and multidirectional influences on substance use patterns depending on each unique situation, setting and time.

In this model, individuals are believed to be impacted by, yet also able to change and adapt to, the environments in which they live (Bandura, 1986). In all possible interactions, cognitive factors (e.g., personal factors) are viewed as mediators of social learning and behavior (Bandura, 1986). Individuals are then viewed as proactive agents that can appraise each situation by weighing the pros and cons before making decisions. The ability to make beneficial decisions is based upon an "ability to make an accurate appraisal of environmental demands, know the strengths and limits of one's repertoire of coping skills, and weigh both the long and short-term positive and negative consequences of projected outcomes" (Abrams & Niaura, 1987, p. 132).

Additionally, it is posited that a combination of factors are often necessary to result in a given effect (Bandura, 1986). For example, a teenager may not decide to start smoking cigarettes just because his peers smoke. It may instead require observing his parents smoke, observing admired celebrities smoke on and off the screen, and peer pressure from friends to actually result in a decision to start smoking. The number of factors requiring the initiation of such behavior varies from one person to the next depending upon their personal factors (including the perceived benefit of such a decision and their coping skills) and the nature and presence of environmental demands.

Another major difference between the SLT perspective of addiction and that of other theories is that, since substance-related behaviors may differ based on the situation, setting, and time, there is a rejection of the inevitable progression of an individual through the stages of alcoholism or substance dependency (Abrams & Niaura, 1987). Situational determinants of drinking, for example, are believed to include stressful life events, work and family pressures, and the availability of proper social support. For this reason, drinking patterns are viewed to vary along a "continuum" from experimentation in childhood or adolescence to abuse, abstinence or controlled use in adulthood (Abrams & Niaura, 1987).

Bandura (1969) described alcoholics as ". . . people who have acquired, through differential reinforcement and modeling experiences, alcohol consumption as a widely generalized response to aversive stimulation" (p. 536). Addictive behavior is then viewed as a maladaptive and habitual way of coping with the stress of both major and common life events (Abrams &

Niaura, 1987). *Stress* is defined as an "adaptational relationship" between an individual and a situational demand (or stressor) (Monti et al., 2002). *Stressors* include major life events (marriage, divorce, birth of a child, etc.) or everyday stresses of life, work, family, and so on. Stressors are, of course, unique to each individual and are contingent upon how a particular event or situation is perceived by the individual based upon their unique social learning history. *Coping* is one's attempt to respond to a demand in a way that relieves stress by restoring balance or equilibrium (Monti et al., 2002). A person's ability to avoid substance abuse is then posited to be related to his or her individual social learning history and acute situational/environmental demands. While genetic influences have been shown to predispose certain individuals to substance abuse, these influences are believed to interact with psychosocial factors, leading to adaptive coping skills and a lower probability of alcohol use, or in coping skills deficits that necessitate coping skills training (Monti et al., 2002).

The central tenets of the CBST model were originally born out of the SLT model of alcohol abuse and follow the primary assumption that if clients with maladaptive coping skills commit to learning new behaviors, they can learn to better handle both genetic and social learning vulnerabilities (Abrams & Niaura, 1987; Monti et al., 2002). There are several important factors posited by SLT and related substance abuse research that impact the development and maintenance of addictive behavior and the ability to alter subsequent behavior. These include reinforcement, modeling, conditioned responding, substance-related expectancies, physical dependence, cognitive factors, and coping skills (Abrams & Niaura, 1987; Monti et al., 2002). Each concept is defined and discussed below in relation to the more specific SLT of substance abuse.

Reinforcement

Reinforcement has to do with the desirability of the outcomes of one's behavior (Rotter, 1982). Research has shown that reinforcement plays a powerful role in the initiation, maintenance and recovery from substance use disorders (Higgins, Heil, & Lussier, 2004). Reinforcement can be experienced socially, physically, or psychologically and can be positive (the experience of something good) or negative (the termination of something unpleasant). Alcohol use, for example, has been shown to increase cutaneous and gastric blood flow, thereby resulting in feelings of warmth or positive physical reinforcement (Monti et al., 2002). Similarly, one may be able to "escape" problems (e.g., depressed mood, anxiety, or tension) by using substances, and in these cases the substance may serve as negative reinforcement.

MODELING

Modeling, or learning from observing what others do and the related consequences of such behavior, is of central importance to social learning theory
(Bandura, 1986). Modeling has been found to be a potent predictor of both the
development and amelioration of substance abuse addictions (Monti et al.,
2002). The effects of modeling can occur in many contexts, from the media
depiction of substance use to directly observing parental and peer substance
use (Bandura, 1986; Barnes, 1977; Caudill & Marlatt, 1975; O'Leary, O'Leary,
& Donovan, 1976). When alcohol use, for example, is modeled by parents or
peers as a way to deal with social anxiety or reduce tension, a young person
may develop an expectancy that alcohol is useful to reduce such problems. As
a result, this young person may begin to drink to cope with his or her own
tension and anxiety and consequently never develop more beneficial coping
skills to deal these stressors. Moreover, if alcohol is successful in dealing with
tension and anxiety, the person may even expand his or her alcohol use to
cope with an even broader number of life's stressors (Monti et al., 2002).
Modeling has also been found to be a powerful way to teach general or
substance-abuse-related coping skills, and is used as a part of the CBST
approach (Monti et al., 2002).

CONDITIONED RESPONDING

In the context of substance use, environmental stimuli or cues elicited through
either classical conditioning (e.g., sight or smell) or operant conditioning
(e.g., situational, social, or emotional situations where drinking was reinforced) play a major role in the maintenance of an addiction and can
make reducing or abstaining from substances very difficult (Abrams &
Niaura, 1987). Cues might include people, places, sights, smells, objects,
internal states, certain times of the day, or holidays associated with prior
substance use (Monti et al., 2002).

SUBSTANCE-RELATED EXPECTANCIES

In SLT, behavior is predicted by the interaction of expectancies regarding the
outcomes of a particular behavior and the reinforcement value (or desirability) of these outcomes (Rotter, 1982). The reinforcement value refers to the
desirability of the outcomes of our behavior. If the anticipated outcome is
attractive and desired, it will have a high reinforcement value. If it is
something we want to avoid or dislike, it will have a low reinforcement
value. There is strong empirical support that suggests that internalized
expectancies for a substance are initially shaped prior to substance use by

socializing and cultural agents, such as parental norms, peer modeling and the media (Abrams & Niaura, 1987). Similarly, an individual's expectancies are also based on past experiences with a substance—the more often the use of a substance has resulted in a particular outcome in the past, the stronger one's expectancy that such an outcome will occur in the future (Rotter, 1982).

PHYSICAL DEPENDENCE

Tolerance and physical dependence are viewed as important indicators of further alcohol use within the SLT model (Abrams & Niaura, 1987). While this model validates the important direct pharmacologic influences on dependence and withdrawal, SLT emphasizes the importance of the interaction of these factors with cognitive and social learning variables to moderate drinking behavior (Abrams & Niaura, 1987). Withdrawal and tolerance are not viewed as static influences that are acquired only because of repeated substance use, but also as behaviors and cognitive and situational responses to environmental cues learned through classical, operant, and cognitive learning models (Abrams & Niaura, 1987). This view stands contrary to the "loss-of-control" perspective, which attributes an entirely pharmacological process that leads to craving and an individual's loss-of-control over subsequent substance use (Abrams & Niaura, 1987).

COGNITIVE FACTORS AND SELF-EFFICACY

Abrams and Niaura (1987) suggest six "critical points" where cognitive information processing deficits could lead to inappropriate decisions regarding whether one should drink and how much one should drink: (1) A problematic social learning history (based upon a lack of healthy role models with regard to alcohol or substance use or cultural/environmental influences), (2) an overemphasis of the short-term benefits of substance use and an underemphasis on the long-term consequences, (3) beliefs that alcohol or substances may improve a person's mood or make him or her more physiologically aroused, (4) a lack of general life coping skills, (5) a lack of specific coping skills to regulate alcohol or substance use, and (6) a lack of attendance to the physiological and behavioral changes and consequences that result from drinking or substance use (e.g., impaired performance, intoxication, etc.). These cognitive beliefs play a major role in whether one uses substances, how much is used, and how a person will behave while using the substance (Abrams & Niaura, 1987).

Self-efficacy, or one's belief that he or she can cope successfully in a particular situation without using substances, is another cognitive factor that plays a major role in one's decision to drink in a particular situation

(Monti et al., 2002). The combination of perceived self-efficacy to cope in a given situation and outcome expectations for substance use have a large influence on whether an individual drinks in a particular situation (Monti et al., 2002). For this reason, it is imperative that clients develop a *"strong* and *realistic* confidence" that they can cope with life's stressors without the use of substances (Monti et al., 2002, p. 7). This is something that develops slowly over time as an individual masters disparate and increasingly difficult situations (Monti et al., 2002). CBST focuses on helping clients develop coping skills to practice dealing with these increasingly difficult situations and to develop a realistic sense of confidence in their ability to cope successfully without the use of substances (Monti et al., 2002).

Abrams and Niaura (1987) propose nine guiding principles for CBST based upon their integration of social learning theory and substance abuse research. Given the specificity of this information to alcohol use, they are adapted within this chapter to reflect the use of all addictive substances. They are presented by these authors within a "developmental framework" but do not constitute a "stage" theory (Abrams & Niaura, 1987):

1. *Early learning plays a role.* How one learns about alcohol and other substances is a part of psychosocial development and socialization within a culture. The views regarding the use of such substances are influenced by the modeling, attitudes, beliefs, and expectancies transmitted by culture, family, peers, and media. Learning often occurs when an individual is very young and before he or she consumes the substance.

2. *Individual differences play a role.* Predisposing individual factors, both biological (genetic) and psychosocial (coping skill deficits, social incompetence, excessive negative emotions, lack of normal drinking models, etc.), may interact with socializing agents mentioned above to increase the risk of alcohol abuse.

3. *Direct experiences with the substance increase in importance with continued use.* The use of substances is reinforced, either negatively or positively, based upon the individual's experiences and reasons for using the substance. Negative reinforcement may involve the ability to escape from tension and stress, while positive reinforcement could include the positive physical sensation related to the substance or improved social interaction.

4. *The interaction of a predisposing individual difference and a current situational demand that exceeds one's perceived ability to cope may result in substance abuse, especially if that person has had positive experiences with the substance in the past.* When a person feels overwhelmed by a particular situation or stressor, believes he or she is unable to cope using his or

her own repertoire of skills (low self-efficacy) and have had positive experiences with a particular substance in the past (high expectancy of the substance's desired effects), he or she is more likely to abuse a substance to cope. This abuse is likely to continue if the individual does not make an effort to develop alternative, more adaptive coping skills. In contrast, individuals who drink at normal levels are more likely to have learned and utilized coping skills that, although they may sometimes be less immediate, are known to be more beneficial.

5. *If substance use is continued, tolerance to its reinforcing properties will occur.* As individuals continue to use a substance, it will take more of the substance to achieve the desired effects. Acquired tolerance to these reinforcing effects, which may also be determined in part by genetic influences, may then contribute to the mediation of further substance use.

6. *If substance consumption increases and is sustained over time, the risk of substance dependence increases.* As one becomes dependent either psychologically or physically, new forms of reinforcement begin, such as the avoidance of withdrawal symptoms or the belief that one cannot cope with life stressors (mood swings, social skills, etc.) without the substance. Cues within the environment, such as associated sights and smells of the substance, may also elicit strong reactions that elicit cravings for the substance.

7. *Reactions of people or institutions within the environment to an individual's substance abuse will cause new life stressors and consequences.* Reciprocal determinism posits that the reaction of others to the person abusing substances (anger, avoidance, etc.) is likely to lead to additional stress, lower self-efficacy and coping ability, less social support, and, consequently, more drinking to cope. This becomes a "vicious circle of negative person-environment interactions" (Abrams & Niaura, 1987, p. 139).

8. *Multiple pathways to substance use, abuse, and recovery are believed to occur, all of which are explained by principles of SLT.* The influence of individual, social, and situational factors related to substance use will vary between individuals and within individuals over time. For this reason, there is no combination of factors that is required to result in substance abuse or dependency and stages of progression through these phases cannot be clearly delineated or generalized across individuals.

9. *Recovery depends on an individual's ability and willingness to explore and choose alternative ways of coping.* It is necessary for an individual to develop general coping skills to deal with life stressors as well as self-control skills to minimize future substance use. According to SLT and Abrams and Niaura (1987), "Through direct practice, verbal

persuasion, modeling, and physiologic pathways, the individual must acquire successfully and practice alternative intrapersonal and inter-personal skills to develop high enough levels of self-efficacy to resist demanding situations" (p. 140). More specifically, the following must happen for an individual with substance dependency: (a) Become more self-reflective in order to indentify risky environmental or personal antecedents of substance use; (b) replace positive expectations about the consequences of substance use with a more balanced set of expect-ancies, including long-term consequences of use; and (c) acquire addi-tional self-regulatory and delay of gratification skills. The goal of abstinence versus controlled drinking for an individual is contingent upon the severity of the drinking problem and the ability to improve cognitive self-regulation as described above so that "quick fixes" are avoided.

The rationale for CBST is based on these tenets of social learning theory. This framework suggests that individuals who have difficulty coping with life's stressors are at an increased risk for developing a substance abuse problem as a coping response (Monti et al., 2002). Similarly, this approach posits that the way to treat a substance abuse problem and prevent relapse is to improve an individual's coping skills (Monti et al., 2002). The focus of this intervention is then to improve coping skills by employing ". . . direct practice, verbal persuasion, [and] modeling . . . [and allowing] the individ-ual . . . [to] practice alternative intrapersonal and interpersonal skills to develop high enough levels of self-efficacy to resist demanding situations" (Monti et al., 2002, p. 140).

IMPLEMENTING COGNITIVE BEHAVIORAL SKILLS TRAINING: ISSUES AND CONSIDERATIONS

There are several important treatment issues that must be taken into account and planned prior to implementing cognitive behavioral skills training (CBST). Monti and colleagues (2002) provide a detailed account of such issues, and this section draws heavily upon their experiences and recom-mendations related to the implementation of CBST. As noted previously, CBST was initially developed for use within a group format, but has since been adapted for use within individual settings. For this reason, issues related to both the group and individual formats will be discussed. Both formats have empirical support for their approach (Monti et al., 2002), so the decision to use individual or group treatment formats likely depends, at least partially, on the resources and time available for treatment as well as the needs of the client. If a client requires more time to focus on his or her unique coping skills or is perceived as inappropriate for group, then an individual approach may be warranted. One potential drawback of using the individual approach, however, is that modeling and role-playing procedures are limited to the therapist and the client, and the client does not observe or receive feedback from other group members (Monti et al., 2002).

In either approach (individual or group), CBST follows a highly structured process during which there is *not* an " . . . exploration of whatever issues come up in the here and now . . . [or the exploration of] underlying psychodynamic conflicts" (Monti et al., 2002. p. 19). CBST is also not a didactic lecture, but rather a process of educating and actively engaging clients in such a way that ensures both the learning and practicing of new coping behaviors (Monti et al., 2002). For this reason, it is important that therapists utilizing this approach are able to be very directive and effective at engaging clients in an interactive learning process.

INDICATIONS, CONTRAINDICATIONS, AND COMBINATION OF TREATMENT APPROACHES

Monti and colleagues (2002) suggest the integration of cue exposure treatment (CET) with CBST and provide detailed information within their manual on how to implement this approach with CBST. Additional information on cue exposure treatment can be found in a book entitled, *Evidence-Based Treatments for Alcohol and Drug Abuse: A Practitioner's Guide to Theory, Methods and Practice* by Paul M.G. Emmelkamp and Ellen Vedel (2006), while a useful discussion of the impact of the urge to drink on the treatment process can be found in an NIAAA article by Rohsenow and Monti (1999), titled, "Does Urge to Drink Predict Relapse after Treatment?"

Cue exposure treatment, like CBST, is consistent with social learning theory principles and is thought to help reduce the intensity of alcohol or substance related cues to improve one's ability to cope with the urge to use or drink (Monti et al., 2002). CET is believed to work for two reasons: (1) Repeated unreinforced exposure to alcohol or substance related cues is supposed to reduce cue reactivity and reduce the chance of relapse and (2) the practice of coping skills while real life cues are less potent should increase the effectiveness of such skills and build the client's expectancies that he or she can cope effectively without using substances (Monti et al., 2002).

Another consideration in combining treatments is to explore new pharmacotherapies that are available to assist in the treatment of substance abuse disorders (Longabaugh & Morgenstern, 1999; Monti et al., 2002). For example, naltrexone has been found to be effective in reducing drinking among alcoholics in the first forty days of treatment, and in a more recent study resulted in less craving for alcohol and a small advantage of less heavy drinking relapse at one year and four months (Anton et al., 2006; Latt,

Jurd, Houseman, & Wutzke, 2002). Naltrexone has also been shown to reduce the feeling of pleasure when opioids are taken and to decrease cocaine use when combined with coping skills training (Comer et al., 2006; Schmitz, Stotts, Rhoades, & Grabowski, 2001). Since such pharmacotherapies offer promise in reducing the urge to drink or use, they may improve clients' chances for treatment success when used in combination with CBST, especially when delivered in outpatient or aftercare settings (Monti et al., 2002). However, the COMBINE study authors recently reported that when offering medication management to all groups, the combination of cognitive behavioral intervention (the combination of motivational enhancement therapy, CBT and self-help groups) and naltrexone did not show incremental efficacy—but rather stood alone as efficacious interventions in the treatment of alcohol dependence (Anton et al., 2006). Therefore, while some of these pharmacologies show promise in treating substance abuse problems, additional research must be done to ascertain their incremental value when combined with CBST.

Finally, CBST was designed to be integrated with other partial hospital and outpatient treatment components such as alcohol or drug education, occupational therapy, individual counseling, involvement in AA (alcoholics anonymous) and NA (narcotics anonymous), and ongoing family groups (Monti et al., 2002). For inpatient clients, Monti and colleagues (2002) suggest that it may be helpful to clarify that the goal of CBST is different from other treatment efforts that are being provided by emphasizing that CBST is largely for skills training rather than the ongoing and frequent processing of feelings (Monti et al., 2002).

This concludes this brief discussion of the issues and considerations of implementing CBST. The following case will be utilized as one of a few case examples throughout the chapter to illustrate various aspects of the CBST treatment process.

A CASE EXAMPLE: SALLY

Sally is a 38-year-old married female who recently completed an intensive partial hospital treatment program for alcohol dependency, and she is now going to start twelve 1-hour individual CBST sessions two times per week for her aftercare treatment. Therapists from her partial hospital treatment program share that Sally is highly motivated to stop drinking and that she had done an excellent job "working the program." Sally's psychosocial assessment identified an additional diagnosis of mild depressive disorder and a common tendency to deal with conflict and life situations in a passive way that led to low self-esteem, depressed mood, and irritability. Her strengths included a supportive husband, who is quite warm and supportive, although he possesses some co-dependent behaviors; a job that has allowed her time off to deal with her alcohol dependency; and a sound financial situation.

Sally is one of the top financial analysts at a major business firm, and although she loves her job, she believes that the stress of this job, and the many job related "happy hour" meetings, may have led her to more problematic drinking. Specifically, she has trouble being assertive at work and has an especially difficult time saying "no" to taking on more work when she is already overwhelmed with things to do. She is also extremely perfectionistic when it comes to her own work, often agonizing over things when they do not turn out the way she envisioned (often because she irrationally believes that others will think she is no longer good at what she does). The combination of an overwhelming workload and a fearful drive toward perfection leads to long hours where she is often at work as late as 11:00 P.M. Additionally, while Sally reports a good relationship with her husband, she has few female friends, little to no contact with her family, and spends very little time doing things she enjoys or spending time with her husband. She believes that building a better social network and finding more enjoyable aspects of life might motivate her to stay sober and set better work boundaries.

OVERVIEW OF CBST TREATMENT: CONTENT AND STRUCTURE OF THE SESSIONS

BRIEF INTRODUCTION TO CBST CONTENT

CBST consists of two kinds of coping skills training—interpersonal and intrapersonal. Interpersonal skills, also referred to as communication skills, are focused on helping clients develop more adaptive ways of dealing with high-risk relapse situations and obtaining and maintaining social support that is important for successful sobriety (Monti et al., 2002). The sessions included in the interpersonal skills training section are listed in order of increasing difficulty: Nonverbal Communication, Introduction to Assertiveness, Conversation Skills, Giving and Receiving Positive Feedback, Listening Skills, Giving Constructive Criticism, Receiving Criticism about Drinking, Drink Refusal Skills, Resolving Relationship Problems, and Developing Social Support Networks.

In contrast, the intrapersonal skills training content is focused on learning to cope with specific, intrapersonal drinking triggers and to incorporate new general lifestyle coping strategies (Monti et al., 2002). According to Monti and colleagues (2002), the skills necessary for coping with intrapersonal drinking triggers include managing urges to drink, anger, negative moods, and planning for emergencies. General lifestyle strategies include learning new ways of problem solving, learning to avoid high-risk drinking situations, and finding ways to balance enjoyable and obligatory activities in one's life (Monti et al., 2002). More specifically, the sessions for the intrapersonal skills section include: Managing Urges to Drink or Use, Problem Solving, Increasing Pleasant Activities, Anger Management, Managing Negative Thinking (and Thoughts about Alcohol and Drugs), Seemingly Irrelevant Decisions, and Planning for Emergencies. As can be surmised from the session titles, this section has more of a cognitive focus than the interpersonal skills section, and for this reason, is not recommended for use with clients who have cognitive or memory deficits or low levels of education (Monti et al., 2002). Although Monti and colleagues (2002) do not recommend a particular sequence or number of sessions, they suggest the following when deciding how to implement the intrapersonal section:

1. It may be useful to present the more complex cognitive restructuring skills (e.g. managing urges, problem solving, managing anger, negative thinking, and planning for emergencies) at the end of the treatment program if temporary cognitive deficits due to the early recovery process are present.
2. If there is little evidence of temporary cognitive deficit, it may be more beneficial to begin with the sessions on managing urges to drink, coping with craving, and problem solving. This will allow clients to implement this information earlier in the treatment process, and thus help them to maintain abstinence. Similarly, if introduced early, the problem-solving content can be used as a framework to discuss issues throughout treatment, thereby allowing the client more opportunities to develop more complex problem-solving abilities.
3. The planning for emergencies session should always come last as a preparation for implementing coping strategies at the conclusion of treatment.

Selection of Sessions for Individuals and Groups

The most recent Monti and colleagues (2002) manual offers seventeen sessions for use in CBST individual or group treatment settings so that sessions can be selected that best meet the needs of individual clients or target populations. The core sessions identified within the NIAAA manual (which are also very similar to those within the NIDA manual) include a combination of intra- and interpersonal coping skills (with a larger emphasis on intra-personal skills): (1) Managing Urges to Drink/Use, (2) Managing Negative Thoughts (3) Managing Thoughts About Drinking/Using, (4) Problem Solving, (5) Drink/Drug Refusal Skills, (6) Planning for Emergencies, and (7) Seemingly Irrelevant Decisions. Four of these sessions are extremely important for dealing with coping with recovery—Managing Urges to Drink/Use, Problem Solving, Seemingly Irrelevant Decisions, and Planning for Emergencies—these sessions should be used in all adapted CBST treatment efforts. Additionally, when selecting sessions, it is important to consider the fact that research has shown that *additional training in inter-personal skills results in significantly and substantively lower alcohol consumption for a broader spectrum of clients than intrapersonal skills training alone* (Monti et al., 1990). The core sessions are primarily intrapersonal, with the exception of drink/drug refusal skills, so it may be beneficial to supplement these core sessions with interpersonal skill sessions.

Beyond the seven core sessions identified above, Longabaugh and Morgenstern (1999) propose a framework for selecting additional CBST treatment sessions based on client strengths and deficits called *Broad Spectrum Therapy.* In this approach, the therapist conducts an assessment of the client's individual strengths and deficits and develops an individualized treatment plan based upon this assessment (Longabaugh & Morgenstern, 1999). If ongoing assessment suggests that new sessions are necessary or that previously selected sessions are now unnecessary, the treatment plan can be altered (Longabaugh & Morgenstern, 1999). This approach then allows for the tailoring of the curriculum, especially in an individual treatment setting, to meet the unique needs of the client. An example of how the therapist might go about selecting and planning treatment sessions for Sally, the case example introduced at the beginning of the chapter, follows.

A CASE EXAMPLE: SELECTING AND PLANNING CBST TREATMENT SESSIONS

This first case study relies on the case information for Sally (presented earlier in this chapter). Based upon Sally's diagnosis of alcohol dependence, the therapist selects the following six CBST core sessions: Drink Refusal Skills, Managing Urges to Drink, Problem Solving, Managing Negative Thinking, Seemingly Irrelevant Decisions, and Planning for Emergencies. Sally's depressive mood may also improve by finding ways to manage her negative thinking. Drink refusal skills will also be very important, as she will need to learn how to refuse alcohol in a business environment that often includes meeting at alcohol-serving establishments. Additional sessions that may improve her mood by helping her become more assertive include: Introduction to Assertiveness, Giving and Receiving Positive Feedback, Giving Constructive Criticism, and Receiving Criticism about Drinking. Similarly, the session on developing social support networks may be useful in helping Sally develop friendships and connections with family members that will support her effort to remain sober and cope better with life in general. The final session selected was the Increasing Pleasant Activities session so that Sally could find ways to balance her work life (which often included drinking) with more pleasurable and social activities.

The therapist begins with an introduction to the CBST treatment approach. Since Sally has already gone through the early phases of recovery, there is no sign of cognitive deficit, and she is receiving treatment while integrating back into her typical life routine, the therapist decides that the first few sessions should focus on managing urges to drink and problem solving. The managing urges session should provide skills to help Sally deal with any urges that may occur early in the treatment process, while the problem-solving session may be useful for helping her deal with a wide array of problems that may occur in her daily life. The therapist believes that the next more urgent and relevant skills for Sally to learn include assertiveness, dealing with negative thinking, and refusing alcohol. These sessions will be utilized to help Sally address her concerns (and affect) related to perfectionistic thinking (and any other identified irrational thinking) and difficulty with being assertive.

After these sessions are completed, the therapist will introduce Sally to the sessions on increasing pleasant activities and developing a support network to help her build positive supports and activities within her life. Since Sally does not have many people within her support network, it may take her some time to build this network. As a part of treatment, the therapist will be encourage her to attend AA self-help groups and explore some pleasant activities that are social in nature in order to identify and get to know persons who may be viable additions to her support network. The therapist will also explore the possibility of including certain family members in the support network. Next, the assertiveness skills that were learned will be further strengthened by introducing the following sessions: Giving and Receiving Positive Feedback, Giving Constructive Criticism, and Receiving Criticism about Drinking. Finally, the therapist will wrap up treatment by providing a termination session focused on planning for emergencies.

STRUCTURE OF INDIVIDUAL AND GROUP SESSIONS

The length of each individual session is 60 minutes, and approximately 15 to 20 minutes should be allocated at the beginning of each session to supportive therapy or the exploration of current client concerns (Kadden et al., 1994). Group inpatient sessions are typically 50 to 60 minutes long, while group outpatient sessions are typically 90 minutes in duration (Monti et al., 2002). Within the 90-minute group session, clients are given approximately 30 to 45 minutes to engage in supportive group therapy, while only 20 to 25 minutes of supportive therapy should be allotted for the shorter inpatient group sessions (Monti et al., 2002). This initial phase of supportive therapy is used to acknowledge the importance of clients' current real-life concerns, assess progress and functioning, and ensure that clients view the session as relevant to their current needs (Kadden et al., 1994). It is important, however, that the therapist maintain a skills-training approach during this discussion. One way to do this is to use the problem-solving format mentioned in the CBST problem-solving session (Kadden et al., 1994). If the client is resistant to moving from the concerns that have been brought up during the brief period of supportive therapy, the therapist should remind him or her of the CBST treatment rationale and focus and emphasize that it is time-limited therapy that is not designed to explore all issues until they are completely resolved (Kadden et al., 1994).

Following the brief supportive therapy, the session becomes more structured, focusing next on a brief review of the skills taught in the prior session and the homework assignment completed by the client (Kadden et al., 1994). Ideally, some discussion of these skills and the assignment will have occurred during the initial 15- to 20-minute supportive therapy session, and effort should be made by the therapist to connect client issues to prior content and skills.

The therapist then introduces the new material, beginning with the rationale for that particular session (Kadden et al., 1994). This is to engage clients in the session by making connections between the specific skill and drinking or using drugs. To increase group member's interest in the session, it is helpful to ask questions that solicit participant's experiences relevant to the presented topic while introducing the rationale (Monti et al., 2002).

The skill guidelines (as shown in the reminder sheet at the end of each individual session), or tips provided to help clients learn the new skill, are then presented in visual format (chalkboard, poster board, handout) and didactically by the therapist, although the therapist should not lecture for an extended length of time and should solicit input and reactions from the clients (Kadden et al., 1994). The goal in introducing these guidelines is to "teach specific coping strategies while encouraging a flexible application of them, consistent with each individual's goals, and with situational parameters" (Monti et al., 2002, p. 43).

Several sessions require that the therapist model the newly introduced skills so that an adequate demonstration of each skill can be observed by the client(s). These sessions include standard vignettes that can be used for this purpose; however, clients within the group may prefer to come up with their own personally relevant vignettes (Monti et al., 2002).

Next, clients are asked to engage in a behavioral rehearsal role-play, or to role-play self-generated scenes in a way that reflects their daily experiences. At least one-third of the session should focus on behavior rehearsal role-playing so that clients get an adequate amount of time to practice the new skill (Kadden et al., 1994). There is often some resistance, at least initially, on the part of the client in participating in the role-playing exercises. For this reason, the therapist should expect to provide a good deal of structure and encouragement to get this process started (Kadden et al., 1994). In a group setting, clients should be paired into dyads and should practice in front of the group so that they can receive feedback and support from the therapists and other group members (Monti et al., 2002). After feedback and support have been provided, the dyad should then practice the role-play again while trying to implement the group's suggestions (Monti et al., 2002). At the conclusion of the group, clients should be provided with the reminder sheets that include a summary of the skill guidelines and the week's homework assignment. Some sessions include detailed information regarding how to introduce the practice exercise. Within the individual session, the therapist can partner with the client in the behavioral role reversal exercises, either as the individual client (to model useful responses for the client to emulate) or the protagonist (to aid the client in practicing their skills within the described situation).

General Treatment Process Issues for CBST

There are several general treatment process issues to consider before implementing CBST group or individual interventions. This section covers several of these issues, including therapist training and role, treatment guidelines, use of a co-therapist in a group setting, treatment contracting, tips on implementing behavioral rehearsal role-plays and practice exercises, use of review sessions, the inclusion of significant others in the treatment process, alcohol and drug use during treatment, the length of the program, and issues germane to a CBST group setting. The general treatment issues covered in this section are borrowed largely from the Monti and colleagues' (2002) and Kadden and colleagues' manuals to ensure that the CBST approach is described with fidelity.

Therapist Training and Role   CBST was designed to be administered by mental health professionals who have at least a master's degree, although Monti and colleagues (2002) report having used bachelor's level professionals to work as group co-therapists. Similarly, they have found it important to have at least one year of experience working in the substance abuse field before administering CBST. Therapists, at a minimum, should:

- Be well-trained in psychotherapy skills and behavioral principles;
- Be able to model good interpersonal skills;
- Be comfortable with being directive and actively involved in role-playing and modeling exercises during the treatment process (Monti et al., 2002).

Therapist Guidelines Therapists are advised to read the content for each session prior to each meeting with the client (Monti et al., 2002). To standardize delivery and to ensure that the session stays on track, therapists are encouraged to bring a copy of the "Skill Guidelines" for each session on a large poster board, blackboard, or some other visual display. Examples of the skill guidelines are listed within the Reminder and Practice Exercise Sheets in Figures 5.1 through 5.4. While it is important that the delivery of the content for each session follows the standard guidelines, it is equally important that this text is not read verbatim or presented in a "cookbook" or mechanistic fashion. Rather, the information should be delivered in a "free-flowing presentation style" (Monti et al., 2002, p. 23). Similarly, it is essential that clients are encouraged to share their own thoughts and experiences regarding each session to ensure that the material is more interesting and relevant to clients. Self-disclosure and a sense of humor, as long as used appropriately, can greatly enhance the therapeutic process and demonstrate that therapists also face their own difficulties in coping with certain situations (Monti et al., 2002).

Use of Co-therapist Teams for CBST Groups Monti and colleagues (2002) suggest that CBST groups be led by co-therapist teams, preferably one female and one male. A mixed gender team ensures that both genders are available for adequate modeling (Monti et al., 2002). It is quite possible, however, that feasibility constraints will preclude the use of two therapists or a mixed gender team, and in these cases, one therapist is sufficient (Monti et al., 2002). If co-therapists are used, one typically takes a "content" role and the other a "process" role. The "content" role involves making sure that all of the relevant content is covered in a given session, while the "process" role involves attending to and responding to group process issues as they arise (Monti et al., 2002). For example, if the overall group becomes less engaged at some point, this therapist may either share a relevant and interesting example or suggest moving to new content (Monti et al., 2002). Therapists should not stay in the same role during the entire treatment process to prevent role stereotyping (Monti et al., 2002). It is essential that a good rapport is established between co-therapists and that they are able to communicate effectively. This can greatly impact the tone of the session and is essential for modeling good communication and interaction skills.

Treatment Contract   A treatment contract is used within the CBST approach to communicate the expectations of treatment and to improve the chances that clients will commit to trying out the intervention for at least four sessions before deciding to stay or drop out (Monti et al., 2002). This contract can include commitment to at least four sessions, consistent attendance and promptness, an agreement to abstain from alcohol and drugs while in treatment and attending sessions, and a commitment to complete the homework assignments. All clients should sign this contract and keep a copy for themselves. A copy of a sample treatment contract for individual treatment settings is included below (see Figure 5.1). This can be adapted for use in group settings by incorporating issues of group confidentiality.

Individual Treatment Contract for CBST

1. I understand that this treatment will last _____ weeks, and I agree to participate for that length of time. If I want to withdraw from the program, I agree to discuss this decision with my therapist prior to taking this action.
2. I agree to attend all sessions and to be prompt. If it is absolutely necessary that I cancel a session, I will call in advance to reschedule. I also agree to call in advance if I will be late to a session.
3. I understand that this treatment is intended for people who want to abstain from drugs and alcohol. I understand that I must work on remaining abstinent for this program to be most effective.
4. I agree that it is essential for me to come to the session drug and alcohol free. I understand that I will be asked to leave any session to which I come after using drugs or alcohol. I will be asked to arrange safe transportation home.
5. I understand that I will be expected to practice and implement some of the skills I discuss in treatment. I agree to bring in the practice exercise sheet each week to discuss with my therapist.
6. I agree to work on the following specific goals during the next _____ weeks.

    1. _____
    2. _____
    3. _____

I have reviewed the above statements with my therapist, and we both agree to abide by them.

Signature   Date

_____   _____
_____   _____

Figure 5.1   Sample Individual Treatment Contract
Reproduced with permission from Kadden et al. (1994).

Behavioral Rehearsal Role-Play Guidelines   Behavioral rehearsal role-play is the central technique used within CBST to help clients acquire new coping skills. Each session should provide a "safe haven" where clients feel comfortable practicing these new skills before they try them in the real world (Monti et al., 2002, p. 24). Because it is so important that the client have the opportunity to practice and repractice these skills, the therapist must ensure that the individual or group does not get sidetracked by discussing problem situations. Rather, the focus of any discussion should be primarily focused on how to improve the use of each specific coping skill (Monti et al., 2002).

It is not uncommon initially for clients to be resistant to or feel uncomfortable about participating in the role playing exercises, especially in front of a group (Kadden et al., 1994; Monti et al., 2002). The therapists may also experience their own resistance for similar reasons (Monti et al., 2002). This should be acknowledged by the therapist as a normal reaction (and if true, an apprehension even on the part of the therapist), and clients should be encouraged that role-playing will get easier as time goes by. If there is a great deal of apprehension, the therapist may need to start the role-play scenario, and it is likely that the client will then begin to participate (Monti et al., 2002). Additionally, the therapist should try to be aware of this resistance and avoid efforts on the part of the client(s) or herself to get sidetracked into discussing other issues instead of implementing the role playing exercises (Monti et al., 2002).

It is important that clients generate their own personally relevant scenes so that the skills practiced will be useful for real-life situations. Initially, these scenes should only be of moderate difficulty (Monti et al., 2002). When the client seems to have mastered moderately difficult scenes, he or she should then be encouraged to select more difficult or complex scenes (Monti et al., 2002). An adequate description of a scene includes the following: where it takes place, the primary problems/goals, whom the role-play partner should portray, and the relevant behaviors of the person portrayed so that the partner can enact the situation (Monti et al., 2002). Ideally, the client will come up with his or her own situation. In the event that the client believes that he or she is unable, the therapist might try, in the following order, to:

1. Prompt the client to recall a situation in the past where the use of the skill might have resulted in a more desirable outcome, or to ask him or her to anticipate a difficult situation that might arise in the future where the skill might be useful.
2. Suggest an appropriate situation based on his or her knowledge of current client circumstances.

3. Self-disclose an appropriate situation based on her knowledge of the client's recent circumstances, or a situation in which she has recently had difficulty within her own life.
4. Create a hypothetical situation for role playing (the very last resort) (Monti et al., 2002).

An example of how the therapist might help stimulate the participation of clients in the behavioral rehearsal role plays is included in the following case example.

It is important that each client experience behavioral rehearsal role-playing in such a way that is "productive and encouraging" (Monti et al., 2002, p. 25). Each individual should have the opportunity to receive praise, recognition, and constructive criticism that is useful for improving his or her own coping skills in both individual and group settings.

A CASE EXAMPLE: STIMULATING PARTICIPATION IN BEHAVIORAL REHEARSAL ROLE PLAYS

Reyna is the therapist for a new CBST group that is being provided in an outpatient setting. She has ten female clients in her group between the ages of 21 and 40 who have all been diagnosed with alcohol dependency. The first group focused primarily on introductions of group members and the therapist, as well as an introduction to the rationale and approach of CBST treatment. Today she began the second group session, which focuses on problem solving. She introduced the rationale and skill guidelines successfully, but noticed that only one or two women in the group were participating. When it came time for the behavioral rehearsal role-plays, she asked each client to come up with a situation or scenario that represented a problem she would like to work on. Each client was asked to describe the problem as accurately as possible so that the group could brainstorm possible solutions, and then identify the best alternative together. Eight of the group members were having a very difficult time coming up with a problem situation. Reyna wanted the group content to be relevant to each individual, so she used some techniques to further encourage and assist group members in identifying such scenarios.

Reyna began by encouraging group members to think about a past situation in which they wished they had better been able to stop, calmly think about the potential options and solutions, and then identify and carry out the best choice. She shared, "This may have been a situation in which you acted too hastily and did something you regretted, or maybe it is a situation that you keep getting stuck in and you aren't sure what to do—like not knowing what to do when someone offers you a drink, how to deal with conflict at work, how to deal with your negative moods, or how to deal with family conflict at home." Some group members were able to think of new situations, but some still had difficulty. Reyna made a special effort to provide social praise and recognition to those group members who were able to successfully identify situations in order to reinforce such effort in the future.

For those group members still having difficulty, Reyna asked group members to think of a situation that might arise in the future where having a problem-solving strategy might be useful. She stated, "While you might not be able to think of something from the past, perhaps there is a situation you are anticipating in which the use of a problem-solving strategy might be useful? For example, is there a person in your life right now that you are having difficulty getting along with? Someone who may not understand your efforts to remain sober? Or maybe you anticipate having difficulty finding a job, obtaining transportation, or finding a good sober friend for support? It can be any potential problem or issue you think you might deal with in the future. . . . "

All but one group member was able to identify a problem situation based on Reyna's second strategy to stimulate participation. For this final group member, Reyna (who is very familiar with all clients on an individual basis as well) suggested an appropriate situation based on her knowledge of this client. Reyna suggested, "Lisa, I know you have mentioned having some difficulty with your landlord in the last month or so. I remember you sharing that he wanted you to pay for a broken window that some kids in the neighborhood had broken while playing ball and you thought this was unfair. Would you like to share this situation, how you chose to handle it, and some potential options for handling the situation?" Reyna specifically chose this situation because she knew that Lisa handled the situation in an assertive manner (she had consulted with Reyna about what to do and shared that the situation had turned out well) and that this would then be an empowering way to encourage her further participation in group activities.

While Reyna was able to get all group members to participate using these first three strategies, further strategies for stimulating participating in behavioral rehearsal role-plays include (1) having the group leader self-disclose about a situation in which he or she had difficulty; and as a last resort, (2) creating a hypothetical situation for role-playing.

Within an individual treatment setting, both the therapist and client should next share their reactions to the performance (e.g., How did each person feel? What was the result and how desirable was it? How was each individual affected?) (Kadden et al., 1994). Next, the therapist should offer comments about the role-play (Kadden et al., 1994). These comments should be both supportive/reinforcing and constructively critical, focused on behavior only, and if there are several deficiencies, the therapist should only choose one or two to work on at one time (Kadden et al., 1994). The client can then be asked to repeat the role-play while incorporating the feedback (Kadden et al., 1994). If necessary, the therapist might decide to model or demonstrate the new skill as necessary by using "role reversal," whereby the therapist plays the client and the client plays the target person (Kadden et al., 1994). This can also be beneficial for the client as he or she is able to experience what it might be like to be on the receiving end of the interaction (Kadden et al., 1994).

Within a group setting, the therapist(s) should do the following after each role-play:

1. Ask both partners to provide their own reactions to the performance (e.g., How did each person feel? What was the result and how desirable was it? How was each individual affected?).
2. Ask group members to provide their comments about the performance. They should be encouraged to remain focused on relevant issues and provide only supportive or constructive feedback. The therapist may find it necessary to only solicit positive feedback from group members at first, while modeling how to give constructive feedback.
3. Provide his or her own comments about the role-play. If there are several deficiencies in the role-play, only one or two should be selected to work on initially. (Monti et al., 2002)

The dyad engaged in the role-playing is then encouraged to reenact the role-play based on the group's feedback (Monti et al., 2002). If the therapist finds that the client or group is having difficulty grasping a key concept, she or he (or a very skilled group member) may decide to model the new skill (role reversal) while the client takes on the role of the target person.

Practice Exercises (Homework)   Each session includes a preplanned homework exercise so that the client can practice newly learned skills in the real-world setting. The practicing of such skills in the real-world increases

" . . . the likelihood that these behaviors will be repeated in similar situations (generalization)" (Monti et al., 2002, p. 27). In addition to practicing the new skill, some homework assignments ask clients to record information about the situation, their response to the situation, and an evaluation of this response (Monti et al., 2002). Homework assignments can be modified as necessary or added to at the discretion of the therapist and can be used in both inpatient and outpatient settings (Monti et al., 2002). Certainly, it is easier for clients to implement "real-world" practice exercises if they are in aftercare or outpatient treatment; however, inpatient clients can be encouraged to practice these skills with staff, other patients, or visitors (Monti et al., 2002).

Compliance with homework assignments is a common problem with CBST, as it is with behavioral therapy in general (Monti et al., 2002). Monti and colleagues (2002) suggest the following to maximize client's compliance with the practice exercises:

- Refrain from calling the assignments "homework" and instead call them "practice exercises."
- Provide a good rationale and description of what is expected for the practice exercise.
- Elicit any problems that the clients foresee in their ability to complete each practice exercise.
- Help clients identify a certain time to work on the practice exercise.
- Start each session with some time on reviewing the prior week's practice exercise and make an effort to praise all efforts to complete the work.
- When the exercise is not completed, brainstorm within the group or individual session to explore what might be done to ensure compliance with the next assignment.

Review Sessions The therapist may choose to schedule review sessions every fourth or fifth session to review the prior skills that have been taught, assess progress, and repractice prior skills (Monti et al., 2002). Such repetition will increase the chance that such information is retained and used in the future. It also offers clients an opportunity to reflect upon and discuss how these skills have since been used in their lives. If problems in the application of these skills have been encountered, the group or therapist-client dyad can discuss potential solutions. Mini-reviews can also occur at the beginning of group or individual sessions as needed (Monti et al., 2002).

Less Motivated Clients Increased attention has been focused within the last decade within substance abuse treatment on the disparate levels of readiness for change (Miller & Rollnick, 2002). According to Velasquez and colleagues (2001, p. 7; also see Chapter 1), the transtheoretical model of behavior change (TTM) consists of the following five stages:

- Precontemplation: Not seeing a problem.
- Contemplation: Seeing a problem and considering whether to act.
- Preparation: Making concrete plans to act soon.
- Action: Doing something to change.
- Maintenance: Working to maintain change.

As noted previously, the immediate use of CBST is contraindicated for clients who are in the precontemplation or contemplation stages of change, as clients who are less motivated for change are also less likely to be interested in learning and practicing new skills to decrease or stop their substance use (Monti et al., 2002). Instead, Monti and colleagues (2002) suggest that clients in these early stages of change may benefit first from one to three sessions of motivational interviewing to assist in moving them into a later stage of change in preparation for CBST treatment. Consistent with this approach, therapists are encouraged to "roll with resistance" and avoid arguing or confrontation. In addition, therapists should also emphasize that CBST skills are also relevant for other areas of their lives in addition to reducing their substance use. Finally, within the group setting, clients often become more motivated for change as a result of group dynamics and the encouragement of other group members (Monti et al., 2002). An example of how to work with a less motivated client is illustrated in the following case example.

A CASE EXAMPLE: THE LESS MOTIVATED CLIENT

Rodney is a 24-year-old male who was recently referred by the drug court to complete a day treatment program for cocaine dependency. A part of the day treatment program includes completing a daily CBST treatment group. Prior to entering the group and after completing his five-day detoxification period, Rodney meets with the therapist for a session to introduce him to the CBST approach and to assess his motivation for change. Rodney shares, "I've thought about quitting quite a bit, and getting arrested for selling it really was a kick in the pants, but I'm still not completely sure I'm ready to let it go. . . ." This statement suggested to the therapist that Rodney was in the contemplation stage of change (thinking about it, but not yet ready to change), and she shared, "Rodney, it isn't uncommon to be unsure about whether you're ready to change. Perhaps it would be good for us to meet a few times together to assess where you're at and what would be most useful for you while you're in treatment." In this case, the therapist is "rolling with resistance" and setting up the treatment process to include one to three sessions of individual motivational interviewing prior to entering treatment (if CBST treatment is eventually agreed on as the right course of action). As a part of these one to three sessions, the therapist will also inform Rodney of the CBST approach and note that many of the skills learned will be useful in numerous situations within the client's life, regardless of whether he decides to stop using. If Rodney decides to enter treatment, other group members may help him get over some of his resistance to change. However, if Rodney does enter the CBST group and remains at a low level of motivation for several sessions, it is probably time to start exploring other treatment options, such as motivational interviewing.

Inclusion of Significant Others   Relational stressors commonly lead to drinking or using drugs (Monti et al., 2002). For this reason, the CBST approach encourages clients to include a spouse or significant other (if present in the client's life) in the treatment process (Monti et al., 2002). For example, in the case of Sally, her spouse would be an essential person to include in treatment so that they can develop or further solidify communication skills that reinforce Sally's effort to become more assertive. Her husband's involvement may also help him to better understand the types of changes she is trying to make and to support her while she is attempting to achieve and maintain sobriety. The focus of these sessions should be on content from the interpersonal skills section, and the session can take place in either individual or group format. If the group format is going to be used, the group should have no more than six to eight clients—or a total of twelve to sixteen—in the group, including significant others. The topics for these interpersonal sessions center on improving communication and reducing conflict among romantic couples that can lead to future relapse for the client (Monti et al., 2002). While Monti and colleagues (2002) ideally recommend including the significant other two or three times a week, they acknowledge that such a time commitment may be too demanding for family members. If this is the case, they suggest holding one extended (2-hour) multifamily group session with family members per week. Additionally, they note that it is not uncommon for some couples to be so conflicted that they have a hard time participating in the role-playing exercises. When this occurs, the therapist is encouraged to role-play the skills with each member of the couple separately, and then have the couple try to replicate the skill with one another (Monti et al., 2002).

Since the inclusion of significant others in treatment is primarily to increase communication and coping skills with significant others to prevent relapse, CBST does not always result in major family systems change or the resolution of extreme marital distress (Monti et al., 2002). While it is essential to explore communication related to substance use, such discussions are likely to also result in the elicitation of more "deep-seated" issues related to trust, anger, intimacy, abandonment, dependency, and narcissistic needs (Kadden et al., 1994, p. 15). Since these issues often require a great deal of time, it is essential that the therapist make an effort to keep each session focused on observable behaviors related to substance use or poor communication skills that can be targeted with the CBST approach (Kadden et al., 1994). Additionally, couples with exceedingly high levels of dysfunction should be referred out to other forms of psychotherapy or marital/family therapy (Monti et al., 2002).

If the CBST intervention is going to be delivered in a group format, it is probably better to create a group in which significant others will participate and a group for individuals who do not have a significant other.

Alcohol and Drug Use during Treatment Clients are asked to remain abstinent from all alcohol and nonprescribed psychoactive substances for the duration of treatment (Monti et al., 2002). The therapist should explain that it is ". . . common for clients to have some ambivalent feelings about accepting abstinence as a goal, and [clients] are encouraged to discuss these feelings, as well as any actual slips that may occur" (Monti et al., 2002, p. 35). Clients are urged to remain in treatment despite relapsing, but are asked to not attend any treatment session while under the influence of alcohol or drugs. Similarly, the therapist should take special care to avoid communicating information about possible relapse in such a way that it can be misinterpreted as validation of future use and to ensure that excessive attention within the group setting for a client's relapse does not reinforce future alcohol or drug use (Monti et al., 2002).

The use of alcohol or drug use testing has been used in combination with CBST. The benefit of a routine testing policy is to avoid unnecessary accusations, guessing, and finding out after the fact that someone is attending a session under the influence (Monti et al., 2002). A routine testing policy, however, takes a great deal of time. Instead, testing may also be implemented at the therapist(s) discretion—this approach takes less time, but may place the therapist in more of a potentially undesirable "detective" role (Monti et al., 2002).

Clients should be informed that if they happen to experience a relapse, they should immediately get rid of the alcohol or drugs that have been used, remove themselves from the situation, and get help from an AA sponsor, friend, or other support person (Monti et al., 2002). They should also be cautioned that they will likely experience guilt, self-blame, and catastrophizing thoughts (e.g., "I've blown it. I'll never be able to change.") and that they should not let these thoughts and feelings lead to further alcohol or drug use. Similarly, clients should be encouraged to use the relapse experience as an opportunity to process and learn more about the triggers—the who, when, and where of the situation, and anticipatory thoughts—so that future occurrences can be easier to avoid (Monti et al., 2002).

Length of Program The original CBST model includes twelve group sessions; however, significant reductions in drinking and other substance use problems can result with only five to eight sessions when integrated with a partial hospital program or as an adjunct with other treatment approaches (Monti et al., 2002; Rohsenow et al., 2001). For guidance on selecting relevant sessions for the length of treatment desired, please refer to the earlier section within this chapter entitled "Selection of Sessions for Individuals and Groups."

Issues to Consider When Running a CBST Group There are several issues that are unique to implementing CBST in a group setting. The first is whether an open (additional group members can be added after treatment starts) or closed (no new members can be added) group format is used. CBST groups can be run as either open or closed groups, as each lesson is unique and has its own rationale, set of skill guidelines, and homework assignments (Monti et al., 2002). Having open groups might also be attractive to agencies that have waiting lists or need to, for financial reasons, maintain a certain number of clients in the group. The benefits, however, of having closed groups are that there is usually greater group cohesion, consistent working relationships between group members, and the ability to maintain a consistent sequence of sessions and build off of prior topics that all group members have been exposed to (Monti et al., 2002).

It is essential, as with any group, to lay down the group ground rules. These rules (attendance, promptness, and alcohol and drug use) should be provided in the form of a treatment contract as shown in Figure 5.1. While this treatment contract is prepared for individual treatment, it can be adapted for use with groups by adding the unique group ground rules, including a request that group members maintain the confidentiality of group member identities and any information that individuals within the group share.

Finally, the size of a CBST group ideally should consist of eight to fifteen clients, but has actually ranged from two to thirty clients in real settings (Monti et al., 2002).

CBST Treatment Settings Cognitive behavioral skills training has been used in partial hospital/intensive day treatment, outpatient, and aftercare settings (Monti et al., 2002). In a partial hospital/intensive day treatment setting, clients benefit from the "safety" of their daily immersion in a partial hospital or day treatment setting. For this reason, therapists can more safely elicit strong feelings related to client high-risk drinking or drug situations, get to know the clients better, and better assess their strengths and weaknesses to adjust treatment accordingly (Monti et al, 2002). Partial hospital sessions are 50 to 60 minutes long and can be scheduled daily or twice daily, depending on the length of the program. A one group per day maximum is recommended, however, so that there is ample time between sessions for the clients to reflect on and complete the practice exercises. If a "rolling admissions" process is being used, new clients can be met with individually for a session or two to prepare them to join the group. As mentioned previously, the therapists can modify topics or eliminate sessions to fit the needs of the specific group members or agency target population (Monti et al., 2002).

The benefit of using CBST in an outpatient setting is the opportunity for clients to apply the skills they are learning in their everyday lives (Monti et al., 2002). They can learn new skills, try them out in personally relevant situations, and then process the outcome of these efforts within the group, thereby assisting them in developing self-efficacy to cope within their natural environment. It also offers the opportunity for support as clients deal with real cravings and temptations to drink or use drugs in their environment, and it also offers early intervention when relapse occurs. There are also drawbacks to having a client attend treatment while in an outpatient setting—there is a greater exposure to stressors and cues that can lead to relapse and distractions or resistance to treatment can lead to less consistent attendance and practice exercise completion than more intensive treatment settings (Monti et al., 2002).

Setting the Stage for Treatment   Prior to beginning the treatment process, it is essential that the therapist orientate the client to the CBST approach. The following script (slightly adapted for use with drugs or other substances) is offered by Monti and colleagues (2002) as a guide when introducing clients to this approach:

> We *all* have some problems getting along with family, friends, and coworkers; meeting strangers; handling our moods and feelings. Everyone has different strengths and weaknesses in coping skills. Because alcohol [or substance use] is often used to cope with problems, interpersonal difficulties and negative feelings are often triggers for relapse. These triggers include such things as feeling frustrated with someone, being offered a drink [or drugs] at a party, and feeling depressed, angry, sad, lonely, and so on.
>
> *An important goal of this treatment is to teach some skills you can use to cope with your high-risk situations.* We will focus on ways to handle various difficult

interpersonal situations more comfortably and honestly. We will teach you some skills and have you practice these skills while role-playing these high-risk situations. In this way, you will learn to cope with high-risk situations and to prevent problems that could lead to drinking [or substance use]. (p. 45)

When introducing clients to this approach, it is important to emphasize that this approach is tailored to their individual needs and that they will get something unique and personally relevant out of the treatment process (Monti et al., 2002). Essentially, the message should be, "You will learn how to cope better with *your* problems" (Monti et al., 2002, p. 45).

This concludes the discussion of general treatment process issues when implementing CBST. The next two sections will provide an introduction to both interpersonal and intrapersonal CBST sessions and four sample CBST sessions (one interpersonal and three intrapersonal). These summaries rely heavily on content obtained from the Carroll (1998), Monti and colleagues' (2002) and Kadden and colleagues' (1994) CBST treatment manuals. Sample Reminder and Practice Exercise Sheets (homework) are included at the conclusion of each individual sample session.

Coping Skills Training Part I: Interpersonal Skills

The first part of the CBST curriculum focuses on the development of interpersonal or communication skills. These skills are important, as they can help clients deal more effectively with both interpersonal and intrapersonal high-risk situations that lead to relapse by offering a way to build a positive social support network that is critical to maintaining sobriety (Monti et al., 2002). The interpersonal skills sessions include the following topics: nonverbal communication, introduction to assertiveness, conversation skills, giving and receiving positive feedback, listening skills, giving constructive criticism, receiving criticism about drinking, drink/drug refusal skills, resolving relationship problems, and developing social support networks.

These sessions do not need to be implemented sequentially and sessions should be selected according to the unique needs of the individual client or treatment group. All CBST treatment efforts, however, should include the session on drink/drug refusal skills, given the universal importance of this skill for maintaining sobriety. An additional consideration when selecting the number of interpersonal sessions is that these kinds of sessions have been shown by research to have a broader impact on a wider range of clients than the intrapersonal sessions alone. Additionally, some of these sessions will be too elementary for some clients who generally have good social or communication skills (e.g., nonverbal communication). For this reason, the therapist should use his or her judgment to select sessions that best meet the needs and draw upon the strengths of the client. A sample session on drink/drug refusal skills is provided below.

Sample Session I: Drink/Drug Refusal and Assertiveness Skills   This session focuses on teaching clients how to assertively refuse alcohol and drugs. One of the most common, high-risk situations occurs when an individual with a substance abuse problem is offered drugs or alcohol (Monti et al., 2002). The therapist should begin the session by asking the client or group members if they have been offered drugs and/or alcohol since beginning recovery, how frequently, and in which situations it occurs (Monti et al., 2002). Their answers may vary based on treatment setting and individual issues, but this discussion will likely illustrate how common this situation is and why it is important to learn how to effectively refuse such offers. The therapist should then introduce the rationale for learning how to assertively refuse alcohol and/or drugs when they are offered. The rationale and context for learning this skill differs between those who have an alcohol problem and those with an illicit drug problem. Given the widespread use and access to alcohol within our culture, it is likely that alcohol will be offered by more people within more social situations than illicit drugs. For this reason, a separate rationale is offered for groups/individuals whose focus is on alcohol abuse versus groups/individuals where illicit drug use is the primary focus.

For Alcohol Abuse

> The social use of alcohol is very common in our culture, and it is encountered in a wide variety of situations and settings. Thus, even the person who totally avoids bars and old drinking buddies will still find him/herself in situations where others are drinking or making plans to go drinking. For example, family gatherings, sports events, office parties, restaurants, and dinner at a friend's home are only a few of the settings in which alcohol may be encountered. Weddings are particularly difficult because of toasting. A variety of different people might offer you a drink, such as relatives, dates, fellow workers, new acquaintances, old drinking buddies, and waiters and waitresses. The person may or may not know of your drinking history. An offer to drink may take the form of a single casual offer of a drink, or may involve repeated urgings and harassment. (Monti et al., 2002, p. 65)

In Sally's case, it will be especially important to ask about her work-related happy hour events and how she plans to handle these situations. Some suggested inquiries include:

"Have you thought about what you might do if you get invited to a work-related happy hour get together?"

"If you do feel obligated to attend a work-related happy hour event for work reasons, how will you refuse a drink? What will you say to your colleagues if they encourage you to drink?"

"Have you gotten rid of the alcohol that you have at home and at work?"

For Drug Abuse

A major issue for many drug users is reducing the availability of the specific drug and effectively refusing offers of this drug. Clients who remain ambivalent about reducing their drug use often have particular difficulty when offered the drug directly. Many drug users' social networks have so narrowed that they associate with few people who do not use drugs, and cutting off contact may mean social isolation. Also, many individuals have become involved in distribution, and extricating themselves from the distribution network is difficult. It is important for the therapist and clients to assess the current availability of drugs and figure out ways to minimize this availability. More specifically, the therapist should explore, with each client, whether they are currently selling drugs, and whether or not persons within their environment continue to use. Some useful inquiries include:

"If you wanted to use [insert drug/substance here], how long would it take you to get some? Is there any in your house? Are you still holding onto [list drug paraphernalia]?"

"The last few times you used, you said Tommy came to your house and suggested you take a drive. Have you thought about talking to Tommy about your decision to stop?"(Carroll, 1998, pp. 65–66)

Similarly, some drug abusers are in intimate relationships with other drug users and they may not be ready or willing to break off the relationship (Carroll, 1998). In these cases, the therapist should explore the best options for the client to minimize exposure to the substance (or other substances) of abuse. One example of what can be said is as follows:

"I hear you say that you feel like you want to stay with Bob for now, but he's not willing to stop using [list drug]. Being there is pretty risky for you, but maybe we can think of some ways to reduce the risk. Have you thought about asking him not to bring cocaine into the house or use it in the house? You've said that you know there's a lot of risk to you while he continues to do that, both in terms of your staying abstinent as well as having drugs around your kids."

Whether a person has a problem with alcohol or illicit drug use, being able to turn down a drink or drug requires more than a sincere decision to stop drinking or using (Monti et al., 2002). It is important to develop assertiveness skills that will help one "quickly and effectively" refuse the substance of choice in real-life situations (Monti et al., 2002, p. 65).

After introducing the rationale for learning how to assertively turn down alcohol or drugs, the therapist should then visually introduce the *skill guidelines* (adapted from both Monti et al., 2002 and Carroll, 1998):

When you are urged to drink (or use), keep the following in mind:

- Say "no" in a clear, firm, and unhesitating voice.
- Make direct eye contact.
- Ask the person to stop offering you a drink or drug and not to do so again.
- Don't leave the door open to future offers (by using excuses or vague answers).
- Suggest an alternative thing to do. If an alcoholic drink is offered, suggest getting together to have coffee or something to eat instead.
- You can change the subject.
- Remember: It's your right not to drink or use!

If the individual or group intervention is focused primarily on alcohol abuse, then the therapist should emphasize the fact that what is needed in any given situation to refuse a drink will vary depending on how the offer is made (Monti et al., 2002). Sometimes, one can simply say, "No, thank you," while in other cases it might be helpful to tell others about the drinking problem in order to enlist support. In most social situations it is OK to simply refuse a drink, as many people don't drink, and the therapist should emphasize the fact that it is a person's right not to drink in any social situation (Monti et al., 2002).

When the intervention is focused on illicit drug use, the therapist should acknowledge the likelihood that the clients will continue to be offered drugs by various individuals within their social network, which may include family, friends, dealers, and so on (Carroll, 1998).

Some individuals, such as dealers, have financial incentives to keep clients using, and for this reason, high pressure from these dealers can make it difficult for clients to remove themselves from this distribution network and refuse drugs. Similarly, a client might be in an intimate relationship with another person who uses and may not be ready or willing to break off this relationship. It is important that the client is able within these situations to negotiate with his or her partner that he or she will not use around the client or bring drugs within the common living environment (Carroll, 1998).

Some possible ways to change the subject and/or suggest an alternative that can be shared with clients include:

> "No, thanks, I don't use [or drink]. This is a great barbeque, and it's so nice to see you and all of the rest of my good friends."
> "No, I don't use [or drink] anymore. Would you like to play a game of darts or pool?"
> "No, I don't use [or drink]. However, I'd love a cup of coffee. Would you like to join me for some coffee at a nearby coffee shop?"

It is possible that it may not be enough to just say "no." In these cases, the client must learn to say "no" again and then request a behavior change. Some possible ways to request a behavior change include:

> "No, I told you I don't drink [or use] anymore. I'd like you to stop offering me alcohol [or drug]. If you can't do that, then I won't be able to spend time with you."
> "I've made it clear that I don't use [or drink] anymore. I wish that you would respect this decision by not asking me to use with you anymore. If you cannot do this, I'll have to ask you to stop coming over to my house."

Finally, clients should be encouraged not to make excuses or provide vague answers for why they are not drinking or using in a particular situation. This may lead others to think that they will use at a later time, increasing the chance that they will continue to be offered drugs and alcohol in the future (Monti et al., 2002). Phrases such as "Not tonight," or "Maybe later," are vague and should only be used as a last resort if someone is not respecting a simple "no" (Monti et al., 2002). In some cultures, especially when it is a family member or close friend who is using/offering, it may be more effective and socially acceptable for the client to provide a reason why he or she has decided to stop using. For example, an individual might state, "I've decided to stop drinking because I have decided to lose weight" or "If I use drugs, I might be randomly drug tested at work and lose my job."

After introducing these skill guidelines, the therapist(s) should *model* an effective and assertive way to refuse drugs or alcohol using the following situation suggested by Monti and colleagues:

The therapist role-plays a situation in which the protagonist is offered a drink [or drug of choice] at a brother's birthday party. Someone offers a drink or the drug of choice and is asked to help "celebrate" by using, and this person ignores the protagonist's first refusal by saying, "Oh, come on, just one drink [or a small amount of this drug] won't hurt you." (2002, p. 66)

Finally, clients should be asked to engage in the *behavioral rehearsal role-plays*. Given the fact that most clients will have already experienced these situations, they are very good at coming up with possible scenarios for this session (Monti et al., 2002). If a client cannot come up with a situation, ask him or her to anticipate a situation in which he or she might be offered drugs or alcohol in the future. The protagonist should offer the drink/drug a minimum of three times to give each client the opportunity to practice different kinds of refusal skills (Monti et al., 2002). Monti and colleagues (2002) suggest that role-plays should only be of moderate difficulty to start out and should encompass a wide range of potential social contexts. They also offer the following advice for therapists:

> In drink refusal role plays, the client asked to play the role of the drink/drug pusher often becomes overly enthusiastic in attempting to outsmart the client playing the role of the refuser. Although this may prove to be fun, and therapists should tolerate some bantering, it is important to ensure that more realistic and subtle situations are also presented. (Monti et al., 2002, p. 66)

Introduce the Reminder Sheet and Practice Exercise for this session (both of which are adapted from Monti et al., 2002; and Carroll, 1998) (see Figure 5.2).

COPING SKILLS TRAINING PART II: INTRAPERSONAL SKILLS

Intrapersonal coping skills are divided into two general categories: skills for coping with specific, intrapersonal drinking or using triggers and general lifestyle modification strategies (Monti et al., 2002). Skills for coping with intrapersonal triggers include managing urges to drink or use, anger, and other negative mood states, and planning for emergency situations. Lifestyle modification strategies include skills for identifying and coping with problems through systematic problem solving, avoiding high-risk situations through improved decision making, and improving the balance of enjoyable versus obligatory activities in one's daily life. These sessions have a more cognitive focus than the interpersonal skills sessions, and for this reason, are more complex and may pose difficulty for clients who have cognitive or memory deficits or lower educational backgrounds. Monti and colleagues (2002) do not recommend any particular number or sequence of the sessions, but do recommend that clients with temporary cognitive deficits (often seen in the early phases of recovery) receive the more complex cognitive restructuring exercises (i.e., managing urges, problem solving, managing anger and negative thinking, and planning for emergencies) in the latter phases of the treatment process. Three sample intrapersonal skills sessions on managing urges, problem solving, and planning for emergencies are provided below.

When you are urged to drink (or use), keep the following in mind:

- Say "no" in a clear, firm, and unhesitating voice.
- Make direct eye contact.
- Ask the person to stop offering you a drink or drug and not to do so again.
- Don't leave the door open to future offers (by using excuses or vague answers).
- Suggest an alternative thing to do. If an alcoholic drink is offered, suggest getting together to have coffee or something to eat instead.
- You can change the subject.
- Remember: It's your right not to drink or use!

PRACTICE EXERCISE

Listed below are some people who might offer you a drink (or drugs) in the future. Give some thought to how you will respond to them and write your responses under each item.

Someone close to you who knows about your drinking/drug problem:

_____

A friend I used to drink or use with:

_____

Co-worker:

_____

At a party:

_____

Other settings (primarily for alcoholics)

Boss:

_____

New acquaintance:

_____

Waitress/Waiter with others present:

_____

Figure 5.2 Reminder and Practice Exercise Sheet: Drink or Drug Refusal Skills
Monti et al., 2002; and Carroll, 1998. Reprinted with permission of Guilford Press.

Sample Session II: Managing Urges to Drink or Use Drugs This session is designed to prepare clients to manage and cope with their urges to drink or use drugs and should be included in all CBST interventions. It is helpful for the therapist to begin by defining what an "urge" is: "desiring, wanting, craving, or even thinking about a drink [or drugs], even though [one] intends not to drink [or use]" (Monti et al., 2002). Therapists should also normalize urges and identify the potential utility of such urges for maintaining sobriety. For example, the therapist might say:

It is normal to have urges, and you should expect them. There is no problem in thinking about drinking or using, as long as you don't act on these urges. These urges can instead serve as an important warning sign that something is wrong regarding the current situation or physical place that one is in. This session will help you improve your ability to deal with these urges by identifying common situations or events that trigger urges and the types of thoughts that can be useful or dangerous in response to such triggers. (Monti et al., 2002, p. 96)

The therapist should then review some of the common situations in which people may have urges to drink or use. Monti and colleagues (2002) share the following common situations and a rationale for each (Adapted and taken verbatim from Monti et al., 2002, pp. 96–97).

- *Remembering life as it was:* Some individuals may think about drinking or using as if it were "some long-lost friend." For example, "I've always celebrated my birthday by going to the bar—it just won't be the same."
- *Triggers in the environment:* Triggers associated with drinking or using are a major source of urges and include the sight of alcohol or a bar, seeing other people drink or use, and time cues, such as a certain time of day (getting off work) or day of the week (Friday night). When you leave a trigger situation, you may still feel urges for some time.
- *Crisis or stress:* During stress or crisis, an ex-drinker (or ex-substance abuser) may say, "I *need* a drink right now. When this is over, I'll stop drinking again." Anger is a very common trigger for drinking or using.
- *Feeling uncomfortable about being sober:* Some people find that new problems arise because of being sober, and they desire to drink or use to end those new problems. For example, "I'm being very short-tempered right now and irritable around my family. Maybe it's more important for me to be a good-natured parent and spouse than it is for me to stop drinking [or using] right now," or "I'm no fun to be around when I'm not drinking. I don't think I should stop drinking, because if I do, people won't enjoy or like me as much."
- *Testing control:* Sometimes, after a period of successful sobriety, ex-drinkers or users become overly confident. For example, "I bet I can have a few drinks with the guys tonight and go back on the wagon tomorrow," or "I bet I can just have one or two hits and it won't do anything."
- *Self-doubts:* You may doubt your ability to succeed at things. For example, "I just have no willpower," or "I tried to quit many times before and none of those efforts worked—why should it work this time?"

Clients should then be asked to attempt to identify their own specific thoughts and excuses related to drinking or using so that they can attempt to modify them (Monti et al., 2002). Some questions that the therapist(s) might ask include the following:

> "What thoughts about alcohol or your drug of choice preceded your last drinking or using episode after a period of sobriety?"
> "Which thoughts about alcohol or your drug of choice seem to be associated with the most frequent or strongest urges to drink or use?"
> "What circumstances, people, or events trigger these urges?" (Monti et al., 2002, pp. 97–98)

On the board, list client responses to these questions under the column headings: Triggers, Thoughts about Drinking/Using, Feelings and Urges, and Behavior.

While engaging in the above discussion during the session, Monti and colleagues provide the following advice when working with clients:

> It is often difficult for clients to grasp the material on analyzing and changing thoughts. If the concept is not understood from the outset, the many benefits of cognitive coping skills can be lost. Clients may initially be unaware of the thoughts or feelings that precede the decision to have a drink. They may simply state that they are not aware of any thought/feeling triggers, and that they "just start drinking, and that's all." This lack of awareness makes it difficult for clients to initiate the use of appropriate coping skills. (2002, p. 97)

To address this lack of awareness and help clients better recall their thoughts and feelings/urges, it may help to begin by exploring the trigger situations that elicited their drinking or using. Monti and colleagues suggest that it may be useful to have them "slow down the action" as in instant replays on TV (2002, p. 97). As clients become more aware of their "automatic thoughts" or beliefs about the situation and how they led to their feelings, they may be better able to examine the chain of thoughts associated with a previous urge to drink or use, improve their ability to self-monitor, and become more ready to learn how to modify their thoughts (cognitive restructuring). According to Monti and colleagues (2002), "The primary goal is to gradually make clients more aware of their thought processes when they have an urge to drink, and of their ability to control or counteract these thoughts with more adaptive coping thoughts that promote abstinence" (p. 97).

Another useful technique, especially when working with individual clients, is to encourage the client to better understand their unique experience of craving so that can better identify appropriate coping strategies (Carroll, 1998). Clients will vary in how they physically experience a craving (e.g., smell vs. physical sensation), how intense cravings are and how long they last, and how they currently cope with the craving/urge. To elicit such information, Carroll (1998) suggests asking the following questions:

What is a craving like for you?
How bothered are you by the craving?
How long does the craving last for you?
How do you try to cope with it?

This information allows the therapist to get a sense of the difficulty a client might experience when managing their urges during treatment and assist the client in identifying coping strategies that will be most useful based upon the client's unique coping style.

Next, the therapist should present the *skill guidelines* for managing urges to drink or use as presented visually in the Reminder Sheet at the end of this session.

- Change the trigger situation. Plan ahead to prevent avoidable triggers or leave the situation.
- Challenge your thoughts: Do you really need a drink or drug? Will you really not have fun without a drink or drug?
- Think of the benefits of sobriety (read list on card).
- Think of the negative consequences of relapse (read list on card).
- Carry photographs of loved ones who would be disappointed if you drank or used.
- Delay the decision: Remind yourself that urges decrease with time.
- Do something else: Find a safe but distracting activity that gives you pleasure or satisfaction.
- Call a sober support and try to talk it out. (Adapted from Monti et al., 2002, p. 118)

While covering this information, it is helpful if the therapist(s) provides examples of replacement thoughts for challenging thoughts about drinking or using. One example of a negative and problematic thought regarding drinking might be, *"I can't cope with this stress right now, I need a drink,"* and a possible replacement thought would be, *"I've learned new ways to cope with my stress, I can call my AA sponsor or go for a walk to deal with my stress. If I delay the decision to drink, this urge will probably pass."* The therapist might also provide examples of ways to engage in each of the suggested actions and encourage clients to maintain phone numbers of sober supports.

After presenting and discussing the skill guidelines, the therapist then asks clients to participate in an in-session *practice exercise* (this session does not include modeling or a behavioral role rehearsal) in which clients imagine difficult, high-risk situations (triggers, thoughts) and practice coping by changing their thoughts and utilizing other methods from the skill guidelines (Monti et al., 2002). It is most useful for clients if they are able to identify their own unique strategies to deal with their urges.

The Practice Exercise (homework) should then be introduced by asking clients to utilize the 3 × 5-inch card (provided by the therapist) to record a list of both the "personal benefits of staying sober" and the "negative consequences that would likely occur if I return to drinking [or using]" (Monti et al., 2002, p. 99). The therapist might introduce this exercise by sharing:

> It is often difficult in the midst of a tempting situation to think of all of the consequences of using and benefits of staying sober. This Practice Exercise will allow you the opportunity to think more in depth about your own personal consequences of using and benefits of staying sober, and to list them for future reference. You can use this 3 × 5-inch card to record this information (hand out card). After you have completed this exercise, you can keep this card with you and pull it out when you find yourself in a situation that you are having thoughts about using or drinking. Reading this card will at least remind you to consider the benefits of not using/drinking and challenge thoughts that may lead to relapse. It will also provide you with time to think about how you might escape the situation and delay drinking/using.

Clients should also be provided with the Reminder Sheet and description of the Practice Exercise for Managing Urges (see Figure 5.3).

Sample Session III: Problem Solving   This session teaches clients a very important skill for preventing relapse—problem solving. The therapist should begin by presenting a *rationale for learning* or improving problem solving in order to have a successful recovery and to become more successful and happy in life in general. It is important to convey to clients that all people find themselves in difficult situations, and these situations become problems when individuals do not know what to do or how to cope to deal with the situation (Monti et al., 2002). Problems might occur when dealing with other people (e.g., social situations, feelings), from one's thoughts and emotions, or from wanting to drink or use. While some problems are easily solved, others require more concentration and time, and the first impulse may not be the best decision (Carroll, 1998). When the proper effort or skills are not

Here are several ways to manage urges to drink or to use drugs:

- Change the trigger situation. Plan ahead to prevent avoidable triggers or leave the situation.
- Challenge your thoughts: Do you really need a drink or drug? Will you really not have fun without a drink or drug?
- Think of the benefits of sobriety (read list on card).
- Think of the negative consequences of relapse (read list on card).
- Carry photographs of loved ones who would be disappointed if you drank or used.
- Delay the decision: remind yourself that urges decrease with time.
- Do something else: Find a safe but distracting activity that gives you pleasure or satisfaction.
- Call a sober support and try to talk it out. (Adapted from Monti et al., 2002, p. 118).

PRACTICE EXERCISE
Provide clients with a 3 × 5-inch index card and ask them to prepare a final list of the benefits and unpleasant consequences of drinking or using. Ask them to read this card whenever they have thoughts of about drinking or using drugs.

Figure 5.3   Reminder and Practice Exercise Sheet: Managing Urges
Monti et al., 2002. Reprinted with permission of Guilford Press.

used to find a good solution to life's more difficult problems, then the pressure can become so great that it triggers drinking or using drugs (Monti et al., 2002).

The therapist should review and present visually the following skill guidelines for problem solving (Monti et al, 2002):

- Recognize that a problem exists.
- Identify the problem.
- Consider various approaches to solving the problem.
- Select the most promising approach.
- Assess the effectiveness of the selected approach.

The therapist should use these skill guidelines, also listed in the Reminder Sheet at the end of this session, as an outline to illustrate the following steps to problem solving (Monti et al., 2002): (1) Problem recognition (reliance on cues listed above); (2) identification of the problem (*"What is the problem?"*; gather as much information as possible and be concrete and define in terms of behavior; break it down into specific parts); (3) consideration of all possible approaches to solving the problem (*"What else can I do?"*; develop as many possible solutions to a given problem by brainstorming and writing them down; think about what has worked best in the past; try to "step back" and become objective as if advising a friend); (4) select the most promising approach (*"What will happen if . . . .?"*; this requires thinking ahead and considering all of the potential consequences—good and bad—that might result from each possible option); (5) assess the effectiveness of the selected approach (*"What happened when I . . . ?"*; implement the selected solution and then evaluate how effective it was in getting the result you anticipated; if it did not seem to work, try something new).

Monti and colleagues provide the following supplemental information for therapists who implement this session on problem solving:

> Problem solving is a skill that provides a flexible coping repertoire in situations that have not been previously encountered. Problem recognition is crucial, especially when the impulse is to minimize or deny problems. The very act of analyzing a problem situation and coming up with a range of possible solutions can also be a direct form of coping that can be used as an alternative to drinking [or using] when one is faced with a difficult situation. Situations requiring solutions can be alcohol [or drug] specific (e.g., at a party where [drugs or] alcohol are available), general (e.g., family illness, conflict at work), intrapersonal (e.g., feeling confused, lonely, depressed, tense) or interpersonal (e.g., family argument).

> Training in problem solving is used to accelerate the process of developing higher-order coping strategies that go beyond situation-specific skills. This enhances generalization of coping skills beyond the treatment situation and, in effect, encourages clients to "become their own therapists" when they are on their own. (2002, p. 100)

For these reasons, the problem-solving curriculum/session is essential to helping clients learn to more independently and effectively cope with all of life's demands on their own and without the use of alcohol and drugs. It is then essential for therapists to teach these skills as early as possible in treatment and to repeatedly reemphasize these skills during supportive therapy offered at the beginning of each session, and throughout all of the CBST treatment sessions.

Following the introduction of the skill guidelines, the therapist(s) should then proceed to the *behavior rehearsal role-plays*. The purpose of this exercise is to collaboratively (as a group or therapist-individual dyad) work through the problem-solving process together. Clients should be asked to begin this exercise by brainstorming and sharing with the group (or therapist) a real-life problem they would like to work on solving (Monti et al., 2002). As each client (or the individual client) shares a problem, ask him or her to describe it as precisely as possible and list each problem on the blackboard (or other writing surface). After each client shares, brainstorm as a group (or individually with the client) all of the possible solutions to the problem. Next, have the group (or work with the individual client) to weigh the advantages and disadvantages of each possible solution, and based on this analysis, prioritize the alternatives and pick the best option. Monti and colleagues suggest the following hypothetical problem if the group or individual cannot come up with a problem:

Your landlord is always crabby when he comes to collect the rent. One of the windows in your bedroom was cracked when you moved in; during a cold night, it cracked all the way, and a section is now out. When the landlord comes to collect the rent, you mention it to him. He screams at you and accuses you of breaking the window, saying that it was never cracked. Whenever he was crabby before, you simply let it go, but this time, he says you must pay to have the window replaced.

Present various definitions of the problem and have clients select the best one:

- The landlord is a real grouch.
- His screaming made you feel real down and hurt.
- You don't have enough money to pay for a new window.
- Your window is cracked and should be repaired by the landlord (correct answer).

Consider various approaches to solving the problem and have clients select the most promising one. Demonstrate the brainstorming process and the factors that go into selecting the apparent best solution (Monti et al., 2002, p. 102). An example of how this dialogue might go after the scenario is provided below:

THERAPIST: So given this situation, which of the following options do you think defines the real problem? One, the landlord is a real grouch. Two, his screaming made you feel real down and hurt. Three, you don't have enough money to pay for a new window. Or fourth, your window is cracked and should be repaired by the landlord.

CLIENT: They are all true. He's a real grouch, he made me feel bad, and my window is cracked and I don't have the money to pay it.

THERAPIST: Yes, all of the statements are true. But which of them is the BEST answer? Try to consider what is specifically causing you to feel down and why you're worried about not having enough money. What is it about the specific situation that is causing a problem for you now?

CLIENT: Well, I have to come up with the money to replace a window and I shouldn't have to do that.

THERAPIST: Right. Who should replace the window?

CLIENT: The landlord. So, I guess the problem is that the landlord is asking me to replace a cracked window and it's not really my fault—he should do it.

THERAPIST: Exactly! Let's brainstorm some ideas of what could be done to solve this problem. What can you (he or she) do about it?

CLIENT: Well, I can't pay for it because I don't have enough money so that's not an option.

THERAPIST: Yes. What other options are there?

CLIENT: I can go with a cracked window, but it will get cold or bugs might get in.

THERAPIST: Yeah, that's an option, but I can see how that isn't a desirable option because it doesn't solve the part of your problem that involves the cracked window.

CLIENT: I guess the other option would be to save up my money and replace the window eventually.

THERAPIST: I guess that's an option, but you would have to deal with the cold and bugs in the meantime. Can you think of anything else that you might be able to do?

CLIENT: Yes, I could talk to the landlord, but I'm not sure what I would say.

THERAPIST: (*If in a group setting, the therapist can solicit feedback from the group. If in an individual format, the therapist might say*) This is a situation in which it is important to use assertive communication. It will be important to think about what you might say beforehand, to be specific and direct, to use confident body language, and be willing to listen to the landlord's point of view. However, in this case, it is clear that it is his responsibility to replace the window, so if he is not hearing you, you will need to restate what you are saying and ensure that he knows that you will contact the proper authorities (which you should research in advance), if this problem is not taken care of.

CLIENT: I think I can do that, but it would be hard.

THERAPIST: Yes, I agree. It is not easy to deal with people who are crabby or to deal with conflict. But it is possible that he just had a bad day, and either way, in order to solve problems, we must often have to do things that we don't like. However, in the end, things usually work out better if we confront our problems head on.

These, in brief, are the steps of the problem-solving process:

- Recognize that a problem exists. "Is there a problem?" We get clues from our bodies, our thoughts and feelings, our behavior, our reactions to others, and the ways that other people react to us.
- Identify the problem. "What is the problem?" Describe the problem as accurately as you can. Break it down into manageable parts.
- Consider various approaches to solving the problem. "What can I do?" Brainstorm to think of as many solutions as you can. Try taking a different point of view. Try to think of solutions that worked before, and ask other people what worked for them in similar situations.
- Select the most promising approach. "What will happen if . . . ?" Consider all the positive and negative aspects of each possible approach, and select the one likely to solve the problem with the least hassle.
- Assess the effectiveness of the selected approach. "How well did it work?" After you have given the approach a fair trial, does it seem to be working out? If not, consider what you can do to beef up the plan and try one of the other possible outcomes.

PRACTICE EXERCISE
Select a problem you expect to find difficult. Describe it accurately. Brainstorm a list of possible solutions. Evaluate the possibilities and number them in the order of your preference.

Identify the problem:

_____

_____

_____

Brainstorm the list of possible solutions:

_____

_____

Figure 5.4   Reminder and Practice Exercise Sheet: Problem Solving
Monti et al., 2002. Reprinted with permission of Guilford Press.

The session should conclude by handing out the Reminder and Practice Exercise Sheets on Problem Solving (see Figure 5.4).

Sample Session IV: Seemingly Irrelevant Decisions   This session is focused on helping clients avoid making seemingly irrelevant decisions (SIDs), or those "decisions, rationalizations, and minimizations of risk that move [clients] closer to or even into high-risk situations, although they may seem unrelated to [alcohol or drug] use" (Carroll, 1998, p. 72). While some exposure to high-risk situations cannot be avoided (e.g., living in a home or area in which drugs and alcohol are common), there are several "minor" decisions that may unconsciously lead one to high-risk situations for relapse (Carroll, 1998; Monti et al., 2002). Clients who seem to benefit most from this session are those who have intact cognitive abilities and an ability to reflect upon their cognitions and emotions (Carroll, 1998).

The therapist(s) should begin by presenting a *rationale for learning* how to avoid seemingly irrelevant decisions. It is helpful for the therapist to point out that many of the choices one makes each day (e.g., going to a particular store to shop, visiting a good friend, etc.) seem to have nothing to do with whether one chooses to drink or use. However, although they may not involve a direct choice to drink or use, they may inch one closer and closer to potential high-risk situations in which the person will need to make such a decision. When these high-risk situations occur, many individuals think that they have become the victim in a high-risk situation they did not anticipate (Monti et al., 2002). They fail to recognize that several "minor" and seemingly unrelated decisions they had made had led them closer and closer to this situation.

In order to avoid such high-risk situations caused by SIDs, clients should be encouraged to *recognize and anticipate the consequences* of each possible choice and how it might be related to an urge to drink or use (Carroll, 1998; Monti et al., 2002). They should also be encouraged to choose the low-risk option and *avoid decisions that lead to high-risk situations*. If they decide not to avoid such a decision, they should at least learn to become more aware of where that decision may be leading them so that the high-risk situation can be avoided (Monti et al., 2002). Finally, if an individual finds him- or herself headed toward or in a high-risk situation, he or she should use *effective skills to cope* with and remove themselves from the situation (Carroll, 1998; Monti et al., 2002).

To illustrate how SIDs can lead to relapse, the therapist can read the following story and ask clients to pick out the seemingly "minor" decisions that led to relapse:

Joe, who had been abstinent for several weeks, drove home from work on a night his wife was going to be away. On the way, he turned left rather than right at an intersection so he could enjoy the "scenic route." On this route, he drove past a bar he had frequented in the past and where he had bought and used cocaine. Because the weather that day was hot, he decided to stop in for a glass of cola. Once in the bar, however, he decided that since his problem was with cocaine, it would be fine to have a beer. After two beers, he ran into a friend who "happened" to have a gram of cocaine and a relapse ensued. (Carroll, 1998, p. 74)

The therapist can then ask and engage clients in discussion using the following questions and comments:

When did you think Joe first got into trouble, or "thought" about using cocaine? One of the things about these chains of decisions that lead to cocaine use is that

Little decisions that seem ordinary can move you closer to relapse. When making any decision, whether large or small, do the following:

- Consider what options you may have.
- Think ahead to anticipate the possible outcomes of each option. What positive or negative consequences can you anticipate, and what are the risks of relapse?
- Select one of the options: Choose one that will minimize your relapse risk. If you choose a risky option, plan how to protect yourself while in the high-risk situation.

PRACTICE EXERCISE
Think about a decision that you have made recently or are about to make. This decision could involve any aspect of your life, such as your job, recreational activities, friends, or family. Identify "safe" choices and choices that might increase your odds of relapsing.

Decision to be made:

_____

_____

Safe alternatives:

_____

_____

Risky alternatives:

_____

_____

_____

Figure 5.5   Reminder and Practice Exercise Sheet: Seemingly Irrelevant Decisions
Monti et al., 2002. Reprinted with permission of Guilford Press.

they are far easier to stop in the beginning of the chain. Being farther away from cocaine, it is easier to stop the decision-making process than when you're closer to cocaine use and craving kicks in.

What do you think Joe was saying to himself at the point he took the scenic route home? We often find that people making Seemingly Irrelevant Decisions can catch themselves by the way they think—thoughts like "I have to do this" or "I really should go home this way" or "I need to see so-and-so because." These end up being rationalizations, or ways of talking oneself into cocaine use without seeming to do so. I've noticed sometimes that you talk yourself into high-risk situations by telling yourself a situation is safe, when it really may not be, like when you told yourself last week that it was safe for you to go hang out in the park with your friends. Can you think of other examples of ways you might have talked yourself into a risky situation? (Carroll, 1998, p. 74)

The therapist should then encourage clients that by becoming more aware of SIDs, they can correct such decisions and avoid high-risk situations (Monti et al., 2002). It is easier to avoid these small decisions (in this example, the "scenic route" home, decision to stop at a bar for a cola, etc.) than it is to deal with temptation in a high-risk situation.

Clients should then be asked to think about their last slip or relapse after being abstinent so that they can describe the situation and the events that preceded the situation (Monti et al., 2002). As the client shares this information, the therapist should help clients identify the decisions that led to a relapse and display these visually on a blackboard or other visual surface (Monti et al., 2002). Processing these situations should help clients become more aware of such SIDs and how to avoid them in the future.

The session should conclude by having the therapist hand out and introduce the Reminder Sheet for SIDS (Figure 5.5).

RESOURCES

READINGS

There are a handful of additional readings that may be of interest to supplement the material presented in this chapter. While this chapter provides an integrated guide for conducting adult group or individual CBST with alcohol and drug dependency, the three CBST treatment manuals relied upon for this chapter provide more in-depth and specialized information pertinent to disparate addictions and treatment formats. Two of these manuals are available for free download from federal government websites (see below). In addition, therapists who are interested in integrating cue exposure therapy with CBST are highly encouraged to purchase the Monti and colleagues (2002) manual, as there is an entire chapter devoted to describing a step-by-step implementation of this approach. Likewise, Monti and colleagues devote an additional chapter to dual diagnosis issues when implementing CBST that would be highly valuable for practitioners and offer more detailed and specific implementation guidance for each session.

- *Cognitive-Behavioral Coping Skills Therapy Manual:* A copy of this manual is available for purchase or free of charge by pdf download from NIAAA: http://pubs.niaaa.nih.gov/publications/MATCHSeries3/index.htm.
- *A Cognitive-Behavioral Approach: Treating Cocaine Addiction:* A copy of this manual is available for purchase or free of charge by pdf download from NIDA: www.drugabuse.gov/TXManuals/CBT/CBT4.html.
- *Treating Alcohol Dependence: A Coping Skills Training Guide:* This manual by Monti, P.M, Kadden, R.M., Rohsenow, D.J., Cooney, N.L., and Abrams, D.B. (2002) is available for purchase from the Guilford Press.

In addition to these CBST treatment manuals, therapists working with substance-abusing clients who struggle more with anger management problems may benefit from the following manual and workbook that also utilize a cognitive behavioral approach:

- *Anger Management for Substance Abuse and Mental Health Clients: A Cognitive Behavioral Therapy Manual* by Reilly, P.M. & Shopshire, M.S. (2002). Center for Substance Abuse Treatment, Department of Health and Human Services publication. No. (SMA) 02–3661. Rockville, MD. Substance Abuse and Mental Health Services Administration, 63 pp. Available online at: http://kap.samhsa.gov/products/manuals/pdfs/angermgmt_manual_2005.pdf
- *Anger Management for Substance Abuse and Mental Health Clients: Participant Workbook* by Reilly, P.M., Shopshire, M.S., Durazzo, T.C., & Campbell, T.A. (2002). Center for Substance Abuse Treatment, Department of Health and Human Services publication. No. (SMA) 02–3662. Rockville, MD. Substance Abuse and Mental Health Services Administration, 49 pp. Available online at: http://kap.samhsa.gov/products/manuals/pdfs/angermgmt_workbook_2005.pdf

REFERENCES

Abrams, D. B., & Niaura, R. S. (1987). Social learning theory. In H. T. Blane & K. E. Leanard (Eds.), *Psychological theories of drinking and alcoholism* (pp. 131–178). New York: Guilford Press.

Anton, R. F., O'Malley, S. S., Ciraulo, D. A., Cisler, R. A., Couper, D., Donovan, D. M., Gastfriend, D. R., Hosking, J. D., Bankole A. J., LoCastro, J. S., Longabaugh, R., Mason, B. J., Mattson, M. E., Miller, W. R., Pettinati, H. M., Randall, C. L., Swift, R., Weiss, R. D., Williams, L. D., Zweben, A., for the COMBINE Study Research Group. (2006). Combined pharmacotherapies and behavioral interventions for alcohol dependence. The COMBINE study: A randomized controlled trial. *Journal of the American Medical Association, 295,* 2003–2017.

Bandura, A. (1969). *Principles of behavior modification.* New York: Holt, Rinehart, & Winston.

Bandura, A. (1986). *Social foundations of thought and action: A social cognitive theory.* Englewood Cliffs, NJ: Prentice-Hall.

Barnes, G. M. (1977). The development of adolescent drinking behavior: An evaluative review of the impact of the socialization process within the family. *Adolescence, 12,* 571–591.

Carroll, K. M. (1998). *A cognitive-behavioral approach: Treating cocaine addiction.* NIDA Therapy Manuals for Drug Addiction, NIH Publication No. 98–4308. Rockville, MD: NIDA.

Caudill, B. D., & Marlatt, G. A. (1975). Modeling influences in social drinking: An experimental analogue. *Journal of Consulting and Clinical Psychology, 4,* 46–54.

Comer, S. D., Sullivan, M. A., Rothenberg, J. L., Kleber, H. D., Kampman, K., Dackis, C., & O'Brien, C. P. (2006). Injectable, sustained-release naltrexone for the treatment of opiod dependence. *Archives of General Psychiatry, 63,* 210–218.

Emmelkamp, P. M. G., & Vedel, E. (2006). *Evidence-based treatments for alcohol and drug abuse: A practitioner's guide to theory, methods, and practice.* New York: Routledge.

Granholm, E., McQuaid, J. R., Fauzia, S. M, Auslander, L. A., Dimitri, P., Pedrelli, P., Patterson, T., & Jeste, D. V. (2005). A randomized, controlled trail of cognitive behavioral social skills training for middle-aged and older patients with chronic schizophrenia. *American Journal of Psychiatry, 162,* 520–529.

Higgins, S. T., Heil, S. H., & Lussier, J. P. (2004). Clinical implications of reinforcement as a determinant of substance use disorders. *Annual Review of Psychology, 55,* 431–461.

Kadden, R., Carroll, K. M., Donovan, D., Cooney, N., Monti, P., Abrams, D., Litt, M., & Hester, R. (1994). *Cognitive-behavioral coping skills therapy manual: A clinical research guide for therapists treating individuals with alcohol abuse and dependence.* Project MATCH Monograph Series, Vol. 3. DHHS Publication No. 94–3724. Rockville, MD: NIAAA.

Latt, N. C., Jurd, S., Houseman, J., & Wutzke, S. E. (2002). Naltrexone in alcohol dependence: A randomized controlled trial of effectiveness in a standard clinical setting. *Medical Journal of Australia, 176,* 530–534.

Longabaugh, R., & Morgenstern, J. (1999). Cognitive-behavioral coping-skills therapy for alcohol dependence: Current status and future directions. *Alcohol Research and Health, 23,* 78–85.

Marlatt, G. A., & Gordon, J. R. (Eds.). (1985). *Relapse prevention: Maintenance strategies in the treatment of addictive behaviors.* New York: Guilford Press.

Miller, W. R., & Rollnick, S. (2002). *Motivational interviewing: Preparing people for change.* (2nd ed.). New York: Guilford Press.

Monti, P. M., Abrams, D. B., Kadden, R. M., & Cooney, N. L. (1989). *Treating alcohol dependence.* New York: Guilford Press.

Monti, P. M., Kadden, R. M., Rohsenow, D. J., Cooney, N. L., & Abrams, D. B. (2002). *Treating alcohol dependence: A coping skills training guide* (2nd ed.). New York: Guilford Press.

Monti, P. M., & Rohsenow, D. J. (1999). Does urge to drink predict relapse after treatment? *Alcohol Research & Health, 23,* 225–234.

Monti, P. M., Rohsenow, D. J., Michalec, E., Martin, R., & Abrams, D. B. (1997). Brief coping skills treatment of cocaine abuse: Substance use outcomes at 3 months. *Addiction, 92,* 1717–1728.

O'Leary, D. E., O'Leary, M. R., & Donovan, D. M. (1976). Social skill acquisition and psychosocial development of alcoholics: A review. *Addictive Behaviors, 1,* 11–120.

Reilly, P. M., & Shopshire, M. S. (2002). *Anger management for substance abuse and mental health clients: A cognitive behavioral therapy manual.* DHHS Pub. No. (SMA)

07–4213. Rockville, MD: Center for Substance Abuse Treatment, Substance Abuse and Mental Health Services Administration. Reprinted 2003, 2005, 2006, and 2007.

Rohsenow, D. J., Monti, P. M., Rubonis, A., Gulliver, S. B., Colby, S. M., Binkoff, J. A., & Abrams, D. B. (2001). Cue exposure with coping skills training and communication skills training for alcohol dependence: 6- and 12- month outcomes. *Addiction*, *96*: 1161–1174.

Rotter, J. B. (1982). *The development and applications of social learning theory*. New York: Praeger.

Schmitz, J. M., Stotts, A. L., Rhoades, H. M., & Grabowski, J. (2001). Naltrexone and relapse prevention treatment for cocaine-dependent patients. *Addictive Behaviors*, *26*, 167–180.

Velasquez, M. M., Maurer, G. G., Crouch, C., & DiClemente, C. C. (2001). *Group treatment for substance abuse*. New York: Guilford Press.

CHAPTER 6

Seeking Safety: An Implementation Guide[1]

LISA M. NAJAVITS

SEEKING SAFETY IS a widely used, evidence-based model (Najavits, 2007b). Originally designed for co-occurring posttraumatic stress disorder (PTSD) and substance use disorder, over time it has been applied to other populations as well. Its core goal is expressed in the title: to encourage clients to attain greater safety—to surmount the chaos and destruction so common in trauma and substance abuse.[2]

This chapter offers ideas on implementing the model—a sort of quick guide that can be used in conjunction with the actual manual. This chapter also addresses themes that have emerged since the publication of the manual in 2002. It has been inspiring to hear how the model has been used over the years by so many different people. Thus, this chapter is part of an ongoing dialogue that has enriched and deepened the work over time. Models of therapy are, in this sense, not static entities, but evolve in relation to clients, clinicians, and programs, with much new learning all around.

OVERVIEW OF SEEKING SAFETY

Seeking Safety was begun in the early 1990s. The manual was published in 2002, after a decade of development based on clinical experience, research, and

---

1. Sincere thanks to all who have contacted me over the years to share their experiences and offer new ideas on how to apply Seeking Safety in different contexts. Also, my deep appreciation to several associates who have worked closely with me on training and consultation: Martha Schmitz, Ph.D.; Kay Johnson, LICSW; and Kevin Reeder, Ph.D.

2. *A note on terms.* For simplicity, "substance abuse" will be used throughout rather than "substance use disorder," although the model can be applied to clients with substance abuse or dependence, as well as other addictions. "Trauma" will be used rather than "PTSD" as the model is applied to traumatized populations broadly, not just to those who meet PTSD criteria.

clinician training. The title of the treatment—Seeking Safety—expresses its central idea: When a person has PTSD and/or substance use disorder (SUD), the most urgent clinical need is to establish safety. *Safety* is an umbrella term that signifies various elements: safety from substances; safety from dangerous relationships (including domestic violence and substance-using friends); and safety from extreme symptoms, such as suicidality and dissociation.

Many of these destructive behaviors reenact trauma—having been harmed through trauma, clients are now harming themselves or others. *Seeking safety* refers to helping clients free themselves from such negative behaviors and, in so doing, to move toward freeing themselves from trauma at a deep emotional level.

Seeking Safety is a cognitive behavioral therapy that can be used from the start of treatment. It can be conducted with males and females, in individual or group modality. It was designed to explore the link between trauma and substance abuse, but without delving into details of the past that could destabilize clients during early recovery. Its goal is a present-focused, empathic approach that "owns" and names the trauma experience, validates the connection to substance use, provides psychoeducation, and offers safe coping skills to manage the often overwhelming impulses and emotions of these co-occurring disorders. It is an integrated therapy that focuses equally on trauma and substance abuse, at the same time, from the start of treatment, but in a way that is designed to be as safe, supportive and containing as possible. The research supporting the effectiveness of Seeking Safety is summarized in Appendix A of this book.

The concept of safety is designed to protect the clinician as well as the client. By helping clients move toward safety, clinicians are protecting themselves from treatment that could move too fast without a solid foundation. Increased substance use and harm to self or others are of particular concern with this vulnerable population. Thus, seeking safety is both the clients' and clinicians' goal.

Key Points about Seeking Safety

Seeking Safety Has the Following Features:

- *Early-stage treatment:* designed to stabilize clients; can be used from the start of treatment.
- *Integrated treatment:* addresses trauma and substance abuse at the same time, although it can also be used for either one alone.
- *Teaches coping skills:* to help build resilience and increase safety.
- *Present-focused:* addresses current issues; does not delve into detailed exploration of the past; however, it can be used concurrently with models that do focus primarily on the past.

- *Idealistic:* strives to build hope.
- *Evidence-based:* the only model thus far established as effective for co-occurring PTSD and substance use disorder.
- *Targets four domains:* cognitive, behavioral, interpersonal, and case management: to help the "whole person."
- *Offers 25 topics:* each topic provides a clinician guide and client handouts; the clinician can do as few or many topics as time allows, in any order.
- *Engaging:* uses quotations, creative exercises, poignant examples.
- *Flexible:* can be used in any setting; for any treatment length; any trauma type; any substance; both genders; and individual or group treatment.
- *Clinician-sensitive:* addresses the clinician role in detail, including self-care and countertransference.
- *Structured:* to use time well and to help clients feel comfortable.
- *Public health emphasis:* low cost to implement; and can be used by almost any clinician, client, and program.
- *User friendly:* organized, easy-to-follow format.
- *Compassionate tone:* honors what clients have survived; respects their strengths.
- *Practical:* focuses on rehearsal of new skills, psychoeducation, and specific tools to help clients move forward in recovery.
- *Relevant to different subgroups:* successfully used with adolescents, military, veterans, homeless, domestic violence, criminal justice, racially/ethnically diverse, mild traumatic brain injury, people who cannot read, and others.
- *Can be combined with any other treatment:* can be used alone or in combination with any other treatments the client is receiving; it also includes an intensive case management component to help clients engage in other treatments.
- *Simple, engaging language:* avoids scientific jargon and long words; the goal is simple, emotionally compelling words, such as "safety," "respect," "honor," and "healing."

See the *Seeking Safety Manual* (Najavits, 2002b) and the website www .seekingsafety.org for detailed background and description of the model.

SEEKING SAFETY TOPICS

There are twenty-five topics, each representing a *safe coping skill* relevant to both trauma and substance abuse (see Table 6.1). The topics address different domains: cognitive, behavioral, interpersonal, case management, or a combination:

Cognitive topics

PTSD: Taking Back Your Power; Compassion; When Substances Control You; Creating Meaning; Discovery; Integrating the Split Self; Recovery Thinking

Behavioral topics

Taking Good Care of Yourself; Commitment; Respecting Your Time; Coping with Triggers; Self-Nurturing; Red and Green Flags; Detaching from Emotional Pain (Grounding)

Interpersonal topics

Honesty; Asking for Help; Setting Boundaries in Relationships; Getting Others to Support Your Recovery; Healthy Relationships; Healing from Anger; Community Resources

Case management

Introduction/Case Management

Combination

Safety; The Life Choices Game (Review); Termination

Table 6.1
Seeking Safety Treatment Topics

(1) *Introduction to Treatment/Case Management*
This topic covers: (a) Introduction to the treatment, (b) Getting to know the client, and (c) Assessment of case management needs.

(2) *Safety [combination]*
Safety is described as the first stage of healing from both PTSD and substance abuse and the key focus of the treatment. A list of over 80 Safe Coping Skills is provided and clients explore what safety means to them.

(3) *PTSD: Taking Back Your Power [cognitive]*
Four handouts are offered: (a) "What Is PTSD?" (b) "The Link Between PTSD and Substance Abuse" (c) "Using Compassion to Take Back Your Power" and (d) "Long-Term PTSD Problems." The goal is to provide information as well as a compassionate understanding of the disorder.

(4) *Detaching from Emotional Pain (Grounding) [behavioral]*
A powerful strategy, "grounding," is offered to help clients detach from emotional pain. Three types of grounding are presented (mental, physical, and soothing), with an experiential exercise to demonstrate the techniques. The goal is to shift attention toward the external world, away from negative feelings.

(5) *When Substances Control You [cognitive]*
Eight handouts are provided, which can be combined or used separately: (a) "Do You Have a Substance Abuse Problem?"; (b) "How Substance Abuse Prevents Healing from PTSD"; (c) "Choose a Way to Give Up Substances"; (d) "Climbing Mount Recovery," an imaginative exercise to prepare for giving up substances; (e) "Mixed Feelings"; (f) "Self-Understanding of Substance Use"; (g) "Self-Help Groups"; and (h) "Substance Abuse and PTSD: Common Questions."

(6) *Asking for Help [interpersonal]*
Both PTSD and substance abuse lead to problems in asking for help. This topic encourages clients to become aware of their need for help and provides guidance on how to obtain it.

(7) *Taking Good Care of Yourself [behavioral]*
Clients explore how well they take care of themselves using a questionnaire listing specific behaviors (e.g., "Do you get regular medical checkups?"). They are asked to take immediate action to improve at least one self-care problem.

(8) *Compassion [cognitive]*
This topic encourages the use of compassion when trying to overcome problems. Compassion is the opposite of "beating oneself up," a common tendency for people with PTSD and substance abuse. Clients are taught that only a loving stance toward the self produces lasting change.

(9) *Red and Green Flags [behavioral]*
Clients explore the up-and-down nature of recovery in both PTSD and substance abuse through discussion of "red and green flags" (signs of danger and safety). A Safety Plan is developed to identify what to do in situations of mild, moderate, and severe relapse danger.

(10) *Honesty [interpersonal]*
Clients discuss the role of honesty in recovery and role-play specific situations. Related issues include the following: What is the cost of dishonesty? When is it safe to be honest? What if the other person doesn't accept honesty?

(11) *Recovery Thinking [cognitive]*
Thoughts associated with PTSD and substance abuse are contrasted with healthier "recovery thinking." Clients are guided to change their thinking using rethinking tools such as List Your Options, Create a New Story, Make a Decision, and Imagine. The power of rethinking is demonstrated through think-aloud exercises.

(12) *Integrating the Split Self [cognitive]*
Splitting is identified as a major psychic defense in both PTSD and substance abuse. Clients are guided to notice splits (e.g., different sides of the self, ambivalence, denial) and to strive for integration as a means to overcome these.

(13) *Commitment [behavioral]*
The concept of keeping promises, both to self and others, is explored. Clients are offered creative strategies for keeping commitments, as well as the opportunity to identify feelings that can get in the way.

(14) *Creating Meaning [cognitive]*
Meaning systems are discussed with a focus on assumptions specific to PTSD and substance abuse, such as Deprivation Reasoning, Actions Speak Louder Than Words, and Time Warp. Meanings that are harmful versus healing in recovery are contrasted.

(15) *Community Resources [interpersonal]*
A lengthy list of national nonprofit resources is offered to aid clients' recovery (including advocacy organizations, self-help, and newsletters). Also, guidelines are offered to help clients take a consumer approach in evaluating treatments.

(16) *Setting Boundaries in Relationships [interpersonal]*
Boundary problems are described as either too much closeness (difficulty saying "no" in relationships) or too much distance (difficulty saying "yes" in relationships). Ways to set healthy boundaries are explored, and domestic violence information is provided.

(*continued*)

Table 6.1
Continued

(17) *Discovery [cognitive]*
Discovery is offered as a tool to reduce the cognitive rigidity common to PTSD and substance abuse (called "staying stuck"). Discovery is a way to stay open to experience and new knowledge, using strategies such as Ask Others, Try It and See, Predict, and Act "As If." Suggestions for coping with negative feedback are provided.

(18) *Getting Others to Support Your Recovery [interpersonal]*
Clients are encouraged to identify which people in their lives are supportive, neutral, or destructive toward their recovery. Suggestions for eliciting support are provided, as well as a letter that they can give to others to promote understanding of PTSD and substance abuse. A safe family member or friend can be invited to attend the session.

(19) *Coping with Triggers [behavioral]*
Clients are encouraged to actively fight triggers of PTSD and substance abuse. A simple three-step model is offered: change who you are with, what you are doing, and where you are (similar to "change people, places, and things" in AA).

(20) *Respecting Your Time [behavioral]*
Time is explored as a major resource in recovery. Clients may have lost years to their disorders, but they can still make the future better than the past. They are asked to fill in schedule blanks to explore issues such as: Do you use your time well? Is recovery your highest priority? Balancing structure versus spontaneity, work versus play, and time alone versus in relationships are also addressed.

(21) *Healthy Relationships [interpersonal]*
Healthy and unhealthy relationship beliefs are contrasted. For example, the unhealthy belief "Bad relationships are all I can get" is contrasted with the healthy belief "Creating good relationships is a skill to learn." Clients are guided to notice how PTSD and substance abuse can lead to unhealthy relationships.

(22) *Self-Nurturing [behavioral]*
Safe self-nurturing is distinguished from unsafe self-nurturing (e.g., substances and other "cheap thrills"). Clients are asked to create a gift to the self by increasing safe self-nurturing and decreasing unsafe self-nurturing. Pleasure is explored as a complex issue in PTSD/ substance abuse.

(23) *Healing from Anger [interpersonal]*
Anger is explored as a valid feeling that is inevitable in recovery from PTSD and substance abuse. Anger can be used constructively (as a source of knowledge and healing) or destructively (a danger when acted out against self or others). Guidelines for working with both types of anger are offered.

(24) *The Life Choices Game (Review) [combination]*
As part of termination, clients are invited to play a game as a way to review the material covered in the treatment. Clients pull from a box of slips of paper that list challenging life events (e.g., "You find out your partner is having an affair"). They respond with how they would cope, using game rules that focus on constructive coping.

(25)*Termination*
Clients express their feelings about the ending of treatment, discuss what they liked and disliked about it, and finalize aftercare plans. An optional Termination Letter can be read aloud to clients to validate the work they have done.

Note: From Najavits (2006). Reprinted with permission.

Key Points about the Topics

It is not necessary to conduct all twenty-five topics. Indeed, significant improvements have been found with clients who attended fewer than half of the twenty-five topics (Hien, Cohen, Miele, Litt, & Capstick, 2004; Najavits, Gallop, & Weiss, 2006; Najavits, Weiss, Shaw, & Muenz, 1998). Conduct as many topics as time allows. Even a few topics during a short stay can help clients improve coping skills and build awareness of trauma and substance abuse. Some programs conduct segments of four, eight, or twelve topics (or any other number); clients come to one segment and then decide if they want to continue to the next segment.

Topics can be conducted in any order. There is no right or wrong sequencing. The clinician may do them in the order listed in the manual or may select whatever feels most relevant at each session. For individual therapy, the client can choose a topic from the list (although many clients prefer the clinician to choose).

Each topic is independent of the others. This allows the treatment to be conducted in open groups if desired (clients can join at any time). It also means that if clients miss any topics, they can return at any point, as each topic stands on its own. These considerations are especially important for substance abuse treatment, where retaining clients is a challenge.

They are called "topics" rather than "sessions" because each topic can be done over several sessions. Indeed, clients often prefer that as it gives them more opportunity to absorb the material.

Each topic has multiple handouts. The idea is to explore whatever is most relevant to clients. Just like the topics themselves, handouts within each topic can be done in any order, using as few or as many as desired.

SESSION FORMAT

Seeking Safety sessions are structured to emphasize good use of time, appropriate containment, and setting goals and sticking to them. For clients with trauma and substance abuse, who are often impulsive and overwhelmed, the predictable session structure helps them know what to expect. It offers, in its process, a mirror of the focus and careful planning necessary for recovery.

Sessions are conducted with the following four parts (see Table 6.2):

1. *Check-in:* Brief questions to find out how clients are doing.
2. *Quotation:* A quotation is read aloud to emotionally engage clients in the session.
3. *Handouts:* Handouts are used to explore a new coping skill.
4. *Check-out:* Brief questions to reinforce clients' progress and close the session on a positive note.

Table 6.2

Session Format

---

1. **CHECK-IN**

The goal of the check-in is to find out how clients are doing (up to 5 minutes per patient). Clients report on five questions: Since the last session (a) How are you feeling?; (b) What good coping have you done?; (c) Describe your substance use and any other unsafe behavior; (d) Did you complete your Commitment?; and (e) Community Resource update.

2. **QUOTATION**

The quotation is a brief device to help emotionally engage clients in the session (up to 2 minutes). A client reads the quotation out loud. The clinician asks "What is the main idea in the quotation?" and links it to the topic of the session.

3. **RELATE THE TOPIC TO CLIENTS' LIVES**

The clinician and/or client select any of the 25 treatment topics (see Table 6.1) that feels most relevant. This is the heart of the session, with the goal of meaningfully connecting the topic to clients' experience (30–40 minutes). Clients look through the handout for a few minutes, which may be accompanied by the clinician summarizing key points (especially for clients who are cognitively impaired). Clients are asked what they most relate to in the material, and the rest of the time is devoted to addressing the topic in relation to specific and current examples from clients' lives. As each topic represents a safe coping skill, intensive rehearsal of the skill is strongly emphasized.

4. **CHECK-OUT**

The goal is to reinforce clients' progress and give the clinician feedback (a few minutes per client). Clients answer two questions: (a) Name one thing you got out of today's session (and any problems with it) and (b) What is your new commitment?

Note: From Najavits (2006). Reprinted with permission.

Key Points about the Format

The format serves many purposes. It keeps the treatment on track and uses time well. Clients consistently state that it helps them feel safe as they know what to expect. In group modality, it promotes boundaries and sharing of time, rather than letting any member overdominate the session. At a deeper level, the structure promotes processes to counteract the impulsivity, chaos, and disorganization of PTSD and SUD (i.e., pacing, planning, organization).

The same format is used for individual or group treatment. The structure works well in both individual and group modalities. Clients consistently say they like the structure and it quickly comes to feel natural to them.

For large groups, the format can be shortened. Some programs have very large groups of twenty to forty clients. For such large groups, you can reduce the check-in and check-out. You could ask just one or two questions with only a few clients responding. For example, at check-in: *"Can anyone name an example of good coping they did this week?" "Does anyone want to share if they had substance use or other unsafe behavior this week?"* For the check-out:

"Does anyone want to share one thing you got from today's session?" If possible, base the size of the group on how much time is available so clients can each go through the full check-in and check-out, but if you need to cut these down, you can. You can also model the check-in and check-out so clients see what level of detail you are looking for.

Try it. Some clinicians believe their clients won't like the format or may themselves feel uncomfortable with a structured session. Keep an open mind. Try it and learn from clients' responses to it.

CLIENT SELECTION

Seeking Safety was originally designed for PTSD and substance use disorder. Over time, it has been applied to a wider range of clients, such as those who could simply benefit from improved coping skills. In part, this is because many treatment programs focus less on formal diagnoses than on general treatments that many different clients can attend. Also, most of the Seeking Safety topics are broad enough to apply to issues beyond trauma and substance use (e.g., Asking for Help, Compassion, Honesty, Creating Meaning, and Taking Good Care of Yourself). Further, both clinical and research experience consistently evidence the model to be safe and thus it can be applied without concern for evoking adverse events (Killeen et al., 2008).

The outcome research on Seeking Safety has also broadened in scope over time. In early studies of the model, all clients met criteria for current PTSD and substance use disorder; later studies loosened these criteria to a wider range of clients and still found positive outcomes (e.g., Desai, Harpaz-Rotem, Rosenheck, & Najavits, 2008, 2009; Morrissey et al., 2005).

In sum, no specific client selection or readiness appear needed for Seeking Safety, other than the guidelines suggested below.

KEY POINTS ABOUT CLIENT SELECTION

Seeking Safety has been successfully used with many different types of clients, including the following:

- Racially/ethnically diverse
- Adolescent
- Seriously and persistently mentally ill (e.g., psychotic)
- Homeless
- Domestic violence
- Military and VA
- Illiterate
- Low cognitive functioning/mild traumatic brain injury

- Complex PTSD
- Criminal justice
- Multiple comorbidity
- Various addictions (gambling, food, internet, sex, pornography)
- Subthreshold PTSD and substance use disorder
- Personality disordered
- Active substance users
- Different settings (outpatient, residential, inpatient, community care, private practice, outreach)

The model is for both men and women. A common misunderstanding is that the model is only for women, based on early research that focused on women. However, by the time the model was finalized and published as a book (Najavits, 2002b), it explicitly targeted both genders. The book includes examples from both men and women as well as gender-neutral language. Four studies on Seeking Safety have been conducted on men, all with positive results. [An article summarizing the use of Seeking Safety with men is now available (Najavits, Schmitz, et al., in press)].

Be as inclusive as possible. It is recommended to invite anyone into the treatment who has an interest, and only remove someone who presents a clear danger to others or is otherwise not able to participate. For groups, clients who are appropriate for any group are appropriate for Seeking Safety—no additional requirements apply. The goal is to monitor clients over time and evaluate whether Seeking Safety is helpful to them, using the check-in and check-out, the End of Session Questionnaire, and the End of Treatment Questionnaire [see Chapter 2 in the Seeking Safety book (Najavits, 2002b) for more on this topic].

Encourage clients to apply the coping skills broadly. The skills can apply to many life problems beyond trauma and substance abuse. For example, Asking for Help may be relevant to finding a job or apartment, dieting, or resolving a relationship conflict.

Use the case management component of Seeking Safety to engage clients in additional treatments. For example, a client with pathological gambling could be referred to Gamblers Anonymous; a client with an eating disorder could be referred to an eating disorder program.

Tell clients to ignore the terms "PTSD" or "substance abuse" in the handouts if these do not apply. This has worked fine, without a need to alter the materials. Clients are guided to use what is relevant and ignore the rest. Also, some clinicians use the terms *trauma* and *trauma symptoms* rather than "PTSD," for simplicity.

Allow clients to try the treatment before committing to it ("Try before you buy"). Encourage clients to participate in several sessions (or, for group treatment, even just sit in and observe), and then decide if they want to join. The key is to respect their decision and empower their choice. If they decide not to participate, it is important to honor that without judgment.

Clients can be at any stage of recovery. Some clients may still be actively using substances; others may have been abstinent for some period of time. They can learn from each other, just as in Alcoholics Anonymous, where participants are at all stages of the recovery process. (Of course, if clients show up for a session intoxicated, they should be sent home and encouraged to come to the next session sober.) Note, too, that motivation to cut down on substance use is not a requirement for participating in Seeking Safety—sometimes motivation is the result of the treatment, rather than present at the beginning. With regard to trauma as well, clients may be at any stage of the trauma recovery process. That being said, some programs have enough clients at different stages of recovery that they choose to create homogenous groups ("early recovery," etc.), which is also fine.

Clients do not need to be stabilized first. Seeking Safety can be used from the start of treatment. It was designed as a first-stage therapy to help create stabilization. Thus, do not assume that Seeking Safety will be "too much" unless it is tried first or there are other reasons for concern (e.g., a psychotic client who needs medication stabilization).

CLINICIAN SELECTION

Seeking Safety has been successfully conducted by a wide range of clinicians—including substance abuse and mental health counselors, social workers, psychologists, psychiatrists, bachelor's level counselors, case managers, nurses, clinical trainees, domestic violence advocates, school counselors, pastoral counselors, and paraprofessionals. We have never heard of adverse events in any setting. The model focuses on coping skills in the present, and thus is safe to use and easy to learn. Originally, various criteria were sought, such as a mental health degree and particular types of background, such as cognitive-behavioral therapy (CBT) or substance abuse. But over time it became clear that far more important than such professional characteristics were more subtle, subjective criteria. Clinicians who genuinely enjoy working with these clients—perhaps perceiving their work as a mission or calling—bring to the work a level of commitment that no credential per se can offer. Similarly, clinicians who are open to the value of a treatment manual, viewing it as a resource that can help improve the quality of the work, are able to make the best use of the material. Because there are no strict criteria for clinician selection, the treatment is usable in a wide range of settings. Many substance abuse programs, for example, do not have staff with advanced degrees or formal mental health training. Also, because the treatment focuses on stabilization rather than trauma processing, it does not exceed the training, licensure, or ethical limits of most clinicians.

KEY POINTS ABOUT CLINICIAN SELECTION

Any clinician can conduct Seeking Safety. No specific degree or experience is required. This is not to minimize the importance of well-trained clinicians, nor to underestimate that this client population can be challenging. However, any clinician in any setting that is legitimately providing treatment to these clients can use Seeking Safety. There are no additional requirements, as there is no evidence to suggest the need for such.

Several clinician characteristics are helpful. The most important qualities are the desire to work with this client population; willingness to use a manual-based treatment; and positive interpersonal characteristics such as empathy, respect, and being "real."

All clinicians need to recognize their limits. Some issues require experts in other areas. For example, bipolar disorder, eating disorders, psychotic disorders, and dissociative identity disorder typically require expert consultation for medications and other treatments. Thus, although any clinician can conduct Seeking Safety, other staff are typically needed as well. The Seeking Safety topic, Introduction/Case Management, offers detailed suggestions for this process. A second area of potential limitation is clinicians' own personal response to the work. If clinicians find that they are excessively triggered when conducting the treatment, have inability to set healthy boundaries, or express aggression or sadism toward clients, they need to step back to determine what personal work they need to do before they are safe to conduct therapy with this clientele.

Consider a try-out using the manual. This can help determine whether a clinician is a good match for the treatment. The clinician reads Chapters 1 and 2 of the Seeking Safety book (which provides background information), then selects one or two treatment topics to conduct with real clients. The clinician can thus get a feel for it without a huge time investment. Similarly, when hiring clinicians, the same procedure can be used, but the session could be audiotaped for a supervisor to listen to and perhaps rate using the Seeking Safety Adherence Scale (see below for more on that tool). For a more detailed description of the try-out process, see www.seekingsafety.org (section Articles, subsection Seeking Safety).

CLINICIAN TRAINING

There are many ways to learn Seeking Safety. Training can occur by simply reading the book, through onsite training, the Seeking Safety video training series, phone consultation, or some combination of these. See www.seeking safety.org (section Training) for various options and a calendar of upcoming trainings. There is also an article on training clinicians in Seeking Safety (Najavits, 2000). The most helpful strategies emphasize direct experience of the model.

When onsite training occurs, it typically ranges from one to two days and covers the following topics:

- Background
- In-depth description of the model
- Clinical demonstration of a session
- Implementation ideas
- Experiential exercises (small-group conduct of a session; grounding exercise; role-play of "tough cases," etc.).

The training can be adapted to focus on particular client populations (e.g., adolescents, military or veterans, prisoners, women or men, domestic violence). There is time for question and answer, and discussion is encouraged. There is no limit on the number of people who can attend training. The training is conducted by Lisa Najavits or an associate who is trained and supervised by her; the list of associates can be found at www.seekingsafety. org (section Training, then Training Calendar, "associates"). Others have created their own training on the model, but we have no way to determine their quality as only the associates provide her training, use her materials, and are supervised by her.

Note, however, that training is not required for Seeking Safety at this point. This is because the model is safe (see earlier in this chapter), it is not hard to learn, and we strongly value a public health focus that puts few obstacles in the way of implementation. Also, from a research perspective, there is no evidence yet of what kind of training, if any, is essential. (This is actually true of almost all models of psychotherapy.) However, some agencies like to provide Seeking Safety training to help introduce the model to their staff, to inspire confidence in using it, and to discuss specific implementation issues at their site. Also, some people learn best through multimodal training rather than simply reading the book. Thus, various training options are offered. Similarly, certification in the model is offered, but is not required (i.e., verifying clinicians' competence in conducting the model).

KEY POINTS ABOUT TRAINING

Various types of training are available. These include video-based training, onsite training, reading the manual, phone consultation, or some mix of these. There is no one way, but many. See www.seekingsafety.org (section Training).

Cross-training can be helpful. If a clinician has no background in trauma or substance abuse, training in these can be sought as needed. Clinicians may also benefit from training in related areas such as domestic violence, gender-sensitive treatment, diversity training, or specific subpopulations such as adolescent treatment, military/VA, criminal justice, or others.

Training can be helpful but is not required. Training can help launch successful use of the model and provide information and engaging exercises to build familiarity with it. It is not required at this point because there is no evidence as yet that it needs to be. Future research will, hopefully, address this issue.

Certification can be helpful but is not required. Certification involves submitting audio- or videotapes of actual sessions and having them rated on the Seeking Safety Adherence Scale. It is sometimes done for research or agency purposes to verify that clinicians are conducting the model in a competent, helpful way, per the manual. However, certification is not required at this point until there is evidence that it is needed. If certification is desired, contact info@seekingsafety.org. Certification can be conducted by our team from a distance. A clinician audiotapes one or more sessions, which are then reviewed by one of our associates and rated on the Seeking Safety Adherence Scale. The clinician receives feedback over the phone and if desired can also receive the completed adherence scale. The goal of this certification process is to provide clinically useful feedback based on real sessions. Once clinicians achieve strong adherence, they can be identified as "certified." This typically takes from one to three tapes.

GETTING STARTED

The best way to get started is to . . . get started. Seeking Safety actually requires only a small amount of preparation. It is now recommended to simply read a small part of the book and then try it. This contrasts with advice in the book, which suggested reading the whole book first. We no longer recommend this as it is not needed and may be overwhelming on the front end given the book's length (400 pages). The key is to just "dive in."

It is equally important to keep an open mind. Clinicians sometimes hold beliefs such as, "My clients won't like some of the topics," "I don't know if this format will work," "What I currently do is good enough," and "A present-focused model can't possibly work as well as a past-focused model." The bottom line is to *learn from clients* what works and what doesn't. Rather than assuming anything at the start, try the manual as written and watch how clients respond. This is part of the empowerment philosophy—to hear their views rather than deciding for them. Thus far, clients are generally highly positive about the model. In sum, take an "agnostic" position—you don't have to believe it will work, but don't assume it won't either.

Finally, know that you can do this. Clinicians sometimes feel intimidated, especially if this is their first time using a manual, or if they have not specialized before in trauma or substance abuse. Sometimes they worry that they need to do it "just right" for it to work. Most find that it quickly feels comfortable and that there is a lot of room for flexibility. Indeed, in a multisite study on twenty-six clinicians' use of the model, the majority (60 percent) reported that it took them less than a month to feel comfortable with the model, and typically about three weeks (Brown et al., 2007). The majority of clients in that same study (n = 157) reported that it took them two weeks or fewer to feel comfortable with the model (Brown et al., 2007). Clinicians from many different theoretical orientations and backgrounds have used it successfully. Try it to discover your own point of view.

Key Points about Getting Started

You do not need a lot of preparation. The simplest way to start is by reading the first two chapters in the Seeking Safety book: Overview (Chapter 1) and Conducting the Treatment (Chapter 2). Then select one of the twenty-five treatment topics that appeals to you. Asking for Help is a good choice as it's the shortest one in the book. Conduct it with a client or group, or role-play it with a colleague, and see how it goes. You can then move on to additional topics one at a time.

Once you are familiar with one topic, the rest follow the same structure. The model was designed to be user-friendly. Each topic provides the clinician guide, followed by the client handouts. Below is a summary of each part.

a. *Clinician Guide:* The clinician guide offers ideas on how to use the session topic. They are 5 to 8 pages and formatted with headers and bold fonts for easy viewing. Each clinician guide has the following parts:
   ○ *Summary:* The gist of the topic
   ○ *Orientation:* Why the topic is important
   ○ *Countertransference issues:* To help notice reactions to clients
   ○ *Goals:* "Big picture" ideas to focus the session
   ○ *Ways to relate the material to clients' lives:* Strategies to help clients learn the skills
   ○ *Suggestions:* Clinical tips for implementation
   ○ *"Tough cases":* Challenging statements clients may say in relation to the topic
b. *Client Handouts:* Client handouts come after the clinician guide. They have the following parts:

○ *Quotation:* An inspiring quote to read aloud
○ *Handouts:* Several pages that relate to the topic; these may include key points; worksheets; coping strategies; exercises; etc.
○ *Ideas for a commitment:* Suggestions for homework

Copy all of the handouts for clients. Some topics have a lot of handouts, and there is not enough time to cover them fully in one session. Nonetheless, it is suggested to give a copy of all of the topic's handouts at the session. Clients can skim them during the session to focus on what matters to them, and they can read the full set of handouts between sessions.

Practice the skills in your own life. Although the topics are simple in concept, they are not easy to do. For example, many people, not just clients, struggle with Taking Good Care of Yourself, Asking for Help, and so on. Clinicians who use the skills in their own lives become better at teaching them to clients.

Elicit client feedback. This is a key principle. Client feedback builds your confidence as you see how they respond, and it offers an opportunity to correct problems. There are three major ways within the model to obtain client feedback:

a. The *check-out* at the end of each session
b. The *End-of-Session Questionnaire* (in Chapter 2 of the book)
c. The *End-of-Treatment Questionnaire* (in the last chapter of the book)

Obtain additional background, if desired. Some clinicians like to obtain information beyond the manual. This may include *formal training* in the model (see the section Training earlier in this chapter), *additional readings* (such as those listed at the end of this chapter), and *watching films* related to trauma or substance abuse (there is a list in the Reference section of the Seeking Safety book). These can all bring to life important background on trauma and substance abuse.

Learn the format first, then the content. This may seems backwards, but it works well. The content of the topics are intuitively understandable (Compassion; Healing from Anger; Coping with Triggers, etc.). However, the format may feel awkward until you try it for a few sessions.

IMPLEMENTATION

Although the model is very straightforward, some points about implementation are worth highlighting. These are based on use of the model in many different settings as well as learning from issues clinicians have raised.

In addition to the points below, see: the manual itself (Najavits, 2002b) and several articles related to implementation listed in the Additional Reading section at the end of this chapter (especially Najavits, 2000, 2002a, 2004b, 2007b).

Key Points about Implementation

Offer many coping skills, rather than "one right way." The model offers many coping skills. Clients can choose what works for them and let go of any that are not helpful. This empowerment approach respects the fact that there is no one right way to cope—what works for one person may not work for another. As long as it is *safe coping*, it is good coping. For example, when craving a substance, one client might call a friend for help. Another might go for a long walk alone until the craving decreases. These are very different ways of coping, but both represent *safe* coping.

Keep the room safe for all. Safety is a broad concept—and part of the work is helping clients experience the feeling of safety in the treatment itself. The clinician is thus ideally like a "good parent" within professional bounds— ensuring that clients do not scapegoat each other, using time well, calming clients who become too distressed, and maintaining a respectful stance. Moreover, because *Seeking Safety* focuses on trauma, the tone of the group may be different than typical substance abuse groups. Clients are encouraged to focus primarily on their own recovery, and to interact with each other using support and problem solving rather than confrontation. Thus, telling a client he is "too self-pitying" or "in denial" would be seen as detracting from the emotional safety of the group.

Identify trauma themes. Most substance abuse clients focus on their addiction because that is what caused the most obvious problems in their lives and is most noticeable to their families and others. They are typically referred to substance-abuse treatment programs, where trauma themes may not be prominent. Thus, the clinician needs to explicitly raise trauma themes so clients become more aware of them. For example: *"The hopelessness you are describing is very common in trauma survivors"; "I wonder if your difficulty taking care of yourself is related to your trauma"; "I hope you will learn to forgive yourself— you have lived through so much pain"; "Your strong startle reflex is common in people with PTSD."* Clients may not bring up trauma on their own even after they have learned about it (e.g., in the Seeking Safety topic, PTSD: Taking Back Your Power).

Find your own style. The flexibility in the model honors clinicians' own styles and preferences when conducting the work. Some clinicians move faster, some slower. Some like to use worksheets, some do not. Some bring in humor, artistic exercises, or other personal touches. The model should feel like it brings out your best work, in ways that suit your personality.

Balance the coping skills and client issues. If the session focuses too much on coping skills, it can feel like school. If it focuses too much on client issues, it can become unfocused without productive movement. The goal is thus to balance between these—interweaving the coping skills and client issues.

Know that you cannot cover all of the material in one session. Many topics have lengthy handouts that cannot be covered all at once. It is fine to cover what you can and what is most relevant that day for clients.

Rehearse the "tough cases." For each topic, there is a list of "tough cases"— challenging statements clients may say in relation to the topic. On the topic Safety, for example, a client may say, "I don't want to stay safe. I want to die." It helps to brainstorm responses to such statements. For example, responses by the clinician might include the following:

"We need to take that very seriously. Do you feel in danger of hurting yourself?"

"I really hear your feelings of wanting to die. I also wonder whether there is another part of you that wants to survive?"

"People who suffer severe trauma sometimes think of suicide. Might your feelings relate to the trauma you went through?"

Teach clients that in any situation, good coping is possible. The basic philosophy of the treatment is that there is always a way to cope safely with any situation. This is not to say that there are easy answers or that good coping is simple. Clients' situations are often complex. But the idea is to keep returning to the idea that good coping is possible—for example, no substances or harm to self or others.

Encourage "headlines, not details." In Seeking Safety, clients are guided to name their traumas (if they choose to) and to explore how these play a role in the present. Discussing trauma is encouraged, as long as it does not move into detailed descriptions of trauma. "Headlines, not details" is a phrase to remember this principle.

Learn ways to redirect and contain. To move through the session, the clinician sometimes needs to interrupt or stop a client. For example, a client who exceeds the time limit during check-in may need guidance. You might say, *"Let me ask you to stop there; I want to make sure everyone gets a chance to check in"*; or, *"I know there's a lot more to that, but please go to the next question. We can return to more details later."* You can also create procedures to keep the session on track. For example, one Native American program had a "talking stick" that was passed to each client during check-in, while another client kept track of the time.

Watch for power dynamics. Many trauma and substance-abuse clients are vulnerable to power dynamics issues. They typically have experienced abuse of power and may have strong reactions to power and control. This includes being overly passive or overly dominant, scapegoating, projecting power issues onto the clinician or group, and reenactments (e.g., roles of victim, perpetrator, bystander, rescuer). It is helpful to watch how power is used in the room and to strive for an empowerment approach—for example, invite, create choices, and ask permission. How the clinician uses power will be closely observed by clients. They are often highly sensitive to issues of fairness, rules, sharing of time, and other implicit power messages. However, just as important as empowerment is not letting clients take over in unhealthy ways—not allowing yourself or others to be mistreated during the session.

Use alternate methods if a client cannot read. The model has been conducted successfully with clients who are illiterate or who have impaired cognitive functioning or mild traumatic brain injury. The concepts are easy to understand: for example, "compassion" and "taking good care of yourself." You can summarize key points for the client and discuss them out loud. If conducting a group, clients who are able can read small sections out loud to help those who cannot read. There is also a complete version of the book now available for the blind and dyslexic (www.rfbd.org).

Give honest feedback. Clients need more than support and validation. They also need honest critical feedback at times. For example, the substance-abuse client who decides to get a job at a bar needs to hear that this is not a good plan. Being able to identify honest strengths and weaknesses helps clients feel that you really see what is going on and want to help them fully.

Understand that working on the present does not mean avoiding the past. There is sometimes an assumption that because Seeking Safety focuses on the present, it is encouraging avoidance of the past. This is not true. Clients are encouraged to name their traumas as part of Seeking Safety and to discuss how they impact them. They are simply asked not to explore lengthy and graphic details about the past, as the primary focus is present-day coping skills. Seeking Safety can, moreover, be used with any past-focused therapy when clients are ready for that (e.g., exposure therapy or eye movement desensitization and reprocessing). Indeed, two studies have used a combination of Seeking Safety and a past-focused model (Najavits et al., 2005; Brown, in preparation). Seeking Safety can help clients better tolerate past-focused models.

Understand that present-focused therapy is not "less than" past-focused. Studies that have directly compared present- versus past-focused PTSD approaches have found both to produce positive outcomes, without significant differences between them (e.g., Marks, Lovell, Noshirvani, Livanou, & Thrasher,

1998; Najavits, 2007a; Schnurr et al., 2003), except for one study, which found a small effect size difference (Schnurr et al., 2007). Thus, past-focused treatment is not the "real" or better treatment at this point. More research is needed to better understand when and under what conditions present- and past-focused PTSD methods are needed, for substance-abuse clients and others. See Coffey, Dansky, and Brady (2002); Coffey, Schumacher, Brimo, and Brady (2005); and Najavits et al. (2005) for more on this issue.

Discuss and rehearse the skills. Clients will readily discuss a skill when given handouts. However, they will not typically move into rehearsal of the skill and thus need guidance from the clinician on that. For example, if the topic is Healing from Anger, clients will easily offer their reactions and comments. But it is up to the clinician to also encourage them to actively rehearse new approaches to anger, such as role-playing staying calm during a confrontation; or doing a think-aloud to coach oneself down from anger. As John Dewey famously said, to "learn by doing" is the most powerful method of growth (1983).

Ask the "big ticket" question: How did you try to cope? The essence of the model is to develop safe coping skills. Thus, a core question is how clients coped with recent situations (e.g., triggers, tough times, negative feelings, challenges). Early in treatment, clients often give answers such as, "I don't cope—I just drift along" or "What is coping?" As they move through the treatment and acquire greater awareness of coping, they will usually provide better answers (e.g., "I tried grounding and talking to my sponsor.") Throughout, encourage clients to notice how they tried to cope (or not), how successful it was, and how they can improve their coping.

Try different ways of rehearsing the skills. Frequent rehearsal of coping skills helps clients use them when new situations arise. There are many different methods, including the following:

- *Do a "walk-through":* Clients identify a situation where the safe coping skill might help, then describe how they would use it. For example, in the topic Asking for Help: *"If you felt like using, whom could you call? What would you say?"*
- *In-session experiential exercise:* The clinician guides clients through an experience rather than simply talking about it. For example, the skill of grounding is demonstrated in a 10-minute exercise during the session.
- *Role-play:* The client tries out a new way of relating to another person by practicing out loud. This is one of the most popular methods for interpersonal topics.
- *Identify role models:* Clients think of someone who already knows the skill and explore what that person does. For the topic Commitment: *"Do you know anyone who follows through on promises?"*

- *Say aloud:* Clients practice a new style of self-talk out loud. For example, on the topic Compassion, *"When you got fired from your job this week, how could you have talked to yourself compassionately?"*
- *Process perceived obstacles:* Clients anticipate what might happen if they try to implement the skill. For example, in Setting Boundaries in Relationships, *"What might your partner say if you requested safe sex?"*
- *Involve safe family/friends:* Clients are encouraged to enlist help from safe people, as in the topic Getting Others to Support Your Recovery.
- *Replay the scene:* Clients identify something that went wrong and then go through it again as if they could relive it. For example, *"What would you do differently this time?"* A Safe Coping Sheet is designed for this process or it can be done more informally.
- *Discussion questions:* For every topic, ideas to generate discussion are offered.
- *Make a tape:* Create an audiotape for clients to use outside of sessions as a way to literally "change old tapes." For the topic Compassion, for example, kind, encouraging statements can be recorded.
- *Review key points:* Clients summarize the main points of the handout that are meaningful to them.
- *Question/Answer:* The clinician asks questions about the topic, for example *"Does anyone know what the letters 'PTSD' stand for?"*

Educate all staff. It is helpful to get everyone "on the same page," even if only some will conduct Seeking Safety. This builds a common language and philosophy, and enhances cohesiveness of the program. Staff education about the model can be done as an in-service, during a regular staff meeting, or as a more formal training. There are also some topics that all staff can learn, such as Detaching from Emotional Pain (Grounding), Safety, and PTSD: Taking Back Your Power. In the trauma field, the concept of trauma-informed treatment also fits this framework—all staff learn the importance of trauma, such as what it is, how common it is, and how it presents in clients' behavior (Fallot & Harris, 2001).

Find a kind way to steer away from overly intense details. Clients will sometimes delve into too much detail about trauma or substance abuse—"war stories" or lengthy narratives. A client may say, "This topic, Coping with Triggers, reminds me of all the horrible body parts I saw in Iraq—I remember coming into a dark town we thought was abandoned, and I stepped on a human leg covered in blood, and there was all this pus oozing, and when I looked to my left I saw. . . . " At this point, the client is describing graphic details that are not necessary for the coping skills work. Thus, validate, but redirect back to the present. For example, *"Mark, I'm going to stop you there. What you're talking about is very important. But let's explore how this relates to the present.*

Our goal is to work on the current impact of trauma and substance abuse." As long as this is done in a compassionate way, clients accept the redirection, and it keeps the session safe for all.

Choose session length and pacing to fit your setting. Sessions can be held weekly, twice weekly, or any other frequency. The length can be 1 hour, 1.5 hours, or any other length. For example, in a jail or inpatient setting where clients leave quickly, some clinicians hold sessions every day so clients can get as much as possible. Do whatever works best in your clinical context.

If time is limited, select key topics. At this point, there is no research to identify which topics are most or least important. However, some suggested ones are: Safety, Detaching from Emotional Pain (Grounding), Asking for Help, Honesty, Taking Good Care of Yourself, Compassion, Recovery Thinking, Red and Green Flags, and Healing from Anger. Also, depending on the client, PTSD: Taking Back Your Power or When Substances Control You may also be priorities. In general, choose topics that clients are not receiving elsewhere. For example, Coping with Triggers can be helpful, but if the client has a lot of other substance-abuse programming, triggers may be covered elsewhere in treatment.

Use a triage approach for deciding what to work on. Clients will come to the session with numerous problems. As you listen during check-in, identify those you may want to return to. Often those will be the most dangerous behaviors, such as substance use and self-harm. However, strive to balance time so that higher-functioning clients get their needs met, too.

Relate process issues to trauma and substance abuse. Some of the most challenging scenarios relate to processes in the session, rather than the overt content. Examples include clients who reject all suggestions, who harshly confront other group members, or who keep failing to do commitments or to keep appointment times. It is helpful to address these behaviors, but in a "face saving" way that is related back to trauma and substance abuse. For example, a client who rejects all suggestions could be told, *"It sounds like you don't like any of our ideas. Many people with trauma and substance abuse feel hopeless about the future—do you think you are feeling hopeless right now?"* The goal is to help clients see how they are coming across, in a compassionate way.

Attend to your experiences. Observe closely what arises as you do the work. This may include the impact of your own experience of trauma and substance abuse, countertransference, self-care issues, and secondary traumatization. (The latter refers to developing trauma symptoms when exposed to traumatized clients.) Also important are negative processes such as neglect, sadism, power struggles, inability to hold clients accountable, and becoming victim to clients' abusiveness. In sum, you are a crucial part of the treatment, one who helps bring it to life. Notice both the gratifications and difficulties that arise.

Interestingly, research indicates that clinicians who treat trauma and substance abuse clients feel more gratification than difficulty with the work (Najavits, Norman, Kosten, Kivlahan, in preparation; Najavits, 2002a).

Note several points about group treatment:

- *Leadership:* Groups can be singly or co-led; either way is fine.
- *Name:* Use a name that will be appealing, such as Seeking Safety Group or Coping Skills Group rather than Trauma Group.
- *Group size:* The size can vary based on your program. Some run small groups of three to eight clients; some run medium-sized groups (nine to fifteen clients) and others run large groups (sixteen or more). Depending on group size and length of the session, you may have to cut down the check-in and check-out (see The Seeking Safety Format earlier in this chapter).
- *Group rules:* Do not review group rules at each session. It is unnecessary for Seeking Safety, and it can alienate clients and reinforce a "one-up" power dynamic. The goal is to create a welcoming, supportive tone. If a problem arises, remind clients of the rules at that point (see the Treatment Agreement in the topic Introduction/Case Management).
- *Contact outside of sessions:* There is no rule about whether clients can have contact outside of sessions—some programs encourage it, some are neutral, and others discourage it.
- *Mixed-gender groups:* Seeking Safety can be done successfully in mixed-gender format. Sometimes this is necessary in settings where there are few of one gender. Make sure all clients know that it will be mixed gender and that they can choose whether to join. If possible, encourage them to try a few sessions before they decide. Also, avoid putting clients with major current perpetration issues in with victims of such perpetration (e.g., sexual abusers with sexual abuse survivors). Note, too, that mixed-gender groups can be very positive for some clients. One female VA client, who had survived military sexual trauma, said that her mixed-gender group helped her develop a more balanced view of men. Their emotional support helped her go beyond seeing them all as predators (Najavits, Schmitz et al., in press).

Consider ways to help clients decrease substance use. Seeking Safety provides various options for reducing use, in keeping with current research and understanding about addiction. These include *abstinence* (clients give up all substances forever), *harm reduction* (decreasing use, usually with a goal of ultimate abstinence), or *controlled use* (decreasing use, with a goal of still being able to use in the future at safe levels). The choice will depend on the philosophy of you and your program, the client's needs, and other factors. An abstinence approach is the most common, but alternative approaches may occur when clients are less severe, are in outpatient care, or when the client is unwilling to engage in abstinence. See the topic When Substances Control You.

If desired, you can be listed as a Seeking Safety provider. If you or your program provides Seeking Safety, you can be listed on the Seeking Safety website. Send an email to info@seekingsafety.org and include specific information: your name, phone, and/or email; whether you provide group or individual Seeking Safety; and any other details you would like to include. Providers listed on the website are not screened for quality; it is simply a resource for those who are trying to locate a Seeking Safety clinician.

Try rating yourself or others on the Seeking Safety Adherence Scale. The scale can be downloaded from www.seekingsafety.org (section Assessment). There is both a brief and a long version. They provide a way to evaluate whether a clinician is "in sync" with the model.

ADAPTATION

Learn from Clients

Some clinicians read the book and say, *"My clients won't like some of these topics," "They won't understand the language," "They won't like the format," "I'd like to change the materials,"* and *"My clients need the materials adapted to their culture."* It is strongly encouraged, however, to try the model as is and *only adapt it based on clients' consistent feedback.* Use the "End of Session Questionnaire" (in Chapter 2 of the Seeking Safety book) and the "End of Treatment Question- naire" (in the topic Termination). If clients consistently provide criticism or suggestions based on these questionnaires, then adapt accordingly. Thus far, the model has been successfully used as is with many different clients. The principle, therefore, is to base adaptation on client responses rather than on preexisting assumptions.

There Are Two Kinds of Adaptation: Within the Model and Outside the Model

"Within the model" means making use of the flexibility that is part of Seeking Safety. Adaptations within the model include varying the session length, pacing, and number of sessions; using examples relevant to your clients; conducting topics and handouts in any order; using group or individual format; going as slow or fast as needed; adding in artwork, games, and other creative exercises; and using it with any other necessary treatments. Adapting "outside the model" means making changes that are not part of it—such as spending the entire session discussing the quotation; changing the check-in and check-out questions; and not giving handouts at all. The bottom line is that the treatment usually goes well by adapting within the model. Adaptations outside the model should generally be done carefully, based on clients' feedback.

EXAMPLES OF ADAPTATION

Below are some examples of adaptations for different types of clients.

Adaptations for Adolescents   Seeking Safety has been used with both male and female adolescents. Thus far, it is the only model for trauma and substance abuse that has shown positive outcomes with adolescents (Hamilton, Vargo, & Najavits, 2006; Najavits et al., 2006). There is no separate version for adolescents, as it has worked as is with them. However, it is helpful to apply it in ways that are appropriate for that age group. This includes the following:

- Use relevant examples, such as school, parents, dating, sports.
- Create fun, engaging exercises:
  - Encourage artwork. For example, the handout "Climbing Mount Recovery" (page 155 of the manual) could be done as a collage, painting, or mural.
  - Try the Seeking Safety card deck and poster (see Implementation Materials earlier in this chapter).
  - Develop a scavenger hunt to collect new coping skills.
- Have sessions with the adolescent's parents, using the topic Getting Others to Support Your Recovery.
- Communicate with the school guidance counselor, teachers, doctors, or others as may be helpful, using the topic Case Management.
- Explore the Seeking Safety topics out loud if an adolescent resists or has difficulty reading the handouts.

Adaptations Based on Gender   Seeking Safety was designed for both men and women. There is sometimes a perception that the model is for females, given that much of the research has been conducted on women. However, both research and clinical experience support its use with both genders (Hamilton et al., under review; Najavits, 2007; Najavits, Liese, & Heath, 2005; Najavits, Schmitz et al., in press; Weaver, Trafton, Walser, & Kimerling, 2007). The published manual uses gender-neutral language and examples from both genders, as it was intended for both. It can also be conducted in mixed-gender groups (see the earlier section Implementation for more on that topic). Thus far, there are no particular aspects that are less useful with one gender than another. Yet, sensitivity to gender is important. Gender-based adaptations include the following.

- Read books and other resources on gender-based psychology (psychology of men and women), especially in relation to trauma and substance abuse.
- Explore how trauma and substance abuse may violate gender roles. For example, men who survive interpersonal violence may feel less manly, strong, and in control. Women substance abusers may feel devalued with stereotypes of "bad mother," "lush," and "loose."
- Identify gender patterns. For example, females are more often the victims of sexual assault; males more often experience combat and crime (Najavits, Weiss, & Shaw, 1997). Males and females may differ in relationship problems (e.g., females more often engaging in unsafe relationships; males more often isolating).
- Read the chapter on use of Seeking Safety with men (Najavits, Schmitz, et al., in press) and also research reports on its use with women and men (see www.seekingsafety.org, section Outcomes).
- Recognize that many aspects of the work transcend gender—for example, developing a recovery identity, reducing symptoms of trauma and substance abuse, and attaining safety.

Adaptations for Military/Veterans   Seeking Safety has been used in the VA since the mid-1990s and is currently implemented in numerous VAs around the country, as well as in active duty military settings. With increasing numbers of returning veterans, there is a now a strong focus on this population. Examples of adaptations include the following.

- Consider the name *Seeking Strength*. Military personnel must go into harm's way, and thus the term *Seeking Safety* may be inaccurate for them. Most military are men, and the term *strength* may be more appealing than "safety." (For others, however, this might imply that they are weak—thus be sensitive to whatever term they prefer.) Also, note that the manual remains the same even if an alternate title is used; there is no separate version.
- In active duty military settings, consider naming the group "training" rather than "treatment," as the latter may be stigmatized.
- Use examples that emphasize the bonding that occurs in military settings (e.g., bonding like warriors or teams).
- Address prominent concerns for military and veterans: difficulty with feelings (which are often devalued or "trained out" in military contexts); issues with perpetuation of violence (feeling "like a monster"); betrayal,

such as when they are not supported on their return; difficulty readjusting to civilian life; and issues with authority and control. Women in the military also have major challenges such as high rates of military sexual trauma, being vastly outnumbered by men, and trying to function in a highly male-oriented culture.

- Understand how trauma and substance abuse may occur in the military. Traumas typical in military settings include military sexual trauma, handling bodies or body parts, watching buddies die, and traumatic brain injury. Substance abuse may be either encouraged (as in the Vietnam era) or discouraged (as in the current era).

Adaptations Based on Ethnic and Racial Diversity   The Seeking Safety book includes examples and language reflective of diverse experiences. Thus far, it has obtained high client satisfaction and positive outcomes with minorities. Rates of diversity in published trials include 100 percent minority in Hamilton et al. (under review); 77 percent minority in Hien et al. (Hien et al., 2004), 65 percent minority in Desai et al. (2008); 61 percent minority in Gatz et al. (2007); 35 percent minority in Zlotnick, Najavits, & Rohsenow (2003); and 21 percent minority in Najavits et al. (1998). Examples of adaptations for diverse populations include the following.

- Explicitly discuss racism, poverty, cultural messages, and intergenerational legacies of trauma and substance abuse. For example, a clinician might ask, "What cultural or family messages did you learn about trauma? Some people hear, 'You must have caused it' or 'Stop complaining.' Substance abuse messages might include, 'It's normal to drink a lot,' 'Our family doesn't have problems,' or 'Live for today— don't worry about tomorrow.'"
- Provide cultural context (e.g., for Latinos, concepts such as *familismo* and *marianismo* and acculturation stress).
- Explore the meanings of trauma and substance abuse within cultural frameworks (e.g., trauma may be so pervasive that it is perceived as a norm; substance abuse may involve culturally specific rituals and meanings).
- Offer extra readings that relate to particular subgroups.
- Use Seeking Safety translations, such as the Spanish version and other languages as described in the appendix to this chapter (Implementation Materials).

General Adaptations   The ideas below were suggested by clinicians all over the country. They are applicable to many different clients and highlight the creativity that can occur in the work.

- A "grounding table" at the back of the treatment room with various small objects and soothing materials. If clients become upset during a session, they are encouraged to use the grounding table to help calm down, while the rest of the group continues.
- Holiday-themed cutouts listing clients' commitments, such as shamrocks for St. Patrick's Day and hearts for Valentine's Day.
- Each of the safe coping skills drawn as artwork and posted on the wall.
- Creating collages using pictures cut out from magazines to illustrate any of the Seeking Safety topics.
- An orientation group to present key Seeking Safety topics in psychoeducational format; this allows the clinician and clients to see if it feels like a good fit.
- An alumni group conducted on a drop-in basis so that clients can return for support as needed.
- Letting clients go through Seeking Safety a second time, if desired.
- Games and experiential exercises. One clinician set up an empty-chair exercise for the topic Integrating the Split Self. The client was encouraged to "speak to another side of you, to offer support and guidance."
- Adding additional materials, such as information on the biology of trauma and substance abuse, and new resources.

ASSESSMENT

Assessment of trauma, PTSD, and substance abuse is a major area in its own right. For a detailed exposition on assessment considerations with these co-occurring disorders, see www.seekingsafety.org (section Assessment). This section of the website provides a book chapter on this important topic (Najavits, 2004a), as well as links to the Seeking Safety Adherence Scales and some other measures.

SUMMARY

It is hoped that this chapter has offered useful ideas for implementing Seeking Safety. We have covered topics such as a basic description of the model, its evidence base, implementation, and how to get started. In addition to providing practical information, the goal has been to encourage comfort with the work and gratification in conducting it. If you would like to communicate about your use of the model, please email info@seekingsafety.org at any time.

RESOURCES

WEB-BASED RESOURCE
Seeking Safety: www.seekingsafety.org

IMPLEMENTATION MATERIALS

Various materials are available to help with implementation of Seeking Safety. Some materials are free; others have a cost. Each is described below and is available from www.seekingsafety.org (section Order). The only required implementation material is the book itself. The optional materials offer ways to enhance implementation, many of which were suggested by clinicians over the years.

1. *The Seeking Safety book:* Also known as the Seeking Safety manual, this is the essential implementation guide (Najavits, 2002b). It has both the clinician guide and client handouts, as well as background chapters.
2. *Foreign language translations:* The complete Seeking Safety book is available in Spanish, French, and German; the handouts are available in Swedish. Translations of the complete book are currently under way in Dutch, Chinese, and Polish.
3. *Version for the blind:* The manual is available in recorded format to qualified individuals at Recordings for the Blind and Dyslexic (www .rfbd.org). It is 22 hours long.
4. *Training videos/DVDs:* The Seeking Safety training videos were developed on a grant from the National Institute on Drug Abuse. They offer an efficient method of training for programs that cannot offer onsite training or that need to retrain clinicians due to staff turnover. All of the videos are available in either video (VHS) format or DVD format and can be obtained as a set or separately. The training videos are as follows. Other training options are described earlier in the chapter (Clinician Training).

Video 1: Seeking Safety.

This is a 2-hour training video in which Lisa Najavits presents a 2-hour version of her standard training on the model. It also includes clips from real clinicians and clients who have used the model. Notes appear on-screen with the lecture, like a live lecture with PowerPoint slides. The video covers background on trauma and substance abuse, an overview of Seeking Safety, and ideas for implementation.

Video 2: Therapy Session: Asking for Help

This is a 1-hour video of Lisa Najavits conducting a group Seeking Safety session with real clients, unscripted, using the topic Asking for Help from the manual. The clients are women with severe PTSD and substance abuse, although the video is relevant for both genders and any setting. The video opens with brief background about the clients in their own words. Throughout, notes appear at the bottom of the screen to highlight teaching points, such as parts of the format as they occur and why specific interventions were chosen.

Video 3: A Client's Story [part 1]

This is a 20-minute video in which a man describes his experiences of childhood sexual abuse and addiction and his recovery process. Males with childhood abuse and addiction remain an underidentified group and this client's honesty helps bring these issues into the open.

Example of Teaching Grounding to a Client [part 2]

This 16-minute video shows Lisa Najavits teaching the skill of grounding to a real client. The client is a man in a correctional setting who had never heard of grounding prior to this video. Lisa reads the grounding script from the Seeking Safety manual and obtains the client's feedback, unscripted.

Video 4: Adherence Rating Session: Healthy Relationships

This 1-hour video shows a social worker conducting a group session with real clients, using the topic Healthy Relationships from the manual. The session illustrates both good and poor elements and serves as the basis for using the Seeking Safety Adherence Scale. Viewers can compare their rating of the session on the Seeking Safety Adherence Scale to the expert rating (which can be downloaded free from www.seekingsafety.org, section Order). This learning exercise is relevant for clinical or research purposes, including interrater reliability estimation.

5. *Poster of the Safe Coping Skills:* The topic Safety in the manual has a list of eighty-four safe coping skills. Examples are "Inspire yourself," "Talk yourself through it," "Persist," "Get organized," "Seek understanding, not blame," and "Leave a bad scene." A poster of the complete list of safe coping skills is available in English or Spanish. It is full color, 24 by 30 inches, professionally produced, with a calming nature scene background.

6. *Seeking Safety card deck:* This deck has 112 cards: all 84 safe coping skills from the Seeking Safety manual, all 24 quotations from the manual, and 3 exercises. The cards can be used as a game or to help remember key points from the manual. An ideas card suggests ways to play games, for groups or individuals. Each card is color-coded (peach = relationship skills, blue = action skills, purple = quotations, etc.). The cards offer a fun way to learn and practice the ideas from Seeking Safety, for both adults and adolescents.

7. *Adherence Scale:* This scale provides a way to rate whether clinicians are using the model per the book. It is also known as a fidelity scale. There are two versions of the Adherence Scale, both available free at www.seekingsafety.org (section Assessment). All the scales below can be filled out either by clinicians themselves as self-ratings to help

monitor their own work, or by someone else such as a supervisor or observer.

   a. *The Seeking Safety Adherence Scale—Brief Version:* This version is one page and designed for clinical use for those who want a brief way to assess adherence (Najavits, Liese, & Heath, 2007). It has two sections: interventions and processes. Examples of items are: "The facilitator did a check-in at the start of the session and worked to keep it brief (up to 5 minutes per person)" and "The facilitator focused the discussion on safe coping skills." All items are rated 0 to 3 ("not done" to "done thoroughly"). This scale has not yet undergone psychometric evaluation.

   b. *The Seeking Safety Adherence Scale:* This version is thirteen pages and was originally designed for research (Najavits & Liese, 2000). It can also be used for clinical or supervisory purposes. It has three sections: format, content, and process. Examples of questions are, "Handouts" (a format item); "Focus on trauma/PTSD" (a content question); and "Level of engagement" (a process item). Each item is rated for two qualities: adherence (how much the clinician did the behavior) and helpfulness (the impact of the behavior). Scaling is from 0 to 3 and includes anchors for each item. A separate score sheet is also available for the rater to list scores and related notes. The scale has shown solid psychometric characteristics in a major multisite trial, using ratings of 257 Seeking Safety sessions (e.g., internal consistency at .82) (Miele et al., submitted).

   c. In addition to the above scales, a one-page *Format Checklist* is available (Najavits, 2003). It was developed early on to rate clinicians' use of the Seeking Safety format. It can still be used for this purpose, or the Adherence scales described above could also be used.

8. *Articles:* A large number of articles can be downloaded for free from www.seekingsafety.org (sections Outcomes and Articles). These include scientific studies of the model, descriptive articles about the model, and articles on PTSD and substance abuse.

9. *Website:* The website www.seekingsafety.org has the following sections: Seeking Safety; Outcomes; Articles; Training; Frequently Asked Questions; Assessment; Order, and Contact.

Key Points about Implementation Materials   *The only required material is the book.* The book provides the clinician guide and client handouts for each topic.

The optional materials can enliven the work or address needs beyond the book. For example, the poster and card deck offer colorful, fun ways to convey the safe coping skills. The videos offer a simple way to train new staff, which can be especially important in programs where there is staff turnover. The Adherence Scale can help keep the work on track.

For information on any materials, see www.seekingsafety.org. Some are available only from the website. This includes most translations of the Seeking Safety book, the Adherence Scale, training videos, poster, and card deck.

You can suggest further implementation materials. New ideas are welcome. E-mail info@seekingsafety.org.

USE OF THE MATERIALS

Questions such as the following sometimes arise about how Seeking Safety materials can be used or adapted:

- Copying the handouts
- Creating new versions
- Translating the book
- Use of the materials for research

The book and all Seeking Safety materials are copyrighted, and it is thus necessary to know about their fair use—how to use the materials within legal bounds. Different treatment manuals vary in these parameters, based on whether they are public domain; who owns the copyright; and general intellectual property issues. For Seeking Safety the key points are outlined below.

Key Points about Use of the Materials   *The Seeking Safety handouts can be copied for personal use.* Guilford Press, which owns the copyright to the Seeking Safety book, offers the following description of how the book handouts can be copied: "An individual (one person) can use the handouts without writing for permission. However, a clinic (or agency, program, institution) does not qualify as the "individual purchaser." The Limited Photocopy License is quite specific about what can and cannot be done. For clinics or multiple users we ask that they write for permission and tell us how many clinicians would use how many books. If it's only two or three, we might approve this at no charge; otherwise, we assess a small licensing fee or ask that they purchase additional copies of the book for multiple users. Part of the reasoning is we want clinicians to have all the necessary background information included in the text when using the handouts. For inquiries, see www.guilford.com (Permissions), or call 800-365-7006.

The materials are available from various sources. The Seeking Safety book can be obtained via the website (www.seekingsafety.org), but also from booksellers such as Amazon.com, local bookstores, or the publisher. Most other Seeking Safety materials (translations, posters, card deck) can only be obtained via Treatment Innovations, which produces them (see www .seekingsafety.org, section Order; orders@seekingsafety.org; 617-731-1501). The audiobook version for the blind and dyslexic is available only from www.rfbd.org.

There is no electronic version of the book or handouts. People sometimes inquire whether it is possible to obtain a copy of the book (or handouts) on CD, in PDF form, as a download from the web, or other electronic versions. There are no such electronic versions of the book, nor any separate version of the handouts alone. Guilford Press, which owns the copyright, does not allow these other formats. They believe that the handouts need to be used in conjunction with the clinician guide and thus do not want to separate them.

Permission is needed to translate or distribute the materials. It is wonderful when clinicians or researchers have an interest in the model. Some have asked whether they can translate the book into another language. Others have inquired about modifying the book or parts of it, such as for domestic violence clients, adolescents, criminal justice populations, veterans, or others. However, the copyright is owned by Guilford Press and it requires formal, written, advance permission for any such translation or modification of the materials intended for distribution. Thus, a clinician could modify the materials for use with his or her own clients, but could not distribute the modified version to any other clinicians or programs, either as a hard copy or electronically. See www.guilford.com (Permissions) or call 800-365-7006. Note that Lisa Najavits does not own the copyright to the book and thus cannot formally give permissions; however, she can help facilitate contact with Guilford if needed. Also, she has assisted with all prior translations and can facilitate communications with Guilford Press, discuss key wording issues to attend to on translations, and, if needed, can distribute the translation from the Seeking Safety website. E-mail info@see kingsafety.org.

Consider creating a separate document—this does not require formal permission. The simplest way to describe and distribute ideas on modifications to the manual is to write a journal article, book chapter, or separate document of some kind. You can refer to the Seeking Safety book, but you may not modify it or reprint any parts of it directly. For example, you could write an article on your experiences conducting the model with adolescents, suggested language changes, examples you used, artwork, or any other modifications. You can publish such a document in any way you choose, as long as none of the actual Seeking Safety content is reproduced there. Also, you may want to contact info@seekingsafety.org if you are interested in adapting the book. It can be helpful to discuss options and learn about current projects.

ADDITIONAL SUGGESTED READINGS

Brady, K. T. (2001). Comorbid posttraumatic stress disorder and substance use disorders. *Psychiatric Annals, 31*, 313–319.

Brown, V. B., Najavits, L. M., Cadiz, S., Finkelstein, N., Heckman, J. P., & Rechberger, E. (2007). Implementing an evidence-based practice: Seeking Safety group. *Journal of Psychoactive Drugs, 39*, 231–240.

Herman, J. L. (1992). *Trauma and recovery*. New York: Basic Books.

Hien, D. A., Miele, G. M., Cohen, L. C., Litt, L., & Campbell, A. N. (in press). *Integrating trauma services for women in addictions treatment*. New York: American Psychological Association Press.

Jacobsen, L. K., Southwick, S. M., & Kosten, T. R. (2001). Substance use disorders in patients with posttraumatic stress disorder: A review of the literature. *American Journal of Psychiatry, 158*, 1184–1190.

Najavits, L. M. (2002). Clinicians' views on treating posttraumatic stress disorder and substance use disorder. *Journal on Substance Abuse Treatment, 22*, 79–85.

Najavits, L. M. (2002). *Seeking Safety: A treatment manual for PTSD and substance abuse*. New York: Guilford Press.

Najavits, L. M. (2004). Treatment for posttraumatic stress disorder and substance abuse: Clinical guidelines for implementing the Seeking Safety therapy. *Alcoholism Treatment Quarterly, 22*, 43–62.

Najavits, L. M. (2004). Assessment of trauma, PTSD, and substance use disorder: A practical guide. In J. P. Wilson & T. M. Keane (Eds.), *Assessment of psychological trauma and PTSD* (pp. 466–491). New York: Guilford Press.

Najavits, L. M. (2000). Training clinicians in the Seeking Safety treatment for posttraumatic stress disorder and substance abuse. *Alcoholism Treatment Quarterly, 18*, 83–98.

Najavits, L. M. (2005). Seeking Safety video training series. Brookline, MA: Treatment Innovations. Includes: Seeking Safety training (2 hours); Example of a Group Session—Asking for Help (1 hour); A client's story (20 minutes); Example of teaching grounding to a client (16 minutes); and Adherence Rating Session: Healthy Relationships (1 hour). See www.seekingsafety.org (section Training).

Najavits, L. M. (2006). Seeking Safety. In V. Follette & J. L. Ruzek (Eds.), *Cognitive-behavioral therapies for trauma* (2nd ed., pp. 228–257). New York: Guilford Press.

Najavits, L. M. (2007). Seeking Safety: An evidence-based model for substance abuse and trauma/PTSD. In K. A. Witkiewitz & G. A. Marlatt (Eds.), *Therapist's guide to evidence based relapse prevention: Practical resources for the mental health professional* (pp. 141–167). San Diego: Elsevier Press.

Najavits, L. M., Ryngala, D., Back, S. E., Bolton, E., Mueser, K. T., & Brady, K. T. (in press). Treatment for PTSD and comorbid disorders: A review of the literature. In E. B. Foa, T. M. Keane, M. J. Friedman & J. Cohen (Eds.), *Effective treatments for PTSD: Practice guidelines from the International Society for Traumatic Stress Studies* (2nd ed.). New York: Guilford Press.

Ouimette, P., & Brown, P. J. (2002). *Trauma and substance abuse: Causes, consequences, and treatment of comorbid disorders*. Washington, DC: American Psychological Association Press.

Najavits, L. M., Schmitz, M., Johnson, K. M., Smith, C., North, T., Hamilton, N., et al. (in press). Seeking Safety therapy for men: Clinical and research experiences. In *Men and Addictions*. Hauppauge, NY: Nova Science Publishers.

Schäfer, I., & Najavits, L. M. (2007). Clinical challenges in the treatment of patients with PTSD and substance abuse. *Current Opinion in Psychiatry, 20,* 614–618.

REFERENCES

Brown, V. B., Najavits, L. M., Cadiz, S., Finkelstein, N., Heckman, J. P., & Rechberger, E. (2007). Implementing an evidence-based practice: Seeking Safety group. *Journal of Psychoactive Drugs, 39,* 231–240.

Brown, S., & Gilman, S. G. (2008). *Utilizing an integrated trauma treatment program in the Thurston county drug court program: Enhancing outcomes by integrating an evidence-based, phased trauma treatment program for Posttraumatic Stress Disorder, trauma and substance use disorder. Executive Summary.* Unpublished report, Lifeforce Trauma Services, La Mesa, CA.

Coffey, S. F., Dansky, B. S., & Brady, K. T. (2002). Exposure-based, trauma-focused therapy for comorbid posttraumatic stress disorder-substance use disorder. In P. Ouimette & P. J. Brown (Eds.), *Trauma and substance abuse: Causes, consequences, and treatment of comorbid disorders* (pp. 209–226). Washington, DC: American Psychological Association Press.

Coffey, S. F., Schumacher, J. A., Brimo, M. L., & Brady, K. T. (2005). Exposure therapy for substance abusers with PTSD: Translating research to practice. *Behavior Modification, 29,* 10–38.

Desai, R. A., Harpaz-Rotem, I., Rosenheck, R. A., & Najavits, L. M. (2008). Impact of the Seeking Safety program on clinical outcomes among homeless female veterans with psychiatric disorders. *Psychiatric Services, 59,* 996–1003.

Desai, R. A., Harpaz-Rotem, I., Najavits, L. M., Rosenheck, R. A. (2009). Seeking Safety therapy: Clarification of results. *Psychiatric Services, 60,* 125.

Dewey, J. (1983). *John Dewey on education.* Chicago: University of Chicago Press.

Fallot, R. D., & Harris, M. (Eds.). (2001). *Using trauma theory to design service systems. New directions for mental health services.* San Francisco: Jossey-Bass.

Gatz, M., Brown, V., Hennigan, K., Rechberger, E., O'Keefe, M., Rose, T., & Bjelajac, P. (2007). Effectiveness of an integrated, trauma-informed approach to treating women with co-occurring disorders and histories of trauma: The Los Angeles site experience. *Journal of Community Psychology, 35,* 863–878.

Hamilton, N., Vargo, M., & Najavits, L. M. (under review). Young African-American men in residential treatment: Outcomes and lessons learned.

Hien, D. A., Cohen, L. R., Miele, G. M., Litt, L. C., & Capstick, C. (2004). Promising treatments for women with comorbid PTSD and substance use disorders. *American Journal of Psychiatry, 161*(8), 1426–1432.

Killeen, T., Hien, D., Campbell, A., Brown, C., Hansen, C., Jiang, H., Kristman-Valente, A., Neuenfeldt, C., Rocz-de la Luz, N., Sampson, R., Suarez-Morales, L., Wells, E., Brigham, G., Nunes, E. (2008). Adverse events in an integrated trauma-focused intervention for women in community substance abuse treatment. *Journal of Substance Abuse Treatment, 35*(3), 304–311.

Marks, I., Lovell, K., Noshirvani, H., Livanou, M., & Thrasher, S. (1998). Treatment of posttraumatic stress disorder by exposure and/or cognitive restructuring: A controlled study. *Archives of General Psychiatry, 55*, 317–325.

Miele, G., Hatch-Maillette, M., Hodgkins, C., Neuenfeldt, C., Schmitz, M., Hien, D., Ball, S., Litt, L., Cohen, L., Nunes, E., Najavits, L., Jiang, H., Robinson, J., & Kropp, F. (submitted). Counselor and supervisor training and fidelity in a multi-site psychotherapy study for women with trauma and addictions.

Morrissey, J. P., Jackson, E. W., Ellis, A. R., Amaro, H., Brown, V. B., & Najavits, L. M. (2005). Twelve-month outcomes of trauma-informed interventions for women with co-occurring disorders. *Psychiatric Services, 56*, 1213–1222.

Najavits, L. M. (2000). Training clinicians in the Seeking Safety treatment for posttraumatic stress disorder and substance abuse. *Alcoholism Treatment Quarterly, 18*, 83–98.

Najavits, L. M. (2002a). Clinicians' views on treating posttraumatic stress disorder and substance use disorder. *Journal on Substance Abuse Treatment, 22*, 79–85.

Najavits, L. M. (2002b). *Seeking Safety: A treatment manual for PTSD and substance abuse.* New York: Guilford Press.

Najavits, L. M. (2003). *Seeking Safety format checklist. Unpublished measure*, Boston: Harvard Medical School and McLean Hospital.

Najavits, L. M. (2004a). Assessment of trauma, PTSD, and substance use disorder: A practical guide. In J. P. Wilson & T. M. Keane (Eds.), *Assessment of psychological trauma and PTSD* (pp. 466–491). New York: Guilford Press.

Najavits, L. M. (2004b). Treatment for posttraumatic stress disorder and substance abuse: Clinical guidelines for implementing the Seeking Safety therapy. *Alcoholism Treatment Quarterly, 22*, 43–62.

Najavits, L. M. (2007). Letter to the editor: Reply to Weaver et al. (2007). *Psychiatric Services, 58*, 1376.

Najavits, L. M. (2007a). Psychosocial treatments for posttraumatic stress disorder. In P. E. Nathan & J. M. Gorman (Eds.), *A guide to treatments that work* (3rd ed., pp. 513–529). New York: Oxford University Press.

Najavits, L. M. (2007b). Seeking Safety: An evidence-based model for substance abuse and trauma/PTSD. In K. A. Witkiewitz & G. A. Marlatt (Eds.), *Therapist's guide to evidence based relapse prevention: Practical resources for the mental health professional* (pp. 141–167). San Diego: Elsevier Press.

Najavits, L. M. (2006). Seeking Safety. In V. Follette & J. J. Ruzek (Eds.), *Cognitive-behavioral therapies for trauma* (2nd ed.) (pp. 228–257). New York: Guilford Press.

Najavits, L. M., Gallop, R. J., & Weiss, R. D. (2006). Seeking Safety therapy for adolescent girls with PTSD and substance use disorder: A randomized controlled trial. *Journal of Behavioral Health Services & Research, 33*, 453–463.

Najavits, L. M., & Liese, B. S. (2000). *Seeking Safety Adherence Scale (revised). Unpublished measure*. Boston: Harvard Medical School/McLean Hospital.

Najavits, L. M., Liese, B. S., & Heath, N. (2007). *Seeking Safety Adherence Scale—Brief Version. Unpublished scale*. Boston: Harvard Medical School and McLean Hospital.

Najavits, L. M., Norman, S. B., Kosten, T., & Kivlahan, D. (under review). Improving PTSD/substance abuse treatment in the VA: A survey of providers.

Najavits, L. M., Schmitz, M., Gotthardt, S., & Weiss, R. D. (2005). Seeking Safety plus Exposure Therapy: An outcome study on dual diagnosis men. *Journal of Psychoactive Drugs*, *37*, 425–435.

Najavits, L. M., Schmitz, M., Johnson, K. M., Smith, C., North, T., Hamilton, N., Walser, R., Reeder, K., Norman, S., & Wilkins, K. (in press). *Seeking Safety therapy for men: Clinical and research experiences. Men and addictions.* Hauppauge, NY: Nova Science Publishers.

Najavits, L. M., Weiss, R. D., & Shaw, S. R. (1997). The link between substance abuse and posttraumatic stress disorder in women: A research review. *American Journal on Addictions*, *6*, 273–283.

Najavits, L. M., Weiss, R. D., Shaw, S. R., & Muenz, L. R. (1998). "Seeking Safety": Outcome of a new cognitive-behavioral psychotherapy for women with posttraumatic stress disorder and substance dependence. *Journal of Traumatic Stress*, *11*, 437–456.

Schnurr, P. P., Friedman, M. J., Engel, C. C., Foa, E. B., Shea, T., Chow, B. K., Resick, P. A., Thurston, V., Orsillo, S. M., Haug, R., Turner, C., & Bernardy, N. (2007). Cognitive behavioral therapy for posttraumatic stress disorder in women. *Journal of the American Medical Association*, *297*, 820–830.

Schnurr, P. P., Friedman, M. J., Foy, D. W., Shea, M. T., Hsieh, F. Y., Lavori, P. W., Glynn, S. M., Wattenberg, M., & Bernardy, N. C. (2003). Randomized trial of trauma-focused group therapy for posttraumatic stress disorder: Results from a department of veterans affairs cooperative study. *Archives of General Psychiatry*, *60*, 481–490.

Weaver, C. M., Trafton, J. A., Walser, R. D., & Kimerling, R. E. (2007). Pilot test of Seeking Safety treatment with male veterans [Letter to the editor]. *Psychiatric Services*, *58*(7), 1012–1013.

Zlotnick, C., Najavits, L. M., & Rohsenow, D. J. (2003). A cognitive-behavioral treatment for incarcerated women with substance use disorder and posttraumatic stress disorder: Findings from a pilot study. *Journal of Substance Abuse Treatment*, *25*, 99–105.

Afterword

ALLEN RUBIN and DAVID W. SPRINGER

I F YOU HAVE just finished reading all the chapters in this book and have not had previous experience with or significant exposure to the interventions they describe, you may be feeling overwhelmed. There is quite a lot to learn if you are considering implementing a new, empirically supported intervention that you've never learned about or provided before. So much to learn, in fact, that even if you have read only one or two of the chapters on just one new intervention approach, you might still be feeling overwhelmed. If you are feeling that way, we urge you not to give up—particularly if the intervention approaches you have been providing to date have not been empirically supported, and especially if they have been studied and found to be either ineffective or much less effective than the interventions described in this book.

No matter how overwhelmed you might feel, we hope you will persevere in trying to master one or more of the interventions described in this book. Perhaps the most important reasons for persevering are your professional ethics and compassion for your clients. A cornerstone of professional ethics is a devotion to serving clients in the most effective way possible.

At the same time, we recognize that clinicians often express reasonable rationales for not switching to empirically supported interventions with which they might be unfamiliar and uncomfortable. Perhaps their agency caseload and other requirements leave them no time to learn to become sufficiently skillful in a new intervention approach, and there are no other clinicians in their area who are adept in the empirically supported intervention. Maybe there are such clinicians nearby, but their clients cannot afford the fees of those other clinicians.

Also, the evidence supporting such interventions may be based on studies with clients whose characteristics or problems are unlike those of the clinicians' clients. Clinicians might perceive such interventions as requiring a manualized and mechanistic approach to practice that deemphasizes and devalues therapist flexibility, expertise, and relationship skills. In that connection, they might cite studies that have supported the importance of the quality of the therapeutic alliance as having as much or more impact on client outcome than the specific intervention approach chosen.

If clinicians provide a rationale for sticking with interventions that are not evidence-based like those similar to the above reasons—or even if it is based on some other reason for thinking that switching would not be in their client's best interest—then even if their reasoning is debatable, they are being professionally ethical in that their reasoning is based on what they think is best for their clients. But one's professional ethics could be questioned if the reason provided for refusing to learn more about a more empirically supported intervention or to refer to a clinician who can skillfully provide that intervention is based merely on what interests the clinician or on the clinician's own unwillingness to invest the work required to try to learn more about something that he or she believes will be more helpful to his or her clients.

For example, occasionally we hear from clinical students near completion of their master's degree studies that they just want to provide the interventions that they find most interesting and with which they are most comfortable, regardless of the research evidence about the relative effectiveness of those interventions versus alternative ones. Admittedly, there is some merit to what they say. Clients will not benefit—and perhaps will fare worse—if clinicians provide an empirically supported intervention unenthusiastically and with skepticism about its efficacy or in an incompetent manner because they have not yet mastered the intervention or perhaps feel very awkward and unsure of themselves in providing it.

But there is no excuse for sticking with interventions that lack adequate empirical support merely because one finds those interventions to be more interesting or personally fulfilling than newer interventions that are known to have a greater likelihood of effectiveness. We often respond to students who express such a reason for disliking evidence-based practice with a medical analogy like the one in the box, titled "Response to Students: Medical Analogy."

Response to Students: Medical Analogy

Imagine going to a physician for treatment for a medical condition that you recently developed and for which you learned that the most rigorous scientific research studies have agreed that Treatment A is by far the most effective remedy—much more effective than Treatment B. Your physician examines you and agrees that you have the condition you think you have and then tells you she or he will provide Treatment B. You then express your consternation about Treatment B in light of the scientific studies you learned about, and your physician tells you that despite knowing about those studies he or she prefers to provide Treatment B anyway because of lack of skill or discomfort with Treatment A. How would you feel about that physician? My guess is that you'd view him or her as inadequately compassionate or ethical. You'd probably insist on being referred to a physician who could skillfully and comfortably provide Treatment A.

What if those studies favoring Treatment A existed, and your physician knew about them, but you didn't. What if he or she then merely provided Treatment B without informing you of the evidence supporting the superior effectiveness of Treatment A or offering to refer you to another physician who could skillfully provide it? What if you subsequently—after receiving Treatment B and not benefiting from it—learned about Treatment A's evidence and found out that your physician knew about that evidence but went ahead with Treatment B anyway for the reasons mentioned above? You might express more extreme terms to describe the physician than "inadequately compassionate or ethical."

Of course, psychotherapy with substance-abusing clients is not the same as treating a medical condition. Therapist relationship skills and the therapeutic alliance have a much greater impact on treatment outcome than in medical treatment. Even the most evidence-based psychotherapies will not be effective without a strong therapeutic alliance. Moreover, even though they may have the greatest likelihood of success, many clients do not benefit from them. Idiosyncratic client characteristics and preferences can have a profound impact on the choice of intervention, and therapist expertise is critical in determining whether an intervention with the best evidence is really the best fit for a particular client in light of that client's idiosyncrasies.

However, the issue is not an all-or-nothing matter. Being compassionate, professionally ethical, and evidence-based does not require that you automatically choose empirically supported interventions in a mechanistic, cookbook fashion and without regard to client preferences. It just means that you will intervene in light of the best evidence and having integrated that evidence with your clinical expertise and knowledge of your client's characteristics and preferences. As is evident in every chapter in this book—and especially in Appendix B—clinical expertise and knowledge of client characteristics and preferences are important elements of evidence-based practice and can rightfully imply that an intervention without the best evidence might be the treatment of choice for some clients. Moreover, being evidence-based does not mean providing an empirically supported intervention in a rigid manner without room for flexibility based on your clinical expertise. Again, the room for such flexibility is evident in every chapter of this book.

Likewise, your level of comfort and skill in providing a new, evidence-based intervention is not an all-or-nothing, black-and-white issue. Every clinician—no matter what interventions she or he is providing—started out being less skillful, less confident, and less comfortable with those interventions than they are now. If you are not yet ready to begin providing an empirically supported intervention due to skill or comfort concerns, that's understandable. But those are not compelling reasons to avoid trying to become more skillful and comfortable with those interventions. And the chapters in this book have identified various additional resources and ways for trying to become more comfortable and skillful with them.

Additionally, it may be helpful to lean on the five steps of the evidence-based process when feeling overwhelmed by all of this. If you are interested in digging in and unpacking the evidence-based process in more detail, we refer you to Rubin's (2008) text on the topic, *Practitioner's Guide to Using Research for Evidence-Based Practice* as well as Appendix B in this book, in which he describes the evidence-based practice process in detail.

Of course, we all encounter shifting pieces as we navigate the EBP process. Despite the reasonable concerns and the real-world pragmatic obstacles that we encounter, many clinicians embrace evidence-based practice. We hope that you, reader, have been spurred by this book to learn more about evidence-based practice and about the interventions described herein. We also hope that this book may have given you enough expertise to begin gaining experience in providing one or more of these interventions.

REFERENCES

Rubin, A. (2008). *Practitioner's guide to using research for evidence-based practice*. Hoboken, NJ: John Wiley & Sons.

APPENDIX A[1]

Research Providing the Evidence Base for the Interventions in this Book

DAVID W. SPRINGER

THE INTERVENTION APPROACHES described in the chapters of this book have had a substantial amount of research empirically supporting their effectiveness in the treatment of substance abuse. Before reviewing the research on the effectiveness of each intervention in this book, it may be helpful to unpack a few things.

First, Guided Adolescent Problem Solving, or GAPS (see Chapter 2), is based on problem solving and social skills training for adolescents. However, GAPS also incorporates motivational interviewing (MI) components (see Chapter 1), so there is overlap in any attempts to discern the effectiveness of GAPS as it relates to MI.

Second, it is worth noting that there are varied concepts of what causes addiction or substance abuse, and a range of definitions that stem from these. Van Wormer and Davis (2008) have nicely summarized some of the ways in which addiction is framed in the relevant literature, from a brain disorder (Leshner, 2006) to an expression of self-determination (Szasz, 2003). Consider, for example, some of the following preferences. The *DSM-IV-TR* (American Psychiatric Association [APA], 2000) avoids the use of the term "addiction" in favor of "dependence." For everyday usage, Moncher, Schinke, and Holden (1992) prefer the word "addiction" in place of the *DSM's* "substance dependence." Stemming from Jellinek's (1960) well-known assertion that alcohol-

---

1. I would like to acknowledge the expertise and substantive contributions of all chapter authors to this appendix, particularly for the sections covering their respective interventions.

ism was "like a disease," many now view alcoholism and other addictions as a disease, including the American Medical Association (AMA). However, McNeece and DiNitto (2005) caution against use of the term "disease" and bring us back to a preference for the term "addiction," as they worry that "if a phenomenon is a *disease* then we expect cure in the form of a drug or other medical treatment" (p. 7). Still others are proponents of a biopsychosocial-spiritual model, or a harm-reduction approach. One thing is certain. Given the impressive developments in brain research in recent years demonstrating the physiological basis in addiction, substance abuse treatment is moving more toward evidence-based practice. The authors of each chapter in this book wisely, in their own way, use the research base to address the conceptualization of substance use that drives the development and implementation of their respective intervention. And, for those readers who are interested in a more detailed exposition on the definition of addiction, I refer you to the following sources (American Psychiatric Association, 2000; McNeece & DiNitto, 2005; van Wormer & Davis, 2008).

Third, I would be remiss if I did not underscore the fact that many clients who present with a substance use disorder also present with comorbid conditions, including conduct disorder in adolescents, depression, or PTSD. Thus, it is worth noting that, fortunately, some of the interventions covered in this book have empirical support for treating clients with comorbid conditions. For example, Family Behavior Therapy (FBT) includes more than twenty behavioral interventions capable of addressing a wide array of problem behaviors associated with, and including, substance abuse and dependence. Along these lines, FBT treatment plans often target co-existing mood, anxiety, and conduct disorders, as well as poor family relationships, child maltreatment, domestic violence, unemployment, poor academic performance, and HIV prevention. Seeking Safety was actually developed with a specific comorbid population in mind—those clients with both a substance disorder and/or PTSD—and all of the research reviewed below on Seeking Safety is on clients with this comorbid condition.

Treatments based in social modeling, social problem solving, or social skills training perspectives have been shown to be successful with adolescent substance-abusing clients with co-occurring conduct disorders. Bender, Springer, and Kim (2006) systematically reviewed randomized clinical trials of interventions for dually-diagnosed adolescents. Results examining both between-group effect sizes and within-group changes indicate the efficacy of several treatment modalities in improving specific aspects of treatment needs, but the findings highlight individual cognitive problem-solving therapy and family behavior therapy as showing large effect sizes across externalizing, internalizing, and substance abuse outcomes in dually-diagnosed youth. Both of these interventions are reviewed below, and are covered in depth in this book (see Chapters 2 and 4, respectively). Seeking Safety (see Chapter 6) was also included in this systematic review by Bender and colleagues and was found to produce moderate effect sizes at post-test and to sustain moderate reductions in substance abuse at follow-up.

Fourth, while pharmocotherapies are not covered in this book (as our focus is on psychosocial interventions), it is important to recognize that there is a growing body of research that supports combining pharmacotherapy and psychosocial treatment and that explores new pharmacotherapies that are available to assist in the treatment of substance abuse disorders (cf. Anton et al., 2006; Latt, Jurd, Houseman, & Wutzke, 2002; Longabaugh & Morgenstern, 1999; Monti, Kadden, Rohsenow, Cooney, & Abrams, 2002).

Finally, in the most recent edition of their well-known text, *Handbook of Alcohol Treatment Approaches*, Hester and Miller (2003) provide us with a large-scale review of hundreds of clinical trials for alcohol treatment. They reviewed and scored forty-seven different treatment modalities that were tested in the literature. For alcohol treatment, the lowest scores were awarded to education tapes, lectures, and films; confrontational counseling; relaxation training; and twelve-step facilitation. The highest scores were awarded to a handful of approaches, including motivational enhancement, social skills training, and cognitive therapy (all covered in this book). The extent to which the outcome research supports the effectiveness of each psychosocial intervention covered in this book is examined below.

MOTIVATIONAL INTERVIEWING

The research on motivational interviewing (MI) is rather impressive. There are currently more than 120 published clinical trials in the literature that demonstrate the efficacy of MI (Miller, 2005). These studies have demonstrated the efficacy and generalizability of MI across a wide range of behaviors and areas of interest—in addition to substance use—such as criminal recidivism, child maltreatment, domestic violence, medication compliance, HIV/AIDS risk behavior, diet, smoking, and behaviors associated with hypertension, diabetes, and obesity.

In addition to its strong evidence base, MI has been found to be effective in a number of different types of encounters, including situations in which the interaction between the counselor and client is relatively brief. In some cases, MI is used as a stand-alone therapy and in others as an adjunct to additional treatment. MI has been particularly useful in managed care settings, where treatment sessions are limited and where early dropout rates tend to be high. When used as a kickoff to longer-term programs, MI increases the likelihood that a person will return for additional treatment (Dunn, Deroo, & Rivara, 2001).

PROBLEM SOLVING AND SOCIAL SKILLS TRAINING

In regard to social problem-solving perspectives, Donohue and colleagues (Azrin et al., 2001) have developed an adolescent substance abuse treatment based primarily on empirically supported problem-solving interventions. You may recall from the beginning of this appendix that the systematic review conducted by Bender and colleagues (2006) revealed that cognitive problem-solving therapy was one of two interventions (along with family behavior therapy) that demonstrated large effect sizes across externalizing, internalizing, and substance abuse outcomes in dually-diagnosed youth.

Guided Adolescent Problem Solving, or GAPS, examined at length in Chapter 2, is based on theory, empirical research, and specific strategies associated with problem solving and social skills training for adolescents struggling with substance use and related behavior problems. GAPS was an NIAAA-funded randomized clinical trial (R01 AA013369) designed to develop and test a school-based alcohol abuse/violent behavior intervention with a multicultural sample of violence-prone alternative school youth with alcohol and substance use problems. Substance-using teens with at least one occurrence of interpersonal violence during the last three months (239 females; 349 males) were randomly assigned to school-based intervention (Guided Self-Change [GSC]) or school-based standard care. The racial/ethnic distribution of the sample was 76 percent Hispanic/Latino, 15 percent African American, 7 percent white non-Hispanic, and 2 percent other. To date, analyses have supported the superiority of GSC to standard care for reducing substance use, substance use problems, and interpersonal violence among predominantly minority teens.

ADOLESCENT COMMUNITY REINFORCEMENT APPROACH (A-CRA)

The first studies (Azrin, 1976; Hunt & Azrin, 1973) on the Community Reinforcement Approach (CRA) were conducted during the early 1970s. Since then, additional studies have examined the effectiveness of CRA with outpatient clients (Azrin, Sisson, Meyers, & Godley, 1982) and homeless individuals (Smith, Meyers, & Delaney, 1998) and combined it with contingency management in the evaluation of treatment for those with cocaine dependency (Higgins et al., 1993). Moreover, several meta-analyses have examined the effectiveness of CRA and other treatments across multiple studies and found it consistently performs among the top five effective interventions (Finney & Monahan, 1996; Holder, Longabaugh, Miller, & Rubonis, 1991; Miller, Wilbourne, & Hettema, 2003).

In 1997, a three-year randomized controlled study with 600 adolescents, funded by the Center for Substance Abuse Treatment, began to evaluate five different outpatient treatments for adolescents who used marijuana and had problems associated with this use (Dennis et al., 2004). While clinical outcomes were similar for all five interventions, A-CRA was one of the most cost-effective interventions. Moreover, thirty-month follow-up data revealed that A-CRA had a significant long-term clinical advantage when compared to one other intervention and a non-significant advantage compared to a family systems approach. A-CRA has also been found effective as a continuing care approach, paired with home visits and case management (Assertive Continuing Care, or ACC) for adolescents following residential treatment, and in a randomized clinical trial targeting homeless, street-living youth (Slesnick, Prestopnik, Meyers, & Glassman, 2007).

A-CRA is now listed on SAMHSA's National Registry of Evidence-Based Programs and Practices (NREPP; www.nrepp.samhsa.gov), which provides independent reviews regarding the research supporting the intervention and the quality and availability of implementation materials.

FAMILY BEHAVIOR THERAPY

FBT has consistently demonstrated positive outcomes in controlled trials involving both adult and adolescent substance abuse (Azrin, Donohue et al., 1994; Azrin McMahon et al., 1994; Azrin et al., 1996; Azrin, Donohue, Teichner et al., 2001; Donohue & Azrin, 2002; Donohue, Azrin, Lawson, et al., 1998). In addition to evidencing significant decreases in both marijuana, "hard drugs" (i.e., cocaine, heroin, methamphetamine, PCP, barbiturates, benzodiazepines) and alcohol use, FBT has resulted in marked improvements in a number of other areas such as depression, anxiety disorders, behavior problems, and family functioning. In short, as indicated in recent literature reviews (cf. Bender, Springer, & Kim, 2006; Carroll & Onken, 2005; Dutra et al., 2008; Waldron & Turner, 2008), FBT is considered one of the most effective drug treatment programs to date.

This treatment approach is rated among the top in its ability to be disseminated into community settings by anonymous reviewers in SAMHSA's National Registry of Evidence-Based Practices and Programs (NREPP), is one of the few evidence-based programs explicitly mentioned in the National Institute on Drug Abuse's Principles of Drug Addiction Treatment (NIDA, 1998), and is recognized as an "emerging developmentally sensitive approach" by the National Institutes of Alcoholism and Alcohol Abuse (NIAAA, 2005).

COGNITIVE BEHAVIORAL COPING SKILLS

The material from the first training manual on cognitive behavioral coping skills (CBST) (Monti, Abrams, Kadden, & Cooney, 1989) was adapted for use in a rigorous five-year study conducted by the National Institute on Alcohol

Abuse and Alcoholism (NIAAA) called Project MATCH (Project Match Research Group, 1993). This well-known study investigated whether varying subgroups of alcohol-abusing or -dependent clients would respond differently to CBST, motivational enhancement therapy (MET), and alcoholics anonymous (AA) twelve-step facilitation. The CBST approach has been found to be one of the most effective approaches for treating adult substance abuse.

There is little evidence that matching unique client characteristics with certain kinds of treatment makes a difference (Longabaugh & Morgenstern, 1999; Monti et al., 2002; Yalisove, 2004). With this caveat in mind, the Project MATCH study (1993) found that CBST (when compared to twelve-step treatment and motivational enhancement therapy) was more effective with clients who were lower in alcohol dependence. It should be noted that only four of the twenty-one matching factors across groups were found to be statistically significant within the Project MATCH study (Monti et al., 2002). Another matching study found that intrapersonal skills training (the second part of the CBST intervention curriculum presented in Chapter 5) was effective only with clients with higher levels of education and lower anxiety and urges to drink, while the interpersonal skills training (the first part of the CBST intervention presented in Chapter 5) was effective across disparate subgroups (Rohsenow et al., 1991; cited in Monti et al., 2002).

If a client is not motivated to change his or her substance use, then it is unlikely that he or she will become engaged in learning the skills presented in the CBST sessions (Monti et al., 2002). Proponents of the CBST approach suggest that the implementation of one to three sessions of motivational interviewing (see Chapter 1) prior to CBST may serve as a catalyst in motivating less motivated clients (precontemplators or contemplators) to improve their readiness for change (Longabaugh & Morgenstern, 1999; Monti et al., 2002). In fact, findings from a recent federally funded study called COMBINE found that a combination of motivational enhancement therapy, cognitive-behavioral therapy, and techniques to enhance mutual self-help group participation (termed Combined Behavioral Intervention) nearly doubled the chance of positive outcome when used with medication management as opposed to a placebo and medication management (Anton et al., 2006). Findings such as these certainly make a compelling case that we should be thoughtful about the integration or packaging of interventions when indicated.

SEEKING SAFETY

Seeking Safety comes with a solid evidence base that demonstrates effectiveness with youth and adults presenting with a range of presenting problems in various settings. To date, four randomized controlled trials have examined and demonstrated the effectiveness of Seeking Safety with adolescent girls with

PTSD and substance use disorders, women with co-occurring disorders and histories of trauma, and homeless female veterans with psychiatric disorders (cf. Desai, Harpaz-Rotem, Rosenheck, & Najavits, 2008; Gatz et al., 2007; Hien, Cohen, Miele, Litt, & Capstick, 2004; Najavits, Gallop, & Weiss, 2006). Seeking Safety was consistently found to be more effective than treatment-as-usual for trauma-related symptoms and for substance use.

Moreover, you may recall that earlier in this appendix I mentioned a meta-analysis that was conducted by Bender, Springer, and Kim (2006), in which we examined the effectiveness of interventions with dually-diagnosed adolescents. We found that Seeking Safety demonstrated moderate effect sizes at post-tests and sustained moderate reductions in substance abuse at follow-up, as well as moderate effect sizes for externalizing disorders (Bender et al., 2006). In short, Seeking Safety is the only model to date for PTSD and substance use disorder that meets standard criteria in the field as an effective treatment (Chambless & Hollon, 1998; Najavits et al., in press).

It is worth noting that Seeking Safety is recognized as a strongly recommended treatment in the Veterans Affairs Uniformed Services Package for Mental Health (Department of Veterans Affairs, 2008), as well as SAMHSA's National Registry of Evidence-Based Practices and Programs (NREPP).

The *Outcomes* section at www.seekingsafety.org provides full published and updated research studies that you can freely download. For additional information, consultation, or collaboration on research, contact Dr. Lisa Najavits at info@seekingsafety.org.

REFERENCES

American Psychiatric Association (2000). *Diagnostic and statistical manual of mental disorders, text revision* (4th ed). Washington, DC: Author.

Anton, R. F., O'Malley, S. S., Ciraulo, D. A., Cisler, R. A., Couper, D., Donovan, D. M., Gastfriend, D. R., Hosking, J. D., Bankole, A. J., LoCastro, J. S., Longabaugh, R., Mason, B. J., Mattson, M. E., Miller, W. R., Pettinati, H. M., Randall, C. L., Swift, R., Weiss, R. D., Williams, L. D., Zweben, A., for the COMBINE Study Research Group. (2006). Combined pharmacotherapies and behavioral interventions for alcohol dependence. The COMBINE Study: A randomized controlled trial. *Journal of the American Medical Association, 295*, 2003–2017.

Azrin, N. H. (1976). Improvements in the community reinforcement approach to alcoholism. *Behavior Research and Therapy, 14*, 339–348.

Azrin, N. H., et al. (1996). Follow-up results of Supportive versus Behavioral Therapy for illicit drug use. *Behaviour Research & Therapy, 34*(1), 41–46.

Azrin, N. H., Donohue, B., Teichner, G. A., Crum, T., Howell, J., & DeCato, L. A. (2001). A controlled evaluation and description of individual-cognitive problem solving and family-behavioral therapies in dually-diagnosed conduct disordered and substance-dependent youth. *Journal of Child & Adolescent Substance Abuse, 11* (1), 1–43.

Azrin, N. H., McMahon, P. T., Donohue, B., Besalel, V. A., Lapinski, K. J., & Kogan, E. S., Acierno, R. E., & Galloway, E. (1994). Behavior therapy for drug use: A controlled treatment outcome study. *Behavior Research and Therapy, 32*(8), 856–866.

Azrin, N. H., Sisson, R. W., Meyers, R. J., & Godley, M. D. (1982). Outpatient alcoholism treatment by community reinforcement and disulfiram therapy. *Journal of Behavior Therapy and Experimental Psychiatry, 13*, 105–112.

Bender, K., Springer, D. W., & Kim, J. S. (2006). Treatment effectiveness with dually diagnosed adolescents: A systematic review. *Brief Treatment and Crisis Intervention, 6*(3), 177–205.

Carroll, K. M., & Onken, L. S. (2005). Behavioral therapies for drug abuse. *American Journal of Psychiatry, 162*, 1452–1460.

Chambless, D., & Hollon, S. (1998). Defining empirically supported therapies. *Journal of Consulting and Clinical Psychology, 66*, 7–18.

Dennis, M. L., Godley, S. H., Diamond, G., Tims, F. M., Babor, T., Donaldson, J., Liddle, H., Titus, J. C., Kaminer, Y., Webb, C., Hamilton, N., & Funk, R. R. (2004). The Cannabis Youth Treatment (CYT) Study: Main findings from two randomized trials. *Journal of Substance Abuse Treatment, 27*, 197–213.

Department of Veterans Affairs. (2008). Uniform mental health services in VA medical centers and clinics. In *Veterans Health Administration* (Ed.), VHA Handbook 1160.01. Washington DC: Veterans Health Administration.

Desai, R. A., Harpaz-Rotem, I., Rosenheck, R. A., & Najavits, L. M. (2008). Impact of the Seeking Safety Program on clinical outcomes among homeless female veterans with psychiatric disorders. *Psychiatric Services, 59*, 996–1003.

Donohue, B., & Azrin, N. H. (2002). Family behavior therapy in a conduct-disordered and substance-abusing adolescent: A case example. *Clinical Case Studies, 1*(4), 299–323.

Donohue, B., Azrin, N. H., Lawson, H., Friedlander, J., Teichner, G., & Rindsberg, J. (1998). Improving initial session attendance of substance abusing and conduct disordered adolescents: A controlled study. *Journal of Child & Adolescent Substance Abuse, 8*(1), 2–13.

Dunn, C., Deroo, L., & Rivara, F. P. (2001). The use of brief interventions adapted from motivational interviewing across behavioral domains: A systematic review. *Addiction, 96*, 1725–1742.

Dutra, L., Stathopoulou, G., Basden, S. L., Leyro, T. M., Powers, M. B., & Otto, M. W. (2008). A meta-analytic review of psychosocial interventions for substance use disorders. *American Journal of Psychiatry, 165*, 179–187.

Finney, J. W., & Monahan, S. C. (1996). The cost-effectiveness of treatment for alcoholism: A second approximation. *Journal of Studies on Alcohol, 57*, 229–243.

Gatz, M., Brown, V., Hennigan, K., Rechberger, E., O'Keefe, M., Rose, T., & Bjelajac, P. (2007). Effectiveness of an integrated, trauma-informed approach to treating women with co-occurring disorders and histories of trauma: The Los Angeles site experience. *Journal of Community Psychology, 35*, 863–878.

Hien, D. A., Cohen, L. R., Miele, G. M., Litt, L. C., & Capstick, C. (2004). Promising treatments for women with comorbid PTSD and substance use disorders. *American Journal of Psychiatry, 161*(8), 1426–1432.

Hester, R. K., & Miller, W. R. (2003). *Handbook of alcoholism treatment approaches: Effective alternatives* (3rd ed.). Boston: Allyn & Bacon.

Higgins, S. T., Budney, A. J., Bickel, W. K., Hughes, J. R., Foerg, F. E., & Badger, G. J. (1993). Achieving cocaine abstinence with a behavioral approach. *American Journal of Psychiatry, 150*, 763–769.

Holder, H., Longabaugh, R., Miller, W. R., & Rubonis, A. V. (1991). The cost-effectiveness of treatment for alcoholism: A first approximation. *Journal of Studies on Alcohol, 52*, 517–540.

Hunt, G. M., & Azrin, N. H. (1973). A community-reinforcement approach to alcoholism. *Behavior Research and Therapy, 11*, 91–104.

Jellinek, E. M. (1960). *The disease concept of alcoholism.* New Haven, CT: Yale Center for Alcoholic Studies.

Latt, N. C., Jurd, S., Houseman, J., & Wutzke, S. E. (2002). Naltrexone in alcohol dependence: A randomized controlled trial of effectiveness in a standard clinical setting. *Medical Journal of Australia, 176*, 530–534.

Leshner, A. I. (2006). *The addiction recovery guide: Your Internet guide to drug and alcohol addiction recovery.* Retrieved February 2009 from www.addictionrecoveryguide.com.

Longabaugh, R., & Morgenstern, J. (1999). Cognitive-behavioral coping-skills therapy for alcohol dependence: Current status and future directions. *Alcohol Research and Health, 23*, 78–85.

McNeece, C. A., & DiNitto, D. (2005). *Chemical dependency: A systems approach* (3rd ed.). Boston: Allyn & Bacon.

Miller, W. R. (2005, November). *Believe your data: Research, theory, practice and training of motivational interviewing.* 39th Annual Convention of the Association for Behavioral and Cognitive Therapies, Washington, DC.

Miller, W. R., Wilbourne, P. L., & Hettema, J. E. (2003). What works? A summary of alcohol treatment outcome research. In R. K. Hester & W. R. Miller (eds.), *Handbook of alcoholism treatment approaches: Effective alternatives* (3rd ed.). Boston: Allyn & Bacon.

Moncher, M., Schinke, S., & Holden, G. (1992). Tobacco addiction: Correlates, prevention and treatment. In E. Freeman (Ed.), *The addiction process* (pp. 222–236). New York: Longman.

Monti, P. M., Abrams, D. B., Kadden, R. M., & Cooney, N. L. (1989). *Treating alcohol dependence.* New York: Guilford Press.

Monti, P. M., Kadden, R. M., Rohsenow, D. J., Cooney, N. L., & Abrams, D. B. (2002). *Treating alcohol dependence: A coping skills training guide* (2nd ed.). New York: Guilford Press.

Najavits, L. M., Gallop, R. J., & Weiss, R. D. (2006). Seeking Safety therapy for adolescent girls with PTSD and substance use disorder: A randomized controlled trial. *Journal of Behavioral Health Services & Research, 33*, 453–463.

National Institute on Drug Abuse, National Institutes of Health. (1998, April). *Principles of drug addiction treatment: A research based guide*. (Publication No. 99–4180). Retrieved August 25, 2008, from NIDA NIH Reports Online via: www.nida.nih.gov/PDF/PODAT/PODAT.pdf.

National Institutes of Alcoholism and Alcohol Abuse. (2005). Adolescents and treatment of Alcohol Use Disorders. *In NIAAA: Social Work Education for the Prevention and Treatment of Alcohol Use Disorders* (Module 10A). Retrieved December 27, 2008, from http://pubs.niaaa.nih.gov/publications/Social/Module10AAdolescents/Module10A.html.

Project MATCH Research Group. (1993). Project MATCH: Rationale and methods for a multisite clinical trial matching patients to alcoholism treatment. *Alcoholism: Clinical and Experimental Research, 17*, 1130–1145.

Slesnick, N., Prestopnik, J. L., Meyers, R. J., & Glassman, M. (2007). Treatment outcome for street-living, homeless youth. *Addictive Behaviors, 32*, 1237–1251.

Smith, J. E., Meyers, R. J., & Delaney, H. D. (1998). The community reinforcement approach with homeless alcohol-dependent individuals. *Journal of Consulting and Clinical Psychology, 66*, 541–548.

Szasz, T. (2003). *Ceremonial chemistry: The ritual persecution of drugs, addicts, and pushers* (rev. ed.). Syracuse, NY: Syracuse University Press.

van Wormer, K., & Davis, D. R. (2008). *Addiction treatment: A strengths perspective* (2nd ed.). Belmont, CA: Brooks/Cole.

Waldron, H. B., & Turner, C. W. (2008). Evidence-based psychosocial treatments for adolescent substance abuse. *Journal of Clinical Child & Adolescent Psychology, 37*, 238–261.

Yalisove, D. L. (2004). *Introduction to alcohol research: Implications for practice, prevention and policy*. Boston: Allyn & Bacon.

APPENDIX B

The Evidence-Based Practice Process

ALLEN RUBIN

As mentioned in this volume's introduction, in its original and most prominent definition, evidence-based practice is a five-step process for making practice decisions. The term *evidence-based practice* (EBP) sprang from the term *evidence-based medicine* (EBM), which was coined in the 1980s and was ultimately defined as "the integration of best research evidence with clinical expertise and patient values" (Sackett, Straus, Richardson, Rosenberg, & Haynes, 2000, p. 1). By including clinical expertise and patient values in the definition, EBM was distinguished from the notion that it was an unchanging list of approved interventions that physicians should implement even if they seemed to be contraindicated in light of the physician's knowledge about the patient. Nevertheless, as the concept of EBM spread to the nonmedical helping professions with the label EBP, some critics disregarded its integration component and misconstrued it as recommending that practitioners mechanistically implement scientifically approved interventions regardless of their clinical expertise and knowledge about client attributes, values, and preferences.

Pointing out the integration component of the EBP process is not meant to diminish the importance of the role of empirically supported interventions in EBP. The best research evidence is a key component of the EBP process. Indeed, this entire volume has aimed to facilitate your ability to find and implement interventions that have the best research evidence regarding their effectiveness with substance-abusing clients. In fact, the ultimate priority of the EBP process is to maximize the chances that practice decisions will yield desired outcomes in light of the best scientific evidence. Thus, the integration component of EBP is not meant to give practitioners so much wiggle room that they can disregard or diminish the importance of the best scientific evidence in making practice decisions. It just recognizes the need to blend that evidence with clinical expertise and client attributes.

There are various practical obstacles to the feasibility of the EBP process often encountered by clinicians. Key among those obstacles are the time, expertise, and other resources required to find relevant research evidence, to critically appraise various studies and sort through their bewildering array of inconsistent findings to ascertain which interventions are supported by the *best* evidence, and ultimately to learn how to implement one or more of those interventions. This volume has been geared to practitioners for whom those daunting obstacles make implementing the entire EBP process infeasible. However, if you would like to try to implement that process, the remainder of this appendix can guide you in a step-by-step fashion.

STEP 1. FORMULATE A QUESTION

The first step in the EBP process involves formulating a question based on a practice decision that you need to make. The question could pertain to any level of practice, including questions bearing on administrative or policy decisions. Here are four common types of EBP questions (Rubin, 2008):

- What intervention, program, or policy is most effective?
- What factors best predict desirable or undesirable outcomes?
- What's it like to have had my client's experiences?
- What assessment tool should be used?

At the clinical level, you are most likely to formulate the first type of question above—one geared to choosing the intervention that has the best chance to be effective for your client. This volume has been geared to that type of question.

In order to make the next step in the EBP process both expedient and productive, you'll need to add as much specificity to your question as possible—without making it so specific that you'll find no evidence bearing on it. To illustrate questions that are too broadly worded, while writing this appendix I went online to the *PsycINFO* literature database and requested that it show each published work that included all of the following three search terms somewhere in its text: *effective, treatment, trauma*. My implicit question was, "What intervention is most effective for treating trauma?" More than 1,000 published works came up. Too many!

My question was too broad. After all, there are many different types of trauma. So I redid my search, substituting *PTSD* for *trauma*. My implicit question was, "What intervention is most effective for treating PTSD?" That reduced the listed results to 677 publications. Still a lot. Assuming that my client was a victim of sexual abuse, I added the term *sexual abuse* to the search, with the implicit EBP question, "What intervention is most effective for treating PTSD among victims of sexual abuse?" That reduced the list to 51 published works—much more manageable and relevant to my hypothetical client.

To illustrate adding more specificity, I repeated my search by adding the term *African American* to the search, with the implicit EBP question, "What intervention is most effective for treating PTSD among African American victims of sexual abuse?" However, no works were found when I added that search term. The same happened when I substituted *Hispanic* for *African American*.

In formulating your EBP questions, it's usually best to go in the opposite direction, formulating a very specific question, and then broadening it in your search if necessary. That way, you can skip the search term tries that give you too many publications that are irrelevant or tangential to your specific practice decision or client, and add (broadening) terms only as needed.

Not all EBP questions about effectiveness are open-ended, without specifying one or more specific interventions in advance. For example, perhaps you know that both EMDR and exposure therapy are accepted as the most effective treatments for PTSD and are wondering which has the best evidence. Your EBP question therefore might be, "Is EMDR or exposure therapy more effective in treating PTSD?" When I asked PsycINFO to find all publications that contained all of the following search terms—*EMDR, exposure therapy*, and *PTSD*—it listed 23 results.

STEP 2. SEARCH FOR EVIDENCE

As a busy practitioner, the least time-consuming way to search for evidence is to use Internet search engines and electronic literature databases. *PsycINFO*, as discussed above, is one useful option. Using it requires a subscription, but there are ways to get around that cost if your work setting does not have such a subscription. One way is to see if you can get free access through any university faculty members or internship students with whom you are affiliated (especially if you serve as an adjunct faculty member or a field internship instructor). Another way is through your local library. Many local libraries provide free access to databases like *PsycINFO* for residents with a library card. You probably will not have to go to the library to use its computers; you should be able to do it all online from your own computer. There are many alternative electronic literature databases, including Google Scholar and MedLine. The nice thing about MedLine is that the National Library of Medicine offers free access to it at www.nlm.nih.gov.

Although different professional literature databases typically require the entering of search terms to retrieve studies, they differ in their search rules and procedures. You'll need to scan their search guidelines before proceeding so that you can expedite your search. For some databases, you can connect the various parts of your search term with words like "AND," OR," and "NOT." Using "AND" limits the number of studies that come up to only those that contain all of the keywords in your search term. For example, if you want to find studies that compare EMDR to exposure therapy, you could enter "EMDR AND exposure therapy." Using "OR" will expand the number of studies that come up. Thus, if you enter "EMDR OR exposure therapy," studies that come up will include those that look only at EMDR, only at exposure therapy, and at both (whereas using "AND" would include only those studies that look at both). If you enter "EMDR AND exposure therapy NOT pilot study," the list of references that come up will include those that address *both* EMDR *and* exposure therapy, but will exclude pilot studies. For some databases, such as *PsycINFO*, you will not have to enter the connecting words like AND, OR, and NOT. Instead, you can enter the keywords in different boxes that are prefaced with the connecting words.

So far I've been discussing the search for evidence in terms of looking for individual studies. Implicit in this approach is the need to critically appraise (in the next step of the EBP process) the quality of the evidence in each of the relevant studies that you find. A more expedient alternative would be to look first for systematic reviews of the studies already completed by others. This would also include meta-analyses, which are systematic reviews that pool the statistical results of the reviewed studies. Systematic reviews are expedient in several ways. First, they save you the time of searching for and reading individual studies. Second, they spare you the difficulty of critically appraising the research methodology of each study, which can be a daunting task for clinicians with limited expertise in research design, methods, and statistics. Third, even those studies that are methodologically rigorous and that supply the best evidence often report findings that are inconsistent from one study to another, and for some EBP questions, that inconsistency can be bewildering. A good systematic review will synthesize the various findings and provide you with a bottom line as to which interventions have the best evidence, for what types of clients and problems, and under what conditions.

Of course, an even more expedient way for busy practitioners to engage in EBP is to rely on volumes like the one you are reading. If you read Appendix A, you saw a synopsis of the ample empirical support—including systematic reviews and meta-analyses—for the interventions selected for this volume. However, if your EBP question is one for which no systematic reviews or books like this have been published, you may have no alternative to searching for and appraising individual studies. When you start your search, you won't know in advance what you'll find. Assuming that time and other practical constraints make searching for individual studies an undesirable option from the standpoint of feasibility, I recommend that you begin looking for systematic reviews and volumes like this and then look for individual studies only as a last resort. That said, however, you need to be careful that the authors of systematic reviews or books like this do not have a vested interested in the interventions that they depict as having the best evidence. If my co-editor and I, for example, had developed or ran workshops on the interventions described in this volume, then the credibility of our previous appendix on the supportive research would be highly suspect, and the value of this book's chapters therefore would suffer. In case you are wondering, we have no vested interests in any of the interventions described in this book.

You should also bear in mind that for some problem areas, different systematic reviews might produce different conclusions regarding which interventions have the best evidence supporting their effectiveness with that problem. For example, some authors with well established reputations in EMDR have conducted reviews that concluded that EMDR is more effective than exposure therapy, while other authors have conducted reviews that reached the opposite conclusion, while still others conducted reviews that concluded that both interventions appear to be equally effective. Systematic reviews should be transparent about the presence or lack of vested interests by the authors of the review. Reviews that lack that transparency should be viewed with suspicion, as should reviews that admit to a vested interest, while reviews in which the authors have no vested interests probably should have the most credibility (all other criteria being equal, as will be discussed below).

Two highly regarded sources for unbiased and methodologically sophisticated systematic reviews are the Cochrane Collaboration and the Campbell Collaboration. Both are international nonprofit organizations that recruit into review teams researchers, practitioners, and consumers without vested interests in the subjects of their reviews. Each of their sites can be accessed on line. If you can find a review bearing on your EBP question in the onsite library at either of those sites, you can probably rely on it to answer your question and thus save you the trouble of searching for and appraising other sources of evidence. Moreover, their libraries also contain comments and criticisms of their own reviews as well as abstracts of other reviews, bibliographies of studies, reviews regarding methodology, and links that can help you conduct your own review. The Cochrane Collaboration focuses on reviews in the areas of health and mental health and can be accessed at www.cochrane.org. Its sibling organization, the Campbell Collaboration, focuses on reviews in social welfare, education, and criminal justice. You can access its website at www.campbellcollaboration.org.

STEP 3. CRITICALLY APPRAISE THE EVIDENCE

The next step of the EBP process involves critically appraising the evidence found in the previous step. Being published is no guarantee that study's evidence is sound. Some studies are better than others, and some have fatal flaws that severely undermine their utility for guiding practice decisions. All studies have at least one or two minor flaws. Your prime task is not looking for the holy grail of a perfectly flawless study; but rather looking for one or more studies (or systematic reviews) whose strengths and relevance to your practice decision far outweigh their minor flaws.

The criteria to use in critically appraising any study depend on the nature of your EBP question. For questions such as, "What's it like to have had my client's experiences?" studies that employ qualitative research methods are likely to provide better evidence than quantitative studies such as experiments or surveys. For questions like, " What factors best predict desirable or undesirable outcomes?" studies that employ multivariate correlation analyses along with survey designs, case-control designs, or longitudinal designs may be your best bet. For questions like, "What assessment tool should be used?" you'll need to examine studies that administer assessment tools to large samples of people and calculate the tools' reliability, validity and sensitivity.

As mentioned earlier, however, the most commonly asked EBP question asks something like, "What intervention, program, or policy is most effective?" For questions about effectiveness, the evidentiary hierarchy table in Table B.1 should guide your appraisal of the evidence.

It is beyond the scope of this appendix to explain everything in Table B.1. If you have had one or more good courses on research methods, perhaps you already have sufficient familiarity with the terminology and standards of research rigor to guide your appraisal. To brush up on that material, you might want to examine my book, *Practitioner's Guide to Using Research for Evidence-Based Practice* (Rubin, 2008). In the meantime, some key criteria to keep in mind when appraising individual studies are as follows:

1. Was a control group used?
2. Was random assignment used to avoid a selectivity bias that would make one group more likely to have a successful outcome than the other?
3. If random assignment was not used (i.e., in a quasi-experiment), do the authors provide solid evidence and a persuasive case for considering a selectivity bias to be unlikely?
4. Was outcome measured in an unbiased manner?
5. Were the attrition rates in both groups roughly equivalent?

Although the above list does not exhaust all the criteria to consider, if the answers to questions 1, 4, and 5 are all *yes*, coupled with an affirmative answer

Table B.1

Evidentiary Hierarchy for Questions about Effectiveness (Best Evidence at the Top)*

Level 1	Systematic reviews and meta-analyses
Level 2	Multisite replications of randomized experiments
Level 3	Randomized experiments
Level 4	Quasi-experiments
Level 5	Single-case experiments
Level 6	Correlational studies
Level 7	Other: • Anecdotal case reports • Pretest-posttest studies without control groups • Qualitative descriptions of client experiences during or after treatment • Surveys of clients as to what they think helped them • Surveys of practitioners as to what they think is effective

*This hierarchy assumes that each type of study is well designed. If not well designed, then a particular study would merit a lower level on the hierarchy. For example, a randomized experiment with egregiously biased measurement would not deserve to be at Level 3 and perhaps would be so fatally flawed as to merit dropping to the lowest level. The same applies to a quasi-experiment with a severe vulnerability to a selectivity bias.

to *either* question 2 or 3, then chances are the study is supplying some relatively strong evidence regarding whether a policy, program, or intervention is effective.

When appraising systematic reviews (including meta-analyses), you should ask whether the reviewed studies were appraised in connection to the above types of evidentiary standards. Reviews can do so in two ways. One way is for the authors of the review to take the strengths and weaknesses of the reviewed studies into account when deriving their conclusions and guidelines for practice. The other way is to exclude from the review any studies that fail to meet certain evidentiary standards, such as the ones listed above.

As mentioned earlier, another important consideration when appraising a systematic review is whether the authors have vested interests in any of the policies, programs, or interventions addressed in the review and whether they are transparent about such vested interests. They also should identify the inclusion and exclusion criteria they used in selecting studies for their review and describe how comprehensively they searched for studies. For example, if they excluded studies of clients with substance abuse comorbidity from their review of treatment for PTSD, and your client has such comorbidity, then their review might have less value to you than one that included such studies. As to comprehensiveness, a key issue is whether the authors searched well for unpublished studies to include in their review, based on the notion that if only published studies are included, the deck might be stacked toward studies with findings supporting the effectiveness of interventions, since studies with null findings often are not submitted for publication.

STEP 4. INTEGRATION, SELECTION, AND IMPLEMENTATION

As mentioned earlier, the EBP process is not merely a mechanistic, cookbook approach in which practice decisions are made and implemented based solely on the best evidence regardless of clinician expertise and knowledge of client attributes and preferences. Consequently, after appraising the evidence, the next step of the EBP process involves selecting an intervention and implementing it only after integrating the critical appraisal of the evidence with your clinical expertise and knowledge of client circumstances and preferences. You might, for example, opt to implement an intervention that has the second or third best evidence because the studies done on that intervention involved clients like yours, whereas the studies done on the interventions with the best evidence involved only clients very unlike yours in ways that you deem to be very important. Likewise, your client might refuse to participate in an intervention supported by the best evidence, such as when some parents cannot be persuaded (through psychoeducation) to permit their child to undergo EMDR or exposure therapy because they fear such treatment would retraumatize their child.

Feasibility issues also must be considered. What if you lack training in the intervention supported by the best evidence? Is it possible to get the needed training? Can you afford the time and money that will be required? Can you get it soon enough? If you cannot get it, can you refer the client to another service provider who has the expertise to provide the desired intervention? If the answers to these questions are negative, the client might be better off if you provide an intervention that has the second or third best evidence but is one that you have the expertise to provide competently. If the preferred intervention is one covered in this volume, perhaps reading the pertinent chapter will suffice to get you started.

STEP 5. MONITOR/EVALUATE OUTCOME

In the final step of the EBP process, you monitor or evaluate the outcome of the intervention (or other practice decision that is implemented in step 4). You might wonder why this final step is needed. After all, haven't you implemented the option that has already been evaluated and found to have the best evidence supporting its effectiveness? There are several answers to these questions. One reason is that even in studies providing the best evidence some of the participants do not benefit from the empirically supported interventions. A related reason is that those studies might not have included participants with some of your client's key attributes. A third reason is that in step 4 you may have opted for an intervention that does not have the best evidence.

Moreover, you might complete all four preceding steps and find no empirically supported intervention that fits your client. You may therefore have to proceed according to theory or clinical judgment, alone, thus implementing an intervention that lacks empirical support. Keep in mind that doing so does not mean you have violated the EBP process. The fact that you completed the preceding steps means you have implemented the EBP process even if your search is fruitless. But if that is so, then it is all the more important to complete the final step of the process; that is, to evaluate whether the intervention you have chosen attains the desired outcome.

A final reason for the final step of the EBP process is the possibility that you might not implement the selected intervention in a sufficiently competent manner. Remember, even the best evidence is only probabilistic. Rather than assure treatment success, it merely means that the chosen intervention has the best *likelihood* of success.

Now that you see the rationale for this final step, you might wonder how to do it. Your options are many, and some might be a lot more feasible for you than you think. The most feasible options pertain to situations where you have implemented an intervention that has already been supported by strong studies. In such situations, you should not feel the need to employ a sophisticated evaluation design aimed at producing causal inferences about whether the chosen intervention is really the cause of any client outcomes. Instead, all you need to do is monitor client outcomes. That is, you just need to see if the client achieves his or her desired outcome, regardless of the cause. That's because previous studies have already produced probabilistic causal evidence about the intervention, and your task as a practitioner (and not as a researcher), therefore, is merely to see if your client gets where he or she wants to go after receiving that intervention and whether (assuming a desired outcome is not attained) a different intervention may need to be introduced.

For a comprehensive guide to monitoring client progress, you can examine Chapter 12 of the book I mentioned earlier (Rubin, 2008). For example, if you are monitoring a client's PTSD symptoms, the client could self-monitor one or more symptoms (including perhaps just one overall rating of the day's symptoms) by completing an individualized self-rating scale each day, such as the one shown in Figure B.1 from Rubin (2008, p. 259)

You could graph the daily ratings chronologically, as appears below to see if the desired level of progress is being achieved. The graph in Figure B.2 (from Rubin, 2008, p. 257) would indicate a successful outcome was being achieved in reducing an undesirable symptom (or overall rating of PTSD symptoms in general).

In contrast, the graph in Figure B.3 (from Rubin, 2008, p. 257) illustrates an outcome in which progress was not being made with the selected intervention (Intervention A), but then after an alternative intervention (Intervention B) was introduced the desired progress was being achieved in reducing an undesirable symptom (or overall rating of PTSD symptoms in general).

If you have implemented an intervention that lacks adequate prior empirical support, you might want to employ a more sophisticated evaluation design that aims to produce causal inferences (assuming, of course, that such a design is feasible for you). Such designs include experiments, quasi-experiments, time-series designs, and single-case experiments.

The above examples were discussed in the context of clinical practice with a specific client. However, they can be adapted to a macro level of practice in

Instructions: At the end of each day, enter the day's date and then circle a number to approximate how depressed you felt on average for that day.

Average Level of Depression[**] for the Day

DATE	Not at all	→		Moderate	→			Severe
____	0	1	2	3	4	5	6	7
____	0	1	2	3	4	5	6	7
____	0	1	2	3	4	5	6	7
____	0	1	2	3	4	5	6	7
____	0	1	2	3	4	5	6	7
____	0	1	2	3	4	5	6	7
____	0	1	2	3	4	5	6	7

Figure B.1　An Individualized Daily Rating Scale for Depressed Mood[*]

[*]The development of this scale was inspired by ideas in Bloom, Fischer, and Orme (2006).

[**]This scale can be adapted for other target problems or goals by substituting those problems (anxiety, anger, etc.) or goals (self-confidence, assertiveness, etc.) for depressed or depression.

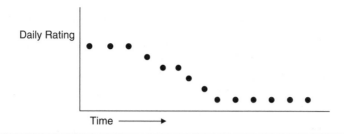

Figure B.2 Illustration of a Successful Outcome in Reducing an Undesirable Symptom

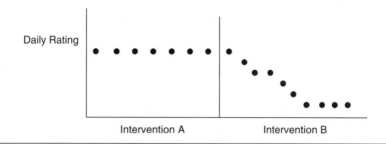

Figure B.3 Illustration of an Unsuccessful Outcome for Intervention A Followed by a Successful Outcome for Intervention B

which you want to monitor or evaluate outcomes with a large number of clients or with an entire community. For example, if you want to see whether a new crisis intervention modality is more effective than previous efforts to prevent PTSD among victims of natural disasters, you could compare the incidence of PTSD among its recipients to the incidence among victims who received alternative or no crisis intervention modalities. To learn more about such macro evaluations, you can read Rubin and Babbie (2008).

The main thing to keep in mind about this phase of the EBP process, however, is to implement it in whatever way that is feasible for you. As a practitioner, you should not feel immobilized just because a rigorous research evaluation design is beyond your reach. Remember, all practitioners routinely have to make judgments as to whether what they are doing is working or not and whether they need to try something different. The same applies regardless of what you find and implement in the previous steps of the EBP process. The ideas presented here and in the suggested reference volumes can help you make your monitoring or evaluation efforts more systematic and doable. Just do the best you can, and good luck!

REFERENCES

Bloom, M., Fischer, J., & Orme, J. G. (2006). *Evaluating practice: Guidelines for the accountable professional* (5th ed.). Boston: Allyn & Bacon.

Rubin, A. (2008). *Practitioner's guide to using research for evidence-based practice.* Hoboken, NJ: John Wiley & Sons.

Rubin, A., & Babbie, E. (2008). *Research methods for social work* (6th ed.). Belmont, CA: Thomson Brooks/Cole.

Sackett, D. L., Straus, S. E., Richardson, W. S., Rosenberg, W. M. C., & Haynes, R. B. (2000). *Evidence-based medicine: How to practice and teach EBM* (2nd ed.). New York: Churchill Livingstone.

Author Index

Subject Index